Praise for

Emperors and Idiots

"An eminently readable history of the combative Yankee–Red Sox relationship, from the turn of the twentieth century . . . through the recent era, with special focus on the infamous 1920 trade that brought Babe Ruth from the Sox to the Yankees and supposedly initiated more than 80 years of jinxed Boston baseball."

—*Bookpage*

"Mike Vaccaro begins his tale by wearing different hats. He chronicles the different way people treat him when he wears a Red Sox baseball cap as opposed to the way people treat him when he wears a Yankees cap. Having captured our attention, he puts on his thinking cap and explains in deft prose the reason for all that noise coming from the red state and the blue state of American sport. Terrific stuff."

—Leigh Montville, author of *Ted Williams* and *Why Not Us?*

"Vaccaro, a sports columnist for the *New York Post,* has written a lively and actually quite marvelous account of the history of the Boston–New York rivalry, infused with his enthusiasm for the game. There's no trashing, gratuitous or otherwise, just an evenhanded account of a century of baseball, as he deftly weaves the history of many encounters between the pinstripes and the Bostons in and around the story of the 2003 and 2004 seasons."

—*Booklist*

"There are very few writers likely to shed new light on the Yankees–Red Sox rivalry at this point in time. Mike Vacarro is a notable exception, and *Emperors and Idiots* is absolute proof and well worth your time and attention."

—John Feinstein, author of *Caddy for Life* and *Season on the Brink*

"Vaccaro writes like a good utility infielder."

"Mike Vaccaro understands the comic, tribal impulses that make Yankee-hating and Red Sox–bashing such worthwhile pursuits. But now, after more than a century of ever-increasing hostilities—an epoch rendered as baseball's version of the Hundred Years War—New Yorkers and Bostonians finally have cause to agree: *Emperors and Idiots* is a hell of a read."

"Vaccaro draws on memories of present and past players, officials and fans for the saga of mostly Yankee triumphs and Red Sox frustrations. The dramatic league play-offs—New York's 2003 win and Boston's final curse-ender in 2004—are fitting highlights."

EMPERORS
AND IDIOTS

EMPERORS AND IDIOTS

THE HUNDRED-YEAR RIVALRY
BETWEEN THE YANKEES AND RED SOX,
FROM THE VERY BEGINNING TO
THE END OF THE CURSE

Mike Vaccaro

Anchor Books
A Division of Random House, Inc.
New York

FIRST ANCHOR BOOKS (BROADWAY BOOKS) EDITION, 2006

Copyright © 2006 by Mike Vaccaro

All rights reserved. Published in the United States by Anchor Books,
a division of Random House, Inc., New York, and in Canada by
Random House of Canada Limited, Toronto. Originally published in
hardcover in the United States by Doubleday in 2005.

Anchor Books and colophon are registered trademarks of Random House, Inc.

Book design by Chris Welch

The Library of Congress has cataloged the hardcover edition as:
Vaccaro, Mike.
Emperors and idiots : the hundred-year rivalry between the Yankees and Red
Sox, from the very beginning to the end of the curse / by Mike Vaccaro.—1st ed.
p.   cm.
1. New York Yankees (Baseball team)—History.   2. Boston Red Sox (Baseball
team)—History.   3. Sports rivalries—United States—History.   I. Title.
GV875.N4V33 2005   796.357'64'097471—dc22
2004065543

Anchor ISBN: 978-0-7679-1910-4

www.anchorbooks.com

147468846

For Michael F. Vaccaro Sr. (1932–2003), who on June 29, 1974, took me to my first baseball game (Mets 4, Cardinals 0), bought me my first knish (with mustard), taught me how to keep a scorecard (in ink), pointed out the press box, and started the whole thing.

CONTENTS

x   **Contents**

ACKNOWLEDGMENTS

This book was born out of a marriage of two wonderful pastimes: baseball and writing about baseball. It's a lucky guy who can make a go of doing what he loves every day, and a luckier guy who gets to write his first book aided by so many terrific people.

This project would not have been possible without the resources and recollections of so many whose words are contained within, notably: Mark Bellhorn, Yogi Berra, Aaron Boone, Ralph Branca, Mike "Mex" Carey, Brian Cashman, Peter Cipriano, Johnny Damon, Bucky Dent, Theo Epstein, John Flaherty, Terry Francona, Jim Frasch, Harry Frazee III, Max Frazee, Nomar Garciaparra, Rich Gossage, Ron Guidry, Tommy

Henrich, John Henry, Reggie Jackson, Derek Jeter, Dave Kaplan, Bill Lee, Grady Little, Jim Lonborg, Derek Lowe, Larry Lucchino, Sparky Lyle, Jeffrey Lyons, Lou Merloni, Gene Michael, Kevin Millar, John Miller, Bruce Mollar, Bill Morgan, Graig Nettles, David Ortiz, Steve Palermo, Jeremy Perelman, Johnny Pesky, Lou Piniella, Manny Ramirez, Jerry Remy, Jim Rice, Mariano Rivera, Mickey Rivers, Phil Rizzuto, Alex Rodriguez, Howard Rosenberg, Frank Russo, Bob Rutchik, Ron Schreier, Buck Showalter, Steve Silva, Alfonso Soriano, Bobby Thomson, Joe Torre, Mike Torrez, Pete Trinkle, Tim Wakefield, Todd Walker, Tom Werner, Carl Yastrzemski, Tony Zannotti, and Don Zimmer.

Jason Kaufman, my editor at Doubleday, was as invested in making this book work as I was, a remarkably empowering thing. Considering he'd edited a little book called *The Da Vinci Code* not long before, it sure set the bar fairly high, and his guidance, wisdom, and friendship were invaluable. Jenny Choi patiently and pleasantly answered a first-time author's million and one questions, for which I'll be eternally grateful. My agents, Greg Dinkin and Frank Scatoni at Venture Literary, showed faith in this project—and nourished a novice author—from the moment Aaron Boone made Tim Wakefield's knuckleball disappear, and for that I am indebted. My deepest thanks also go to Adrian Wojnarowski, who set this project in motion and whose friendship, wisdom, and talent have all contributed greatly to this finished product.

Lou D'Ermilio at Fox Sports and Andrew Fegyveresi at YES Network both eagerly supplied me with video resources that proved invaluable to this book. Rick Cerrone and Glenn Geffner, the PR honchos for the Yankees and Red Sox, were great sources of assistance and patience, and Pamela J. Ganley, the Red Sox' coordinator of alumni and archives, was a big help as well. The kind folks at both the Boston and New York Public Libraries, too many of them to name, were consistently helpful during my primary research. So was Frank Vaccaro (no relation), whom I was lucky enough to sit next to at the library one gray December Saturday and who opened up a whole new Society for American Baseball Research flavor to this project.

I wouldn't have been in a position to do this book at all had so many folks not helped at so many stops along the way. George Evans and Russ Jandoli encouraged me to take a whack at journalism at St. Bonaventure University, and once I was there I was lucky enough to learn the tricks of the trade and the craft of writing thanks to the generous hands of Mary Hamilton, Rick Simpson, Jim Martine, and the late Pete Barrecchia. Chuck Ward was the first man ever to pay me for a story I'd written, at the *Olean Times-Herald*, Chuck Pollock gave me my first sportswriting gig there later on, and Tom Missel showed me every day how to do the job right. Bill Burr rescued my career in 1993, giving me a second chance at the *Middletown Times Herald-Record*. Dinn Mann and Mike Fannin gave me a taste of the big time at the *Kansas City Star* before Kevin Whitmer and Chris D'Amico brought me home, to the *Star-Ledger*. And all Greg Gallo and Dick Klayman did after that was give me the only job I'd ever wanted, at the *New York Post*, which has been like being asked to sit in with the E Street Band.

The baseball crew at the *Post* makes me look a lot smarter than I am, starting with Joel Sherman, sounding board and friend. Michael Morrissey was especially helpful lending his eyes and ears when mine were elsewhere; George King, Mark Hale, and Kevin Kernan all make the *Post* a must-read every morning for baseball fans in New York City. Lenn Robbins and Dan Martin are an essential part of our playoff team, and Dave Blezow lent a vital helping hand while I was trying to procure photographs for this book. Ian O'Connor, Joe Posnanski, Marc Berman, and Les Carpenter always provide wisdom and support during the column-writing process; they worked overtime during the writing of this book. Dominic Amore and Scott Mackenzie were both kind enough to give the raw version of this book a careful read, so you wouldn't have to, and I am grateful for their skill and friendship. And an amazing batch of newspaper friends were there to provide support and counsel, among them Pete Caldera, Jack Curry, Jon Heyman, Jerry Izenberg, Steve Politi, Ed Price, T. J. Quinn, Lawrence Rocca, Steve Serby, and Wright Thompson.

Lastly, I want to salute the two women in my life: my mother, Ann McMahon Vaccaro, who ceded me not only her grammar gene but also an unyielding belief that her boy could write a book someday. And, of course, to Leigh Hursey Vaccaro, best friend and best girl, whose smile on the day I sold this book is matched in my memory only by the one I wore the day I met her.

INTRODUCTION

It was no great surprise that Yogi Berra would be the one who described the situation best, at the start of my journey, inside the museum in Montclair, New Jersey, that bears his name. This was a couple of weeks after the end of the 2003 baseball season. Across the next few months, I would pose variations of the same basic question to dozens of baseball players, some active, some retired, all of them having logged some hard time on either side of baseball's Great Fault Line.

The question, essentially, was this: What does it feel like?

What makes the Red Sox–Yankees rivalry so compelling, so seductive, so absorbing? Why do the passions run so deep on both sides, much deeper than anywhere else in American professional sports? Why is there more electricity attached to a meaningless spring training game between these two in Fort Myers, Florida, than to half the playoff games contested every October by other teams? And how can one possibly understand what it is to play high-pressure baseball games under the glare of this unrelenting spotlight?

What does *that* feel like?

The Red Sox and the Yankees have been feeding this festering feud for a hundred years already, from the moment on May 8, 1903, when a New York Highlanders outfielder named Dave Fultz hit a harmless ground ball to Boston Pilgrims first baseman Candy LaChance. Fultz, a former football player, stormed down the first-base line with little regard for whatever was standing in his way—in this case, Boston pitcher George Winter, who had dashed over to cover the bag. The collision was ugly, the contact audible to everyone inside the Huntington Avenue Grounds, and a hush fell over the small ballpark in southwest Boston. Winter was knocked nearly senseless. Fultz, unapologetic, simply dusted his uniform off and growled at Pilgrims manager Jimmy Collins: "Tell your pitcher to pitch or get him the hell off the field." It was the second baseball game ever contested between American League teams representing the dueling harbor cities of Boston and New York. New York won the game, 6–1; five months later, Boston wound up capturing the pennant and the first-ever World Series. The rivalry's first blood had been drawn, and it had been bad, and it would stay that way.

"It's a different kind of rivalry," Derek Jeter would explain a century later.

"It's hard to put it into words, really," the normally loquacious Kevin Millar would say.

"You just always knew they were the biggest games of the year," Phil Rizzuto would chirp.

"Bigger than the World Series, when we played 'em," Johnny Pesky would insist.

"I guess I hate the Yankees now," an unsuspecting Curt Schilling would quip on the day in November 2003 when he was introduced as the Red Sox' new pitching ace, mouthing a politician's line but holding no real enmity in his heart; that would come later.

All of the participants can talk for hours about old stories, old games, old arguments, old brushbacks, old resentments, and yet they tie their tongues into stopper knots describing what it's like to live square in the eye of baseball's perfect storm. All but Yogi, of course, who'd already summed it up quite eloquently, providing a dash of his own specific Zen.

"You got to go through it," he'd said, "to know what it's like to go through it."

It wasn't until a few months later that I would completely grasp what he meant. During one especially manic two-week chunk of February 2004, I shuttled back and forth between the Yankees' spring training headquarters in Tampa and the Red Sox' in Fort Myers, making the four-hour round-trip drive along I-75 every day. At each location, I'd bought official caps from the official team stores, which I'd intended to give away as gifts (it was surely no coincidence, either, that at $33, the Yankees hat cost eight bucks more than the Red Sox hat, a percentage that fairly mimicked the difference in the teams' starting payrolls for the 2004 season).

The caps never did make it to the gift boxes. It was a few days later that I wore the Red Sox cap into a downtown Tampa casino, where I sat at a low-stakes poker table. An hour or so in, with maybe $20 of my money shoved into the pot, as I was waiting to rake it back after revealing queens full of jacks, I was horrified to see the player three seats over from me lay down kings full of sixes. They call that a "bad beat" at any poker table on the planet. The guy who robbed me nodded sympathetically as he neatly stacked his chips.

Then added: "Shit, dude, you must be used to losing heartbreakers by now, right?"

My first reaction was a cocktail of curiosity cut with anger, wondering how this smarmy little shit could possibly know about my long and inglorious history with seven-card stud. It took only a few moments to realize what he meant, when I remembered what I had worn to that table, how the dark blue cap had developed into a universally accepted symbol for suffering and torment, the Old English *B* on the front literally a scarlet letter representing baseball bereavement.

"First Boone," said another guy at the table, laughing, referring to the Yankees third baseman whose epic eleventh-inning home run had broken a fresh set of hearts all across New England four months before. "And then kings full of sixes. Tough."

And I understood.

This was exactly the kind of visceral feeling that had drawn me to this subject in the first place. Having grown up a fan of neither team but an admirer of both, I'd seen this ancient squabble reach its zenith in the American League Championship Series in October 2003, seven games that captivated two cities and captured the imaginations of millions of observers both passive and passionate. It is impossible to grow up an acolyte of baseball in this country, as I did, and not have at least a passing fascination with the Yankees, the sport's dynastic ruling class, and the Red Sox, the perennial sparring partner, the team the Yankees are most closely identified with—and, through 2003, dominated—from the moment they moved to New York from Baltimore before the 1903 season. Ever since, players have come, gone, retired, died. Generations of fans have been turned over. And still, there is an unmistakable aura about these two teams when they enter each other's space, now more than ever.

I'd only felt it from a distance before. Suddenly, a table of card-playing strangers had looked at my headwear and made an absolute judgment about me. And I eased into the role with little difficulty.

"Yeah," I said, aping the words I'd heard from dozens of legitimate Red Sox fans the prior few months. "*Aaron Fucking Boone . . .*"

A few days later, I was flying to Arizona, neutral territory for both camps, and I decided to have a little fun. I kept both caps at the ready and switched them every few hours, just to see what would happen.

When I was wearing the Red Sox cap, people would nod to me knowingly, as if they understood the unspoken wounds I'd suffered during what had surely been an unending apprenticeship of angst.

Some wore Sox caps of their own, and the looks they flashed were so real, so obvious, so *empathetic*, I nearly copped to being an imposter, a fraud, an actor wearing a prop. But I didn't. Which entitled me to this greeting from the guy who drove the rental-car shuttle at the Phoenix Airport, who'd done little to chisel away the Brooklyn still hanging all over his syllables: "The Red Sox blow, man. Can I take your bags?" He smiled, his rough words clearly etched in respect. After boarding, I found myself seated across from a man wearing a black and orange Baltimore Orioles cap. He was laughing. "Screw the Yankees," he said. I nodded. *Yeah. Screw 'em.*

Switching caps was more surreal. No one looks you in the eye when you wear a Yankees cap, unless, of course, the other guy is wearing a Yankees cap, too. Then you might get a high five, as I did walking through the Phoenix Metro Mall, or a fist bump, as I did in the airport lounge. Red Sox sympathizers, both behatted and bare-headed, either cower or glower. And everyone else just kind of stares straight ahead, trying either to ignore you or to vaporize you with their contempt. But everyone, *everyone*, reacts to you if you wear one of those two hats, dark blue with red *B* or darker blue with interlocking white *NY*. I wear a lot of hats. No one has ever commented on my bright green 2002 Masters hat. No one has ever said a word about my vintage blue Brooklyn Dodgers cap. Not once.

And then I recalled the words of a wise old man.

"You got to go through it," he'd said, "to know what it's like to go through it."

He was right. Suddenly, I understood. And, as Yogi might also have said, "You don't have to be in it to be in it." You don't have to be a player, a manager, or an owner to be fully engaged—although it doesn't hurt to be any of those things, either. If you enter this fray, if you endorse one side or the other, then it makes you who you are, and what you are— forever—as much as any declaration anywhere in sports. And in the twenty-three months stretching from December 2002 through October 2004, there came an even more startling stream of contempt, antagonism, respect, fear, anger, joy, and sorrow—on both sides—than ever before. Given the history that already preceded all of this, that would have seemed virtually impossible. As we shall see, it was anything but.

What follows is an appreciation for all the color, all the characters, all the craziness that has fueled this wonderfully American bond between the Yankees, baseball's unmatched empire, regal and dominant and preeminent for decades, and the Red Sox, who dubbed themselves a merry band of carefree idiots, eager to challenge the establishment Yankees, determined not to rest their bearded, hairy, free-spirited selves until they'd unseated not only their nemesis but eighty-six years of torment as well.

Mike Vaccaro
Hillsdale, New Jersey
November 2004

EMPERORS
AND IDIOTS

CHAPTER

1

NOT AGAIN

I don't know if I believe in curses, or jinxes, or anything like that.
But I'll tell you what I do believe: I believe in ghosts. And we've got
some ghosts in this stadium. —*Derek Jeter, October 17, 2003*

Every day you sit in front of your locker and ask God, "What the hell
is going on?" —*Rick Burleson, September 17, 1978*

He'd been asleep for only a second or two, the kind of restless, involuntary slumber that arrives only after you've stretched your work-night bedtime way too long. Through much of working-class America, millions of people were fighting a similar battle, not wanting to give in to their eyelids, certain that something unforgettable would soon fill their television screens. Clocks up and down the East Coast had just clicked to 12:15 A.M. on this morning of October 17, 2003, including the digital Armitron chronometer that dominated the center field scoreboard at Yankee Stadium, right above where the most important numbers were posted: Red Sox 5, Yankees 5, bottom of the eleventh inning, seventh and deciding game of the American League Championship Series.

It was quiet inside the eighty-year-old stadium, a spooky silence having long before seeped into the bleachers and grandstands, where 56,279 had gathered to watch these two old foes play out the final moves of their sweaty chess match. It was a duel that had ground

1

two cities to a halt, reduced millions of fingernails to the quick, even captured the imaginations of otherwise sane citizens who spend their days blissfully unaffected by baseball. This was why so many people in so many parts of the country were trying to blink away their exhaustion as Thursday night bled into Friday morning, as Yankees third baseman Aaron Boone stepped to the plate to face a Boston knuckleball specialist named Tim Wakefield, as all those timepieces ticked over to 12:16.

The exact minute, as it happens, that Bucky Dent fell asleep.

It was the shouting that jarred him back to life.

"What happened?" Marianne Dent yelped.

"Huh?" her husband sputtered.

"Look at the TV! They're mobbing somebody! The Yankees just won the game! They won the pennant! I think someone hit a home run!"

They were showing replays, and Dent, wide awake now inside his Boynton Beach, Florida, home, watched Wakefield deliver a flat, fat knuckleball, watched Boone all but jump out of his spikes as he dove into the pitch, watched the camera follow the baseball as it sketched a beautiful white path against the black Bronx sky, watched it settle into the lower left-field stands, watched Wakefield march solemnly off the mound, watched Boone jump onto home plate with both feet, watched as the crowd, suddenly liberated from nearly four hours of unbearable tension, exploded in a giddy rush of joy.

"Look at you," Marianne Dent said. "You're beaming."

It was more than that, of course. Dent's eyes remained locked on the TV, but the moment he saw it all unfold, his soul had immediately drifted. . . .

Suddenly, he was rounding first base on another October day, exactly twenty-five years and fifteen days before, the last time the Red Sox and Yankees had met under these circumstances, one game for a championship, only then the game was played in the middle of a glorious afternoon, in another grand old ball field called Fenway Park. Dent had greeted Mike Torrez' fastball with the sweet spot of his borrowed Max

44 bat, and now his eyes were trained on the left fielder, Carl Yastrzem-ski, who was drifting back toward the left-field wall, only 310 feet from home plate. Nobody ever played that thirty-seven-foot-high wall at Fenway like Yaz, everyone knew that, so Dent waited for a sign as he started chugging into second. *Did I really get enough of it?*

When Yastrzemski's knees buckled, Dent knew he had.

He looked up in time to see the ball settle softly against the net behind the wall. He thrust his right fist into the air, clapped his hands together, and floated the final 180 feet of his journey home. A 2–0 Red Sox lead had become a 3–2 Yankees lead with one swing of Dent's bat, with two outs in the bottom of the seventh inning. The Yankees would win, 5–4. It was October 2, 1978, and Bucky Dent was twenty-six years old, and if you had told him that he would ever feel the same rush that bubbled his bloodstream that day, when he staggered Old Man Yaz' legs and broke New England's spirit and fueled the New York Yankees on to their twenty-second world championship, he would never have believed you.

Except that's exactly how he felt all these years later, inside his bed-room, watching mayhem tumble out of his television.

"You called it earlier, didn't you?" Marianne asked.

Dent laughed. It was true. Before he'd even washed the champagne from his hair that afternoon a quarter century earlier, Dent acquired an instant appreciation for the link he'd just crafted for himself within the long chain connecting the Yankees and the Red Sox. He quickly embraced the humbling reality that a twelve-year career that included two World Series rings and three trips to the All-Star Game would for-ever be reduced to and remembered for that singular trip to the plate, one of 4,512 official at-bats he would accrue as a major leaguer. That was fine with him. Dent had been born in Savannah, Georgia, and raised in Florida, but he had rooted for the Yankees as a kid. He knew all about the Yankee mystique before he ever added to it. He believed in the almost mystical way the Red Sox taunt the Yankees, and the Yankees haunt the Red Sox, how they've stubbornly refused to exit each other's shadow from the first time they encountered each other, on May 7, 1903, a 6–2 Boston victory.

Hell, how could he *not* know?

By 1983, Dent had been traded away to the Texas Rangers, though he still owned a house in Wyckoff, New Jersey, which he rented out during the season. That year, the lease belonged to the man who'd recently been hired as the Yankees' third-base coach, a baseball lifer named Don Zimmer, the same man who'd been the Red Sox manager on October 2, 1978, and whose professional fate was irreversibly sealed with that one swing of Dent's bat.

"First time I go in there," Zimmer recalled years later, during his second tour of duty on the Yankees coaching staff, "I notice a picture on the wall, and guess what? It's a picture of that son of a bitch hitting that home run. I go into the next room—same thing, another picture. And the next. And the next. Every fucking room. You know what I did? I turned 'em all around. Then I called him up on the phone and I told him I'd turned 'em all around."

So Dent, having done as much as any one man could to stir the Red Sox–Yankees embers, understood better than anyone that something different was bound to happen in this game, eventually. He had become something of a student of the Red Sox' tortured history, one whose unholy trinity of infamy involved three separate incidents—the selling of Babe Ruth, the Bucky Dent home run, and the fabled ground ball that leaked through Bill Buckner's legs in game six of the 1986 World Series—with one notable thing in common.

"As the game is building up," Dent would say a few months later, "I'm going, 'OK, who's going to do something? Who's got a *B* in their name—Bernie [Williams] or [Aaron] Boone—to keep the *B*'s going?' And then after I dozed off for a second, then woke up, I said, 'God dang, somebody hit a home run!' They showed Boone had hit it, and I was like, 'Oh, right!' Yeah, I was thinking to myself, 'Who's got a *B* in their name that's going to keep Babe, Bucky, Buckner alive?' It was Boone."

No further explanation is needed for why this man, who entered the world as Russell Earl Dent on November 25, 1951, had at least once on every New England day that passed from October 2, 1978, through that early morning hour of October 17, 2003, in every precinct of Red Sox Nation, from Cambridge, Massachusetts, to Concord, New Hampshire, from Winooski, Vermont, to Waterville, Maine, been referred to by his more common name.

Bucky Fucking Dent . . .

The joy was not limited to Bucky Dent's bedroom in South Florida. Back at Yankee Stadium, in the South Bronx, nobody wanted to leave, nobody wanted to let go of the night, nobody wanted to walk away from the latest installment of this most remarkable baseball passion play. On the field, Boone was mobbed by his teammates, by television microphones, by his manager, Joe Torre. "What I want to know," Boone would gush, "is this: What are all these people doing in my dream?" Mariano Rivera, the peerless Yankees relief pitcher who'd thrown three brilliant innings, "waiting the whole time for one of our guys to make a ball disappear," as Torre described it, had collapsed at the pitcher's mound, far apart from the joyous pile forming around home plate, and it took a two-man tandem of coaches Lee Mazzilli and Willie Randolph to finally pry him from the dirt. The public address system blared "New York, New York" fourteen straight times, and with every replay, 56,279 voices joined an old Dodgers fan named Sinatra when he stretched out the words "Ayyyy-num-berrrrr-oooooone . . ."

The clubhouse was delirious, incorporating all the restraint and dignity of a Delta House rush party. Baby-faced Yankees general manager Brian Cashman, who could easily be mistaken for a freshman pledge, doused everyone he could find with gleeful two-fisted vengeance, and when he spoke of it a few months later he would call it "the happiest room I've ever seen in my life." Later, the party would spill out of Yankee Stadium and cross the Macombs Dam Bridge into Manhattan, to Scores and the China Club and Jay-Z's new place, the 40-40 Club, all the late-night palaces where these princes of New York City were always welcomed. Being a New York Yankee means always being on the right side of life's velvet rope, never more so than now, in the first few hours of their reign as American League champions.

Jason Giambi, the Yankees first baseman who'd hit two home runs off Pedro Martinez that night to keep his team close, pointed at Boone and smiled. Not only had Boone just hit a home run for the ages, but his wife, Laura Cover—also known to readers of *Playboy* magazine as Miss October 1998—had just entered the clubhouse to congratulate her husband on his heroics.

"That lucky son of a bitch," Giambi said, "should head straight to Vegas."

It was a feeling shared by most New Yorkers, even those not married to centerfolds. "What a great night to be a Yankees fan!" a longtime Yankees booster observed as he entered the clubhouse, before he was engulfed by a two-armed Joe Torre hug. Rudolph Giuliani, formerly New York City's mayor, forever its highest-profile Yankees fan, accepted a brand-new cap and exclaimed, "There's nothing sweeter than beating the Red Sox! Nothing!"

A hundred steps down the hallway, past the photographs of bygone Yankee immortals and bygone Yankee celebrations, through the narrow blue-walled corridor that leads to the third-base side of the stadium, there couldn't have been a more jarring juxtaposition. Inside the visitors' clubhouse, grown men still clad in their Red Sox vestments were openly weeping, not caring who saw them, oblivious to the cameras clicking away, recording their pain for posterity. Professional locker rooms never look this way, or feel this way, or sound this way.

"It was like we were all back in high school, like we'd just gotten beat in the state playoffs, and everyone was gonna graduate, and we weren't ever gonna see each other again," is the way Kevin Millar, the Boston first baseman, would describe it. "When you're a teenager and you lose the big football game, that's when you see guys cry uncontrollably. You don't see that much at this level."

The cramped room was solemn and funereal, no music, no television, no chatter that rose above a hoarse whisper. The Boston Red Sox had been five outs away from winning this game, winning this series, sending all of New England into a spin cycle of glee that would have lasted forever, suffocating once and forever the relentless talk of jinxes, hexes, poxes, and curses. They'd had a three-run lead with the best pitcher in baseball, Pedro Martinez, on the mound and the hottest bullpen in the playoffs warmed up and ready to go. Five outs to go, three runs to protect. And they couldn't do it. They couldn't beat the Yankees.

Again.

Again.

"I let us down," said Wakefield, who'd pitched so brilliantly in the series but would forever be remembered as the man who served up Boone's game-winner. His voice, reduced to a rasp, was barely audible, even in the silence of the room. "All I can say is, I'm sorry."

There was exactly one man in the country who could understand what Wakefield was feeling, the specific emotions at war within his heart. At that exact moment, he was sitting on a sofa in his living room in Naperville, Illinois, watching ESPN as it replayed the home run again and again. Half an hour earlier, he'd been in the same exact spot, a fresh soft drink in his hand, a queasy sense of inevitability swirling in his stomach, as if he knew exactly what was coming. It hadn't taken long. Wakefield's first pitch had made him cringe, even before Boone stepped into it. Too flat. Too straight. Too inviting.

"Jesus," Mike Torrez said. "Not again."

All this time later, Torrez laughed as he remembered the ball he threw to Bucky Dent, laughed as he said, "I thought I'd gotten the ball in plenty enough, I really did. I'd gotten him out on almost the same exact pitch two innings earlier." Ah, but the vagaries of baseball are sometimes measured by the width of a hair. A pitch that yields a harmless pop-up to the shortstop in the fifth inning can bear a home run in the seventh. All it takes is one less mile per hour in velocity, or a centimeter's tail toward the fat part of the plate, or a generous gust of wind properly timed. Torrez had owned Dent his whole career. Wakefield? He'd gotten Boone out easily five times in this series, three weak fly balls and two strikeouts. He'd made Boone look utterly foolish. Right up to the last pitch.

"Sometimes," Mike Torrez said, "you just have to understand and accept that the other guy beat you. That's what baseball is. One guy wins, one guy loses. It's a little trickier when you factor in all the feelings and all the emotions, of course. And with the Red Sox and the Yankees, shit . . ."

He laughed a little louder.

"When those two get together, it makes a holy war seem like a cocktail party."

Torrez has long accepted his role in the Yankees–Red Sox melodrama. He's been much closer to Ralph Branca than to Donnie Moore on the sliding scale of pitchers who surrendered epic postseason home runs. Twenty-seven years before Torrez delivered his fateful 1–1 fastball to Dent, Branca, a pitcher for the Brooklyn Dodgers, had thrown another fastball, this one on an 0–1 count, in the bottom of the ninth inning of a National League playoff game at the Polo Grounds in upper Manhattan. Bobby Thomson connected, a radio announcer named Russ Hodges wailed "The Giants win the pennant!" into baseball eternity, and the two of them, Thomson and Branca, rode off into the rubber-chicken sunset together, earning a fortune on the after-dinner speaking circuit. "I think Ralph's pain was eased by all the money we made through the years thanks to that one pitch," Thomson said fifty summers after that fabled "shot heard round the world," laughing.

"Hey, the way I look at it, when you're a part of a moment like that, you should consider yourself blessed," Torrez says. "People are always going to talk about me and Bucky, Ralph and Bobby, and now Tim and Aaron. It's good to be remembered. I guess Donnie Moore [a California Angels pitcher who, three years after allowing a home run to Dave Henderson that rescued the Red Sox from oblivion in the 1986 playoffs, committed suicide] didn't feel that way. And look, I know Red Sox fans don't feel that way."

No. Red Sox fans had already amassed plenty of memorable moments in their collective scrapbooks of misery, so many of them against the Yankees, building layer upon layer of scar tissue. They didn't have to hear Wakefield's stand-up apologies, because they'd heard the same words, the same sentiments, the same apologies so many times before. They'd heard Yastrzemski mutter after that '78 playoff game: "Those bastards always have a little bit extra." They'd heard from Ted Williams, Teddy Ballgame, after the final weekend of the 1949 season, when he'd lamented, "If you can't win one game in two tries with the season on the line, maybe you'd just better admit you were beaten by the better team." If they were feeling especially masochistic, they could have gone all the way back to January 5, 1920, when a theater impresario named Harry Frazee, who also happened to own the Red Sox, said this after selling Babe Ruth to the Yankees for the astonishing sum of $100,000: "I am well-satisfied to let him try his fortune in New York."

Still, in so many ways, this was more than just another night in an endless string of torturous loyalty tests. All Aaron Boone did at sixteen minutes after midnight that awful morning was ring in the longest night, the longest morning, and the longest off-season in the history of that anguished confederacy known as Red Sox Nation.

Bill Lee, who in another life was one of the great Yankee-killers of all time, winning twelve of the fifteen decisions he recorded as a Red Sox pitcher against New York from 1969 to 1978, listened to the game's final seven innings on his car radio, driving from a television studio in Boston to his home in Vermont.

"I was just pulling into my driveway when the bottom of the eleventh inning started," Lee said. "And I mean, you could hear the crack of the bat hitting the ball coming right through my speaker. All I heard was that crack. It's all I needed to hear. I turned the radio off and said, 'There goes the pennant.'"

Back in greater Boston, the melancholy was far more vivid, and it bled everywhere. Inside the Tequila Rain sports bar on Lansdowne Street, right across the street from the Fenway Park bleachers, a gnawing sense of inevitability had already crept into the room once the Yankees had evened the game at 5–5.

"We just know these things," said Steve Silva, a marketing specialist who has followed the Sox for over thirty years and spilled more than a few pints of blood along the way.

Some uninitiated souls would hear a quote like that and shake their heads. Red Sox fans were self-fulfilling prophets, they insisted, whose inherent cynicism provided the ultimate karmic blockade for the team they purport to love so much. Who could succeed in a place populated by so much ghastly gloom? But the newbies never understood. They hadn't seen their own grandfathers live out long, otherwise prosperous lives without once seeing their Red Sox win a championship. They hadn't heard their fathers' sad tales about waiting for the Red Sox to hurry up and clinch the 1949 pennant so they could run to Fenway and buy World Series tickets for a World Series that never came. They hadn't been on the receiving end of Bucky Dent. These prophecies needed no help from the faithful. For eighty-five consecutive years, they succeeded quite nicely all by themselves.

"Even when Pedro was struggling, I thought, 'If they can just get through this, we'll be okay,'" said Mike Carey, a thirty-two-year-old Red Sox fan who suffers the great misfortune of both living and working in Queens, New York. "Seriously. I kept saying, 'Just get by here . . .'"

Long pause. Long sigh. Bitter laughter.

"When they tied it . . . it's like getting kicked in the nuts, it really is. I mean, you can't possibly feel worse, you know? At least you think that's the way it is. And then Boone hit the home run . . ." Another pause. "Let me put it this way. That game was played on Thursday. The previous Saturday, I'd had to go to a funeral. And I felt a lot worse on Thursday. A lot worse."

Carey's wife, Cassie, summed it up even better.

"It's a sickness," she said. "It should have a name."

It **never ends,** of course. Not for Sox fans. Not for the Yankees fans who lord over them. One hundred forty-three days passed from the moment Boone's ball disappeared into the blurry glee at Yankee Stadium to the instant Bronson Arroyo fired a first-pitch strike to Kenny Lofton, leading off the top of the first inning in the first spring training game between these teams, at City of Palms Park in Fort Myers, Florida. Tickets for the exhibition had been going for as much as $1,000 on eBay in the morning, and for only slightly less from ticket scalpers outside the small ball yard. A Yankees official engaged in a heated parking-lot argument with a Red Sox worker. It was only March 7, yet it already felt like October 17.

"Only in this rivalry," Derek Jeter said, shaking his head in wonder. "It's crazy."

Those 143 days, of course, constituted the most eventful off-season in the history of organized baseball. The Red Sox, still smarting from their ALCS defeat, fired the first shot, pulling off a staggering Thanksgiving Day trade for Curt Schilling. Across eighty-five years of abject frustration, the Red Sox have had a better pitching staff than the Yankees in maybe ten of those seasons, probably fewer. Suddenly, they had Pedro Martinez and Curt Schilling at the top of their starting rotation, while the Yankees lost Andy Pettitte, Roger Clemens, and David Wells to, respectively, free agency, temporary retirement, and contractual treachery.

Somehow, within weeks, the Red Sox reduced the buzz caused by the Schilling trade to a dull roar, because they were hours—some insisted minutes—away from closing the biggest deal in the 103-year history of the franchise. Alex Rodriguez, the best player on the planet, was on his way. The pieces were in place. The Red Sox and Texas Rangers would swap Rodriguez and Manny Ramirez, baseball's only $20 million-per-year fat cats. To make room for A-Rod, the Sox would then send Nomar Garciaparra—the most popular everyday Red Sox player since Yastrzemski—to Chicago in exchange for outfielder Magglio Ordonez. The chatter was so laced with confidence, even the most skeptical lot of Red Sox fans had a difficult time disbelieving it. It was going to happen. Any day now. Any hour now. Any minute. It was going to happen.

It was definitely going to happen!

It didn't happen.

The Red Sox froze, asking Rodriguez to restructure his contract to ease the immediate fiscal burden on the club. Rodriguez, eager to escape Texas, desperate to be paroled from last place, agreed. Commissioner Bud Selig gave his conditional approval. Rodriguez' agent, Scott Boras, did the same. But the Players Association, fearful of setting what it felt would be a dangerous precedent, balked. They wouldn't let Rodriguez, in essence, buy his way up the American League food chain. They would make him accept every penny of his $25 million annual salary, whether he liked it or not. Rodriguez, seeing the light the way most do after being paid a visit by a *caporegime*, said he would never betray his union brothers. He was going back to Texas. The Rangers named him captain. Both sides swore this would be a more prosperous corporate marriage than Sears and Roebuck. Red Sox fans sighed about what might have been.

And waited until February 17—the day Alex Rodriguez officially became a New York Yankee—before deciding to throw up.

"I said the Boone thing was like being kicked in the balls?" Mike Carey said. "This is like getting kicked, getting back up, and getting kicked again."

By the same guy, too.

For the only reason why the Yankees even thought about entering the A-Rod sweepstakes was because Boone, the man who delivered them in October, shredded his knee playing pickup basketball in January. So Boone hammered the Red Sox twice in the space of three months: once in the ALCS, once with his ACL.

The season hadn't been decided, of course; it was barely under way. But this was just one more Yankee victory eked out at the eleventh hour, one more critical crossroads when the Red Sox couldn't hold a lead late in the game. Only this time it was winter instead of autumn, February instead of October. And you wonder why Bill Lee didn't even wait for confirmation that the crack he heard over his car radio wasn't just a long foul ball? You wonder why Mike Carey, poor guy, went to watch *Mystic River* in a theater the night the Rodriguez-to-the-Yankees stories began to heat up—Valentine's Day, naturally—and, after noticing in the opening scene that one of the kids is wearing a Red Sox cap, found his mind wandering helplessly away from the film and onto other important matters, such as: *Why does this always happen to us?* You wonder why the Tequila Rain was filled by that death-watch pall a full hour before Boone hit his home run, why people steadily started to leave, knowing they'd rather witness the final, unavoidable heartbreak in the privacy of their own automobiles, apartments, dens?

Oh yes—and you wonder why Yankees players (to say nothing of Yankees fans) felt more bulletproof than Clark Kent over the course of eighty-five years?

No need to wonder. All you needed to do was watch the way these two warring cities reacted in the wake of those seven wonderful games that constituted the ALCS. The way they both recovered—the Sox from another Yankee drilling, the Yankees from a disappointing six-game loss to the Florida Marlins in a decidedly anticlimactic World Series— within a matter of days, eager to resume hostilities. And the way they stayed well within each other's shadow for the entire length of the 2004 season, kicking their decadent duel into the stratosphere once and forever. Much would be made about whether this was truly a rivalry or not—after all, something so one-sided was more of a feud, no? An extended quarrel?—but the semantics mattered little. The owners knew that to be so. The players certainly did.

The fans?

They're the greatest benchmark. After all, months after the fact, a radio engineer named Peter Cipriano was willing to say of game seven: "I confess that I was physically ill early on when the Yanks were down, thinking about the concept of the Red Sox winning the ALCS—at Yankee Stadium, no less."

And, perhaps most telling of all, there was this message, posted at the Boston fan Web site www.nextyear.blogspot.com at 5:08 on the morning of February 2, 2004. The New England Patriots had won Super Bowl XXXVIII less than eight hours earlier, and most of the board's messages over the weekend had been devoted to that glorious achievement. The Pats' charge to glory included a fifteen-game winning streak that closed out the season, and for many Bostonians it was a necessary salve for their wounded sporting souls. Only an insomniac with the simple screen name of Rob realized the time to celebrate was over. And so he repeated the mantra that had echoed throughout New England for three full months: "Timlin in the 8th. Williamson in the 9th. Is that so fucking hard to understand?"

2

STRIKING BACK AT THE EMPIRE

> Oh, when it comes down to whom I'm rooting for, the Red Sox or
> the Yankees, there's no question about it—the Yankees. Once a Yankee,
> always a Yankee. I've never seen this team play except on TV a few times.
> I don't know enough about them to be able to say how great they are
> compared to the players I had. But I know a little bit about what happens
> when Boston plays New York. New York wins. —*Joe McCarthy,*
> *September 14, 1977*

> Last year I was assaulted by George Steinbrenner's Nazis,
> his brownshirts. He brainwashes those kids over there and they're led by
> Billy Martin—Hermann Goering the Second. They got a convicted felon
> running that club. What do you expect? —*Bill Lee, March 2, 1977*

Not that it matters, but Larry Lucchino invented neither the term nor the analogy.

"I'm not that clever," the Boston Red Sox' president said. "I wish I were. Maybe I could have had a lot more fun with my life, you know?"

No, as early as 1983, baseball pundits had likened the New York Yankees to an "evil empire," sometimes going so far as to employ capital letters for emphasis. Dozens of columnists, essayists, commentators, and fans had linked the two. It was easy, really. George Steinbrenner had fostered an image for himself as baseball's Darth Vader, sinister in his unquenchable desire to conquer all that lay before him. The truth is, Steinbrenner relished the role, not only from his perch atop the Yankees' organizational flow chart, but throughout his business affairs and personal life.

"The man thinks he is Vito Corleone," one former Yankees employee quipped in the summer of 2003. "The problem is, he treats everybody else like Fredo."

Steinbrenner had seen his team called the Evil Empire long before Christmas Day 2002; if anything, he courted the scorn, taking great delight in throwing his team's relentless success back in the faces of his envious critics. "Evil Empire" references were all but impossible to miss. In fact, if you do a LexisNexis search connecting May 25, 1977—the day *Star Wars* was released in theaters—with December 24, 2003, you get eighty-eight different hits connecting "Yankees" and "Evil Empire." During the 2000 playoffs, *Newsweek* magazine ran a story under the headline "The Most Hated Team in Baseball," and there wasn't a soul in the United States who had to read a word to know that the author, Mark Starr, was not referring to the Kansas City Royals.

Lucchino himself had casually used the term at least once before in public. In October 2002, not long after he arrived in the Red Sox' offices, following a disappointing, out-of-the-money finish for his new team, Lucchino had told a gathering of Boston writers: "We recognize that the Evil Empire is always out there willing to do what's in their best interests. We can't control that, but we recognize that the threat is always there, and the force will be with us." Again, there was no need for Lucchino to qualify his statements; he was not indicting the Tampa Bay Devil Rays. And yet Steinbrenner let the remark pass, even though he undoubtedly saw it, because even into his seventies Steinbrenner manages to read every syllable written about him, maintaining an extensive clip file.

Two and a half months later, that policy of benign indifference officially changed. Maybe forever.

For on Christmas Eve, the Yankees announced they had signed

Cuban émigré Jose Contreras to a four-year, $32 million contract. This had set off a full-scale angst attack in Boston, for the Red Sox had targeted Contreras from the second he'd arrived in Nicaragua, his new homeland, in late summer. They'd exhausted every bell and whistle in their possession, too. They'd learned where Contreras was staying in Managua, and they'd gobbled up the other fourteen rooms at the Hotel Campo Real, making sure no other interested club could get that close to him. They'd assembled a traveling party that included not only their freshly minted, twenty-eight-year-old general manager, Theo Epstein, but also Spanish-speaking organizational stalwarts Euclides Rojas (bullpen coach), Luis Eljaua (director of Latin American operations), and Luis Tiant (a fabled Sox alumnus who'd also fled Castro's Cuba). They'd made what they thought was a generous offer to a man who'd never thrown a single pitch in the major leagues, $27 million for four years.

And been overtaken, in the end, by the Yankees.

How many times had Red Sox fans been taunted by that very sentence across the years?

Lucchino had been on the job less than a year, but he'd gotten an instant sampling of what life in this rivalry is all about. So on Christmas morning, as Steinbrenner snapped open his copy of the *New York Times*, he saw this observation from the Sox' chatty executive: "The evil empire extends its tentacles even into Latin America."

And this time, Steinbrenner seethed.

"That's bullshit," snorted the Yankees' principal owner. "That's how a sick person thinks. I've learned this about Lucchino: He's baseball's foremost chameleon of all time. He changes colors depending on where he's standing. He's been at Baltimore [where the seeds of this feud were planted] and he deserted them there, and then went out to San Diego [and helped lead the 1998 Padres to the World Series, where they were promptly swept by the Yankees], and look at what trouble they're in out there. When he was in San Diego, he was a big man for the small markets. Now he's in Boston and he's for the big markets.

"He's not the kind of guy you want to have in your foxhole. He's running the team behind [Red Sox owner and former Yankees limited partner] John Henry's back. I warned John it would happen, told him, 'Just be careful.' Lucchino talks out of both sides of his mouth. He has trouble talking out of the front of it."

Lucchino, figuring he was already all in, countered, "Is that the best he could do? I don't think he even gets the reference."

Steinbrenner fumed for weeks. Around the office, he wouldn't even refer to the Red Sox by name, calling them "that team from north of here." He railed against Lucchino so often and so vividly, the commissioner's office finally ordered him to shut up. Chastened, Steinbrenner settled instead for a satisfying belly laugh when, on January 15, the Yankees engineered a three-way trade that delivered Montreal Expos right-hander Bartolo Colon—the other pitcher besides Contreras the Red Sox had coveted for months—to the Chicago White Sox. The Yankees received two players in the deal who would barely be heard from again, and yet Steinbrenner's mirth could be heard up and down the eastern seaboard, all the way to Fenway Park. Revenge was his, served ice cold, a feeling more gratifying than he could do justice to with words.

This grudge match was *so* on.

"I was just trying to be funny," Lucchino would say incredulously eight months later. "I guess George didn't find it so funny."

Maybe Steinbrenner had finally grown weary of the Darth Vader references. Maybe, as a rock-ribbed Republican (who'd been famously convicted for illegal contributions to Richard Nixon's 1972 reelection campaign), he understood that despite Red Sox fans' instant fascination with stretching the *Star Wars* metaphor as far as it would go, the empire in that film was never once referred to as "evil" (although the implications were surely there). No, it was on March 8, 1983, that Ronald Reagan, speaking to the National Association of Evangelicals in Orlando, had said, "I urge you to beware the temptation . . . to label both sides equally at fault, to ignore the facts of history and the aggressive impulses of an evil empire, to simply call the arms race a giant misunderstanding and thereby remove yourself from the struggle between right and wrong, good and evil."

And no, Reagan was not referring to Luxembourg.

"I don't think George ever once thought Lucchino was talking about *Star Wars*," one longtime Steinbrenner observer said. "I honestly think he believed Larry was calling him a commie."

For fans on both sides of this acrid baseball chasm, this was a dream come true. All the loathing, all the contempt, all the suspicion that Red Sox fans and Yankees fans felt for each other, all of that festering bile, rarely worked its way up the corporate ladder. Oh, occasionally it would flare up on the field. Bill Lee would call the Yankees "George Steinbrenner's Nazis" or refer to Billy Martin as "Hermann Goering the Second." Thurman Munson would try to drive his shoulder clear through Carlton Fisk's solar plexus. Johnny Pesky would deliver a double-play relay throw right into Joe DiMaggio's shoulder and would be mad because he'd really aimed for his head.

But through all the years, across all the pennant races, with all the bad blood that had been spilled since 1903, somehow the men at the top of each franchise had mostly managed to get along famously. Indeed, the American League would long bear the notorious tag as the "brother-in-law league" because its intramural battles tended to be far less bloody than the ones taking place in the National League. It may seem an odd paradox to think of the Red Sox and Yankees, these long-standing adversaries, as baseball bedfellows, but for much of the last century, that's often what the executive-suite relationships were like.

This first manifested itself during the very first summer-long duel between the two clubs, in 1904. That season would come down to a climactic five-game clash between the Yankees (then known as the High-landers) and the Red Sox (then known as the Pilgrims), but long before that showdown there would be hints of cronyism and allegations of collusion, and it would be just the first of many times when a Boston owner seemed to be wandering a little too close to the social orbit of the club that was supposed to be his chief antagonizer.

It had begun the previous off-season when Boston, fresh off winning the first-ever World Series, agreed to swap Long Tom Hughes in exchange for Jesse Tannehill. At the time, no one could forecast that Tannehill would go 21–11 for the '04 Pilgrims, or that Hughes would muddle through a dreadful 7–11 season for the Highlanders; all Boston baseball fans knew was that this seemed like a pillaging of the highest order. Hughes was Boston's best pitching prospect, fully five years younger than Tannehill. There was talk of a fix, the kind of unchecked chatter that abounded in those looser, laxer days, especially in places like Boston's Third Base Saloon—so called because it was "the last stop on the way home"—operated by outspoken Boston fan Michael "Nuf Ced" McGreevy, the head of the team's famed Royal Rooters booster club. Such wild speculation was common tavern patter in the aught years of the last century.

Only, in this case, it happened to be true.

Ban Johnson, the founder of the American League, desperately wanted a competitive team in New York City, not only to rival the National League Giants but also to establish a foothold in what already was the nation's burgeoning economic center. It was why he'd moved the bankrupt Baltimore Orioles north in the first place, and why now, in December of 1903, he'd arranged a meeting between Harry Killilea, the Boston owner, and the New York partnership of Frank Farrell (a poolroom king who controlled a gambling syndicate valued at $3 million) and William "Big Bill" Devery, former chief of police for the city of New York, who somehow had managed to cobble together enough scratch on his constable's salary to hold a significant chunk of New York real estate.

Farrell and Devery had made their respective fortunes, both within the law and without, by relying on sure things; Johnson was trying to extend them a similar baseball courtesy, hoping to turn their $18,000 investment in the franchise into a winning lottery ticket. And so the trade was done, over the deafening howls of the Royal Rooters and everyone else who cared about the team immodestly referred to as the "world champions" on everything from the club's own literature to the local newspaper headlines to the marquee at Huntington Avenue Grounds.

"Anything to strengthen New York!" they crowed, echoing a cry their great-great-grandchildren would still be bellowing a century later, although in 1903 the only thing resembling an Evil Empire was the Tammany Hall Democratic machine in New York City that had helped yield both Highlanders owners their fortunes. Devery, after all, was best known during his shakedown salad days with the NYPD for his personal credo of gluttony: "Hear, see, and say nothing; eat, drink, and pay nothing." That, in essence, became the Highlanders' own motto as 1903 became 1904.

Killilea's successor, John I. Taylor, extended the chummy relations with the men who should have been his chief adversaries. After purchasing the Pilgrims in late April, Taylor—scion of a prominent Boston newspaper family—watched his club promptly vault to the top of the American League, much to the chagrin of Johnson, much to the outrage of Frank Farrell and Big Bill Devery. Once again, Johnson arranged a sit-down, plied the parties with Cuban cigars and snifters of brandy, and smiled as the trio hit it off beautifully. By the end of their first meeting, Taylor agreed to part with his best offensive player, Patsy Dougherty, who'd hit .342 as a rookie in 1902 and paced the world champions with a .331 mark in '03, in exchange for an undisclosed sum of cash and an unremarkable infielder named Bob Unglaub.

And as much as another transaction between these clubs would cause something of a stir fifteen and a half years later, at least the selling of Babe Ruth encouraged a healthy debate on both sides of the issue. In Boston, the exiling of Patsy Dougherty was greeted as nothing short of a criminal act of sedition.

Such was the outcry that Taylor was forced to shield himself against an immediate onslaught of accusation, insisting, "The trade of Dougherty for Unglaub was made to help the Boston club and for no other reason." And Boston manager Jimmy Collins, targeted as an unindicted co-

conspirator in this mess, defensively declared, "I have always done the best I could behind the Boston club and have never injured our club to the benefit of anyone. I have always given Boston the best I could according to my knowledge of the game, and I have done so in this instance."

Ah, but in 1904 fate had yet to select baseball Boston as its primary target of torture, so it naturally happened that the Pilgrims clinched their second straight American League pennant on the last day of the season, in New York, when Boston pitcher Big Bill Dineen ended the game with a three-pitch strikeout of Patsy Dougherty, setting off a wicked celebration back home in Boston, where it was clear the local nine would always hold sway when matters of baseball proficiency needed to be settled with their civic rivals from the southwest.

New York City would have to wait another seventeen years before an American League flag would fly above one of its ballparks, and that would happen only as the result of the greatest display of Boston munificence in the franchises' long, cordial association. Although history has loudly (and wrongly) reduced the sale of Babe Ruth to a simple matter of Harry H. Frazee's need to finance a solvent Broadway show following a long string of failures, the truth is far more complicated than that. Civil war had racked the American League by the winter of 1919–20, with the Red Sox, White Sox, and Yankees sitting on one side of the philosophical border, rebels to Ban Johnson's long tyranny, and the other five clubs in Cleveland, Detroit, Philadelphia, St. Louis, and Washington serving as loyalists in Johnson's army.

So when Frazee wanted to unload Ruth, who'd grown too loud, too ornery, and too obnoxious for him to handle—Frazee, used to the ways of the theater, had little regard for divas—he had a limited supply of trading partners. He briefly inquired about a straight-up swap of Ruth for Joe Jackson with Chicago but planned all along on doing business with his closest allies in this patchwork axis, the Yankees. The one part of the Frazee-Ruth legend that the curse's carnival barkers actually got right was the notion that Frazee and the Yankees' owners—Colonel Jacob Ruppert and Colonel Tillinghurst l'Hommedieu Huston—were a little friendlier than competing owners should ever be. Ruppert, after all, agreed to a $300,000 loan on favorable terms as part of the Ruth deal, and when Ruth made his first appearance in Boston the next April, Frazee was following the game via wireless telegraph in the company of Huston, one of his closest friends, from the comfort and safe remove of Huston's New York offices.

And it never truly stopped. Thomas Yawkey, who owned the Red Sox for forty-three years, counted among his friends and drinking partners a string of Yankees owners, from Larry MacPhail to Del Webb to Dan Topping. Even George Steinbrenner was known to enjoy the social company of Haywood Sullivan, who served as a de facto owner when Yawkey's trust ran the ballclub in the 1980s.

And now this: Steinbrenner and Lucchino fully engaged in a public pissing match, fully locked at a public impasse.

"Let's just say that on the list of top people with respect and affection for me," Larry Lucchino would say in the summer of 2003, "you will probably not find George's name there. I don't expect a dinner invitation anytime soon."

And that was perfectly acceptable to Red Sox fans. For once, they could look to their club's leadership and see the same passion, the same fire—the same *ire*—that they'd felt, almost from the womb. And Yankees fans, who in less than a decade had gone from loathing Steinbrenner to wanting him—and his bottomless coffers—canonized, were equally pleased. Who loves a gutter fight more than New York? Gone for now, maybe for good, were gentlemanly baseball disputes decided on fields of play and toasted in private barrooms later on. There was nothing genteel about this rivalry anymore. There was nothing convivial about this connection.

The Red Sox would not be parting with Patsy Dougherty in 2003.

"For the first time," said John Miller, a longtime Red Sox fan and an investment adviser from Grafton, Massachusetts, "it seemed to me that the people who ran the Red Sox hated the Yankees every bit as much as I did."

Of course, there was a reason the Yankees were so eminently hatable.

They were an awfully good baseball team again.

So good that they'd lost shortstop Derek Jeter, the soul of the club who would soon earn a captain's *C* to formalize his unofficial standing, to a grisly shoulder injury in Toronto on opening day and still won twenty-four of their first twenty-eight games without him. So good that Kansas City Royals manager Tony Pena would say, "Some teams are so intimidating, they start out with a 1–0 lead before a pitch is ever thrown; the Yankees are so strong, they start out with a 2–0 lead." So good that the rest of baseball seemed willing to officially cede them a sixth straight American League Eastern Division championship before April had even yielded to May.

With one notable exception.

"Shit," Boston first baseman Kevin Millar said in early April. "How about we play the damned season before anyone sizes 'em up for a ring?"

They played the damned season, all right, and in New England, it turned out to be as enjoyable a baseball ride as anyone could remember. All across the summer of 2003, the Red Sox kept winning games that Red Sox teams never win. They were relentless. They were resilient. They rescued games by scoring bunches of runs in their last at-bat. They displayed a camaraderie rarely seen in a franchise that had long ago invented the concept of "twenty-five players, twenty-five cabs." They had three superstars—pitcher Pedro Martinez, left fielder Manny Ramirez, and shortstop Nomar Garciaparra—who were at least the equal to any other player at their positions in all of baseball.

Yet the soul of the team consisted of players like Millar, Bill Mueller, Todd Walker, and David Ortiz, all of them low-profile, almost anonymous off-season pickups, all of them certified role players, all of them the kind of "clubhouse guys" for which all successful teams thirst. Johnny Damon was a classic leadoff hitter. Jason Varitek was a catcher who seemed to be plucked out of a 1930s newsreel: hard-nosed, crewcut, tough as an old set of spikes, with an insatiable appetite for hard work and a knack for hitting in the clutch, so old-school his at-bats should have been televised in black and white. Red Sox fans developed a quick, abiding affinity for this team from the beginning, one that ran even deeper than usual. And they had a convenient—and familiar— measuring stick against which to compare them, because all season long, the Yankees were either a half step ahead or a half step behind, these dueling shadows never terribly far from each other.

"Just like the old days," Phil Rizzuto, the old Yankees shortstop, said. "The years fly by and it's always us and those huckleberries, the Yankees and the Red Sox. It's hard to believe. They never go away. And neither do we."

The Red Sox would finish second in the AL East in 2003, the sixth consecutive time they would finish second, *the sixth straight time they would finish second to the Yankees.* That had never happened before in the history of American team sports, one team serving as another's personal understudy that long, that often, that consecutively. And yet, in so many ways, that was exactly as it should have happened. Since 1938, after all, the Red Sox had finished in second place in seventeen seasons; fourteen of those years, it was the Yankees who had finished ahead of them. Those roles had been reversed exactly twice: once in 1986, once in 1995.

The Red Sox had tried everything in that time. In the 1930s, Tom Yawkey had opened up his checkbook and imported future Hall of Famers Jimmie Foxx and Lefty Grove from the Philadelphia Athletics, a team that had figured out how to overtake the Yankees three straight times from 1929 to 1931; Fox and Grove never could replicate that trick in Red Sox uniforms, with the team finishing second four times. In the late 1940s, the Sox had one of the best lineups ever assembled and came within a game of winning the 1946 World Series (a season in which the rebuilding Yankees finished third), yet never again made it out of the regular season. And in the 1970s, after Boston had once again built a batting order that could knock over buildings with its brute force, it still couldn't hold off the Yankees down the stretches of hard-fought pennant races. In 1977, the Sox faded in September; a year later, they would wait all the way until October 2 before melting under the last rays of summer.

"Second place suits Boston," Billy Martin had cracked in 1977, after the Yankees had taken a critical September series at Yankee Stadium. "A second-place baseball team for a second-rate town."

That was one wound that never closed, and one of the reasons why Boston, as a city, and Red Sox fans, as a group, maintained such a wicked obsession with all things New York.

Civic pride—and paranoia—suffers still from a decades-long hangover, a lingering inferiority complex that underlines, and undermines, everything about the baseball relationship between the two cities. It doesn't matter that the New England Patriots won two Super Bowls in three years, regularly beating both the New York Giants and New York Jets along the way. It doesn't matter that the Boston Bruins beat the New York Rangers in the 1972 Stanley Cup hockey finals, or that the Celtics have sixteen NBA banners hanging in their arena's rafters while the Knicks have but two limply dangling from theirs, or that the Boston Marathon remains the premier road race in the country, dwarfing in importance and popularity the marathon that suffocates New York's streets and agitates its citizens' tempers each November.

"All that other stuff is terrific," said Tony Zannotti, who, with his father, operates a trophy and plaque store in Worcester, Massachusetts. "But baseball is different. Don't ask for reasons. Don't ask for explanations. Just understand: It's different. It goes back a long way. And it represents something more than just winning a championship. It's bad enough we haven't won since 1918. It's worse that they've won *twenty-six times* since then. Much worse. It's New York. Goddamned New York."

Those are feelings that have long permeated the avenues and boulevards of Boston, a city founded in 1630 by a band of a thousand

Massachusetts colonialists led by English Puritan John Winthrop. For much of the nation's first century and a half, Boston was the ideal, the cultural, spiritual, and philosophical hub of the nation. In 1858, in fact, author and philosopher Oliver Wendell Holmes dubbed Boston "the hub of the solar system," and, at a time when Boston's self-confidence was unmatched, that expression actually grew to "hub of the universe."

Through most of those years, Boston rarely gave its coarser, earthier Northeast corridor neighbor 230 miles to the southwest much of a second glance. For one thing, New York had been a British stronghold during the Revolution, lousy with Tories and turncoats, while Boston had been a breeding ground for patriots and politicians. Boston, for one, was little surprised when Civil War riots broke out in lower Manhattan in 1863. Boston bred statesmen, scholars, artists, actors, musicians, master planners; New York was a place where Tammany Hall could exist, thrive, and dominate as no American political machine ever had before.

Even into the early decades of the twentieth century, Boston clung to its place as the setter of the American social agenda. It had, after all, built the nation's first public library. It had founded the first successful public school system. While New Yorkers were clumped together in seedy tenements or exiled to outer boroughs, unable to traverse their complex geography, Boston built the country's first subway system. So it followed that Boston also became the epicenter of the nation's growing fascination with baseball. The Red Sox won five of the first fifteen World Series ever contested and would have been favored to win a sixth if the New York Giants of the National League had agreed to face them in 1904. Hell, even the Boston Braves, the other team in town, had pulled off one of the most spectacular baseball stories ever written, rallying from last place on July 4, 1914, to win the National League pennant that year before sweeping Connie Mack's mighty Athletics in the World Series. Better, whenever New York had dared challenge Boston supremacy—the Highlanders in 1904, the Giants in the 1912 World Series—its representatives were summarily vanquished.

"We are," the *Boston Globe* sniffed in a 1919 editorial, "the capital of many things, baseball chief among them."

Still, there were fissures in the foundation of Boston's ancient standing. Slowly, New York began asserting itself. Boston Harbor, long America's jewel of trade, suffered from choking pollution as the century turned, and that permitted New York Harbor to forever seize the mantle of the nation's most important entry point, a conversion that had begun in 1825 with the opening of the Erie Canal. Wall Street began to flourish as the nation's economic epicenter thanks to the arrival of J. P. Morgan, who in 1907 invented U.S. Steel out of a billion-dollar merger hatched there. In 1902, the Hotel Pabst was razed near a strategic patch of midtown Manhattan known as Longacre Square, and on April 8, 1904, it was rechristened Times Square. It rapidly became the seed around which all of Broadway was planted.

Theodore Roosevelt, whose strong will and youthful bluster personified everything that turn-of-the-century America wanted to be, ascended to the White House in 1901 and brought the burgeoning cocktail of New York style, savvy, and street smarts with him. In fact, even as the Pilgrims were outlasting the Highlanders to win that 1904 pennant, the *New York Times* had already clearly defined which of the two cities it believed ruled the republic's roost. In an editorial following the Pilgrims' pennant triumph, the *Times* wrote: "Though the metropolitan fan may be temporarily distressed and even impoverished, the metropolitan philosopher will be ashamed to grudge Boston one championship out of two. Their necessity is greater than ours."

By 1923, Babe Ruth was a New Yorker, the Yankees were world champions for the first time, and there wasn't a soul still living who believed there was even a question anymore which province was considered the quintessential American town. The simultaneous loss of Boston's two great birthrights—both to the same municipality—has never been forgiven. Or forgotten. Seventy years later, Jerald Podair, a history professor at Lawrence University in Appleton, Wisconsin, may have best summarized the towns' respective fates: "The Sox' chase of the Yankees is a modern version of Melville's *Moby-Dick*. Ahab never lands the great white whale, but his futile attempts produced great art. The Sox are great art and bad baseball. The Yankees are great baseball and bad art."

Somehow, that has been of little concern to Yankees fans through the years. And of little consolation to Red Sox fans.

Until expansion first arrived in the American League in 1961, the Red Sox and the Yankees would play each other twenty-two times out of 154 games, the kind of familiarity that inevitably bred contempt, and contretemps. After that, the number was eighteen, and it stayed eighteen even after another batch of expansion split the league into two divisions in 1969. By 1978, two more teams had been added, and the number of meetings had been further reduced, to fifteen, although the teams did play a sixteenth time that season, their one-game playoff counting in the regular season statistics. And the advent of interleague games in 1997 meant that over the next three years, the fiercest rivals in all of baseball squared off only twelve times a season, six in Fenway, six in Yankee Stadium.

That was absurd, an example of progress setting the game back decades, and though it took a while, baseball finally recognized that. In 2001, a new "unbalanced" schedule was introduced to all six divisions, a system that automatically assigned greater weight to the games teams played with their division rivals, since they would now play just under half their entire schedule against those four teams. This was a bonanza for the Yankees and the Red Sox. Now they would play nineteen times a year, and it bothered no one that this meant that each year, one team would receive an extra home game out of the match-up.

"I think if you ask any of the players, they'll say you don't even have to play these games at either ballpark at all. Play them in a big field somewhere in the middle, all nineteen games, and they'll get after it there. And that's not a joke." Joe Torre made that observation on May 26, 2003, Memorial Day, in New York City, a few minutes after the Red

Sox and Yankees had played their first watershed game of the season. Roger Clemens, who'd spent thirteen years in a Red Sox uniform, who'd won three Cy Young Awards for Boston, who twice struck out twenty hitters with a red *B* on the front of his cap (ten years apart, no less, against the Mariners in 1986 and the Tigers in '96), and who led the Sox to the precipice of a world championship in '86, was trying to take a giant leap into one of baseball's most exclusive clubs that day, a drizzly, drafty afternoon.

Five days earlier, at Fenway, Clemens had secured the 299th victory of his career with a gritty 4–2 win over the Sox, where he'd been showered with the usual rain of ugliness from 35,002 of the 35,003 fans in attendance, many of whom continued to take Clemens' presence in pinstripes as a personal affront. The lone holdout was a visitor who watched the game from the newly built Monster Seats that now crowned the famed left-field wall.

"I was very happy for Roger," Bucky Dent had said that night, sitting in almost the exact spot where his home run ball would have landed twenty-five years earlier, fending off the commentaries—most of them good-natured, some not so much—of his neighbors in the pricey bleachers.

Now, five days later, as the midafternoon sky spit a steady stream of rain, Clemens had gathered seventy-five family members and friends from points all across the country, including his mother, Bess, who suffered from emphysema and rarely ventured far from her Katy, Texas, home, to witness him becoming the twenty-first member of major league baseball's 300-victory club. Even in a city as baseball-mad as New York has become during this latest Yankees renaissance, the past few days had been a testament to the town's hype machine smoking into overdrive. After all, it seemed so perfectly predestined, the man known as the Rocket entering pitching's most rarefied air against the team that drafted him, then defamed him, then ditched him.

Clemens' rancorous departure from the Red Sox in 1996—and former general manager Dan Duquette's assessment of him as being in the "twilight of his career"—had fueled Clemens for seven years. He'd doubled his total of Cy Young plaques, earning the first two with the Toronto Blue Jays back to back in 1997 and '98, the last with the Yankees in 2001. Just a few days earlier, he'd all but dared the Hall of Fame to force him to wear the Boston *B* on his Cooperstown plaque when that date inevitably arrived, vowing that he "just might not show up" if he wasn't permitted to wear the interlocking Yankees *NY* into eternity.

Now here came the Red Sox, history's perfect patsies, lined up to perform their traditional task, serving as a Yankee sparring partner.

There was one problem with this precise piece of planning: The Red Sox wanted no part of it. They battered Clemens, who threw 133 pitches across five and two-thirds decidedly uninspired innings. The final was 8–4. History was put on blocks for a few days. And a feisty band of Bostonians was moved to clear their throats inside New York City's baseball borders for one of the first times ever.

"This game wasn't just hyped as 'Come see Roger Clemens go for his 300th win,'" said Millar, the spare part who'd rapidly evolved into a reliable first baseman as well as the Red Sox' unofficial press secretary and truly relished what they'd just done against Clemens, a fellow Texan. "It was hyped as a sure thing: 'Come watch the old Red Sox star get number 300 against his old team.' A sure thing? Our job was to try and win a frigging game. We did a great job with great at-bats. The odds are against you. The Rocket's home, he's going for his 300th win, the storybook's there."

Millar's grin grew as big as his home state.

"I think you have to tip your hats to us," he said. "We shit all over the storybook."

As the season slowly unfolded, more and more baseball observers would do just that. It wasn't just the defiant way the Red Sox refused to concede the upper hand to the Yankees; it was the way they went about that insolent itinerary. For the first time in over eighty years, the Red Sox had decided to break with their traditional business plan, which had always been fairly simple: build a fence-busting roster that could take advantage of Fenway Park's cozy dimensions. You would have thought someone would have steered clear of these identical blueprints after the first sixty or seventy empty seasons, but the Red Sox were like the stubborn school of fish who, one after the other, keep choosing to bite the worm, damn the bloody consequences.

For this, of course, generations of Red Sox fans had the Yankees to thank.

"The Red Sox," commented Yankees fan Frank Russo, an East Brunswick, New Jersey, Web site operator, "were so envious of the Yankees for so many years, they tried to *be* the Yankees. And, of course, they never quite got it right."

Aggravating, but true. The Yankees dynasty was born in the 1920s out of the ashes of Red Sox ruin, and for many years the Red Sox fruitlessly tried to overcome the Yankees by copying the Yankees.

The Yankees had the best slugger in the game, the biggest drawing card in sports, Babe Ruth? Fine. The Sox, therefore, would import a past-his-prime Jimmie Foxx to take aim at the Green Monster. Foxx would hit 222 of his lifetime 534 home runs in a Boston uniform, but the Sox never came within eight games of first place the whole time and never got closer than seven games behind the Yankees, who by now had groomed a kid named Joe DiMaggio to be their next Ruth.

The Yankees always believed in collecting the best pitching? Fine. The Sox, therefore, would trump them by finding the best pitcher, and there were few better in the game's history than Lefty Grove, whom the Sox traded for in time for the 1934 season. And while Grove did win the final 105 games of a 300-win career while playing for the Red Sox, he would average barely more than thirteen wins per season, after averaging more than twenty-three wins a year in his previous seven seasons. And Grove could never push the Red Sox past the Yankees, either.

The latest Red Sox regime finally put an end to this, led by Theo Epstein, an honors graduate from the New School of Baseball Thought, a philosophy popularized during the 2003 season by Billy Beane's continuing success in Oakland and his ability to craft winning teams with a minimum of fiscal resources and a maximum of raw statistical data. The Red Sox hired Bill James, the author of the wildly influential Baseball Abstract series, to help build this blueprint throughout the organization, to craft success scientifically, heavy on numbers, heavy on statistics. They acquired players accordingly, which is how Millar, Mueller, Ortiz, and Walker, among others, found themselves in Boston.

Slowly, what the Sox discovered about themselves was that for whatever pitching miseries they might endure—and there would be many of them, especially early, especially in the bullpen—theirs was an offense that was pesky, powerful, and clever. By the end of the year, it would be compared with the '27 Yankees for its efficiency; at the start, all anyone knew was that there weren't many easy outs to be found in a batting order whose chemistry was subtle yet unmistakable. All of which stood in stark contrast to the Yankees' long-held belief that you identify the best players, you acquire them no matter the cost, and you find a way to make all of that work. Into their lineup, alongside Jeter, was stuffed a gaggle of top-dollar All-Stars such as Jason Giambi, Bernie Williams, and Jorge Posada. Alfonso Soriano had quickly emerged as the best young slugging infielder in the American League, and in the winter they'd added the man who'd dominated the Japanese Central League for the past ten years, left fielder Hideki Matsui.

All this did was ratchet up the intensity of all nineteen Red Sox–Yankees meetings during the regular season and ensure that not one seat in either ballpark would go unsold during those get-togethers. It was impossible to ignore the sense of inevitability that permeated the six-month dance the teams engaged in, since it looked so stunningly similar to all that had come before.

In early July, the teams split a four-game holiday weekend series whose electricity and volatility nearly caused a blackout at Yankee Stadium. David Ortiz, a Minnesota Twins castoff just a few months earlier, provided the appropriate fireworks early on, slamming four homers in the first two games, propelling the Sox to victories in both, counting among his victims an infuriated Clemens, who, after getting shellacked in the second game, seethed, "Ortiz has too much plate coverage. I am going to have to make adjustments the next time I face him." This after Clemens had already hit Millar with a pitch that sure didn't seem like an accident.

"I don't know what he means when he says that," Ortiz said, whose knowing smile shouted that he understood *exactly* what Clemens meant. Ortiz wasn't done haunting the Yankees. In fact, two months after his holiday outburst, a jittery George Steinbrenner would summon to his Yankee Stadium office Joel Sherman, the baseball columnist for the *New York Post*, and insist that he'd advised Cashman in the off-season to pursue Ortiz after the Twins had failed to tender him a contract, making Ortiz available to any team that wanted him. "But Cashman told me we already had two first basemen [Giambi and Nick Johnson]. I said, 'Find a way, he's going to be tough.'" Not only had Ortiz worked Steinbrenner's nerves, but he'd worked his way into the Yankees' heads, especially Clemens'.

Nobody needed to draw a map for Pedro Martinez, who pulled the assignment to start the series finale on Monday, July 7, opposite the Yankees' best pitcher, Mike Mussina. Both aces turned in masterful performances in a game the Yankees would win, 2–1, in the bottom of the ninth after both starters were long gone. If Clemens had earned a reputation as the modern pitcher most likely to adhere to baseball's old code of frontier justice—which reads, in part, "You pitch inside, and you pitch with purpose, and you pitch to protect your teammates, or you might as well spend your time pitching beer-league softball"—then Pedro was the heir apparent, Bob Gibson to Clemens' Don Drysdale.

Of the first eleven pitches Martinez threw on that steamy afternoon, two of them sent the Yankees' star middle infielders, Soriano and Jeter, to the hospital.

"I wasn't trying to hit anybody," Martinez said, none too convincingly. "I didn't have any reason to do it."

The Yankees disagreed, although their complaints were muted by the game's outcome and by the fact that Steinbrenner, watching all of this from his owner's box, actually began weeping as he talked about the way "his boys" had fought "those other guys."

"You know, I'm getting older," he said. "As you get older, you do this more."

Three weeks later, Steinbrenner's emotions undoubtedly spiked once again when he read the comments of Leslie Epstein, chairman of the creative writing department at Boston University and father of the general manager of the Boston Red Sox, in the Tuesday, July 29, edition of the Bergen (New Jersey) *Record*. The Red Sox had won two out of three at Fenway the previous weekend, both wins coming in dramatic, late-inning fashion, and *Record* columnist Adrian Wojnarowski caught Epstein at an especially giddy moment, amid reports that Steinbrenner had summoned Cashman to his Tampa office for a corporate scolding.

"I don't like to gloat over Brian getting reamed by his boss, because I know he's a good guy, but if Darth Vader the Convicted Felon should be discomforted, well, it pleases me to no end. The fact that my son is part of doing that to him is even better," Epstein told Wojnarowski.

Epstein was just clearing his throat. "I've always been a Red Sox fan. I hated the Yankees so much. To me, rooting for them would be like voting Republican. The Yankees are not good for baseball. One hundred eighty million bucks [the Yankees' payroll] is not good for the sport."

But the Yankees–Red Sox rivalry, as bitter and as beautiful as ever, *was* good for the sport. That was easy to see. Across the second half of the season, the Red Sox never could catch the Yankees, but throughout much of the summer they maintained a fairly comfortable cushion for themselves in the wild-card race. Suddenly, a notion that had been on millions of baseball minds across New York and New England from the earliest hours of spring began to work its way into conversations all across the region: What if these teams met in the American League Championship Series? Seven games to settle these little difficulties, once and for all?

"You could tell it was coming," Yankees fan Peter Cipriano said. "You just knew it had to end up that way."

"Destiny," said Red Sox fan John Miller. "Pure and simple. Destiny."

And for once, the players weren't ashamed to get caught up in the madness, certainly not the one player who understood what this rivalry meant to the franchises—and the fans—more than any other.

"I hope it happens," Roger Clemens said. "That would just be awesome."

This was two days before Clemens would pitch his final regular-season game at Fenway Park, on August 31, a place where he'd won ninety-two times in a Red Sox uniform. Fenway had become a chamber of horrors for Clemens since his arrival in New York four years earlier, but he would walk off the mound in triumph, on the long end of an 8–2 victory, and when he left the game, taking a slow amble toward the dugout, he was rewarded with a standing ovation from Red Sox fans who set aside their anger long enough to say thank you. And Clemens returned the favor a few minutes later.

"These are great fans," he said. "They deserve having these two teams play a few more games here. If this was my last time pitching here, I'm happy it had to end this way. But I have a funny feeling we'll be back. I have a funny feeling I'll get another chance to pitch here again."

CHAPTER

3

IT'S SECOND TO BREATHING

I have my doubts about Ruth ever eclipsing his home run record.
I'm not alone in believing that 1919 will be his best year. At any rate, I
am well-satisfied to let him try his fortune in New York.
—Harry H. Frazee, January 5, 1920

If someone had announced the Old South Church was to be
transformed into a billiard hall, the news wouldn't have created half as
much astonishment in Boston as did the report that Babe Ruth had been
sold to the Yankees. A 45-rounder between the Crown Prince and the
Kaiser on Bunker Hill would scarcely have raised any more disturbances
among Boston sports followers. —Editorial, Boston Post, January 6, 1920

The guests couldn't help themselves, couldn't hide their restlessness. They wanted to be happy for the bride and groom; they wanted to fill the upstairs ballroom at Georgetown Country Club with the kind of merriment the happy couple would be able to hear ringing in their ears for the next fifty or sixty years.

The hosts just had a lousy sense of timing, that's all.

Not that they could have known. Not that they could have guessed that October 4, 2003, the date of their blessed union, would happen to fall on a day when the Boston Red Sox were trailing the Oakland Athletics, two games to none, in a best-of-five American League Division Series, or that their reception would coincide with game three, which would be taking place thirty miles south of here, in front of 35,460 desperadoes, the largest Fenway Park crowd in thirteen years. Nobody could blame them for failing to forecast this most unfortunate conflict of interests.

Well, almost nobody.

"Who in their right mind schedules a wedding in Boston in October?" one of the guests had inquired earlier, letting the last word roll off his tongue with a disgusted, exaggerated New England bounce: *Ahc-tow-bah.*

This wasn't the first time John Miller had found himself forced far away from the action while his favorite baseball team forged its way through a fabled autumn. Seventeen years before, as a ten-year-old, he'd been exiled to the lonely coffee shop that adjoined the Campanelli Grafton House, the restaurant and saloon his parents owned and operated in Grafton, forty-two miles west of downtown. All through the night of October 25, 1986, into the morning of the twenty-sixth, John Miller had sipped Cokes and ginger ales and watched the Red Sox play game six of the 1986 World Series against the New York Mets, all by himself. He was untouched by the cynicism in which so many Sox fans were eventually baptized, unaware of any tortured history. When Dave Henderson hit a tenth-inning home run, giving the Red Sox the lead, nudging them three outs away from Valhalla, young John Miller ran around the coffee shop with a joy he'd never known before. His team was about to win the World Series.

"Well, you know what happened then," the all-grown-up John Miller said, laughing, even though he still doesn't find the memory terribly funny. "I guess every Red Sox fan has that moment that stays with them forever, right? That moment when you understand, for the very first time, that maybe it is a little different rooting for this team than for any other team in baseball, or in sports for that matter. I guess for me, the moment was when the wild pitch skipped past [Rich] Gedman [allowing the Mets to tie the game in the bottom of the tenth], more than [Bill] Buckner's error [which is how they wound up winning it]. After you have that first initial shock, nothing else that happens surprises you."

This is why so many people in the upstairs ballroom at Georgetown Country Club were dizzy with despair on the evening of October 4. If this most magical of Red Sox seasons was truly going to expire, they wanted to know the precise hour of death. Only that wasn't possible. Because not only had the happy couple failed to consult a baseball post-season schedule before planning their nuptials, they'd managed to find the one country club in Boston that had a bar with no television set.

"We were shit out of luck," John Miller said.

Fans manage, though. They adjust. They adapt. Someone got a text message on a cell phone early in the evening, reporting that the Red Sox had taken a quick 1–0 lead. Someone else received a phone call and tried to piece together the bizarre events that had helped the A's tie the game in the sixth. What had happened? One of the A's was tagged out because he'd forgotten to touch home plate? Another had failed to even reach home plate? What? The information bounced kinetically around the room, which only made the frustration that much greater. *Biggest game of the year, and we can't see one inning of it. Not a single, solitary pitch . . .*

"John!"

A friend was grabbing Miller by the arm, hurrying him away from the reception. He'd made an impossibly serendipitous discovery as he wandered the club, looking for better cell reception. In his travels, he'd meandered downstairs, to the lounge area where the club's golf members wound down after a round. And there it was, big, beautiful, and blown up on a large-screen television: the ball game. It was still tied. It was the late innings. Alive! The Red Sox were still alive! The friends could hear the muffled sound of music bleeding through the ceiling, and occasionally they'd feel a twinge of guilt that they'd abandoned the party. But it always passed quickly. They lost themselves in the game, in the pitch-by-pitch agony of elimination baseball, and so it wasn't until a bit later that John Miller looked around and noticed something quite astonishing.

"There must have been forty or fifty people milling around the TV screen," Miller says. There were two weddings going on at the same time, in the two huge halls upstairs, and it seemed like half the guests from both parties were in this cramped room, staring at the screen, screaming at the Sox, stammering with nervous energy. "It was like being in the stands at Fenway," Miller said. "Only, you know, everyone was dressed a little better."

Ah, but the game was careening toward extra innings now, and this is where John Miller's conscience finally got the better of him. The game could last all night, and they couldn't stay away from the wedding all night; it was, after all, only a baseball game. His friends agreed. They decided to take turns going on scouting missions every so often, racing downstairs for updates, standing sentry as the season stared down extinction. In the meantime, the others would go upstairs, they would drink, they would dance, they would toast the newlyweds, they would pretend they were having a hell of a good time, and they would try to keep their imaginations from making the simple thirty-minute hop down U.S. 1 and I-95.

And then they discovered they'd been touched by another dash of gold dust.

"One of the waitresses had found this tiny little five-inch black-and-white, and she'd set it up on the right side of the bar, and that's where I set up with three of my friends," Miller said. "And that's where we saw it."

That's where, at exactly 11:18 P.M., the four of them saw Trot Nixon smoke a fastball from Rich Harden, and even on the minuscule screen, they could see it was going to carry into the center-field bleachers. Even thirty miles away, they could feel Fenway Park rocking on its ninety-one-year-old foundation, because that was the same way the Georgetown Country Club soon felt as the news bounced around the two wedding halls, spilling out the doors into the crisp New England night.

"We had a lot of fun at that wedding the rest of the night," John Miller recalled. "Good times. Good, good times."

For the first time, there was a sense of something greater at work. For the first time, the idea of a New York–Boston championship series officially emerged from the mothballs of the fans' fantasies. All season long, fans and players and coaches and front-office executives and writers and broadcasters had speculated that something like this could happen. Why not? The Yankees and the Red Sox were clearly the two best teams in the American League. They had the two largest payrolls in the league. Their lineups had both proven to be slump-proof, and both rosters seemed to enjoy the give-and-take and constant stress of a pennant race.

The Yankees had pulled away at last in September, clinching the division on September 23 when Jose Contreras—who else?—threw eight shutout innings against the Chicago White Sox and the Yankees enjoyed a 7–0 romp and a champagne bath in the visiting team's clubhouse at U.S. Cellular Field, the faceless, charm-free ballpark that dominates Chicago's South Side. It was the Yankees' sixth straight AL East Division title. Throughout the team's long and dominant history—which included, through that moment in Chicago, twenty-six World Series championships and thirty-eight American League pennants—the Yankees had never finished in first place six straight seasons. It was their thirteenth win in sixteen games, and it left the Red Sox battling the Seattle Mariners for the wild-card berth. Yet it caused only the slightest ripple of excitement among the Yankees core, who believed you saved your bawdier celebrations for the deeper dates of fall.

"You don't want to get too crazy," Derek Jeter warned, "because this is only the first step. We have three more playoff series we want to win. We have eleven postseason games we have to win. When we do that, then you'll really see a celebration."

Bernie Williams had lived through even more of these impromptu parties than his captain had. Since 1995, Williams had celebrated two wild-card clinchings, seven division championships, five division series wins, five championship series victories, and four World Series clinchings. Those were the most memorable moments of merriment, when you were likely to see George Steinbrenner weep, Joe Torre hand out cigars from his private stock, or Wade Boggs commandeer a police horse and steer it around Yankee Stadium in a triumphant victory lap.

"Once you've experienced a World Series celebration," Williams coolly observed, "the others don't really compare."

Two nights later, the Red Sox respectfully, and raucously, disagreed.

For on that night, they thrashed the Baltimore Orioles, 14–3, securing themselves a spot in the postseason for the first time since 1999. They hadn't been able to keep up with the Yankees across the long baseball summer, but that hardly mattered to any of the 34,526 people who crammed Fenway Park that night, or the millions of others who giddily watched the proceedings on New England Sports Network's feed to living rooms, saloons, and satellite dishes all over the country. And it certainly didn't impede the happiness the Red Sox themselves were feeling. They may only have been a wild card, meaning they'd have to open the playoffs three thousand miles away in Oakland, meaning they'd have to face any decisive game on the road for as long as they stayed alive in the American League bracket, meaning . . . well, meaning nothing to anyone. They were in. That's all that mattered.

"Let's go, Red Sox!" the people crowed.

"Bring on Oakland!" they cried.

"Yankees suck!" they screamed.

The players sprayed each other and hugged each other and poured beer and champagne down each other's throats, but the tiny clubhouse couldn't contain their glee. So a good half hour after the final out, five of them—Todd Walker, Derek Lowe, Lou Merloni (who grew up a Sox fan in suburban Framingham), Gabe Kapler, and Kevin Millar—bolted out of the locker room, sprinted out of Fenway Park, and, ringed by a nervous contingent of security men who were officially entering virgin territory, sprinted down Yawkey Way to the corner of Boylston Street. They had street clothes on, but they'd all wrapped brand-new wild-card T-shirts over the civvies, and when they passed the threshold into the Baseball Tavern it took a few moments for the people inside to understand what was happening.

Were these really Red Sox, honest-to-gawd Red Sox, embracing them, buying them beers, handing out high fives? Really? Was this a joke? It was no joke. It was them. And they were here to party with the rank and file.

"They were drenched in sweat, champagne, and beer," Sue Desgrossielliers, of Manchester, New Hampshire, gushed to the *Boston Globe*. "You could smell it all."

"You can probably smell it on me," her friend Staci Hicks, of Pembroke, giggled. "I hugged all of them."

Millar was the one who ran up to the bar, jumped behind it, reached into a cooler, and started distributing bottles of beer, stopping to shake a few up, spraying the Baseball Tavern regulars. They stayed ten, fifteen minutes, and it was the grandest example of a team bonding with a city that anyone, anywhere, could ever remember. You couldn't have displayed a starker difference between the Yankee Way and the Red Sox Way if you'd managed to open the brains of both George Steinbrenner and Larry Lucchino and allowed the contents to spill out onto Yawkey Way.

"What I want to know is this: Who wrote the script?" Millar asked a few days later, after word of the Fun Five's bar hop had spread everywhere. "Who wrote the script for celebrations? What is it? Clinch wild card, no beers? Clinch Division Series, four to nine beers? Clinch LCS, six to twelve beers? Win the World Series, no limit? I never had more fun in my life, running down Yawkey Way in my spikes with Derek and Todd and heading into that bar with a couple of thousand people behind us chanting. I wish we could have stayed four hours. And we might have, if we didn't have a bus and a plane to catch."

Millar had long since established his place in Fenway folklore. It was on August 13 that he'd first uttered for public consumption the phrase that would embody this team the rest of the way. Speaking of Lowe, who'd shut down the A's in the Oakland Coliseum that night, Millar said, "It was time to cowboy up, and we needed someone to cowboy up, and D-Lowe did it for us." Over the next three months, "cowboy up" would sweep across Boston. It would cause instant agitation among Yankees fans. And it sealed forever Millar's status as the most popular Everyman ballplayer Boston had seen since Johnny Pesky.

"Hell, don't compare me to him," Pesky, the former Red Sox short-stop, manager, coach, and broadcaster, would say months later, point-ing across the Boston spring training compound. A crowd of kids surrounded Millar, patiently seeking the autograph of a player they'd never have been able to pick out of a lineup less than twelve months before. "That kid, he made a whole city realize how much fun a pennant race can be. That's a hell of a gift. A hell of a gift."

Pete Trinkle hadn't always been trapped behind enemy lines. He'd grown up a New Yorker in the purest sense, raised on Manhattan's Upper East Side, on Seventy-fourth Street and Third Avenue. His par-ents' apartment was just around the corner from Rusty Staub's restau-rant, a rib joint that attracted every Mets fan in the tristate area; Trinkle resisted those tugs. What did he know about good ribs? What he knew were the Reggie! candy bars that filled the shelves of neighborhood candy stores in that summer of 1978, when he was seven years old. Underneath the wrapper was a calcified mixture of nuts, chocolate, and caramel. But the wrapper! It was bright orange. The letters spelling out Reggie! were in dark Yankee blue. And there was a photo of a pinstriped Reggie Jackson, swinging from the heels as always.

"Once I saw the Reggie! bar," Trinkle said, "I was a Yankee fan. I was hooked forever."

That was the summer the Red Sox jumped out fourteen games ahead of the Yankees, and it was also the summer that Pete Trinkle's parents took the family to Rhode Island on summer vacation. For the first time, Trinkle came face-to-face with the enemy, these loud, laughing kids who wore the enemy's colors on their backs and a bright red cap with a dark blue *B* on their heads (proving that even a classic uniform like the Red Sox' wasn't immune to the occasional late-'70s fashion faux pas). It's useful to learn who your enemies are at an early age. From that summer forward, Trinkle knew. The borders of his baseball existence had been secured. He understood. It was simple, really: Yankees fans stayed in New York. Red Sox fans stayed in New England. That was the way of the world. That, and the fact that being a Yankees fan meant never having to say "Wait till next year," a truth he learned that October, when he ran the two blocks home from the Buckley School in time to watch Bucky Dent deliver for him.

"I had it all figured out," Trinkle says, laughing.

Only he never figured on this: In the summer of 2003, thirty-two-year-old Trinkle, now a writer, found himself living, with his wife and his dog, in a handsome apartment on Boston's South End. Living among . . . *them*. He'd resided in Boston for nine years. This was his—gulp—*home*.

"The embedded Yankee fan," he called himself.

His was a lonely contrarian's voice as the Red Sox began to rescue themselves against the A's, winning game four just as dramatically as they'd won game three, flying to Oakland for game five with a plane-load of confidence, leaving behind a fan base just as convinced that they were going to keep this season alive for at least another week. The trash talk was already spilling out of the radio stations: *Bring on the Yankees!* Trinkle had watched with quiet satisfaction as the Yankees had dispatched the Minnesota Twins in four games in their division series. His team was already in the American League Championship Series. Now, before game five of the Boston-Oakland series had even begun, he was surrounded by certainty of what was sure to come.

"That's what I really don't understand about Red Sox fans," Trinkle said. "I mean, it was an amazing thing. The whole city was convinced they were going to win, even when they were down 2–0. I mean, they absolutely *knew* it, and that's the way they always are, and I've never been able to put that together with their history. I mean, if that was my team, I wouldn't expect that. It's kind of sad to watch how they throw their heart into it every time and every time it's . . . well, it's pure tragedy."

So a part of Trinkle enjoyed this manic behavior breaking out all around him. And another part of Trinkle—a larger part than he or any other Yankee fan would willingly admit—wanted the Red Sox to lose 11–0. Not because they hated the Red Sox—although, make no mistake, they *do* hate the Red Sox with every fiber of their being—but because they (*Sssshhhh! Not too loud!*) feared the Red Sox.

"I mean, let's be honest," Pete Trinkle said. "Sooner or later, the laws of probability are gonna catch up to you. Sooner or later the Yankees are going to play the Red Sox in a game that really, truly matters, and the Red Sox are going to win that game. Sooner or later, Babe Ruth's ghost is gonna say: 'The hell with it. Enough is enough.'"

Years later, an old friend and teammate named Jumpin' Joe Dugan would have this to say about George Herman (Babe) Ruth: "That big son of a bitch could never have played his whole career in Boston. He was born to play in New York. That swing, that ambition, that appetite? There was just no way a small town like Boston could contain him. What town could? Maybe Chicago. Maybe. No, the Babe was built for Broadway, for the big time. There was only one place for him."

Fact is, Ruth had spent much of his early career auditioning for the Yankees and for New York City, even if he didn't realize it at the time. Raised in a Catholic orphanage in Baltimore, placed there by a saloon-keeper father who hadn't a clue how to control his son's already outsized appetites, Ruth seemed destined for a career as a shirtmaker until a tall cleric named Brother Mathias taught him how to throw a baseball very fast and how to hit it very hard. The Baltimore Orioles signed Ruth out of St. Mary's Industrial School for Boys, then sold him to the Red Sox, who sent him out to Providence for a brief apprenticeship on the farm before recalling him. He was a pitcher. In that dead-ball era, teams placed far more value on the men who could get hitters out than on hitters who could reach distant fences. Ruth's hitting prowess was a bonus, and the Red Sox' perceptions never would change. To them, he always would be a pitcher first.

On Friday, October 2, 1914, Babe Ruth took the mound for his second-ever start as a big-league pitcher, a meaningless late-season game at Fenway Park between the Red Sox, bound for second place in the league that year, and the Yankees, headed for seventh, and the fourth of five consecutive nonwinning seasons. There were a few thousand fans dotted throughout the stands that day to watch the Red Sox beat the Yankees, 11–5. The occasion of Babe Ruth's second career start was not enough to fill the park that day; perhaps if they'd known what else lay in store that afternoon, more would have felt the need to make the pilgrimage.

For in the seventh inning, Yankees pitcher Leonard "King" Cole, who'd won twenty games as recently as 1910 for the Cubs but was pitching in the final game of his career, grooved a fastball to the kid the next morning's *New York Times* would describe as "Boston's rangy lefthander, who recently helped the Providence Grays to the International League championship." Even at age nineteen, Ruth wasn't about to let a lousy fastball go unpunished, and he smoked a double into the rightfield corner, the first of his 2,873 career hits.

It was also the first first he would collect as the central figure in this Red Sox–Yankees mini-drama, a role he would gleefully serve for twenty years, on both sides of the divide. More would soon follow. Seven months later, now firmly entrenched as a member of Boston's pitching rotation, Ruth would hit the first of his 714 career home runs. It came against the Yankees at the Polo Grounds, the stadium that would become his own personal paradise over the next few years. Yankee Stadium may have been conceived with an eye toward becoming "the house that Ruth built," but it was at the Polo Grounds, the horseshoe-shaped baseball depot on 155th Street and Eighth Avenue in upper Manhattan, that Ruth truly began to appreciate the substantial reach of his hitting powers—and the even more significant consequences of being able to do something so impressive in front of New York City's watchful gaze.

Leading off the third inning, Ruth took advantage of another fading

Yankee pitcher, Jack Warhop, who was muddling through his final year as a big leaguer. Ruth's mighty swing propelled a drive high over the right-field fence. According to the *Boston Post*, "The blast went so far into the stands that the ushers never made any attempt to recover it," deep into the second tier that towered over the field. Ruth trotted around the bases with a wide grin on his face and added two hits to the Red Sox cause. Ruth also pitched a splendid game, throwing all thirteen innings in a 4–3 Red Sox win. The reason Ruth's workday was extended four additional innings was thanks to a ninth-inning, game-tying run driven in by Yankees second baseman Dan Boone, who was related neither to the famed American frontiersman nor to a future Yankees third baseman who would someday wreak additional late-game havoc on the Red Sox.

Interestingly, that was game one of a twenty-one-game, twenty-nine-day road trip for the Red Sox that wouldn't end until Wednesday, June 2, again at the Polo Grounds, again with Ruth hitting a homer off Warhop (his second) in the second inning that the *Post* described as "a record breaker for distance, as it carried away the top of a chair in the Section One of the pavilions, and when the ball was last seen it was headed for the [Harlem] River." Yankee manager Bill Donovan may have been the first manager to ever be officially spooked by the Babe: He ordered him intentionally walked twice that day as Ruth—who would finish his first full season with an 18–8 record—went the distance in the 7–1 victory. Twenty-three days later, Ruth smacked his third home run of the year, again victimizing the Yankees, this time at Fenway Park, this time moving Donovan to mutter, "I am curious what Manager [Bill] Carrigan feeds that boy in the Boston dressing room, he does seem to have it in for us."

Actually, soon enough, Ruth deployed his considerable talents on the rest of the American League, too. The Red Sox won the World Series in 1915 and again in 1916, with Ruth rapidly evolving into a big-game pitcher. In fact, across parts of three World Series, he would string together twenty-nine and one-third scoreless innings, a record that remained intact for forty-three years, nine years longer than he held the mark for most homers in one season, four years longer than his 714 homers would last as the standard for a career. It never occurred to anyone in Boston that Ruth was anything other than the next Cy Young, so they kept his bat in mothballs between starts. During his first three full seasons, Ruth hit a total of but nine home runs. Nobody in Boston felt they were missing out on anything.

But there was one man in New York who did.

As early as 1917, Colonel Jacob Ruppert, the co-owner of the Yankees, publicly marveled at the displays Ruth would put on in batting practice. He was especially grateful that the presence of the Babe would usually swell his attendance figures by five thousand to seven thousand customers, since New York baseball fans had caught on quickly that Ruth had a special affinity for the close-in right-field fence at the Polo Grounds, which lay only 258 feet away from home plate. So moved was Ruppert that on the occasion of the Red Sox' first visit to New York in 1918, he could no longer contain his lust. He contacted Harry Frazee, the Red Sox' owner, and made him a flat offer of $100,000 for Ruth's services. Frazee, a theater impresario, was no rube. And he certainly knew there was no way to put a price tag on his star's value to the Red Sox.

"I might as well sell the franchise and the whole club as sell Ruth," Frazee said in turning down the colonel's proposition. "The sum named was three times as much as any figure that has been used in baseball. But it is ridiculous to talk about. Ruth is our big ace. He's the most talked of, most sought for, most colorful ballplayer in the game."

Ruth, ever the showman, developed a habit of saving personal firsts for New Yorkers. On May 4, losing 4–1 in the top of the seventh, he walked to the plate with two out and Everett Scott standing on first base. The Yankees pitcher was Allen Russell, a Baltimorean that Ruth had known, and competed against, for years. On Russell's first pitch, Ruth unloaded a mammoth blast into the upper deck that sailed just foul; agitated, Ruth turned to the home plate umpire, Billy Evans, and said, "I'll hit this one right back there, Bill, and it'll be fair by such a wide margin there'll be no doubt about it."

Which is exactly what he did; thus, Babe Ruth had delivered the first—if decidedly not the most famous—"called shot" of his career.

Two days later, before the finale of their three-game series with the Yankees, early-arriving fans noticed the Red Sox had a novice first base-man fielding ground balls before the game: Babe Ruth. World War I was raging, and major-league ballplayers were receiving call-ups every day. The Red Sox' roster was ever-changing, and they felt the need, finally, to adapt. Manager Ed Barrow relented at last, and for the first time in his professional career Babe Ruth's name appeared on a lineup card with something other than a *P* next to his name. Hitting sixth, he celebrated by drilling a two-run homer into the upper deck in the fourth inning.

Slowly, ever so slowly, the circumstances that would soon transform Babe Ruth into the most recognizable American name in the world were beginning to settle into place. For the rest of the season, Ruth would play thirteen games at first and fifty-nine in the outfield in addi-tion to his twenty starts as a pitcher. He would hit eleven home runs, an astonishing total for an era when the baseballs resembled overboiled potatoes, and it brought him the first of the twelve home run titles he would win over the next fourteen years. And after briefly receiving a scare from the Yankees, who moved into a first-place tie with the Sox on June 27 but were soon hit harder than any other major-league team by the draft (typical Yankees bad luck, New Yorkers moaned), the Sox would win their unprecedented fifth World Series that September.

"The Red Sox dynasty lives, and there is no end to it in sight!" crowed John "Honey Fitz" Fitzgerald, the former mayor of Boston, longtime Red Sox fan (whose son-in-law, Joseph P. Kennedy, had tried to buy the team when it was awarded to Frazee), and grandfather of the future thirty-fifth president of the United States.

Just as slowly, but just as relentlessly, the gears had begun to grind that would turn Honey Fitz' words—and Red Sox fans' hearts—inside out and upside down.

In the fall of 1918, if you'd uttered the name "Harry Frazee" anywhere in New England, you were almost certain to elicit a smile and warm sense of good cheer, for Frazee was an unmatched baseball hero in Boston. For one thing, where many baseball owners had fretted about potential ruin during the war, Frazee had seen only opportunity. First, he'd fleeced Connie Mack's Philadelphia A's of Amos Strunk, Joe Bush, and Wally Schang in exchange for $60,000, all but ensuring his team the pennant, then he'd made sure there would be a pennant for them to win. There was serious talk of shutting baseball down early in 1918, "for the duration." Ban Johnson, the American League president, had made a ham-fisted attempt to convince Congress of baseball's "essential value to the home front" and had, in fact, made matters worse because many citizens already believed ballplayers were "slackers" who played a game for a living even as thousands of American boys had begun to die in the trenches and forests of Western Europe. Frazee would rectify the mess. He paid a personal visit to Newton Baker, the secretary of war, making a passionate and convincing argument that baseball, like theater, was good for morale and provided patriotic workers with a most-needed diversion.

"The season should be allowed to continue," Frazee argued, "not for the sake of baseball but for the good of the country." This carried the day, but it also sealed the animosity between Johnson and Frazee forever.

Frazee's rise to prominence had a distinctly American flavor to it. Born in Peoria, Illinois, in 1880, he'd been a high school third baseman who left home at sixteen to find his fortune, settling at first for a job sweeping floors in the Peoria Theater. But he was a born hustler, and he was soon promoting a play called *Mahoney's Wedding,* from which he cleared a tidy $14,000 profit. He never looked back. By 1910, he put on his first Broadway hit, *Madame Sherry,* which ran for 231 performances and landed him a quarter million dollars in the black; he followed with a string of simple musical comedies that always seemed to play to packed houses. He branched out. He promoted prizefights. He tried to buy the Boston Braves, then the Chicago Cubs, then the New York

Giants. He targeted baseball as a natural progression of his own enter-
tainment interests, vaulting ahead of that curve by at least eighty years.

"Baseball is, essentially, show business," Frazee said in 1917. "If you have
any kind of production, be it a music show or a wrestling bout or baseball
games that people want to see bad enough to pay money for the privilege,
then you are in show business. And don't let anyone tell you different."

Within two years of finally finding a baseball outlet for his growing
empire, after purchasing the Red Sox along with partner Hugh Ward for
$675,000, after returning the team to its rightful perch atop the sport's
kingdom, Harry H. Frazee was bulletproof in Boston, and he knew it.

"The toast of the town," his grandson, Harry Frazee III, would say
more than seventy-five years later, with more than a little pride in his
voice. "My grandfather really was the prince of the city."

Frazee's ego, never small to begin with, expanded accordingly, at
almost precisely the same time that another supernova's self-esteem
began bursting at the seams. Nobody would have believed you in the
fall of 1918 if you'd told them that within a year, this escalation of warring emotions would culminate in the most ill-fated deal in the history
of American sports, no matter how inevitable it all seems today.

For Frazee wasn't the only one who'd started reading—and believing—his press clippings. When Ruth reported for work in the spring of
1919, he announced that he was through with pitching, that he wanted
to concentrate all of his energies on offense. He'd reached this epiphany
after getting large on the off-season banquet circuit, noticing that the
eleven home runs he'd hit the previous year had fattened his bank
account more than any of the eighty pitching victories he'd collected
the past four years. The Red Sox, of course, were horrified. They really
didn't even want Ruth to continue his between-starts playing regimen.
The war was over, and American League rosters would be fully stocked
with legitimate ballplayers again. Everyone knew Ruth wouldn't hit
eleven home runs again. He was a pitcher, for crying out loud. This was
baseball. It wasn't the circus.

"I am no longer a pitcher," Ruth declared. "I am a baseball player."

He had also started to rankle his boss, squawking about his salary, and now he had someone to squawk on his behalf: Johnny Igoe, a bootlegger and drugstore owner who served as Ruth's manager and de facto agent. Igoe advised Ruth to ignore his $7,000 contract for 1919, so Ruth informed Frazee he wanted either a one-year contract for $15,000 or a three-year contract for $30,000. Frazee didn't take him seriously, even after Ruth threatened to retire. How many prima donna actors had pulled similar empty threats on him through the years? The play is always bigger than the player.

"If Ruth doesn't want to work for the Red Sox," Frazee vowed, "we can make an advantageous trade."

They were so many hollow words. The public demanded Ruth be allowed to play and to hit, and Frazee had little choice. He agreed to the three-year deal, at $10,000 for that season, serious money for the time. But Ruth began earning it almost immediately. On opening day, April 23, he hit a home run in the Polo Grounds—where else?—and it was the first of twenty-nine he would slam that year. Ruth was no longer a mere amusement, no curiosity. He was a sensation. Every time he swung his bat, a stadium—and, by extension, a nation—held its breath, not knowing what would happen next.

All the standing single-season home run records began to fall, in rapid order: those of Socks Seybold (American League record, sixteen, with the 1902 A's), Gavvy Gravath (modern major-league record, twenty-four, with the Philadelphia Phillies in 1915), and Ned Williamson (a name dragged out of an attic somewhere as Ruth continued his assault, who'd hit twenty-seven for the 1884 Chicago Cubs while taking aim at a 215-foot right-field porch).

This was completely untamed territory. Twenty-nine home runs? *By a pitcher?* It would be like Pedro Martinez showing up one season, grabbing a bat, and hitting a hundred of them. It was that implausible. It was that impossible.

It was also entirely appropriate, because Ruth himself was turning increasingly impossible.

He was always given to tantrums, prone to pouting, unskilled in handling life's daily little challenges. But in 1919, fueled by the public's unyielding affections, Ruth became intolerable, insolent, insubordinate. Barrow couldn't discipline him. His teammates couldn't rein him in. His appetites for beer, food, and women expanded exponentially. He stubbornly refused to pitch until the Red Sox made it worth his while to do so. He talked his way out of games when the hangover wouldn't dissolve by the 3:00 P.M. game time. Then, late in the season, after he'd secured the all-time home run title, after the Red Sox had held a Babe Ruth Day in his honor in which an all-time Fenway Park crowd of 31,000 had turned out (after which, typically, he'd hit a home run off Chicago's Lefty Williams, one of the White Sox players who, just a few weeks later, would conspire to throw the 1919 World Series), after hitting number twenty-nine in Washington on September 27, he'd unceremoniously jumped the Red Sox, opting to play a lucrative exhibition game forty-five miles down the road in Baltimore on the season's final day.

Frazee seethed.

He also sat down, looked at his books, and noticed something else: For all of Ruth's mass appeal in other cities, Boston's attendance lagged, at just over 417,000 for the season, fifth in the eight-team league. Frazee interpreted this only one way: Boston fans were far more apt to flock to the ballpark when the team was winning. And in 1919, the Red Sox had fallen flat: a 66–71 record, sixth place in the American League, twenty and a half games behind the pennant-winning White Sox.

"The Red Sox," he'd said, ever so cryptically, a week after the season ended, "are not, and never will be, a one-man team."

Still, in Ruth's case, surely an exception would be made. How could it not? Ruth's fame spread daily. Every day, it seemed, his name popped up in the newspapers. The New York *Daily News* reported on October 30 that Ruth was pondering an early retirement so he might pursue his second career as a cigar maker. "A ballplayer's career is basically ended when he reaches the middle thirties," Ruth noted, "whereas a fellow can make cigars all his life." On November 19, news of Ruth's arrival in San

Francisco led every sports section in the country, amid reports that, as a member of Buck Weaver's barnstorming team, which was packing stadiums throughout California on an exhibition tour, Ruth would earn an unbelievable (but true) sum of $500 per game.

The diva was, officially, out of control.

On December 24, Frazee told an interviewer he was prepared to shake up his entire team, willing to part with anyone besides outfielder Harry Hooper, who'd hit .267 with three home runs and forty-nine runs batted in for 1919.

"If I am satisfied that I can make a stronger team than I had last season by a shake-up, you may be sure there will be a shake-up," Frazee said. "The Boston baseball public wants a winner, and it is my business to provide one, if I can."

Surely, he was asked, Babe Ruth was also an untouchable.

"The only untouchable," Frazee repeated, "is Hooper."

Who could believe that? Posturing is all that was. Ruth continued his West Coast tour and entered negotiations to star in a motion picture when the expedition reached Hollywood. Story after story repeated his belief that "I'll top that record again this year, you'll see." Ty Cobb stirred up a fresh controversy when he dismissed Ruth's year, calling him "a contract violator," prompting Ruth to fire right back.

"Cobb must be jealous of me because the newspapers have played me up this year as the biggest attraction in baseball," he said. "A player is worth just as much as he can get. And Cobb has been paid all he is worth, believe me, for quite a few years. I wouldn't say anything of Cobb if he held out for $100,000, so why should he say anything about me? He ought to be tickled to see another player get as much as he can. I'll settle the question when I see Cobb. Cobb? Why, he gets on beating out bunts and the scorers help him out. He gets fifty, seventy-five hits every season he isn't entitled to."

Babe Ruth could say anything he wanted. He could do anything he wanted. He was rapidly approaching a place where he could buy anything he wanted. Bigger than the game? He was becoming bigger than all of American pop culture. What could Harry Frazee do about that?

Well . . . he could trade him, for openers.

The deal was done with amazing swiftness, on the day after Christmas. The terms were most agreeable to Frazee: $100,000, paid in four $25,000 installments, the first of which was due immediately. Ruppert would also lay out a low-interest, $300,000 loan, for which Frazee named Fenway Park as the security. The men agreed to keep the deal quiet for eleven days, and in those primitive informational times, that was not an issue. Ruppert dispatched his field manager, Miller Huggins, to Los Angeles to inform Ruth of the deal, and also to receive assurances that he would honor the contract that still had two years and $20,000 to run. If Ruth became difficult, Huggins was told to offer him a one-shot $20,000 bonus to mollify him. He did that.

And it was done.

On January 5, 1920, the Red Sox and Yankees made a joint announcement, letting the rest of the world in on their little secret.

"We offered $100,000 for Ruth some time ago and were turned down," Ruppert admitted. "The purchase is in line with our policy of giving New York a pennant-winning team in the American League."

Said Frazee: "It would have been an injustice to keep him with the Red Sox. We would have become a one-man team."

From the coast, telegrams began arriving in the newspaper sports departments from "G. Ruth," a stroke of public relations that was decades ahead of its time. "Will not play anywhere but Boston," the telegram insisted. "Will leave for the East Monday." Ruth, of course, had already agreed to the trade, in addition to his tidy $20,000 bonus. But he already knew Frazee would hold nothing back in trying to justify the trade. He'd seen Frazee's ego up close. He'd seen how he'd tried to ruin performers who'd crossed him. Ruth knew Frazee, now Ruth-less, had long been ruthless, and would be vicious. He was right. Frazee issued a staggering 1,500-word screed.

"Had Ruth been possessed of the right disposition, had he been willing to take orders and work for the good of the club like the other men on the team, I would never have dared let him go, for he has youth and strength, baseball intelligence and was a public idol," Frazee said. "But lately this idol had been shattered in the public estimate because of the way in which he has refused to respect the contract and his given word. During the season, he regularly refused to obey the orders of the manager and finally became so arrogant that discipline in his case was ruined. He would not pitch but insisted upon playing in the outfield. He has no regard for anyone but himself and was a bad influence upon the young players on the team. He left us in a lurch many times and just because of his abnormal swatting power and the fact that he had been given such tremendous advertising he obeyed none but his sweet will.

"For the past two years he has come so rapidly to the front that the individuality of every other member of the Red Sox club has been swallowed up. I might say that the New York club was the only outfit in baseball that could have bought Ruth for cash. Had they been willing to trade players, I would have preferred the exchange but to make a trade for Ruth, Huggins would have had to wreck his ball club. They couldn't afford to give me the men I wanted. Ruth's gate value did not appeal to all the club owners. I could not get Joe Jackson for him in a trade, and I know of at least two other stars that Ruth could not be traded for. I am willing to accept the verdict of all baseballdom, and I think that fair-minded patrons of the sport will agree with me that Ruth could not remain on the Boston team under existing conditions.

"Ruth had become impossible and the Boston club could no longer put up with his eccentricities. While Ruth is without question the greatest hitter the game has seen, he is likewise one of the most inconsiderate men that ever wore a baseball uniform. A team of players working harmoniously together is always to be preferred to that possessing one star who hugs the limelight to himself. Ruth is taking on weight tremendously. He doesn't care to keep himself in shape. He has a floating cartilage in his knee which may make him a cripple at any time."

Ruth, for his part, was more than happy to volley back, in between the fifty-four holes of golf he was logging per day in southern California.

"I have given my best," he said. "Frazee tries to [justify the trade] by saying I will be an obstacle to the club winning pennants. . . . I have been with the Red Sox for six years and in that time we won three pennants. Not so bad? I am not a disturbing element. I have always played in the interest of the public and the players and Frazee knows it. He'll be lucky to have anybody at all in the park next year. If he even owns the ballclub. Frazee put me on the block. I have not lost anything, only the association of the people who matter least of all. I am refused the privilege of playing in my favorite city all because the man who owns the club is money-mad. He cares nothing about Boston people. He does not belong there, and when he sells out, which I expect will be the next big piece of news emanating from the East, he will not care if the Red Sox finish first or last.

"Frazee is not good enough to own any ballclub, especially one in Boston. It is not necessary for me to say he is unpopular, for that's a fact well known by anybody within the game. He has done more to hurt baseball in Boston than anyone who was ever connected with the game in that city. The Boston people are too good for him and it will be a blessing for them when he steps down."

The reaction of the fans was instantaneous. Most loathed the deal. "I figure the Red Sox club is now practically ruined," Charlie Lavin wrote to the *Post*. "With the sale of Babe Ruth, the Red Sox lost their mainsail. The team's future looks gloomy," Micah Murray wrote to the *Globe*. Johnny Keenan, the leader of the Royal Rooters, was everywhere denouncing the trade.

"Ruth was ninety percent of the Red Sox club last summer," Keenan groaned. "It will be impossible to replace the strength Ruth gave to the Boston club. Ruth is a wonderful player, loved the game and gave his all to win. Management will have an awful time filling the gap caused by his going. Surely the gate will suffer."

Still, to maintain, as many have for so long, that this was universally perceived as a steal is just wrong. Fans were just as contemptuous of spoiled, entitled athletes in 1920 as they are today, and so Orville Dennison, a longtime Red Sox fan from Cambridge, spoke for a small but sturdy minority when he said, "I admire Frazee's willingness to incur the enmity of the fans, at least temporarily, in his effort to produce a happy, winning team."

And the Boston press was hardly united in its appraisal of the deal, either, although the *Post* did lead the cries of agony: "The average patron cannot view with great equanimity the transfer of a star of the first magnitude, the greatest drawing card in the game. Boston fans, therefore, are bound to be disgruntled," the newspaper wrote in a bold-face editorial. Franklin Collier also drew the now-famous editorial cartoon for the *Boston Herald* that showed FOR SALE signs on Boston Common and the public library. But other cartoons weren't as kind. One depicted Ruth as an overfed bull rattling through a china shop; another showed him standing alongside the Flatiron Building (home of the American League offices) with a scowl on his face.

"I agree with Frazee," pitcher Fred Tonney said in a statement, moments after the deal was made public. "He knows his business best. A team is as strong as its weakest link. A player that fits a team is of more value than any star not working in harmony with his club. No player is indispensable."

The fact that Ruth turned out to be the most indispensable player in the whole tapestry of baseball is often held up as proof that Frazee either (a) had no idea what he was doing, (b) was in cahoots with the Yankees (he'd already dealt them top-flight pitcher Carl Mays during the 1919 season, and would soon unload a stream of players to one of the two teams—the White Sox were the other—still willing to do business with him in those years of American League civil war), or (c) was desperate to receive an infusion of cash in order to save what history has insisted was a foundering theatrical career.

It's worth taking a closer look at these three charges

Perhaps the most reasonable indictment is the first one, because if there is one thing that even Harry Frazee himself might admit, if he could, all these years later, it is that he truly did not have any idea what he was doing. Nobody could. And nobody did. Remember, the Babe Ruth that Frazee sold still had a far deeper résumé as a pitcher than he did as a hitter, and as a pitcher, he was coming off a season in which he'd won but nine games. As a hitter, he'd had only one season to date where he'd logged as many as 400 at-bats. He'd only hit forty-nine home runs for his whole career, and he would soon be turning twenty-five (as a point of comparison, a future Red Sox home-run hero named Tony Conigliaro would have 160 homers by the same age; Ted Williams had 127; Carl Yastrzemski had 79).

On January 5, 1920, there wasn't a soul alive who could make even a reasonable guess how Babe Ruth's career would shake out; surely, no one would be foolish enough to think he still had 665 career home runs left in his bat. And in fact he would never have come close to that number had he stayed in Boston, taking aim at the vast right-field spaces in Fenway Park seventy-seven times a year, rather than the hitter-friendly paradises of first the Polo Grounds and later Yankee Stadium. In truth, for a long time, this wasn't even considered the worst trade in Red Sox history. For years, Red Sox fans shook their head in fury when recalling the date of April 12, 1916, when the Sox shipped Tris Speaker, indisputably the best player in the American League, to the Cleveland Indians for $55,000 and two low-level players. Speaker was twice the player at the time of his trade that Ruth was, a .337 lifetime hitter who would raise his average to .345 before he would retire, sixth on the all-time list.

Frazee's friendship with Colonel Huston is a matter of record, as was his warm relationship with Colonel Ruppert. Did that cloud his judgment? No. The Red Sox, remember, were embroiled in a war among the American League states in 1919. Nobody would do business with them other than the Yankees and the White Sox, and Charlie Comiskey, owner of the White Sox, had enough misery on his hands with the growing whispers surrounding the possibility that his team had thrown the World Series. That left the Yankees. That's why Carl Mays became a Yankee. It's why Frazee agreed to send the Yankees Ernie Shore and Duffy Lewis, two Sox returning from the war who'd lost their jobs in

Boston but were a big help for the Yankees. There is no doubt that as the years passed, Sox fans grew bitter that Frazee spent most of his year in New York, close to his other business interests. But selling Ruth had nothing to do with friendship.

One other thing to consider: Given the restraints that Frazee was working under, once he decided to make a deal, any deal, to rid himself of Ruth, he actually made the better of the two he sought. He did get his cash, after all, and he did try to reinvest it in other ballplayers, although none could come close to measuring up to a ghost of Ruth's girth. Still, the alternative was a straight one-for-one deal, Ruth for the White Sox' Joe Jackson. Within ten months, Jackson would be exposed as a fixer and would be banned from the game for life; what would Red Sox fans have thought about *that* swap?

The subject that always draws the most ire from Red Sox fans is the idea that Frazee sold Ruth to save himself, to keep his theater operations from going under. The shortened version goes something like this: Frazee, desperate for cash, deals Ruth for enough money to open *No, No, Nanette,* which becomes a huge hit and saves the day for the Frazee family fortune while subjecting the Red Sox to a century stuffed with misery.

Which is just plain wrong.

Frazee was simply *not* on the brink of financial ruin, as he's long been portrayed. The fact is, the Red Sox turned a profit in 1919, cashing in mightily on Ruth's pursuit of history. This also happened to be when Frazee was at the peak of his business interests. He had his own theater chain. He had three Shubert theaters, which he leased. He had a real estate investment firm, a management company, a stock brokerage company. And at the same time he was trading Ruth, he was actually thriving as a theater impresario as never before. Twenty-three days before the trade, his newest play, *My Lady Friends,* opened to rave reviews and played for nine months. It earned Frazee $3,000 a week. He took it on the road and made even more money.

No, No, Nanette, the play that brought you the standards "Tea for

Two" and "I Want to Be Happy" while simultaneously filling generations of Sox fans with fury and angst, wouldn't open for almost six
years, although when it did premiere at the Globe Theater on Broadway
and Forty-sixth Street, starring Louise Goody and Jack Barker, the
reviews were breathless and glowing. "It is full of much vigorous merriment," gushed the *Times*. "A triumph," cooed the *Herald-Tribune*. It ran
for 321 performances, a stunning number for its day, and it did make
Harry Frazee even richer than he already was. For the record: During
the play's run, covering parts of the 1925 and '26 seasons, the Yankees
went 53–24, the Red Sox 24–50. Forty-five years later, the play enjoyed a
smashing two-year run as a revival, and the Sox finally exacted a measure of revenge, compiling a 170–147 mark to the Yankees' 161–156.

Still, to Red Sox fans, the most critical numbers turned out to be this:
In Ruth's final year in Boston, the Yankees finished twelve games ahead
of the Red Sox. It was only the fourth time the Red Sox had ever finished
behind the Yankees in the American League standings. It would be
another twenty-seven years before the Red Sox would again finish ahead
of the Yankees in the standings, and over the next eighty-four years, the
Yankees would finish ahead of the Red Sox a staggering sixty-four times.

It wasn't a very good trade.

The 2003 Red Sox did complete their comeback, in nerve-fraying
fashion, holding off a late Oakland rally at the end of a decisive game
five, sending New England into a complete spasm of joy.

New York?

Sure, Yankees fans understood that these Red Sox weren't your great-
grandfather's Red Sox. Intellectually, they realized the spell the Yankees
had held would end sooner or later. But they were also soothed from an
unlikely place. George Steinbrenner had watched his team dispatch the
Twins with cool efficiency. He was happy. He was proud. He was chatty.
And when all of these planets align, sometimes he can produce magic.

"The win against Minnesota demonstrates the spirit of our Yankees,"

Steinbrenner said in a statement that should have been accompanied by a fife and drum corps. "We were treated beautifully by Minnesota, but our team had the mental toughness that only the Yankees can show. New Yorkers are battlers, and so are we. The victory was great for New York and for our fans, and I'm proud of our guys.

"New Yorkers support our team with their hard-earned dollars, and I want our team to understand what we owe them by the way we dress and how we play on the field. One thing that we hold dearly is that quitters never win and winners never quit. For us, winning isn't the only thing. It's second to breathing. As MacArthur said, 'Victory is essential.'"

Actually, the general's exact quote had been "In war, there is no substitute for victory," but nobody was much inclined to point this out to Steinbrenner. The man was on a serious roll.

CHAPTER

4

THE WORST POSSIBLE THING

It was a tough game to lose, and a tough pennant to see go by the board through one wild pitch. However, I am not crying. Boston won the game fair and square and Boston deserves the flag. I take my cap off to Collins and all his players. Their steady play on Saturday and today was nothing short of wonderful. You have a great baseball city and a great ball team.
  —*Clark Griffith, manager, New York Highlanders, October 10, 1904*

I'm not really a big believer in the Curse of the Bambino. I don't think we're battling the Curse of the Bambino here. We're battling the New York Yankees, and this group of renegades that I'm putting on the field, they don't care. They care about their Harley-Davidsons running good enough that they won't run off the Tobin Bridge over there in Boston, and playing baseball. *—Grady Little, manager, Boston Red Sox, October 8, 2003*

The arrival of the Red Sox, via red-eye charter from California, signaled an unambiguous transformation among the people of the city of New York. It happens every year. New Yorkers take great pride in their ability to affix a studied detachment to everything: the arrivals of popes and presidents, the opening of Broadway blockbusters, the successes and failures of their sports teams. It simply isn't cool to get so giddy over the things that make New York what it is: writers strolling through Washington Square Park amid the hackey-sack-booting college kids; actors running the reservoir loop at Central Park alongside early-rising attorneys, stockbrokers, and waiters; musicians stepping into the dive bars of Greenwich Village, seeking—and expecting—anonymity.

"This isn't Ames, Iowa," no less a source than Donald Trump had said earlier in the summer, before ascending to his regular Yankee Stadium perch inside George Steinbrenner's personal box. "New Yorkers aren't blown away by much of anything."

Ah, but the Yankees in autumn are a different story. Over the past eight years, the Yankees had become such a ubiquitous part of the city's soul that there was no use denying certain facts of life: During October, the Yankees managed to turn the most sophisticated city in America into earth's most oversized, overstuffed college town. The back pages of the city's normally grizzled tabloids fell over themselves to offer breathless encouragements to the local nine. Even the front page—or "the wood," the old-time term even new-age editors clung to—could sometimes become an undisguised bastion of cheerleading. On the morning of October 8, 2003, the *Daily News'* cover featured a large picture of Babe Ruth, with a simple message superimposed: "No Way."

All across the city on that Wednesday afternoon, people treated their workday like schoolchildren wishing away the last hours before summer. In law firms and brokerage houses, workers kept staring at clocks, peeking at their watches, peering out office windows. Inside university classrooms, along the halls of government buildings, outside scaffolding-encased high-rise towers, professors and lawmakers and hard-hats and students all readied themselves for what would arrive later that evening—an athletic Armageddon none of them could quite articulate.

The Red Sox were playing the Yankees: best of seven. Winner takes the American League flag. Loser gets to endure a sleepless winter, followed by an endless spring.

You know how you could tell this was a big deal? Because once you stepped away from the clamoring city and walked into the clubhouses underneath Yankee Stadium, you still couldn't lose the electricity. These are places of business, peopled by calm, unruffled professionals. Long ago, they had the little boy beaten out of them, the wide-eyed innocent capable of enjoying the wonder in just taking part in such a magnificent spectacle. Joe DiMaggio had summed it up best more than fifty-five years earlier. "If you convince yourself that today is the biggest game of your life," he'd told his friend, columnist Jimmy Cannon, "then how in the world do you get excited about tomorrow?"

Joe D.'s words disintegrated in a deafening din of pre-series anticipation.

"We play them nineteen times in the regular season and it's always very intense, almost like nineteen different wars," Yankees pitcher David Wells said. "To get this match-up, all hell is going to break loose. It's good for New York and Boston. Both cities love their teams."

In a surprise to no one, Larry Lucchino was more than willing to concur.

"We still refer to them as the Empire from time to time, and we have some fun with that," the Red Sox president chuckled, standing amid a thick crowd of writers a few hours before the series' first pitch. "But how do we view them? We view them with a lot of respect and appreciation for what they have accomplished and what their recent history has been. I think there's an intense rivalry between the cities, between the teams, between the front offices. There's no question about that. But that's now background to the main event. The main event is what happens out on the field between the white lines. It is poetic that it comes down to the Nation against the Empire."

Red Sox–Yankees spiked an avalanche of odd, ancillary anecdotes, testimony to just how personal the fans viewed this series. John MacCormac, for instance, had been a lifelong Yankees fan living in Woodbridge, New Jersey. He grew up to become his home state's treasurer, responsible for the safeguarding of billions of dollars of state funds, charged with making sure the nation's most densely populated state ran its business with fiscal precision. And yet even a man with such a staid, sober outlook on life was not immune to hardball hyperbole.

"You always try to avoid the worst possible things in life," MacCormac said, straight-faced, before game one. "And the worst possible thing for the Yankees is to lose to the Red Sox."

Meanwhile, on Beacon Hill, Massachusetts state representative Barry Finegold, a Democrat from Andover, attempted to introduce a bill into the state legislature that would help eradicate the sale of pro-Yankees merchandise around Fenway Park for games three, four, and five. Finegold's resolution called on hawkers within a mile of Fenway to turn their backs on any merchandise that smacked of support for the New York club.

"Every so often," Finegold said in his finest statesman's voice, "you need to put people over profits. Our dearly beloved Red Sox fans have suffered quite a bit." It was an impressive pitch but ill-fated; the measure stalled in the House counsel's office, which said such a move was "unprecedented."

Fans place no such limits of restraint on their own daily meditations. And so it was that Mike Graves found himself making an odd pilgrimage to a grassy sanctuary twenty minutes north of Yankee Stadium, a few hours before Mussina would fire the first pitch of this series, a knee-high strike to Todd Walker. Graves was a twenty-nine-year-old Red Sox fan who was born in Providence, Rhode Island, but now lived and worked where the enemy ate: He managed a Cheesecake Factory restaurant in nearby White Plains, New York, a favored eatery of both Bernie Williams and Derek Jeter.

He'd lived with plenty of Red Sox–inflicted scar tissue lining his soul already and had mostly kept his mouth shut around his customers, the better not to get a drink thrown into his Red Sox–loving face. He'd endured this quiet desperation long enough. So he ventured to Gate of Heaven Cemetery in Hawthorne, stopped by the visitors' office (always helpful with directions to the gravesites of James Cagney, Dorothy Parker, or Billy Martin), and been pointed down the familiar path to the graveyard's most famous tenant.

Which explains why he was on his knees, praying in front of Babe Ruth's headstone.

"I just want this curse to be over already," Graves explained. "Maybe me coming here will help the Red Sox."

Graves arrived bearing a peace offering: a Red Sox cap, which he left atop the marble marker, a keepsake for the Babe filed alongside the other bits of bric-a-brac presently festooning his eternal resting place: assorted American flags, Yankees caps, game-used bats, newspaper clippings, baseball cards, a bottle of Old Slugger Pale Ale ("Brewed in Cooperstown!" the label proudly proclaims)—even a rapidly decaying ballpark frank appropriately dressed with sauerkraut, thus far untouched by the birds soaring overhead.

"I'm willing to try anything," Graves said.

"Leave it to a Red Sox fan," Frank Russo moaned, "to try and defile a holy place."

Russo, as you may already have guessed, is not a Red Sox fan. He is a Yankees fan, has been one since at least August 8, 1969, the day his father brought him to Yankee Stadium to see his first major-league game. It was a Friday, and Russo's dad closed his dry-cleaning shop early so they could hurry across the river from their home in East Brunswick, New Jersey, and make the second game of a doubleheader between the Yankees and the Oakland A's. Catching for the Yankees in that game was a young Ohioan making his major league debut, wearing number 15. Thurman Munson crashed through the door in a mad rush, getting two hits in three at-bats, scoring a run, driving in two, powering the Yankees to a 5–0 victory.

"It wasn't until years later," Russo says, "that I realized the irony that day, the fact that Thurman got his first hit off his future teammate and friend, Catfish Hunter."

Russo is a former radio personality and a full-time Web designer these days, although that really just describes the way he makes his living. The way he fuels his life is with a marvelously quirky Internet page devoted to baseball's dear departed, www.thedeadballera.com. To qualify for a slot on Russo's site, you need only fulfill two basic requirements.

1. You must have played major-league baseball.
2. You must be, to quote Casey Stengel, dead at the present time.

Yes, there is more than a trace of the macabre involved here. There are, after all, more than a thousand pictures of gravestones, headstones, and mausoleum markers here. There are more than a thousand obituaries. The site's motto? "Where every player is safe at home." Its logo? Two bats, crossed, with eagles' wings on each side.

This means you need to fulfill a few requirements of your own if you wish to enjoy this site to its fullest.

1. An appreciation of baseball history.
2. An appreciation of gallows humor.
3. An ability to feel not the least bit guilty stifling a laugh at the misfortunes of the likes of Jim Creighton, a pitcher for the Brooklyn Excelsiors who, in 1861, died after rupturing his bladder while swinging at a pitch and who, given his fate, may well have been the first inspiration for the advent of the designated hitter.

"This isn't supposed to be a sick site, and I don't think it is," says Russo. "I think it's a place to recognize and memorialize people who played major-league baseball. They did something that millions of us dream about doing, playing in The Show. This is a tribute to them. And I've heard from families of some of these players. They see it that way, too."

Russo is not a fan of the make-the-trip-to-Babe's-grave method of rooting for either of these teams, however. This is a sacred place for him, after all. Baseball's all-time biggest star is also its all-time biggest curiosity. People want to know where the Babe is, even fifty-five years after his death. Russo has no quarrel with baseball fans leaving their mementos behind. But using them as talismans?

"Like I said," Russo said, "leave it to a Red Sox fan. It's been so long since they were able to beat the Yankees when it mattered, they're willing to try anything."

It was true. The last time the Red Sox had beaten the Yankees in a meaningful win-or-go-home October situation, the teams were known as the Pilgrims and the Highlanders. It was 1904. Babe Ruth was a boy of nine, just starting his second year at St. Mary's Industrial School for Boys in Baltimore. New York City was just getting used to the idea of a second professional baseball team inhabiting the northern Manhattan hinterland, and Boston was settling into its self-titled role as "capital of baseball." It had earned this distinction with a victory in the first World Series the previous autumn, a title it would retain for the better part of the next two decades.

Tensions between the teams began to simmer right from the beginning. The first game pairing American League representatives of Boston and New York took place on May 7, 1903, at Boston's Huntington Avenue Grounds, a relatively uneventful 6–2 Boston victory as Bill Dineen bettered Snake Wiltse, enabling the Pilgrims to leapfrog over the Highlanders into third place. There was already an underlying friction between the franchises, given that the Highlanders had spent the previous two seasons as the Baltimore Orioles, and Baltimore had long been Boston's most bitter municipal enemy on baseball diamonds.

The next day, though, the paying customers at the Huntington Avenue Grounds received the first hint that a fresher, fiercer feud had officially arrived, the moment New York's Dave Fultz barreled into Boston's George Winter at first base. The vicious collision knocked Winter silly, and it was only after Fultz began barking at him to pitch or quit that the Boston pitcher resumed throwing, ultimately taking the loss in a 6–1 New York victory. In those heartier times, there was little chance of a bench-clearing brawl leaking onto the field, but the first blood of this rivalry had officially been spilled. Boston recovered any-way, going on to win ninety-one times, taking the American League flag by fourteen and a half games (seventeen over the 72–62, fourth-place Highlanders), and earning the first-ever World Series title by beating Pittsburgh in eight hard-fought games.

By 1904, New York desperately wanted to settle the score.

The team's owners, Frank Farrell and Big Bill Devery, had already begun to make shrewd (Bostonians screamed crooked) deals that seem-ingly strengthened New York while weakening Boston. They also began eyeing acquirable players of Irish descent, the better to take advantage of the ethnic group that had taken the quickest liking to baseball—although most of those emerald émigrés had flocked instead to the Polo Grounds to root for the National League Giants, a team stuffed with surnames (Devlin, Bresnahan, McGraw, O'Rourke, McGinnity) who seemingly had arrived in the majors by way of Galway Bay. The Giants already looked upon the Highlanders suspiciously, deriding the upstart American Leaguers as "the Invaders," for having trodden on their city with their inferior style of ball.

"It is simple," Clark Griffith, the Highlanders' fiery manager, said on the eve of the 1904 season. "We want an exciting team that New York will be excited about. But most of all, we want the Bostons' flag."

His players immediately stoked that optimism on opening day, when they thrashed the world champions, 8–2, jumping all over Cy Young with five first-inning runs, much to the delight of the 69th Regiment Band and the 15,840 people who'd jammed Hilltop Park, the tiny tinder-box on the corner of Broadway and 168th Street, thirteen blocks north of the Giants' majestic Polo Grounds. Jack Chesbro picked up the vic-tory for the Highlanders, the first of forty-one wins Happy Jack would record on the year, a single-season standard that will likely stand forever.

It was Chesbro's right arm—and his most reliable pitch, a wicked spitball that all but rained on the hitter as it wiggled past the plate—that fortified New York's pennant aspirations all summer. Between May

14 and July 4, he won fourteen consecutive starts, which is the biggest reason the Pilgrims—who tempered the Highlanders' opening-day enthusiasm by winning the next two, getting a head start in the pennant chase—were never quite capable of running away and hiding from the rest of the American League. So it was that when New York traveled to Boston in early May, with the Pilgrims already out to a 13–3 start and the Highlanders sputtering at 8–7, Griffith—a fiery manager who was in many ways a spiritual antecedent of the man who would occupy the same office seventy years later, Billy Martin—would make a bold, unabashed proclamation.

"We are not afraid of the world champions," Griffith declared before the teams took to the Huntington Avenue Grounds May 6. "We believe we are at least their equal."

Two days later, after his team had taken two out of three from the first-place Pilgrims, Griffith all but flew back to the train station propelled by sheer ecstasy, telling anyone who would listen, "We did what we said we would. Keep your eye on the Invaders! We took two from the world champions and can do it again!"

And if they couldn't do it on the field across the long season, then the men in the ownership suites were doing their damnedest to make it possible everywhere else. The Pilgrims were in Chicago that June 18, the day word began to spread that the club had dealt Patsy Dougherty to the Highlanders. It was a crushing blow to Pilgrims fans, but also a perceptible strike at the heart of the sport itself. Baseball had long been shadowed by rumors that it wasn't played on the level, and gamblers were welcome guests (and reliable customers) at every major-league ballpark. Indeed, one of the Highlanders co-owners, Frank Farrell, had fortified his fortune through the dimes and dollars of unlucky card players, while his partner, Devery, the former police chief, had made his by turning a blind eye to such mischief.

Now the Pilgrims had traded away their best everyday player. The Highlanders had a marquee star, one who brought the happy bonus of bearing a Gaelic moniker.

And the cries of "Fix!" were everywhere.

"The fans are greatly disturbed over the change made by John I. Taylor by which we lose a peerless wielder of the stick and get in return an untried player [Bob Unglaub] in fast company," bemoaned an anonymous Boston correspondent in the *Sporting News*. "There is not the least doubt in my mind, and the vast majority of people who are interested in the world champions, that we got the worst of the exchange. Inability to bat is a common disease this season."

The spinning was endless. Boston officials immediately described Dougherty as "aloof, unsympathetic," which put him at odds with a Pilgrims team described as being "full of compassionate men." This did nothing to stem the anger flooding the streets around Huntington Avenue Grounds. Both Taylor, the owner, and Jimmy Collins, the manager, retreated into defensive positions.

"The trade was made only after consultation with manager Collins and on his advice," Taylor wailed. "We are doing what we can to win the pennant for Boston." Added Collins, suddenly thrown under the bus by his owner: "Mr. Taylor made the trade of Dougherty for Unglaub with my sanction and I think the deal will prove to be in the best interest of the Boston club."

That was of little consolation a week after the trade, when the Highlanders, with Dougherty anchoring the middle of their lineup, went into Boston and took two more from the staggering champs, drawing to within a half game of first place. It was clear from that moment on that Boston and New York were on a collision course, and it exploded in historic fireworks late on the afternoon of August 5. That day, New York blanked Cleveland, 5–0, while the Red Sox fell to Detroit, 4–3, and when all the reports were filed to the league office, the standings in the American League read this way:

NEW YORK	54–34	.614
CHICAGO	57–36	.613
BOSTON	55–35	.611

It was the first time ever that the sun set with a New York team sitting atop the American League standings. It was a heady baseball time in New York City, a feeling undiminished by the increasingly stubborn words emanating from the Polo Grounds, where the Giants had begun to grumble that they would not participate in a World Series that autumn, no matter who emerged from the other league. "We are content to rest on our laurels," Giants owner John Brush declared, his team sitting ten full games ahead of the pack in the National League.

Since that race was all but finished, even before September, Brush's vow was swept aside by the growing fever surrounding the pennant chase in the American League. Chicago quickly fell aside, allowing Boston and New York to emerge as the lone participants in a two-team dash. All of baseball pointed to two key series that lay ahead: a four-game set in Boston from September 14 to 17, and a five-game series that would cover the final weekend and take place in both cities, knowing these were likely to be as close to "playoff" series as they were likely to see in that most divisive season. Leading into the homestretch, Griffith, ever the pugnacious optimist, crowed, "My team is in the best condition it's been in all year. I cannot see at all where the Bostons have us beaten."

The first encounter was a scheduled four-game series that grew into a six-game series, with each team winning twice, losing twice, and, due to darkness, tying twice. It was a merry showcase for the team's stars. Dougherty scratched out eight hits and was given a rousing ovation each time he stood at the plate, even as he was continuing to single-handedly slaughter his former team. Chesbro pitched twice in the series, winning both of New York's games, and Young won the finale for Boston, adding another jewel to what would be one of the greatest seasons of his long and distinguished career, a 26–16 record that yielded a 1.97 ERA and included the first modern perfect game, pitched on May 5. Boston had entered the series leading by one percentage point; somehow, the series managed to pull the teams even closer together:

| BOSTON | 81–51 | .6126 |
| NEW YORK | 79–50 | .6124 |

New York went back home to play a single game against the Senators, then embarked on a seventeen-game, eighteen-day road trip to Washington, Cleveland, Detroit, Chicago, and St. Louis, and they kept themselves in the race, going 10–6 with one tie.

The season was reduced to a weekend.

But what a weekend! From late summer on, with the Giants having already lapped the field in the National League, more and more New Yorkers had begun to find their way to the rickety wooden stands at Hilltop Park. American League founder Ban Johnson's dream of supplanting the National League in the nation's media capital suddenly seemed less a stretch and more a possibility. So while the city prepared to welcome the defending champions to town, caught in the clutches of serious pennant fever, the Giants decided to do what they could to drown out the noise.

They officially called off the World Series.

"The people of New York have been kind enough to give me some credit for bringing the pennant to New York, and if there is any blame for this club's action in protecting this highly-prized honor, then blame should rest on my shoulders for I and I alone am responsible for the club's actions," said John McGraw, the Giants' tempestuous and blustery manager. "Never, while as manager of the New York club, and while this club holds a pennant, will I consent to enter into a box office grafting game with Ban Johnson and Company."

So as the Pilgrims and Highlanders prepared to meet on that first weekend of October 1904, they did so knowing the season would extend no further. There would be no championship series. There would be no best-of-nine, no best-of-seven, no one-shot winner-take-all between the warring leagues. Nothing. The entire season would be reduced to these five games for the right to claim the American League pennant. For Boston, there was the additional motivation of knowing that by winning the league pennant, they would retain the title of "world's champions" by default.

"If we win and the New York Nationals don't care to play us," Collins said, "then we will be perfectly happy to wear the crown unchallenged for another calendar year."

In New York, there was an additional slab of outrage to lay atop McGraw's furious gall. It turned out that despite all their dubious dealings, despite pulling every string within their grasp in an effort to secure a pennant for themselves, Farrell and Devery never quite believed in their team's chances. They certainly never expected the final series of the season, the five games at Hilltop Park, to be anything more than meaningless exhibitions. Boston was too powerful.

So the owners made an appalling decision. Early in the summer, they agreed to rent their ballpark to Columbia University for its Saturday, October 8, football game against Williams College (the future alma mater of one George M. Steinbrenner III). Compounding that calamitous gaffe, October 8 was a scheduled doubleheader. When the Pilgrims agreed to switch sites with the Highlanders, they got two extra home games, a bonus they might not have appreciated in June but one that took on extraordinary significance in October. Flustered, Farrell and Devery tried to persuade Taylor, their pal in Boston, to let them reschedule the doubleheader for Friday in New York and play only a single game Saturday in Boston, but Taylor, understanding that such a transaction would sign his own death warrant among Pilgrims fans still steamed by the Dougherty trade, wouldn't hear of it. And so it was set: There would be one game in New York on Friday, two in Boston on Saturday, an off day on Sunday in deference to local blue laws, and then a season-ending doubleheader on Monday, October 10, at Hilltop Park.

The Pilgrims, traveling to the big game by train from Chicago, stopped in Buffalo for a meal and were besieged by reporters. Collins, a veteran of dozens of past baseball wars, said, "There is nothing left now but to go ahead and do our best. It's now a case of who can win three out of five, and should we lose we will have no excuse to offer."

Ten thousand fans showed up at Hilltop Park for game one, and the Highlanders sent them home happy with a 3–2 win, helping Jack Chesbro to his forty-first victory. Delirious Highlanders fans carried Happy Jack on their shoulders, firmly believing there was nothing he couldn't do, no team he couldn't beat when absolutely necessary.

"There's nothing like taking the starter!" Griffith gushed. "We've got Boston on the run!" So exhilarated was the New York manager that before the teams left the ballpark, he'd approached Jimmy Collins, already dressed in a smartly pressed suit, and laid out a proposition.

"There isn't going to be a World Series, Jimmy," Griffith said. "So let's play one of our own, no matter what happens here. Best of five. We'll even play three in your park if you'd like. For the world's championship."

Collins, fresh from a thorough beating, seemed intrigued.

"We'll see," he said. "Let's see how the weekend goes."

To the press, Collins flashed a far more confident pose.

"We have yet to lose the flag," he said. "We are not defeated. New York, to win the flag, must beat us two more games. Tell the Boston fans not to lose hope. We will be there tomorrow fighting with all our old-time spirit."

With four games left in the season, for only the second time all year, Collins' team had been knocked into second place:

NEW YORK	91–56	.619	—
BOSTON	92–58	.613	½

Now all the Highlanders needed was a split. Griffith was pleased. He'd keep Chesbro home, the better to make sure he'd be ready on Monday. It wouldn't be out of the question for his team to split the doubleheader in Boston, right? They'd won 66 percent of their games since July 25; was it such a stretch to ask them to play .500 ball for one day? And then he'd have Happy Jack Chesbro, on full rest, with a standing-room-only crowd at Hilltop Park, one win for the flag . . .

"Who are you going to pitch in Boston tomorrow?"

Griffith snapped out of his daydream as he stepped onto the platform at Grand Central Terminal, waiting to board the train that would take the Highlanders to Boston. There, in front of him, stood Jack Chesbro.

"What the hell are you doing here?" the manager asked his meal ticket.

"I asked you a question," Chesbro said. "Who are you going to pitch in Boston?"

Griffith, still startled, stammered. "I figured Al Orth in the first game and Jack Powell in the second," he said. Between them, Orth and Powell had won thirty-five games that season for New York.

"What the hell's the matter with me?" Chesbro asked.

Griffith said nothing.

"Don't I work for this club anymore?" the pitcher chided.

"But you worked today," Griffith said. "You can't pitch them all."

That logic wasn't going to work with Chesbro. He'd already appeared in fifty-three games and started forty-nine of them, and he'd already thrown well over four hundred innings, and even in a time when pitchers were expected to finish what they started, that was an astonishing total.

"You want to win the pennant, don't you?" Chesbro asked, his voice rising. "I'll pitch. And I'll win."

What could Griffith do? He'd ridden Chesbro all year, handed him the ball three times a week on occasion, sometimes twice in one day. How could he keep him home now, with the pennant so close, with him demanding the ball?

"OK," Griffith said. "It's your game. Give 'em hell."

Saturday afternoon, the Highlanders took a quick 1–0 lead when Dougherty scored his 113th and final run of the season—the 80th in the 106 games he'd played for New York. But Chesbro was working on fumes and had nothing. Boston shelled him. And the fans taunted him. There were, by most estimates, 30,000 of them in or around the Huntington Avenue Grounds that afternoon, arriving as early as six o'clock in the morning. Rows of schoolboys took turns dropping to their knees, straining to peek under the center-field fence. Hundreds of others climbed the telegraph poles that ringed the outskirts of the ballfield. All of them jeered Chesbro as he allowed hit after hit, run after run, all the way to a 13–2 rout that vaulted the Pilgrims back into first place by a half game. Worse, Young pitched a 1–0 gem in a nightcap shortened by darkness to six innings. The Pilgrims had themselves a sweep and a one-and-a-half-game lead.

And suddenly the Highlanders were in deep, deep trouble.

Griffith was angry at himself as he took a carriage to Back Bay Station, in time for the Highlanders' eleven o'clock train home. Chesbro shared the cab, silent and sullen. New York's margin for error had vanished. A Monday sweep was now imperative. And somehow, Griffith would have to perk Chesbro's psyche after the pitcher had absorbed his worst beating of the season. Chesbro tried to do it for him, speaking for the first time since trudging off the mound hours before.

"Don't worry," he said as the two men boarded the train. "I'll trim 'em on Monday if it costs me an arm."

It was a difficult trip home for Griffith. He was angry at his owners for giving up on his team earlier in the summer, selling out a crucial doubleheader at Hilltop Park. He was annoyed at his ace pitcher for putting his ego above the team. And he was furious with himself for listening to Chesbro and not the inner voice in his head that had told him to leave the pitcher home, do the right thing, the conservative thing, the *smart* thing.

Years later, after he'd established a family dynasty with the Washington Senators, Griffith was still angry about it. "They said the Yankees dynasty began with Ruth," he groused a few years before his death in 1955. "Well, it shoulda been another group of New Yorkers. And who knows: If we'd have won it, maybe they'd forever be known as the Highlanders."

Griffith's uneasy journey stood in stark contrast to another train that would soon traverse the Northeast corridor. The Royal Rooters decided they would treat this season-ending doubleheader as their own de facto World Series, and over three hundred of them overran the clerks in the American League's offices with ticket requests. The long, circuitous trip took much of Sunday to complete, stopping frequently in small Connecticut towns where the merriment spilled over into local eateries. The Rooters came with their vocal cords primed, and practiced the cheers and chants they would aim at the Highlanders the next afternoon. Years later, Boston opponents could still hear, ringing in their ears, the Rooters' most famous song with its dreadfully banal lyrics:

> *Tessie, you make me feel so badly*
> *Why don't you turn around?*
> *Tessie, you know I love you madly*
> *Babe, my heart weighs about a pound.*

By the time they arrived at the Marlboro Hotel on 166th Street, just two blocks south of Hilltop Park, the Rooters were hoarse and hysterical. But New York City, fully trapped now in the pull of a pennant race, was also ready for the big day. There was some concern that dark skies might be blowing in from the west, and it had been decided by the league office that the season would not be extended. If there was a rainout, the Pilgrims would win by default. That was the second ruling that threw a wrench into the morning festivities; Collins had already sent word to Griffith that his team would not accept Griffith's five-game challenge. They would abide by the outcome of the regular season. Griffith, hardly surprised by that, told his team that morning: "Boys, it's all or nothing for us today."

Thirty thousand baseball fans marched upon upper Manhattan as the sun defiantly lit the Monday afternoon sky. Today, a full century later, the complex of buildings making up New York–Presbyterian Hospital dominates the corner of 168th Street and Broadway, where Hilltop Park once stood. The original hospital's older brick building shares the sidewalk with a modern specialty wing named for a brokerage house. The streets here converge with St. Nicholas Avenue, and the city has carved out a small green space, Mitchell Park, at the triangular intersection. A small branch location of a major bank, a deli, a pizzeria, and a donut shop line the northwest corner at street level, serving doctors, patients, and local residents. The neighborhood teems with foot and automobile traffic.

Yet that singular patch of Manhattan has never again known the wonder and energy that filled its air some two hours before the first pitch on October 10, 1904. Every seat was occupied. Aisle space was nonexistent. The fans had begun to rev themselves into a fevered pitch. The Royal Rooters settled comfortably into their seats behind the Pilgrims' third-base bench and started singing "Tessie" soon thereafter. Highlander fans responded with appropriate retorts, the specifics of which have been lost to time, although they were probably similar in tone, if not temerity, to the "Boston sucks!" chants that would fill another New York City stadium a century later.

Their passions were rewarded, too. Chesbro was back to his dominant self in the early innings, his spitball dipping and diving around Boston bats. Trying to be true to his vow, he also made a contribution with his stick, smoking a one-out triple in the bottom of the third. But with the park pleading for a hit, he was stranded there, Big Bill Dineen fanning the tandem of Patsy Dougherty and Wee Willie Keeler, escaping the jam.

The delirium reached a peak two innings later when Chesbro stepped to the plate for his second at-bat. Before he could, a small contingent of fans from Chesbro's hometown of North Adams, Massachusetts, stormed the field and presented their man with a sealskin coat and a matching cap. Chesbro, startled and touched, smiled for photographs as the crowd roared its approval—save for the three hundred Royal Rooters, who screamed "Traitors!" at their fellow New Englanders.

Duly inspired, Chesbro rapped out a single, which helped ignite a two-run rally keyed by RBI singles from Dougherty—Boston couldn't keep its former fair-haired boy down for long—and Kid Elberfeld. This, at last, was what New York's American League fans had been so ardently hoping for. The best pitcher on the planet had himself a two-run lead, and he set the Red Sox down in order in the sixth. Nine outs to go. He retired the first hitter in the seventh. Eight outs to go. The Rooters had grown dumb. The remaining 29,700 inside Hilltop Park had officially drowned them out and begun the final countdown toward the all-or-nothing nightcap.

One hundred years later, seen through the prism of all that came later, we can understand how the Red Sox and Yankees we've come to know now are, in fact, photographic negatives of the Pilgrims and Highlanders who spawned them. For in 1904, it was New York fans who believed the worst would inevitably occur, somehow, some way, and it was Boston's fans who trusted always in the guiding hand of a greater baseball providence.

On October 10, 1904, Highlander fans would see a second baseman named Jimmy Williams commit three abysmal mistakes in one inning that completely underlined why they believed they would never, ever be able to figure a way to beat the Bostons when it mattered most. Williams, in essence, gave the Pilgrims six outs and two gift runs that tied the game. Chesbro recovered, retiring the side before staggering back to the dugout, glassy-eyed and exhausted.

Griffith approached Chesbro. Ninety-nine years on, another star-crossed manager would approach another spent pitcher in a crucial spot involving these teams, would ponder whether to keep him in the game. Ninety-nine years before Grady Little would have a fateful conversation with Pedro Martinez, Clark Griffith had one with Happy Jack Chesbro.

"Do you have anything left?" the manager asked his pitcher.

"No," Chesbro answered, finally understanding the value of complete honesty in this pennant race. "I'm finished."

The answer didn't satisfy Griffith. He turned to Red Kleinow, his twenty-four-year-old catcher, and asked, "What do you think?"

Kleinow, with exactly sixty-eight games of major-league experience to his name, said, "He hasn't got anything, but he's getting along all right. It's a toss-up."

That was what Griffith wanted to hear. So after the Highlanders went out meekly in the bottom of the eighth, he sent Chesbro out for his 454th inning of work in 1904. To a man, there were 29,700 petrified Highlander fans who could have predicted what would happen next.

Lou Criger led off with a routine grounder to short, which Kid Elberfeld booted for his forty-eighth error of the season. Dineen sacrificed Criger to second, but Chesbro, his arm screaming with every pitch, induced Kip Selbach to ground out to Elberfeld, who carefully fielded the play and allowed Criger to advance to third without incident. Chesbro was now one out away from getting out of the inning, handing the game over to his hitters. Only Freddy Parent, Boston's leading batter on the year at a modest .291, stood in the way. Chesbro had already struck Parent out twice, and on three straight spitters he jumped ahead of the count, 1 and 2.

Everyone in the ballpark knew what Chesbro would do next, because Jack Chesbro's spitball in 1904 was as devastating a pitch as the game has ever seen. Chesbro went for the kill, wetting the tips of his fingers, squeezing a little extra hard on the ball, winding up, and then, keeping his wrist and forearm stiff as a starched collar, snapping his arm straight down. It was a routine that had already resulted in 239 strikeouts and scores of puzzled hitters all season.

This time, it betrayed him.

This time, the ball sailed out of Jack Chesbro's fingertips, and it soared some fifteen feet over his stunned catcher's head, rolling seventy feet behind, to the chicken-wire backstop. Criger, dancing off third, could hardly believe what he was seeing and didn't run right away. But even with the delay, he dashed home easily, touching home plate in the encroaching silence of the Highlanders fans and the piercing guffaws of the Royal Rooters.

On the New York bench, Clark Griffith first collapsed to his knees and then fell prostrate in the dirt. He never saw Parent scratch a single off Chesbro—*would he have gotten the hit if the game were still tied? Did that render Chesbro's wild pitch moot? No one will ever know*—and never saw Parent get forced at second for the final out. He also never saw his ace pitcher trundle off the field, crumple onto the bench, and begin to sob uncontrollably, gales of sadness no teammate could contain.

Naturally, the Highlanders had one more tease left. With one out, Dineen walked Wid Conroy, putting the tying run on base. Kleinow popped to second for the second out, but now Chesbro would have a chance for the ultimate redemption. Griffith, his eyes once again fixed on the matters at hand, fully intended to let his pitcher hit, especially since Chesbro, a .236 hitter that season, had done well against Dineen all afternoon. But now, for the first time, he looked over and saw what a mess Chesbro was. He opted to let Deacon McGuire, a forty-year-old catcher, pinch-hit. McGuire drew a walk.

Two out. Two on. A pennant hung in the balance.

And Patsy Dougherty strode to the plate.

Surely, New York fans wailed, no baseball god could be this cruel. If not for Patsy Dougherty, the Highlanders never would have gotten anywhere near first place. They stood and they roared, even as Dougherty looked at strike one, even as he took ball one, even as he swung through a curveball for strike two. Behind the Red Sox bench, even the Royal Rooters could take no more, covering their eyes with each Dineen pitch, waiting for a crowd reaction to let them know what was happening. The fourth pitch resulted in another soaring howl from the locals as Dougherty took ball two.

Dineen had enough gas left for one more challenge pitch. He had won sixty-four games in the previous three years, but he was already feeling the effects in his arm; over the last five years of his career, he would have only one winning season, and he would retire with a thoroughly mediocre lifetime mark of 170–177. But the glory of baseball is that numbers mean nothing in the moment. It's your best against the batter's best, a simple equation. That's all.

Dineen threw. Dougherty swung. And caught nothing but air.

The Rooters stormed the field. The Highlanders fans gasped audibly, most of them filing out of the park immediately, not caring to wait around for the second game (a thoroughly meaningless New York victory).

Chesbro continued to sob softly, cursing himself for his stubborn insistence on pitching in Boston and for his rotten luck with the wild pitch. His record-breaking season had worn him out, and by 1908, after losing twenty games, the Highlanders would ship him away—to Boston, of all teams, where he would lose the only game he ever started for the newly rechristened Red Sox before retiring with 198 wins and a 2.68 life-time ERA. Forty-two years after uncorking one of the most famous wild pitches in baseball history, he was voted into the Baseball Hall of Fame. Griffith would manage for sixteen more seasons with the Highlanders, Cincinnati Reds, and Washington Senators and would never again come so close to first place. He, too, gained entrance to the Hall of Fame in 1946, still harboring sadness for the pennant that got away.

A few months after this awful end to a wonderful season, Griffith and Chesbro went dove hunting together in upstate New York. Chesbro could barely lift the gun off his shoulder.

"Why don't you look for something to shoot?" Griffith asked.

"I was thinking," Chesbro said.

"About the wild pitch?"

"Yes."

"Now look here," Griffith said. It had taken him this long to forget about the disastrous turn the season had taken. He would only rarely speak of it again the rest of his life. Here in the woods, he would take the stand with his ace that he should have taken on the platform at Grand Central months earlier.

"If you ever mention that pitch again," Griffith said, "I'll shoot you as I would a muskrat. Now shut up and hunt."

Two days shy of ninety-nine years later, the Red Sox finally won another October showdown with the Yankees. Dog tired after their fourth cross-country flight in less than a week, missing their starting center fielder, Johnny Damon, who'd suffered a concussion in a frightening collision with teammate Damian Jackson in game five of the Oakland series, they nevertheless found the energy to beat the Yankees, 5–2, silencing a rabid Yankee Stadium throng, seizing a 1–0 advantage in this best-of-seven American League Championship Series.

Knuckleballer Tim Wakefield threw six strong innings, retiring fourteen in a row at one point. David Ortiz, who had been 0 for 20 lifetime against Yankees starter Mike Mussina, clubbed a two-run homer into the upper deck in right field, breaking the ice. But the moment for which this game was destined to be best remembered came in the fifth inning when Boston's Todd Walker, leading off, stroked a high fly ball that hugged the right-field foul line and then disappeared into a maze of arms and bright lights somewhere near the foul pole. First-base umpire Angel Hernandez initially called it foul; home plate umpire Tim McClelland quickly overruled, saying a fan had reached across the pole, and awarded Walker a home run.

The fan in question was eighteen-year-old Josh Mandelbaum of Fair Lawn, New Jersey, who was sitting in Seat 7, Row A of Box 655 of the right-field upper deck. Stunned by his sudden celebrity, he begged an onrush of reporters to leave him alone, saying, "I just want to enjoy the game," but adding, "I just didn't want to get hit in the face with the ball. It would have been foul, clearly."

Televised replays indicated differently, which is why Steve Palermo, major league baseball's supervisor of umpires, would later say, "We wanted to make sure we had twelve eyes on anything that might be considered controversial. McClelland would be 150 percent sure he was right to overrule on that."

Red Sox fans should be forgiven if they saw ethereal implications from that one play. For the first time anyone could remember, the Yankees had been victimized by one of their own. The image was still clear, after all, of twelve-year-old Jeffrey Maier plucking a fly ball out of the sky before it could hit Tony Tarasco's mitt in the 1996 ALCS between the Yankees and Baltimore Orioles; Maier's play had been ruled a home run for Derek Jeter, and seven years later Orioles fans were still bitter about that, even as Maier grew up and went on to play college baseball at Wesleyan University in Middletown, Connecticut.

But there was one other thing.

On October 2, 1978, Palermo, the umpiring supervisor, had been the third-base umpire at Fenway Park, so he was the one who raced down the left-field line as Bucky Dent's blast cleared the Wall. He was the one who saw the ball nestle into the screen in back of the fence, the one who twirled his right index finger in the air, indicating a home run. In essence, Palermo was the one who'd officially signaled to Red Sox fans that one of the worst moments of their lives was real and not some dreadful nightmare.

Twenty-five years after that, ninety-nine years after the wild pitch, those Red Sox fans suddenly had reason to believe all those mystical forces that had conspired against them all these years were taking a few days off.

It was about time, too. Red Sox supporters had long carried dual burdens in this matter. The obvious one, of course, revolved around their team's regular inability to beat the Yankees when absolutely necessary. Such is the kind of misery that informs all manner of fan frenzy. But the other part, the secret part, was even worse: Red Sox fans never quite saw the same kind of obsession in Yankees fans. And this *killed* them.

It's one of the things that always made this one of the most curious competitions in sports. Can a rivalry truly be a rivalry if one team wins all the time? Is Lucy and Charlie Brown a rivalry? Did Perry Mason and the district attorney engage in a true rivalry? In most rivalries, the only emotional rush that surpasses the prospect of sweet victory is the looming specter of wrenching defeat. At West Point, losing a football game to Navy casts a pall on the campus that lasts for months. If the Green Bay Packers walk into Soldier Field and beat the Bears in an important football game, then all of Chicago becomes the City of the Slumped Shoulders for days at a time. Red Sox fans have certainly felt this way enough times through the years. But had the Yankees fans? Ever? Even once? That infuriated Red Sox fans the worst. They were Ugarte in *Casablanca.* Yankees fans were Rick.

Ugarte: "You despise me, don't you?"

Rick: "If I gave you any thought, I probably would."

This was different, though. This changed things. Yankees fans woke up the morning after game one lacking the smug confidence with which they'd awakened the day before. They weren't fooling around any longer. And their emotions, venomous as they may have seemed, were like sweet songs in the ears of Red Sox fans.

"Regardless of the bluster and general wisecracks, I have a lot of respect for the Boston franchise history—emphasis on *history,*" said Peter Cipriano, the rabid Yankees fan. "But a lot of the reasons why I hope they die like dogs on a regular basis *is* their fans. They're just plain crazy. If there were ever a batch that puts the 'fanatic' back in 'fan,' it's them. When their team is doing well, they expect them to collapse. Then if they collapse, they blame a ghost."

Observed Frank Russo, growing increasingly agitated at Red Sox Nation declaring unofficial squatter's rights on the gravesite of George Herman Ruth: "As a whole, sportswise, I have no use for them."

This was good news for Red Sox fans, whose own fears and frustrations finally found an acceptable dance partner, whose own feelings toward the Yankees could probably best be summed up by Mike Carey, the Red Sox fan living in Queens, New York: "I hate them with the white-hot passion of a thousand suns. I loathe them. I hate them more now, but detested them when I was a kid. I used to bet chocolate milks with my priest back home [near Albany, New York], who was a big Yankees fan and had a dog named Mickey. I brought my daughter to church back home last summer and hoped to see him just so I could say 'Meghan, Yankees,' and hear her let out a big raspberry.

"This," he reported proudly, "is exactly what she did."

Even though the Yankees answered back the next night, winning 6–2 behind Andy Pettitte, the Red Sox had come into Yankee Stadium and gotten a split, which was all they really wanted. They would head home to the welcoming embrace of Fenway Park knowing they'd broken the Yankees' serve, if not the New Yorkers' spell over them. They would have Pedro Martinez on the mound, and while Martinez refused to speak with reporters, he did offer a message through pitching coach Dave Wallace: "Buenos fuerte mañana." *Very strong tomorrow.*

The words sounded like a song to the local baseball citizenry. An unmistakable love song.

DOES HE LOOK LIKE HE WAS HIT WITH A PURSE?

All these months later, I still can't believe no one in the bullpen went
after Pedro Martinez. He got off easy, the son of a bitch. If it was me,
I would've gone right for him. We would've finished it right there.
That skinny little gutless shit, he threw right at us! It's too bad he doesn't
have to hit, because I guarantee you he wouldn't be throwing at hitters
like that. These guys think they can intimidate the Yankees? Fuck 'em.
No one does that. All they did was wake the Yankees up.
—*Rich "Goose" Gossage, February 27, 2004*

It's like these two teams were supposed to share the same brain.
When I was playing, it was always, "What did the Yankees do today?
What did the Yankees do this off-season? Who did the Yankees trade for?
We gotta keep up! We gotta catch up!" Jesus, that was over fifty years ago.
And it's still going on! It's like every time something good happens
to them, we're the other guy in the picture. —*Johnny Pesky,
February 27, 2004*

The morning dawned bright, sunny, warm, perfect. Every now and
again, you get an October day in New England that satisfies everybody's purposes: The college kids can play Frisbee with their shirts
off, they can toss Nerf footballs or hold hands in the quad. The poets
and the artists can laze on a bench in the Common, sketching furiously

on their pads. The traffic on the Charles River is almost as dense as the mess on the Mass Pike. And almost everyone has a transistor radio nearby, or a portable television, or a freshly charged cell phone, the better to keep up with the proceedings across town.

Because these are also perfect days to play baseball at Fenway Park.

October 11, 2003, was one such day. The sun sat high in an endless blue sky, summer's last gasp. Fans who figured they'd be the first to congregate around Lansdowne Street and Yawkey Way discovered they weren't even close, that some of the more fervent disciples had already beaten them there the night before, spreading sleeping bags on the pavement.

"We didn't have to do this," a nineteen-year-old Northeastern University student named Brent Keebler said. "We already had our tickets. But the other day, we all kind of looked at each other and said, 'What the hell, let's camp out outside Fenway.' And so we did."

The Yankees team bus arrived to the usual assortment of hoots and chants and catcalls, showered in various slanders. Some Red Sox fans craned their necks, hoping for a good glimpse of Roger Clemens, the Yankees' starting pitcher that afternoon, but they were wasting their time. Clemens took a cab right up through the private players' entrance. It was a veteran's move.

Inside, groundskeepers were busily tending to the grooming of the oldest ball field in the American League, and there was an odd sense of serenity blanketing the lawns as the first few Red Sox peeked out of the dugout. Workers painted foul lines, raked the infield dirt, watered the outfield grass, touched up the American League Championship Series logo behind home plate. In the distant outfield bullpens, maintenance men, including a moonlighting special education teacher from Derry, New Hampshire, named Paul Williams, carefully prepared for the coming festivity.

"Hell," Kevin Millar said, his words practically echoing in the hushed park, "let's just play all five of the games we have left here today. Like one of those softball tournaments. You think the Yankees would go for that?"

Lou Merloni grew up a Red Sox fan in suburban Framingham, Massachusetts. Now he was serving a second tour of duty for the team of his childhood obsessions, filling a backup role as a utility infielder. He was having a catch along the first-base foul line with Nomar Garciaparra, and in the empty yard the popping sounds of ball hitting mitt sounded like gunfire. Every so often, Merloni would stop, take a long, deep look around the park, and smile.

"Hey!" Garciaparra yelled at one point, laughing. "Stop gawking! It's embarrassing!"

Merloni only smiled wider.

"Shit, I grew up coming to Red Sox–Yankee games," he said. "That was it; the city shut down. You grow up around here, your dream isn't just to play for the Red Sox, it's to play against the Yankees. Those Wiffle ball games in the backyard, you played the Red Sox against the Yankees, man. You never played against the Kansas City Royals, you know what I mean?"

Joe Torre surely knew. The Yankees manager had grown up in Brooklyn on East Thirty-fourth Street and Avenue T, square in the heart of Dodgers territory, yet he'd been a New York Giants fan, inheriting his siblings' affinity for their neighbors' most hated rivals.

"That's the only thing I can even remotely compare what this is like, when we play the Red Sox," Torre said. "The key thing to remember is, you weren't just a Giants fan; you *hated* the Dodgers. You hated Jackie Robinson, because you couldn't ever get him out. You hated Duke Snider, because he would hit one nine miles off you in the ninth inning. I know that's the way Red Sox fans and Yankees fans feel about one another now. Red Sox fans are always all over Derek Jeter, because they know he's gonna kill them somehow. And Yankees fans live in fear that one of these days, Pedro's gonna throw a perfect game against us. You don't get a lot of *personal* rivalries in baseball. I know Dodgers-Giants was like that, because I was forever at odds with the Fanelli brothers, and Vinny Esposito, and the other guys in my neighborhood who were Dodgers fans. And I know that's how Red Sox fans and Yankees fans feel about each other's teams now."

In fact, each time Torre came to Boston, he was reminded of just how intimate the locals' relationship with baseball really was. Early in 1999, Torre returned to the Yankees after spending six weeks fighting prostate cancer, and his first game was at Fenway Park. That night, Red Sox fans gave Torre an extended standing ovation when he took the lineup card out to home plate for the pregame meeting with the umpires.

"That," Torre said, "was the most emotional I've ever been on a baseball field."

Five months later, with the Yankees and Red Sox embroiled in their first-ever American League Championship Series meeting, Torre went to Sunday Mass with his wife, Ali, and their daughter, Andrea, at St. Francis Chapel in downtown Boston. Andrea was three years old and fascinated with the long banks of candles lining one side of the altar. Torre, ever the doting dad, kept throwing coins in the prayer box as his daughter lit five, six, seven different candles.

Suddenly, from behind, somewhere in the church, came a voice.

"If one of those candles is for a Yankee win," the disembodied voice said, "I'm going to blow it out."

The Yankees won that day, so Torre is fairly convinced it wasn't God speaking. But on the morning of game three, he'd received another indication of just how fearless Red Sox fans were, even in encountering the great manager of the hated Yankees. Torre stepped into an elevator at the Ritz-Carlton Hotel so he could meet Don Zimmer for breakfast. A man and a woman were already in the car. The doors closed.

"Are you Joe Torre?" the man asked.

Torre, always publicly polite to a fault, nodded, said, "Yes."

"We're gonna beat you tonight," the man said.

Torre smiled. "Well," he said, "I hope you're wrong."

There was a pause, and Torre could sense that the man was wondering whether he should say what was on his mind, then saw him come to the conclusion: *What the hell.*

"You know," the guy said, "if it came to a choice between beating the Yankees or capturing Osama bin Laden, I think I'd take beating the Yankees." With that, on cue, the doors opened, the couple walked out, and Torre was left alone for the rest of the trip to the restaurant, laughing uncontrollably.

"It was like a scene from a movie," he said.

The kid's head was buried in a newspaper, so he never saw the light towers from the backseat of the taxi. This was early May of 1984. The kid had sipped a brief cup of coffee in the minor leagues, but the Red Sox hadn't drafted him out of the University of Texas with the idea of keeping him on the farm. No long-term, soft-glove apprenticeship for him. The Red Sox looked at him and didn't just see a live right arm; they saw greatness. Too often across the years, the Sox had gone entire decades without seeing anything resembling greatness on their pitching staff. Jim Lonborg had one magical season, in 1967, before a skiing accident pilfered all his pixie dust. Luis Tiant had a nice run in the 1970s, but he was well into his thirties by then. This kid, he was different. He had attitude. He had swagger. He had gasoline in his right arm. He was twenty-one years old.

"We're here, buddy," the cabdriver said, screeching alongside the curb.

The kid pulled his nose out of his newspaper, looked out the window, saw this unsightly mass of red bricks and green paneling.

"Hey," Roger Clemens finally said, his voice still full of Katy, Texas. "I'm not looking for a warehouse. I'm looking for the baseball stadium."

That drew a big laugh from the hack.

"This is it, pal," he said. "This is Fenway Park."

Nineteen and a half years later, as Roger Clemens slipped into Fenway, he tried to savor everything, take mental snapshots of every detail. As much as he'd put New England in his career's rearview mirror, this was still a special place to him. "Fenway," his wife, Debbie, said, "was where we grew up."

To the people of Boston, that mattered very little. Clemens was dead to them.

"And he always will be," noted Steve Silva. "He made his choices. We've made ours."

Clemens understood perfectly well the politics of his present situation.

"Going out to lunch today, the people who were my fans when I was here were great," Clemens had said at Friday's workout. "I understand, and they understand, the situation now, that I'm pitching against the Red Sox. That's totally understandable. I've kind of distanced myself from everything that's gone on here. It's been great for the most part. I have to go out and pitch well and pitch against a good lineup and try and get guys out. The fans were great to me when I worked here. But I work for the Yankees now."

The hard feelings lingered, though they were somewhat diluted thanks to the man who would oppose Clemens in game three. For as much of a folk hero as Clemens had become during his time in Boston, he had already been replaced, and surpassed, in the eyes and the souls of Red Sox Nation by another pitching deity.

Pedro Martinez, traded to Boston by Montreal prior to the 1998 season, had long since established residence on his own island as the most feared pitcher in baseball. Martinez had won a National League Cy Young Award with the Expos and added two more as a member of the Sox, but his credentials transcended such earthly pursuits. Pedro wasn't merely the Red Sox' best pitcher.

He was the team's nervous system.

He was their lifeline.

More than any other player—with the singular exception of Carl Yastrzemski in 1967—Martinez was the one man in whom Red Sox fans placed an almost otherworldly trust. Even Ted Williams, for all his brilliance, never captured the hearts and minds of New England that completely, due to his hot-and-cold relationship with Boston's baseball culture. The same way Yaz made anything seem possible in that long-ago summer of impossible dreams, so, too, did Pedro instill a sense of invincibility among the faithful. In 1999, at Cleveland's Jacobs Field, Martinez had lumbered in from the bullpen dragging a sore right arm and threw six no-hit innings at the Indians in game five of the American League Division Series, an examination of pain tolerance and will and exquisite pitching genius that Sox fans still whispered about with a hushed reverence.

Better, early in his Boston career, he'd often saved his best for the Yankees.

On September 10, 1999, in Yankee Stadium, Martinez struck out seventeen Yankees and outdueled Andy Pettitte in a 3–1 Red Sox victory that may have been the most dominant pitching performance in the history of this rivalry—including the no-hitter New York's Dave Righetti threw against the Red Sox on the Fourth of July in 1983, and the one Allie Reynolds had thrown late in the '51 season, which clinched the pennant for the Yankees. Martinez retired the final twenty-two Yankees that night, after Chili Davis reached him for a home run with two out in the second. He struck out eight of the final nine batters.

"That," said Yankees pitcher David Cone, who'd pitched a perfect game earlier that summer, "was the best game I've ever seen in person."

"I won't lie," Martinez himself had said that night. "That's about as well as a game *can* be pitched."

It didn't hurt Martinez' status in the eyes of the truest Boston believers that he'd also enjoyed a fair measure of success at Clemens' expense. On May 28, 2000, he'd engaged Clemens in one of the most stirring pitching duels Yankee Stadium had ever seen. Clemens, then thirty-seven, struck out thirteen Red Sox and was sailing along splendidly until Trot Nixon touched him for a two-run home run with two outs in the top of the ninth. Martinez, at the peak of his physical powers, struck out nine and got the game's final out by inducing a Tino Martinez ground ball with the bases loaded in the bottom of the inning to preserve a 2–0 Boston victory.

But the moment Pedro Martinez may have truly latched onto the heart and forever plugged himself into the visceral spirit of New England came exactly one year and two days after that gem, on May 30, 2001, when he teamed up with Derek Lowe to shut the Yankees out on a five-hitter, 3–0. Afterward, as reporters crowded around his locker, Martinez uttered what may be the seminal sentence in the entire history of the Red Sox–Yankees conflagration.

"I don't believe in rivalries," Martinez said, clearing his throat.

"I don't believe in curses," he insisted, gathering momentum.

"Wake up the damned Bambino and I'll face him," he declared defiantly, jutting his jaw out like Charles Bronson. "Maybe I'll drill him in the ass."

Throughout New York and New England, fans manned their battle stations. For some, that meant seeking out a favored couch or bar stool, the same place where they believed they'd engineered hundreds of rallies across the summer. For others, it meant stealing quick snippets of the game on the radio, or getting updates from friends on cell phones, since they'd agreed to spend one of the last great-weather days of the year in the outdoor company of spouses, friends, or other assorted rogues with little interest in what was happening at the Fens.

John Miller, for instance, spent all of game three at an outdoor gathering in Southbridge, Massachusetts, celebrating the end of his softball team's season. Mike Carey spent the day driving from Albany to Queens following a family funeral, steadfastly keeping his car radio tuned to Boston's WEEI-AM broadcast, even as the signal began to sputter and die on the Cross Bronx Expressway, because the mere thought of listening to John Sterling and Charley Steiner on WCBS-AM, the Yankees' flagship station, was enough to make him nauseated. And Steve Silva brought his seventy-four-year-old father to the game, sitting not far from where the Red Sox' most famous fan of the moment, Ben Affleck, would take in the game alongside his fiancée of the moment, Jennifer Lopez, even though Silva's father reminded him, "Every time you take me to a game, we lose."

Their counterparts on the other side of the Great Divide were no less distracted and no less committed. Frank Russo had agreed weeks before that he'd run errands that afternoon with his fiancée—a well-intentioned gesture that immediately turned sour when she began complaining about the static that accompanied the radio broadcast. Jim Frasch, Peter Cipriano, and Pete Trinkle all blocked out the afternoon so they could watch the entire Fox telecast with, respectively, their fiancée, wife, and cousin.

"A big game like that," Frasch said, "you'd better be ready to go the distance on the couch."

The Red Sox jumped on Clemens quickly, snatching a 2–0 lead in the first inning, but that provided only a brief spasm of hope, since it was quickly evident that Martinez hadn't brought his best stuff to the ballpark that day. His first few fastballs barely registered in the high eighties on the radar gun, so he went with a heavy diet of breaking pitches. And Pedro's breaking pitches aren't nearly as devastating when you know they're coming.

"The air came out of the park early that day, even when we were still ahead by a couple of runs, because we saw Pedro wasn't throwing his fastball," Steve Silva said. "Any savvy fan knew Pedro didn't have it when they saw that."

If there were any doubts, Derek Jeter squashed them. The Yankees had gotten a run back in the second when Jorge Posada doubled and Karim Garcia knocked him in with a two-out single, but it was Jeter who announced that they were officially back in the game an inning later when, with one out, he connected with a hanging curveball that vaulted the Wall, cleared the screen, and wouldn't land until it crossed Lansdowne Street. It was an epic blast, the kind you see in batting practice, not the top of the third inning, not off the most intimidating right arm on the planet.

The assault happened quickly. Martinez threw six straight breaking balls to Posada, who walked leading off the fourth. He threw four more to Nick Johnson, who singled on the last to push Posada to third. And when Hideki Matsui followed with a ground-rule double (off still another hanging curve), the Yankees had a 3–2 lead with men on second and third and nobody out. Fenway was suddenly quieter than it had been back when the grounds crew was watering the grass in the morning.

Martinez changed that with one cock of his right arm.

It was his first real fastball of the inning, only it was headed nowhere near the plate, speeding instead toward Karim Garcia's batting helmet. Instinct took over, and Garcia dipped his head out of the way, but the ball grazed his back, ricocheted off his bat, then squirted toward the backstop. For half a heartbeat, nobody moved. Nobody breathed. The quiet was palpable. And then Garcia's voice lifted above the spooky silence.

"You threw the fucking ball at my head, you crazy fuck!"

Suddenly, in a flash, the small ballpark exploded in a burst of noise and light. An element of Red Sox fans cheered; most just screamed as the full impact of what they'd just seen finally hit them. Yankees jumped on the top step of the dugout; Red Sox players did the same. Pitchers edged to the front of both bullpens, waiting to dash forward if things grew darker and reinforcements were necessary. Dave Wallace jogged out of the dugout to calm Pedro down; the pitcher was uneasily eyeing one member of the Yankees' top-step battalion, who was screaming so loud spit was splashing between the syllables.

"Throw that asshole out of the game!" Don Zimmer yelled at umpire Tim McClelland, the crew chief. Then he turned right to Martinez and yelled, "You're a gutless son of a bitch!"

Calm returned for a few moments, long enough for Alfonso Soriano to bounce the ball to shortstop, starting a routine double play that, naturally, turned out to be anything but. Johnson scored to push the Yankee lead to 4–2. Garcia, working on adrenaline overdrive, went into second base spikes high, upending Todd Walker who, understanding his place in this burgeoning epic, said nothing, despite the fresh burst of boos. But Garcia couldn't resist. As he jogged off the field, he passed Martinez.

"Fuck you, punk," he said. "That was for you."

So much for the calm. Both teams returned to the top step of the dugout, the front edge of the bullpen. Martinez, shaken, furious, looked furtively toward the Yankees dugout, saw Posada standing there fully armed with his catcher's gear, and screamed: "*What* the *fuck* are *you* looking at?"

That flipped a switch inside Posada, whose eyes grew big as satellite dishes.

"Why don't you have the balls to throw at *me*?" he yelled back.

"The *next* one's for you, asshole," Martinez snapped.

And then he pointed to his head. And this is where all ninety-nine years of this Red Sox–Yankees chronicle began to funnel in a furious rush to the field at Fenway. It was all there, naked, exposed, flopping like a fish in a dry well. The crowd, now fully engaged, broke into an ear-splitting rendition of "Yankees suck! Yankees suck!" Roger Clemens, even more engaged, wandered out of the dugout, his face flushed, cursing nonsensically, overcome with rage. Mel Stottlemyre finally grabbed his left arm and pulled him back. "This isn't your fight, Roger!" he shouted over the din. "This isn't your fight!"

McClelland issued a warning to both benches: One more close call and there would be ejections. This quickly drew Torre's wrath.

"Tim, this is bullshit, my guy hasn't thrown a ball anywhere near them," Torre said, his nose maybe two inches away from McClelland's. "*That's* the son of a bitch"—he pointed at Martinez—"that you gotta run out of here."

"Joe," McClelland said, "you know the rule."

Calm was restored, *again*. Martinez—fortified now by raw adrenaline coursing through his right arm—threw three fastballs to Enrique Wilson, in the lineup because of his .476 lifetime average against Martinez, and on the third pitch Wilson popped out to Walker at second. The inning was over. Fenway was coiled like a spring, but it seemed the worst had finally passed. Clemens stalked to the pitcher's mound, angry at the incident, angrier still that McClelland had essentially put him on notice that he wouldn't be allowed to pitch inside, where Clemens had made his living for almost twenty years. Still, he settled to the task at hand and jumped ahead of Manny Ramirez, 1 and 2. Posada put down his sign for the next pitch: fastball. Clemens tried to get an extra yard on it, and it sailed on him, crossing the plate high, even with Ramirez' eyes. To almost everyone watching, it appeared to be a routine ball two.

To Ramirez, it was Fort Sumter.

"He's out!" Ramirez yelled, walking toward Clemens, pointing his bat menacingly at the pitcher. "Throw that motherfucker out of the game!"

Clemens answered that oath with one of his own. And now it was *really* on. The dugouts emptied. The bullpens emptied. Ramirez was restrained, and so was Clemens. It looked like it was going to end there.

Only now there came an odd-shaped blur of blue lumbering out of the Yankees dugout, crossing to the other side. Pedro Martinez, standing in front of his own dugout, saw the shadow heading his way. "What?" he asked of the onrushing blur. *"What?"*

But Don Zimmer couldn't hear Martinez. Zimmer came charging right at him. Martinez, clearly stunned, cradled Zimmer's head in his hands ever so slightly, then pushed him aside. Zimmer fell to the ground in a heap, rolled over twice, and collided with Ramirez' discarded bat. Then he came to a halt, lying in a heap, a trickle of blood oozing down his face.

Andy Pettitte rushed over, not believing what he'd just seen, the way nobody in the ballpark could believe what they'd just seen. He crouched over his fallen coach.

"Zim," Pettitte whispered, "are you OK?"

Fights, brawls, brouhahas, rhubarbs—however they've been described through the years, on-field altercations are the ugly underbelly of any sports rivalry, and the natural by-product of what happens when you mix decades of conflict into a combustible cocktail alongside the usual ingredients of adrenaline, ego, and testosterone. Pick your way through the nastiest rivalries in sports over the past twenty-five years—Knicks-Heat in the NBA, Cowboys-49ers in the NFL, Senators–Maple Leafs in the NHL, North Carolina–Duke in college basketball—and it's clear the games often aren't enough to contain the passions spouting out of the athletes' pores. Invariably, something else happens. More often than not, the confrontations are almost comical in nature, more posing and posturing than any actual pugilism.

From the start, Red Sox–Yankees has been different.

When these two fight, they *fight*; they don't pair up and dance and exchange locker-room epithets and leave it at that.

"Part of that," Reggie Jackson said, "is because this wasn't just a calm dislike between two ardent foes. We *hated* those fuckers, and they hated us."

Said Carlton Fisk: "You don't generate the kind of passions this rivalry has generated without going to a deeper place in your soul. And it wasn't a coincidence that the Yankees were usually on the field when we arrived at that place."

For the first twenty years of the rivalry, the on-field mores of the time kept any major disputes from breaking out during games. It was simply an accepted part of the sport that you played hard, you slid with your spikes high, you occasionally delivered a fastball under the chin of a hot hitter, you treated the catcher like a tackling dummy if he had the ball in his mitt and was blocking the plate. If the Dave Fultz–George Winter collision that enlivened the second American League game ever played between Boston and New York had happened thirty, seventy, a hundred years later, people would still be talking about the after-effects and the long-term ramifications. In 1903, all the parties involved simply played on without comment. And from 1920 through the mid-1930s, as the Red Sox devolved into one of the most pathetic outfits in organized baseball, there was never a chance that brushfires would replace baseball between the white lines. The Yankees won 266 of the 395 games they played against the Red Sox from 1920 to 1937, a staggering .673 winning percentage that hardly hinted at any looming enmity.

In 1938, however, the Red Sox split the twenty-two-game series with the Yankees, and while they still landed a distant nine and a half games out of first place, their second-place showing was the Sox' highest finish in the twenty years that had passed since their most recent championship. The Red Sox were finally emerging from a long winter's slumber, having acquired Jimmie Foxx and Lefty Grove, having called up a future Hall of Famer named Bobby Doerr that year, knowing there was another kid playing for their farm team in Minneapolis that summer, a mouthy phenom named Williams, who was going to add some pop to the lineup soon. The teams were as close as they'd been since Babe Ruth was a full-time pitcher living on a farm in Massachusetts, and so perhaps it was simply a natural matter of course that these rivals, so closely tied by geography and by one epic player transaction, would finally invade each other's space in a big way.

May 30, 1938, was Memorial Day in New York City, and all across the five boroughs there was cause for an overflowing civic celebration. The Great Depression, after nearly nine agonizing years, had finally loosened. More people were working in New York than at any time since October 1929, and while a glimpse of the international sections of the morning newspapers would provide a daily dose of discomfort, the items could be quickly discarded as distant problems on distant shores.

The Yankees began the day in fourth place, three and a half games behind the Indians, but they were notorious slow starters anyway and were just getting used to the return of Joe DiMaggio, who had missed the season's first two weeks because of a salary dispute. That was one of the reasons the doubleheader in the Bronx that afternoon was attracting heavy advance notice. Lou Gehrig was another, since if he played both games—and he hadn't missed one in over thirteen years—he would appear in his 1,998th and 1,999th consecutive games, and all of New York was anticipating the 2,000-game milestone he would reach the next day if all went well. Almost incidental to the revelry was the appearance of the Red Sox on the Stadium marquee, even though they had bolted out to a solid start and were a game up on the Yankees after the season's first six weeks, sitting in second place; the fact that a fine pitching match-up between Lefty Grove and Red Ruffing would kick the day off right was also a nice bonus.

Whatever their reasons, there were 83,533 people who filled Yankee Stadium on a blazingly hot afternoon, more than would ever legally be permitted inside the park again. Five thousand additional fans were turned away, because there was simply no place to cram them in, and another 511 people who actually had standing-room-only tickets were given reluctant refunds because there was literally nowhere left to stand.

The pitching duel they expected in the opener never materialized, although most of the fans hardly cared because the Yankees pulled out to a 3–0 lead by the third inning when Grove, frustrated, decided to send a message whirring past Jake Powell's head. Powell ducked out of the way, but the Yankees outfielder registered the purpose pitch in his memory bank. An inning later, the Yankees chased Grove with four more runs; Archie McKain, replacing Grove, was promptly greeted by back-to-back singles by Bill Dickey and Myril Hoag; and the Stadium crowd began taunting the hapless Red Sox as Jake Powell again stepped to the plate.

Powell was hardly a beloved figure in baseball, not by his teammates, certainly not by his opponents. Almost two months to the day after this game, he would go live on WGN radio in Chicago before the Yankees played the White Sox at Comiskey Park. Bob Elson, the announcer, lobbing innocent softballs, asked Powell what he did in the off-season, and Powell responded that he was a policeman in Dayton, Ohio. It turned out later that Powell had never spent a day in a police uniform, but Elson was unaware of that lie. Intrigued, he asked, "So, what do you do as a policeman?"

"I crack niggers on the head," Powell replied.

Even in a far less enlightened time, the WGN switchboard lit up immediately, and Powell, instantly shunned by the other Yankees, spent much of the final seven years of his career answering for that, often ducking out of the way of balls aimed for his head.

Here, McKain's first pitch, a slow curve, sent Powell sprawling to the ground. His second, a fastball, drilled Powell in the stomach, the third straight pitch thrown his way with malicious intent, and even in the more primal codes of baseball in 1938, that was enough to snap a man's patience. Before walking to first base, Powell took a detour toward the mound, bat in hand, spewing profanities. McKain, itching for a fight, welcomed Powell's advances, but before he could reach him, the Red Sox' shortstop, Joe Cronin, who also happened to be the team's manager, got in the way.

Cronin, eager to protect his player, reached Powell and began the negotiation with a right-handed uppercut that landed squarely on Powell's jaw. Powell, out of his mind with rage now, landed his own right cross to the manager's temple, and what followed was as frenetic a baseball brawl as anyone could recall.

But that was just the undercard, as it happened.

Because after umpire Cal Hubbard doled out instant ejections to both Cronin and Powell, and after Cronin had handed his lineup card over to one of his coaches, the Sox' skipper headed off to the sweltering visitors' clubhouse. But in order to reach that room at Yankee Stadium in those days, you had to first walk through the Yankees' dugout and proceed down a long, dark runway.

Powell was waiting for Cronin in the runway.

Herb Pennock, the former pitcher who'd played for both the Red Sox and the Yankees and who was now serving as a Boston coach, described what happened next.

"When I ran down the steps, Joe and Powell were going at it with several of the Yankees crowding around them, not doing much of anything," Pennock said. "So I tried to separate them. Just then, Cal Hubbard led the umpires into the dugout steps. Joe had several gouges on his face that didn't come from punches, and the best information I could obtain was that he had a headlock on Powell and was ready to give him the business when a band of Yankees pulled him off and grabbed his face in the process. The only Yankee who tried to break it up was Joe DiMaggio."

It was later erroneously reported that Judge Kenesaw Mountain Landis slapped each man with a ten-game suspension for his part in the melee, but the lordly commissioner of baseball adhered to the same statutes of frontier justice the players subscribed to. The umpires decided that Cronin, despite throwing the first punch, had entered the fray merely as a peacekeeper, so he was acquitted without so much as a fine. Powell, meanwhile, was docked $25 and slapped with a three-game ban, which began on May 31, when the Yankees completed their three-game sweep of the Red Sox and Gehrig, to much joy, played in his two thousandth consecutive game.

Over the next fourteen years, the Red Sox–Yankees match-up evolved at last into one of sports' greatest continuing tales. Boston, in fact, emerged from World War II with the stronger club, winning the 1946 pennant and, it was assumed, serving notice that the Red Sox were prepared to overtake the aging Yankees as the game's standard-bearer. That never happened, primarily because the Sox never could seem to figure out the final chapters of their seasons, while the Yankees rebuilt, reloaded, and reenergized their dynasty. By May 24, 1952, the teams had reverted to their prewar places in the baseball stratosphere. The Yankees were well into a stretch of five straight World Series championships and were making a seamless transition to life without Joe DiMaggio, who'd retired the previous winter. The Red Sox' pitching had collapsed almost immediately after 1946. Bobby Doerr had retired after the 1951 season. Dominic DiMaggio was playing his final full year. Johnny Pesky would soon be traded away to Detroit. And just twenty-two days earlier, Ted Williams had reported to Willow Grove Naval Air Station in Pennsylvania to begin his second tour as a war pilot; soon enough, he would be in Korea.

It seemed the Yankees and Red Sox were through being blood enemies for a while. The Yankees were too good. The Sox were too young. So it was the perfect moment in time for two of the most combustible personalities in baseball history to splash-land right into the core of this rivalry.

Billy Martin was a street kid from Oakland who had always overcome his physical limitations by the sheer force of two natural resources: a steely-eyed, unbending will and a set of cast-iron, unbleeding fists. The secret to Martin's success was best summarized in the passage etched on his gravestone (located just a few steps away from Babe Ruth's at Gate of Heaven Cemetery): "I may not have been the greatest Yankee to wear the uniform, but I was the proudest." Jimmy Piersall, meanwhile, grew up in Waterbury, Connecticut, the son of a demanding, perfectionist father who drove him relentlessly to become a major-league ballplayer and, ultimately, helped drive him into a sanitarium. Piersall managed to cobble together a fine career that was marked by a quirky streak. He was known to hide behind the on-field monuments in deepest center field at Yankee Stadium during pitching changes, and on the occasion of his one hundredth career home run in 1963, as a member of the New York Mets, he commemorated the milestone by jogging backward around the bases.

On this Saturday afternoon, however, both players were still trying to make their way in the majors. Martin, the more established of the two, thanks to the two World Series rings he'd already earned, had made an instructional movie during the spring on how to properly slide into a base. Much to Martin's great misfortune, he'd broken his ankle doing it, had missed the rest of spring training, and was just now working his way back into the New York lineup. Naturally, the thought of a professional baseball player maiming himself while performing a simple task like sliding—while in the process of teaching a nation of Little Leaguers how to do it the right way—made Martin the instant target of every bench jockey in the American League. And there was no one in all of baseball who took to that job with greater aplomb than Piersall, still early in his rookie year with the Red Sox, who figured the quickest way to gain his teammates' acceptance was to needle the hell out of every opponent he could.

But Piersall saved his A game for Martin.

Two weeks earlier, in fact, during a game at Yankee Stadium, Piersall and Martin had exchanged so much trash talk that Lou Boudreau, the Red Sox manager, warned Piersall to back off the relentless riding or risk getting sent back to Louisville. Piersall dialed it down, for a little while anyway. But now, at Fenway Park, with a few more weeks of big-league life under his belt, Piersall was feeling a bit friskier. He was taking ground balls at shortstop when Martin stepped out of the dugout to have a catch with Mickey Mantle. Suddenly, a shrill voice pierced the lazy late morning.

"Hey! Martin! How'd you break your ankle? You trip on your garter belt?"

Martin ignored him, though he was ready to jump through his skin. Piersall raised the volume.

"Your fuckin' bloomers get in the way, Martin?"

He'd tried. But Billy Martin's buttons weren't so terribly hard to find if you really wanted to push them.

"Piersall," he fired back, "you're crazier than a shithouse rat. Shut up or I'll shut you the fuck up."

"I'd like to see that, Miss Billy."

"You don't have to ask me twice."

And before anyone knew what was happening, Piersall had slammed down his glove and sprinted to the tunnel that led from the Red Sox bench and in those days provided the only field exit. Piersall, a son of suburbia, was no match for Martin, the street tough from the Bay Area, even though Piersall was an inch taller and twenty-five pounds heavier. Martin landed two quick right hands as soon as they ducked out of sight; Piersall was out on his feet almost immediately, recovered, then started to grab Martin.

"I didn't like some of the things he was saying to me," Martin said. "I couldn't take such insults. He made some pretty bad remarks. I may be smaller than him, but I'll fight anybody who makes those remarks to me. I had hit him good twice and then he grabbed me and started to wrestle."

Two coaches finally broke up the fight, Bill Dickey of the Yankees and Oscar Melillo of the Red Sox, who both grabbed hold of Martin and pulled him off Piersall. That day's starting pitcher, Ellis Kinder, was also in the dugout, and he was nearly trampled before peace was restored.

"Jim rushed at me and says, 'Hold my hat.' I thought he was kidding with Martin," Kinder said. "But then I see it's no joke and I tried to step between them. Then Dickey comes along and grabs Martin while I held on to Piersall. They stepped all over me. I'm lucky I didn't get spiked."

Piersall wasn't done for the day; as he was getting into a fresh uniform, his teammate, pitcher Mickey McDermott, began riding him from across the clubhouse, and Piersall jumped after *him*, too. But even this didn't bother Boudreau, who'd grown enamored of his rookie's spunk, especially on a team filled with passive, placid personalities. "I told Jim to stay on the bench and watch his language during the game," the manager said. "Other than that, I didn't stop him from riding Martin. They're both scrappy kids, quick-tongued and quick-tempered."

Piersall kept it up, too. Though he sat out the game (a 5–2 Red Sox win), Piersall spent much of it on the top step of the dugout, taunting Martin by pretending to train a movie camera on him. Later that season, he would suffer a nervous breakdown that nearly ended his career, a development that drew a morsel of remorse from Martin years later.

"Hell," Martin said, "if I knew he was crazy, I sure wouldn't have fucked with him. Who the hell knows what he was capable of?"

Martin, of course, would go on to partake in a slew of other public bouts before dying in a car accident on Christmas Day 1989. This was the first one people noticed, and remembered, and it earned him a place in his manager's heart.

"If Martin wants to fight, I'd suggest he wait until he has regained the fifteen pounds he lost while his ankle was mending," Casey Stengel said, draping his arm around his favorite player. "Still, this should wake my other tigers up. It's about time they realize they've got to fight harder than ever to win this year. Everyone wants to see us licked. I just hope some of that kid's fire spreads to the others."

The Red Sox finished in sixth place that year, the dynasty-that-never-was suffering public death spasms throughout the remainder of the 1950s, deep into the '60s. Between 1952 and 1966, they would never finish within twelve games of first place, and the longtime romance between Boston and its Red Sox came shockingly close to divorce. On June 20, 1967, in fact, Tom Yawkey, the beloved owner of the Sox, granted an interview to Will McDonough of the *Boston Globe* that would send shock waves up and down the American League when his words were printed in the next morning's editions. Fenway Park, Yawkey said, had deteriorated to the point where it was unfit to serve as a home to any major league team, much less one with the deep tradition of the Red Sox. He revealed that Milwaukee, which fifteen years earlier had wooed the Braves out of Boston before itself being abandoned in favor of Atlanta in 1965, had already begun a full-court press, seducing Yawkey with an armful of promises.

"This is not a threat," Yawkey said. "This is a mere statement of fact. I cannot indefinitely continue under present circumstances. I am losing money with the Red Sox and no one—unless he's a damn fool—likes to lose money."

"Can you see the Red Sox playing in Fenway in five years?" McDonough asked.

"No," Yawkey said. "I don't intend to bankrupt myself."

The very night Yawkey uttered these vows (which turned out to be as hollow as the Ted Williams Tunnel), the Red Sox arrived in New York for a two-game series, a vastly improved product over the recent vintage at 31–31, six and a half games behind the first-place White Sox. Before the season was over, the Red Sox would engineer one of the great turnarounds in baseball history, authoring an Impossible-Dream roll that wouldn't be halted until game seven of the '67 World Series. For the time being, though, all the magic that would enrapture New England's summer was completely in the future. Hardly any notice was paid to this Red Sox–Yankees gathering in the Bronx.

In fact, it may be entirely possible that that very day—June 20, 1967—represents the absolute low ebb in the teams' relationship. There was no juice any longer, no fire, no fury. In 1966, the Yankees had finished tenth in the American League, the first time in fifty-five years they had finished in last place; the Red Sox wound up in ninth, a half game better. These were two lousy teams with two lousy farm systems who promised to be lousy for years. Barely ten thousand people came to Yankee Stadium that night, many of them Red Sox fans. The fifty thousand empty seats sent a much louder message.

The rivalry, such as it was, was dead.

The Red Sox had arrived in New York on June 19, taking the train up from Washington. When they got in, their third baseman, Joe Foy, took a subway up to his parents' house at 846 Timon Avenue, out in the East Bronx. Foy had been a star athlete at nearby Evander Charles High School, and whenever the Sox came to town he eschewed the team's Manhattan accommodations in favor of his childhood room; from there he would walk the thirteen blocks to Yankee Stadium. When Foy emerged from the subway, around 10:30 at night, he was immediately met by a neighborhood kid who delivered a terrifying news bulletin: "Hey, Joe, your house is on fire!"

"I got my mother and father out of there and went back inside," Foy would recall the next day. "I thought maybe I could get some of my stuff out but the smoke hit me."

He lost his scrapbook in the fire, lost all his clothes and most of his trophies and plaques. He brought his parents to his sister's house in another section of the Bronx, then returned to the Sox' team hotel at around 4 A.M. Later that night, in the fifth inning of a scoreless game, he clobbered a drive into the left-field seats off Mel Stottlemyre for a grand slam that propelled the Sox to a 7–1 win that put the Sox at 32–31; they would spend the rest of the year above .500. And Joe Foy, unwittingly, had already stirred the resurrection of the fiercest rivalry baseball ever knew.

The Yankees, already helplessly out of the race, were determined to save themselves from further embarrassment. The next day, June 21, the Sox jumped to a quick 4–0 lead thanks in part to another clutch hit from Foy, a first-inning single. Thad Tillotson, a marginal major-leaguer making one of only five starts he would get in his career, was desperate to stay in the game and prove his worth to Yankees manager Ralph Houk, a tough, no-nonsense ex-Marine. So in the second inning, with Foy waving a red-hot Louisville Slugger in the batter's box, Tillotson zipped a fastball under his chin. Foy jackknifed out of the way, no harm, no foul.

The next pitch crashed right into Foy's helmet.

Foy stewed as he dusted himself off and trotted down to first base, but he didn't say a word. Not the time. Not the place. That would have to wait a half hour or so, until the Yankees came to bat in the bottom of the third.

First up: Thad Tillotson.

Jim Lonborg was on the mound for the Red Sox. Nobody would embody the Joe Hardy spirit of those 1967 Red Sox the way Lonborg would. Carl Yastrzemski was the clear MVP of that team, and he would carry the Red Sox on his shoulders as few ballplayers ever have. But Lonborg was the gift that fell out of the sky. He would win twenty-two games that year, easily the best season of a solid but unspectacular career. Partly, this was due to a young pitcher finally harnessing his talents. And partly it was thanks to the tutelage of Sal Maglie, a Red Sox spring training instructor who'd been dubbed "the Barber" as a player and who'd earned both his nickname and his paycheck by unabashedly throwing inside, damn the consequences.

"Basically, Sal's message was simple," Lonborg would remember thirty-seven years later. "You want to pitch in semipro ball, go on and lay it over the plate, hard as you can. You want to win in the majors? Make them afraid you'll stick one in their ear."

Lonborg would hit nineteen batters in 1967, tops in baseball. One of them was Thad Tillotson, who never had a chance to duck out of the way. Tillotson, lacking Foy's savvy, walked slowly to first, clutching his bat, pointing it at the pitcher, telling him, "I'll be waiting for you next time, you son of a bitch." Finally, Foy snapped. He'd take one in the temple in silence, but threaten his pitcher? All bets were off. He charged after Tillotson: "If you want to fight, fight *me*, motherfucker!"

The third-base umpire tried to keep Foy away, but by this point the benches were empty, the bullpens were empty, and the sleepy crowd of

13,061 was instantly roused to its feet. Reggie Smith, a Red Sox outfielder, caught up with Tillotson, and the two men exchanged punches. New York's Joe Pepitone and Boston's Rico Petrocelli, both Brooklyn natives who'd known each other for years, started jawing at each other. At first, it was nothing more than friendly trash talk. But as the anger swirled around them, the two neighborhood guys began swinging at each other, too, and Pepitone found himself at the bottom of a pile with a sprained wrist.

"All I know is twenty guys are on top of me and one guy keeps pulling my hair," the perfectly coiffed Pepitone remembered. "*That* pissed me off more than anything."

Adding to the oddness and the intrigue, one of Petrocelli's older brothers, Dave, was a special security cop at Yankee Stadium that night, stationed—as he always was when the Red Sox were in town—in the visitors' dugout, and he was one of the first men who raced onto the field to help restore the peace. Several Yankees swore they heard a voice screaming from the middle of the madness: "You hurt my brother, I'll break your leg!" Yankee shortstop John Kennedy, in fact, raged angrily afterward: "I know that guy. He was out on the field, he's a special cop, and he's yelling, 'I'll kill all you guys.' That's a hell of a thing to say! What right did he have to be on the field, anyway?"

"Over the years, people asked me about that," Rico Petrocelli insisted much later. "I think people think my brother was out there fighting, helping me. But the truth is, he didn't come out until it was just about over. That was really it. We had a few laughs about it over the years, but it was no big deal. Just another baseball fight, that's all."

The pitchers, of course, would have the final say, both on the field and in the clubhouse. Tillotson did hit Lonborg the next time up. And Lonborg, looking for the last word, drilled Yankee second baseman Dick Howser late in the game.

"There isn't a doubt in anybody's mind who knows anything about baseball that Tillotson was trying to hit Foy," Lonborg later explained.

Said Tillotson: "The truth is, I wasn't pitching a good game. I wasn't putting the ball where I wanted it. Think about it a second. There's a man on first and Yaz, one of the best hitters in the American League, is coming up. Anyone who thinks I'm going to hit Foy on purpose and put another run on the board must be stupid. No one gets hit on purpose in the head. If you're going to hit a guy, the best place to do it is here." He pointed to his backside. "Like where I got hit."

"Things between the teams were dead at that point, I mean completely dead," Lonborg recalled. "Suddenly, after that, it was like people started saying, 'Oh, right. It's the Red Sox and the Yankees.' I'd like to think it would have heated back up without me throwing the ball at Tillotson's ass, though."

He's probably right. The Red Sox' ascent in 1967 was no one-year fluke; from then through 2004, they would suffer losing seasons in only six of thirty-eight years. And the Yankees were soon to enjoy a major renaissance when, on January 3, 1973, a group headed by a young shipping magnate named George M. Steinbrenner III purchased the team for $10 million. Better teams meant better games, and better games meant a higher likelihood of high tension. So it was no coincidence that just under eight months later, on August 1, Carlton Fisk and Thurman Munson—the cornerstone catchers around whom both teams were constructed—had a high-spirited collision at home plate.

The seeds for that encounter were probably planted the night before, when the Yankees, clinging to first place in a heated three-team race with the Red Sox and Orioles, scored three times in the ninth to stun the Sox, 5–4. In that game, Fisk had purposely tripped Roy White as the Yankees outfielder attempted to score in the fateful ninth. So when Mel Stottlemyre took the mound the next day, the first time he faced Fisk he sent a fastball straight for his bright red batting helmet.

"I didn't think he was throwing at me at the time," Fisk would say later. "But in retrospect, he probably was."

Thirty-one years later, Stottlemyre remembered that at-bat as if it had happened thirty-one seconds before.

"Fisk," he said, "was correct in his assumption."

The next day, with Munson on third base, Yankees shortstop Gene

Michael attempted a suicide squeeze but failed to get his bat on the ball. Munson, hung out to dry, never slowed down and crashed square into Fisk, and Fisk responded by flipping Munson over onto his head. Munson was pulled away from the melee by Carl Yastrzemski and three other Sox after Fisk pounded his back with a few wild punches, and he wound up just outside the dugout, pinned by the Red Sox posse.

From there, he saw his roommate keep the bout alive. Gene Michael— six foot two, 180 pounds, aptly nicknamed Stick—had missed the bunt that led to the collision, and he felt awful about it.

"I just started pummeling Fisk," he remembered. "I just started swinging and landing, and I'm so small he probably doesn't even feel the impact, but he does know I'm there and he started screaming, 'Get this crazy bastard off me!' And the funny thing is, Larry Barnett, the umpire, he threw out the catchers, and he never threw me out."

Fisk noticed that, too.

"Michael came at me from the blind side and stuck a finger in my eye," Fisk said. "That skinny fucker was the guy who should have been thrown out."

Michael's use of Fisk's head as a speed bag produced a few ugly scratches and bruises, and more than a little frivolity in the Red Sox clubhouse.

"He cheap-shotted you, Pudge," pitcher John Curtis said.

"You should have killed that son of a bitch," coach Ed Popowski added.

"Don't worry," Fisk replied. "Next time, I will."

Just then, Bill Lee wandered past Fisk's locker for an official inspection, and in his inimitable way, the man his teammates called "Spaceman" was about to define the underlying tensions that would exist between these two teams for the rest of the decade.

"You know how I know you were in a fight with Michael?" Lee asked, bursting with laughter. "Your face is scratched. Michael must have hit you with his purse."

Three years later, Lee would hear those words quoted back to him, only he wouldn't find them quite so amusing. On May 20, 1976, the Red

Sox paid their first-ever visit to the newly refurbished Yankee Stadium. The Sox, the defending American League champions, had stumbled to a 13–16 record, while the resurgent Yankees were already at 19–10, threatening to lap the field in the six-team AL East Division, and eager to send the Sox an early-season message. Lee was on the mound, pitching a splendid game, although the Yankees held a 1–0 lead in the bottom of the sixth inning when rookie Otto Velez stroked a base hit into right field. Dwight Evans, owner of one of the biggest outfield arms in baseball, charged the ball and fired a perfect strike home, one bounce into Fisk's glove. Lou Piniella, never to be confused for a world-class sprinter, came barreling around third and was an easy mark for the waiting Fisk.

So Piniella did the only thing he could do.

He flattened Fisk with his shoulder and rolled over him, trying to jostle the ball free.

"He stuck his elbow over my eye and started kicking," Fisk said. "I don't know if he was punching or not. What you've got to remember is, it's been that way between the Red Sox and the Yankees ever since I started playing."

Fisk held on to the ball with his bare hands, showed it to the umpire, Terry Cooney, then shoved Piniella. Piniella shoved back. Here came the benches. Here came the bullpens. There was a lot of pushing, a lot of wild cursing and threatening, not unlike any other baseball brawl. The 28,418 people inside Yankee Stadium were screaming for blood, yelling at Fisk, but it wound down in a hurry, and it looked like nothing bad was going to come of it.

But Bill Lee had a few things to get off his chest.

Lee had been backing up the plate, and when Piniella rolled over Fisk, the Spaceman snapped. He screamed at umpires. He screamed at Yankees. He screamed at teammates. He called Piniella "a gutless prick," and he started taunting other Yankees as they passed him into the fray.

"It sure looked like he was spoiling for a fight," said Billy Martin, the Yankees manager, who knew better than anyone what a guy spoiling for a fight looks like.

And Lee got one. Graig Nettles had been on the field in Boston three years before. He'd read the newspapers the next morning, digested Lee's pithy quips about Gene Michael and his pocketbook. And he remembered every syllable.

"Lee came in from the mound, and it looked to me like he was swinging at someone in the infield," Nettles said. "I grabbed him, pulled him away, and we fell to the ground. Lee landed on his shoulder and I knew he was hurt, and I thought it was over. But he just kept yelling at me. I shook it off one time. The man had tears in his eyes. I don't like to hit someone who's crying. But I did."

Lee, naturally, saw things a bit differently.

"It's hypocrisy when a guy says he wasn't trying to hurt me and does to me what he did. All I was doing was trying to keep Velez off Fisk," he said later, his arm nestled in a sling, his season over with ligament damage. "Nettles grabbed me from behind, body-slams me down, and then grinds my shoulder in the dirt. Then he pleads innocence."

Nettles laughed when he heard that rebuttal. He had one of his own.

"I was sorry at first, but if he says that, then I'm glad I hurt him. Did he say he was hit by a purse? That's how he said the Yankees fought the last time our teams fought. I'd like to know. Does he look like he was hit with a purse?"

But Nettles should have realized: No one in history has ever gotten the last word off Bill Lee. A year later, before making his first comeback start against the Yankees, Lee was handed a gift box in the clubhouse, and it was signed, "Best wishes, Billy Martin." Lee unwrapped the ribbon, tore open the package, and discovered a dead mackerel.

Lee obtained his revenge the best way he knew how. On May 23, 1977, a year and three days after shredding his shoulder, Lee pitched a masterful game in beating the Yankees, 4–3, at Yankee Stadium, enduring chants of "Lee sucks!" and similar tidings from the crowd. He didn't mind. Afterward, his locker crowded with reporters brandishing notebooks and cameras, he cracked open a beer and held court.

"How can I hold anything against them?" he asked of the Yankees. "They're just tools of that madman Martin."

Asked if he had any hobbies to keep himself busy during his long rehab, Lee said: "Yeah. I'm trying to figure out a way to get George Steinbrenner incarcerated."

And lastly: "I had a terrible dream the other night, a vision, the ghost of Christmas past. It came into my room and had Steinbrenner's face on Billy Martin's body."

An uneasy calm descended over Fenway Park as the shadows grew long this afternoon of October 11, 2003. Zimmer lay on the ground. Pedro stood a few feet away, an anxious look on his face. Three full minutes after starting this whole mess, Manny Ramirez was still yelling at Clemens. David Ortiz and Kevin Millar finally blanketed him, brought him back to the bench, calmed him down.

Zimmer, stunned but unhurt, finally got to his feet. Clemens draped one arm around him, then walked with his catcher, Posada, back to the mound. Soon enough they'd have to start playing baseball again, and the Fenway faithful had already crunched the calm with a fresh wave of foundation-rattling boos and chants, loud enough and scary enough that Red Sox officials immediately cut off beer sales. It took thirteen minutes for the umpires to restore peace, and when they did, they decided to throw no one out of the game. Ramirez dug in again. Fans had to remind themselves of the count: It was 2 and 2.

Clemens threw a fastball. Ramirez waved at it weakly.

And that was, in many ways, the end of the Red Sox this day. They would get a run back in the seventh to creep to within one, but Mariano Rivera wasn't going to give them anything else. They were about to go down in a wisp of anticlimactic smoke.

The commotion in the right-field bullpen changed that.

Few people noticed at first, because the general tumult of the ballpark had drowned out the initial confrontation between Jeff Nelson, the right-handed relief pitcher for the Yankees, and Paul Williams, a special-education teacher moonlighting as a grounds crew worker in the Red Sox bullpen. While the Red Sox prepared to bat in the ninth,

Williams began to wave a towel, as he had much of the day, much to the annoyance of the Yankees relief corps. Nelson told him to stop. Williams said something in return. Exactly what happened next would take more than a year to sort out.

What the people inside Fenway Park saw was Karim Garcia, who'd already had a full day, leaping over the short fence in right field. They saw Posada, in full catcher's regalia, sprint toward the ruckus. They saw cops vault the back bullpen fence and pull Williams away from the two agitated Yankees. And they saw Garcia led off the field, blood trickling from his cut and bruised left arm.

Afterward, very little of the postgame chatter centered around the final score.

There was Pedro . . .

"There's no question in my mind that Pedro hit him on purpose," Joe Torre said. "Second and third, nobody out, left-hand hitter, right-hand hitter on deck? He can thread a needle at any time he wants. He was frustrated that we hit some balls hard. You know I respect Pedro's ability to pitch, but I didn't care for that."

"I know my pitcher," Grady Little countered. "I can't believe he would do something like that with such a big ball game on the line. I don't believe that."

There was Manny . . .

"You guys saw it," Clemens said. "I was trying to strike him out inside. The pitch was actually over the plate. I was OK with it until I looked up and he was coming towards me, mouthing me. Anybody is going to react when that happens."

"Emotions are high," Trot Nixon said, since Ramirez had made himself scarce. "It really did feel like a powder keg out there."

There was Zimmer . . .

"I would never hit him," Pedro said meekly in his own brief defense. "I would never do it. I was just trying to move him away. I hope he is OK."

"We won, that's all that counts, and I feel good enough to have a hot dinner," said Zimmer, though he would soon be detoured to the hospital.

And there was the preposterousness in the bullpen, which nobody would fully comprehend for another day, but which would nevertheless provoke Yankees president Randy Levine to fume: "It's unacceptable. If an employee of the New York Yankees jumped into a bullpen and hit a player, he would be fired, he would be prosecuted and we would be on the phone apologizing to the other team's ownership. Any kind of hostile interaction is over the line. It's so outrageous, it's beyond belief. What disturbs me is a lawless attitude permeating here, a total lack of security."

It was, in many ways, just the beginning. A day later, after rain washed away game four, angry accusations flew between the offices of New York City mayor Michael Bloomberg ("If that happened in New York we would have arrested the perpetrator. Nobody should throw a seventy-year-old man to the ground, period. You just cannot assault people, even if it's on a baseball field") and Boston mayor Thomas Menino ("It wasn't anybody from Boston who attacked the worker in the bullpen, it was the Yankee players. They can't even be poor winners. It's their players who attacked the staffer. I'm asking for a public apology from the Yankees to the Boston police and the staff at Fenway Park for the way that they outright attacked them").

Talk radio was electric. The newspapers ate it up. The front page of the *New York Post* summarized Gotham's take on the matter: "Pedro the Punk." The New England Patriots, at the start of a winning streak that would extend all the way to the Super Bowl, were humiliating the New York Giants in the quagmire at suburban Foxboro's Gillette Stadium, settling at least a portion of a civic score, and yet hardly anyone paid attention, other than to punctuate the long television time-outs with chants of "Yankees suck!"

From across the decades, former Yankees and former Red Sox chimed in, starting with the old-timers like Johnny Pesky ("What a terrible shame") and Yogi Berra ("Someone shoulda been kicked out") and continuing all the way down the line. Graig Nettles and Rich Gossage, veterans of the Yankee–Red Sox battles of the '70s, sounded eager to don uniforms (if not battle fatigues) when contacted by Bob Klapisch, baseball columnist for the Bergen *Record*.

Nettles: "Manny Ramirez is a dog who does nothing but loaf on the bases, in the field, he loafs all the time. For all the money he makes, he should buy a book about how the game is played. We would've chased Pedro right into the stands. There's no way we would've been milling around like that. Garcia should've been the first one to go after Pedro. There's no way you let a seventy-two-year-old man do your dirty work for you."

Gossage: "When Ramirez started walking to the mound with a bat in his hand, I jumped up and started screaming at the TV set, 'Kill that son of a bitch!' Manny Ramirez is a chickenshit, and I hope he reads that. If he pulled that stuff in the old days, he would've gotten back in the box and I guarantee you he would've had the next pitch in his earlobe. Ramirez might've gotten one of us, but he wouldn't have gotten all 10. You wouldn't have seen him the rest of the series, I promise you, because we would've put him in the hospital. Give me a break."

Red Sox alumni were equally hot. Luis Tiant, who'd been in the center of so many battles with the Yankees (before himself defecting to the Bronx in 1979), said, "I've never seen anything like that before in my life. Zimmer was so mad with Pedro, but that wasn't good for the game. It was the craziest thing. I hope it never happens again. The fire is always there, all you need is a little gasoline for it to blow up. The intensity is like that. When Pedro threw over the guy's head, that's all it took, but that kind of stuff has been happening for years. It just carries over from one year to the next."

Bill Lee, not surprisingly, had the most unique take.

"I thought Manny's reaction was a joke, because Clemens' pitch wasn't even in the same area code," Lee said. "But I have to say, all kidding aside, that I was pretty proud of Zimmer. Watching him waddle across the field, going after Pedro, I honestly don't think he's lost a step. Although he doesn't bounce quite as high as he used to."

Zimmer, fined $5,000 for his part in the Saturday's absurdity—along with Martinez (who was docked $50,000), Ramirez ($25,000), and Garcia ($10,000)—made a public apology.

"First of all, last night, we won a hell of a game, and the media gathered around me and I didn't want to be rude. I was hurting and I had to get to the trainer's room, and I didn't want nothing to take away from the win that we had last night."

By now, tears were streaming down Zimmer's cheeks.

"I'm embarrassed by what happened yesterday. I'm embarrassed for the Yankees, the Red Sox, the fans, the umpires and my . . . my . . ."

Torre put his arm around Zimmer's shoulders.

". . . my family. That's all I have to say, I'm sorry."

With that, Zimmer stumbled off the podium and out of the room. Everyone was ready for the circus to leave town and for baseball to resume, and when it did, the teams would split the next two games thanks to a couple of pitching gems—Tim Wakefield against the Yankees in game four, David Wells against the Red Sox in game five. The teams would head back to Yankee Stadium, the Yankees ahead in the series, 3–2, but before they did, Wells would leave one last parting shot for the denizens of Fenway, who'd greeted the Yankees bus on three successive days with single-fingered salutes, and worse.

"Whenever they are ready to get rid of this place," the Yankees' zaftig lefty said, "let me push the button."

6

THIS IS WHAT THE BASEBALL GODS DEMANDED

If we played 100 times, I think we'd win fifty and they'd win fifty.
—*Derek Lowe, October 17, 2003*

*Go back to Boston, boys. Goodbye. They didn't treat us very well
in Boston, but, you know, we get the last laugh.*
—*George Steinbrenner, October 17, 2003*

No matter where they go in the world, New Yorkers forever believe there is but one city, "the city." Folks from Hempstead and Hackensack, Chappaqua and Massapequa, Greenwich and Greenpoint, it doesn't matter whom they're talking to or where they're talking to them. When they speak of "the city," there is never any ambiguity, to them, about which city they're referring to.

"A guy from New York could be talking to a guy from Chicago and a guy from Detroit inside a bar in San Francisco," said Red Sox fan Mike Carey, who now lives among New Yorkers in the borough of Queens. "And the guy from New York will go on and on about 'the city,' and he expects everyone in the bar to know what city he's talking about. It's like there isn't another place on the globe that also deserves to be called a city. Drives me nuts."

It's a simple matter, the New Yorker will reply. There is New York City. And there are a lot of cute little towns scattered everywhere else.

Similarly, if you ask a Yankees fan where his favorite team plays its baseball games, he will tell you, "The Stadium." In the same way Madonna, Pele, and Prince do not require surnames for instant identification, neither does Yankee Stadium necessitate a first name.

"I'm going to the Stadium this afternoon," the Yankees fan will say.

God help you if you ask, "Which stadium?"

The differences between Yankee Stadium and Fenway Park are bold and boundless, a fair irony if you consider they were both conceived in the same place: in the boardrooms and sketch pads of Osborn Engineering, a Cleveland firm that had also rebuilt the Polo Grounds when its original wooden frame was razed by a devastating fire on April 14, 1911. When the Yankees committed at last to building their own home in 1923, Colonel Jacob Ruppert searched exhaustively for the ideal place to headquarter his newly fashionable ballclub. Until Yankee Stadium began to rise out of the South Bronx' soft granite bedding, Fenway Park was the model for most of the places that housed major-league baseball: cozy fields that fit neatly into the cramped street-and-avenue geography of an urban grid, safe havens that recalled the game's rustic roots. Ruppert wanted to obliterate that blueprint, because he knew he had Babe Ruth, a player people wanted to see, and a team that would inspire fierce devotion once it learned how to win.

The Bronx wasn't Ruppert's first choice. He explored a lot in Long Island City, in western Queens, then fixed his gaze on the site of the Hebrew Orphan Asylum in upper Manhattan, and even pondered for a time a vast amphitheater over the Pennsylvania Railroad tracks in downtown Manhattan (which might have yielded a sports complex decades ahead of its time if the War Department hadn't intervened). Finally, Ruppert turned to an old ten-acre lumberyard in the undeveloped South Bronx wilderness owned by the Astor family. The colonel paid $600,000 for the site, which was easily visible from the Giants' offices across the river.

This delighted certain segments of New York City baseball.

"If they move to the Bronx," the Giants' quarrelsome manager, John McGraw, huffed loudly, "they may never be heard from again."

Ruppert took his chances anyway. "I want the greatest ballpark in the world!" he demanded of the representatives of Osborn Engineering. He wanted his new place of business to shout majestically across the city, louder still across the country. The Yankees' ballpark would be the first in the United States to call itself a "stadium," a word derived from the Greek *stadion,* referring to the length of the track at Olympia, or about one-eighth of a mile. Original plans called for three decks to enclose the entire structure, which would have borne some 80,000 seats. Even when those ambitions were scaled back, crowds topping 70,000 were not uncommon. Adding to the grandiose aura already surrounding the stadium—which would take an astonishing total of only 284 working days to complete—was the copper frieze, designed by Osborn's imaginative engineers, that would hang from the upper grandstand roof for the first fifty years of the Stadium's life. Even now, some thirty years after that façade was removed during the stadium's mid-'70s facelift—a white steel facsimile now hangs above the scoreboard in center—it remains the very symbol not only of the stadium but of the team itself.

"When I see that façade," Derek Jeter says, "I shudder."

"I got chills the first time I saw it," Phil Rizzuto says, "and I still get chills."

The players aren't alone. Yankees fans may fancy themselves as savvy, cynical street toughs, impervious to whim or whimsy, immune from being too impressed by any one team, player, game. Yet to a man, or woman, when you ask about Yankee Stadium, every one of them channels Robert Frost, issuing lyrical, poignant memories of lost youth and past summers, of trips taken with fathers and doubleheaders shared with siblings. The first look stays with them forever.

"I was only four or five years old the first time I went to Yankee Stadium, and it was the 'old' version, before they renovated it," recalled Peter Cipriano, a thirty-six-year-old radio engineer and a lifelong Yankees fan. "But there's one thing I do remember: looking around and thinking, 'Gosh, this is like a different planet.' I mean, it was *humongous.* Of course, we sat behind one of those old poles that used to keep the roof from falling down, and that pissed off my father, so what I remember is this: huge stadium, angry father. I still have the ticket stub."

Even after the Stadium went under the plastic surgeon's scalpel, the sensations remained the same for Yankees fans. Seating capacity was slashed by nearly 15,000 when the new place was reopened on April 15, 1976. Gone were those awful, sight-impairing support poles, but so, too, was the façade, as well as the monuments that used to stand sentry in center field. Death Valley, that endless patch of left-center field, had also been reduced by some thirty feet. It looked quite different in many ways except one: the enormousness of it all. The height of the upper deck; the lushness of the playing field. There was a time when Yankee Stadium was the only place a city urchin could come to see what green grass looked like. Yet even today, with so many younger fans commuting in from upstate, from Jersey, from Connecticut, from Westchester and Bergen and Fairfield Counties, suburban havens with backyards the size of football fields, you still see kids with eyes the size of the sewer covers their grandfathers used to take aim at during city stickball games.

"One thing that's never changed is the feeling I get walking in through the ramp, walking down the tunnel, the first glimpse I get when I see the field for the first time," Cipriano said. "It still takes my breath away. It still gives me a rush."

It's a high that can be easily and legally shared, too. Cipriano's wife, Monica, grew up the daughter of a Red Sox fan; her modest act of teenage rebellion was to root for the Yankees, which is one of the reasons she and her husband get along so well.

"The first time I took her to Yankee Stadium, she'd heard me talk about it so much, she couldn't wait to see for herself," Cipriano said. "Next thing you know, she's running up the tunnel ahead of me, because she wanted to get a glimpse of that field. And she started shrieking, 'That's so awesome!' Just like everyone else I know who goes there for the first time. It's like a rite of passage. There's no place like it anywhere."

For Yankees fans, that's true anytime.

For everyone else, it's especially accurate in October.

No other place in baseball understands October the way Yankee Stadium does, no place wears it quite as well, the way it carries the festive red, white, and blue bunting like an elegant evening gown, the way it invites just enough autumnal chill through its doors to remind you how vital, how significant these games really are, since a long, cold winter awaits the loser of these games. No other venue, in any sport, at any time, has ever borne silent witness to more important moments. On the night of October 15, 2003, game six of the 2003 American League Championship Series, Yankee Stadium would host its 142nd postseason game; Fenway Park, by comparison, though eleven years older, had to that point been the site of forty-five, not including the one-game playoffs in 1948 and 1978 that counted as regular-season games.

In the Stadium's very first taste of October, held exactly eighty years and five days earlier, Casey Stengel's inside-the-park home run had lifted the Giants to a 5–4 win over the Yankees in game one of the 1923 World Series. From there, you could cull a fairly exhaustive history of October moments that had been conducted exclusively on the Stadium's featured lawn. Don Larsen threw his perfect game here. Al Gionfriddo stuck his glove over the left-field fence in 1947, inspiring the usually dispassionate Joe DiMaggio to kick the dirt near second base; eight years later, another Dodger named Sandy Amoros would make a forever stab at a ball hit off the bat of Yogi Berra, on the day when Next Year finally arrived for the Brooklyn Dodgers. Chris Chambliss had taken a Kansas City Royals pitcher named Mark Littell deep here one night in 1976, ending a twelve-year pennant famine for the Yankees; Reggie Jackson would hit three balls out on three straight swings a year later, ending their fifteen-year World Series drought. Roger Clemens threw the business end of a splintered bat at Mike Piazza here in 2000, and a year later, on successive nights, Tino Martinez and Scott Brosius hit two-out, ninth-inning, game-tying home runs against the Arizona Diamondbacks at a time when the entire country, even Yankee-haters, seemed to be pulling for New York, since there was still a terrible pile of steel smoldering in the ruins of lower Manhattan.

The sheer size of it all can take your breath away.

"The first time I trotted out to right field at Yankee Stadium, wearing a Yankees uniform, I was already a veteran ballplayer," Paul O'Neill says. "I'd seen a lot. I'd already won a World Series ring in Cincinnati. I was no kid. And about halfway out there, it occurred to me that this is exactly the spot where Babe Ruth used to play. He used to hit home runs into those bleachers right behind me. That's when I really looked around, and noticed how enormous it all is."

On this sunny late afternoon, the Red Sox, one game from elimination, tried not to dwell on any of that. The wind was blowing hard, swirling in thick gusts overhead. Andy Pettitte, one of the great money pitchers in recent playoff history, would be trying to usher them into oblivion. The Yankees, up 3–2 in this best-of-seven series, needed only to win one of two, at home, in this cathedral of American sport. If the prospect of this overwhelmed the Red Sox, they did a wonderful job of hiding it.

"Let's just play the damned game," Johnny Damon said. "Let's see who's got what today. We've got a curse to crush, man. We've got a curse to crush."

Curse.

Jesus, just looking at the word would drive a Red Sox fan to distraction. Hearing it tumble off the tongue of one of the less savvy members of their own ranks caused the synapses in the brain to snap. Hearing it from a Yankees fan inspired fantasies of violence.

Hearing *their own players* even *acknowledge* it?

"Unbelievable," Sox fan John Miller said.

"Unfathomable," Tony Zannotti said.

But few Sox fans can put their feelings into words better than Steve Silva, who operated the Boston Dirt Dogs fan Web site, who seethed when people who should know better—and, worse, when people who don't know enough to know better—started slinging around the word *curse,* as if the majority of Red Sox fans believed in the word, accepted that some magical, mystical force had kept the Red Sox from winning the World Series since 1918. You want to call it "the curse of the Bambino," the way so many poets, documentary producers, and radio call-in show hosts did? You are taking the simpleton's approach to what afflicted Boston's baseball fans for all those many years. And you risk really, *really* pissing off the ward heelers of Red Sox Nation.

"People think we're just this crazy group of loyal puppy dogs who believe God doesn't want us to win because of a trade that happened eighty-five years ago," Silva said early in the summer of 2004. "Gee, why would we be angry about that kind of portrayal? Everybody wants to be looked at as a pathetic bunch of self-pitying, self-loathing losers. It doesn't fit into the plan that maybe we understand there are plenty of logical reasons why the Red Sox haven't won in so long. Sure, we've been unlucky. But cursed? Come on. Get a life."

And it got worse the longer the drought continued, because while players may have been the first to deny that their present had anything at all to do with the Red Sox' past, while they were quick to snap at an inquiring reporter who dared ask about the alleged hex/pox/jinx/curse, they sure didn't mind embracing it for their own comedic purposes or—worse—their own profit. In the spring of 2004, for instance, newly acquired Boston pitcher Curt Schilling starred in a Ford commercial that appeared continually during Red Sox telecasts on the New England Sports Network, where he'd toss his equipment bag into an F-150 truck and talk about heading to Boston "to break an eighty-six-year-old curse."

There was also this: The Sox are trendy.

And what happens when a team becomes trendy? You get "fans" who aren't really fans, but extras in some live-action play. These new patrons surely helped fatten the Red Sox' revenue streams. But they drove regulars like Silva to distraction.

"You have these assholes who are walking around and e-mailing me with this FROM CURSED TO FIRST crap shirts, and a Web site," Silva groused. "Give me an effin' *break!* We're not in effin' first yet, a-holes. And we're only 'cursed' when effin' ass-clowns like them are running around Fenway with their effin' cookies and T-shirts with the C-word on them. [Broadcaster Jerry] Remy too, he's pitching CURSE THIS! T-shirts. Hey, shithead: When you put the C-word on your goddamned shirts, no matter how you use it, you give the friggin' myth hype. You want to talk about the curse of alcoholism, bad managers, owners, GMs, and players at times, fine. But the Babe Ruth crap is for every clown that believes everything he reads or sees on ESPN. Spare me."

For Red Sox fans, it had been bad enough to endure another postseason where every broadcast, every national magazine article, every postgame press conference contained multiple references to the dreaded C-word; that happened whenever Boston made it to October. They were numb to it. In 2003, though, it was doubly troublesome, because over in the National League, the Chicago Cubs had also made a splendid postseason dash, and the Cubs' run of futility dated back ten years beyond the Red Sox', all the way to 1908. In many ways, the Cubs' ninety-five-year drought was even more troubling than the Red Sox', because throughout most of those years the Cubs engaged in some horrifying baseball. They hadn't even appeared in a World Series since 1945, and in the fifty-eight years that connected that season—when, on October 6, a goat named Murphy, owned by local saloon owner William Sianis, was denied entrance to Wrigley Field for a World Series game with the Tigers, thereby igniting the alleged "billy goat curse"—with this one, the Cubs had winning records only fifteen times.

But the Cubs were primed to do something about that.

In fact, as Red Sox fans emptied out of Fenway Park after game five of the 2003 American League Championship Series, as they started lighting up the switchboard at WEEI radio to fill fifty thousand clear-channel watts with their many anxieties, their brothers in baseball anguish, half a continent away, were getting ready to light the Illinois night with a storm of unqualified glee. This, of course, only added to the collective misery in New England. The Cubs were the one team that had always allowed Red Sox Nation to feel good about the previous eighty-five years.

Now the Cubs were six outs from the World Series.

And now a comedian named Bernie Mac, a high-profile Cubs fan, grabbed the microphone in the public-address booth at Wrigley Field. The mood in Chicago was positively transcendent. Thousands of fans crammed the narrow streets around the tiny old ballpark, waiting for the biggest baseball party in the city's history to commence. Inside? Thirty-nine thousand fans eagerly readied to shout out the words to "Take Me Out to the Ballgame." Harry Caray, the Hall of Fame broadcaster, used to lead this daily sing-along; since his death in 1997, the Cubs opted for guest stars at every game, be they Chicago icons or visiting celebrities. This time, it was Bernie Mac's turn, and the crowd never sounded louder, never, never sounded happier . . .

Until Bernie Mac reached the part of the song that normally goes, ". . . always root, root, root for the home team, if they don't win it's a shame . . ." Caray had always personalized it: ". . . always root, root, root for the Cubbies . . ."

But Bernie Mac added a new twist. Caught up in the glee of the moment, enraptured by the fact that the Cubs were up 3–0 in the bottom of the seventh with their best pitcher, Mark Prior, still throwing smoke on the mound, needing only six outs to qualify for their first World Series since 1945, Bernie Mac . . . well, he lost his mind. He decided to arm-wrestle baseball's gods. And so, to the horror of Cubs fans everywhere, this is what Bernie Mac sang: ". . . *always root, root, root for the champions . . .*"

In Boston, there were people who literally laughed out loud when they heard that. They knew what was coming next.

"I remember so many of my friends, back in 1986, telling stories about how they'd woken their sons up, infants at the time, and they'd propped them up in front of the TV set to watch the Red Sox get the final out of the World Series," a lifelong Red Sox fan named Bruce Mollar would say a few weeks later. "And I would hear that and tell them: 'Jesus, what did you *expect* would happen? You root for a team that hasn't won a championship since nineteen-fucking-eighteen, and you're this close to doing it, and then you pull a cheap stunt like that? Are you out of your freaking mind?'"

Mollar laughed.

"And then Bernie Mac pulled that wonderful piece of bullshit at Wrigley, and I turned to my wife and I said, 'Write this down: The Cubs are losing this game.' She laughed. She told me, 'You tell me there's no curse on the Red Sox, and now you're telling me there's one on the Cubs?' And I shook my head and said, 'That ain't a curse. That's freaking stupidity.'"

What happened next was almost too cruel to be real: With one out in the Marlins' eighth—five outs away—a foul ball off the bat of Luis Castillo, about to nestle safely into the glove of Cubs left fielder Moises Alou, instead wound up in the hands of a twenty-seven-year-old Cubs fan named Steve Bartman, sitting in the stands along the left-field line; Castillo promptly walked. A few moments later, a tailor-made double-play grounder ate up Cubs shortstop Alex Gonzalez. Later still, the Marlins started parading across home plate, eight runs in all. The Marlins would win, the series would be tied, and even though game seven loomed the next night, everyone in Chicago—and Boston— knew the Cubs had a zero percent chance to win that game.

"He was begging for trouble," Bruce Mollar said of Bernie Mac's folly. "I mean, he was just *begging* for it."

You would think the Red Sox would learn from this audacious example of mindless hubris. You would think.

Of course, for much of game six, it seemed like these Red Sox were bound for that most inglorious of Boston dénouements: they weren't even going to bother breaking their poor fans' hearts this time. There would be no need to summon the great authors of Greek tragedies. The Red Sox were getting their asses good and kicked, and Yankee Stadium would soon be deep into a victory lap of deafening celebration.

Pettitte wasn't at his best, but he had enough to keep the Yankees in the game until they seized a 6–4 lead after five innings. The Red Sox had twelve outs left in their season. They knew the last six would have to come against Mariano Rivera, who was only the greatest relief pitcher in the history of baseball and an October assassin of the highest order. They understood if they were going to find the runs they needed to extend their season, they would have to come in the next two innings.

Against Jose Contreras.

Of course it had to happen this way. How many times through the years had the Red Sox finished second during the off-season, dealing with and against the Yankees, then watched the fruit of those botched winter negotiations come back to doom them to second place during the summer? Contreras, the object of both teams' affections the previous December, had famously set off a bear market on EVIL EMPIRE T-shirts. Six days earlier, during game two, Joe Torre had removed Pettitte with the Yankees leading, 4–2, with Nomar Garciaparra batting, representing the tying run. In from the bullpen jogged the craggy, weather-beaten face Red Sox Nation had had seared into its brain for eleven months.

Joe Torre, through his catcher and interpreter, Jorge Posada, told the new pitcher, "You just throw strikes and do what you do best, you understand?"

"*Sí,*" Jose Contreras said.

Growing up in Castro's Cuba, the son of a revolutionary who believed in the cause deep in his bones, Jose Contreras had little understanding of what Red Sox–Yankees was truly about. In Havana, in his hometown of Las Martinas, everywhere in the island nation, the biggest rivals were everyone else. Cuba dominated international competitions, and Contreras was the country's baseball icon. In a 1999 exhibition, he threw eight innings of two-hit, shutout ball at a Baltimore Orioles lineup that featured Albert Belle, Cal Ripken Jr., and Brady Anderson. Afterward, he reaffirmed his commitment to his home nation, while revealing he had recently been offered a $50 million contract to defect to the United States, as sixty countrymen before him had.

"For this sum, nor any other, would I turn my back on my family, my people, or my homeland," he said. "I have a lot of respect, confidence, and admiration for Fidel."

Things change. Situations change. People change. Tensions mounted within Cuba's baseball federation. Contreras' status dimmed. Small insults festered. And Contreras could feel the clock ticking on his career. He was thirty. He had been told by an American agent, Jaime Torres, that there would be a bidding war for his services if he ever changed his mind about playing in the United States. Now, his mind was changed. There was an international tournament in Mexico; on October 1, 2002, the Cubans trounced the team from the Dominican Republic, 6–0. Contreras slipped away from the Hotel Camino Real in Santillo afterward, walked a few blocks, and climbed into a car sent over by Torres. Within an hour he was on a plane to Tijuana.

One full year later, he stared right at Nomar Garciaparra, who kicked the dirt in front of him with both feet, his signature quirk. "Once I was declared a free agent and those two teams were bidding to sign me," Contreras had said earlier in the season, "maybe then is when I realized what a big rivalry this really is."

Contreras threw one pitch, a blazing fastball. Garciaparra swung. He got under it. The ball sailed high over first base before plopping into Nick Johnson's glove. One pitch, one swing, one out, end of threat. And he was even better in the next inning. On a full-count pitch, Contreras threw a split-finger fastball that magically dipped under Manny Ramirez' bat for strike three. The crowd was beside itself, and grew even louder when Contreras brushed back David Ortiz a few moments later, before inducing him to pop up meekly to third. Then Kevin Millar followed with another weak pop-up, this one to Derek Jeter at short. Contreras had thrown fourteen pitches, eight of them for strikes, and had blitzed through all four hitters he faced. A folk hero was born in the Bronx.

"It gave me a lot of satisfaction and confidence as a pitcher that they believe in me and trust in me in a tight situation," Contreras said later on, through a translator. "I'll be a little more at ease when I go into a game from now on."

Luis Eljaua, the Red Sox' director of international scouting, who'd been a part of the Sox' clandestine Nicaragua operation, was impressed and distressed all at once.

"He's throwing great now," Eljaua said. "I wish him well, but obviously I wish he was in our rotation. Actually, we're probably lucky he's not in *their* rotation."

That he wasn't was evidence of Contreras' mystifying inconsistency, which had actually landed him in the low minors, at the Yankees' Class A Tampa facility, for a small stretch during the regular season, and cost him a spot on the Yankees' postseason starting staff. But none of that seemed to matter now, in the critical hour of game six. Here came Contreras, who had helped elevate this rivalry beyond the boiling point, the pitcher whom Fidel Castro himself had nicknamed "El Titan de Bronze," after Cuban general Antonio Maceo. He retired the Sox in order in the sixth; now all he needed were three outs to clamp the Red Sox in a straitjacket before he could hand the ball to Rivera.

All it took was three *pitches* in the seventh to turn the game upside down.

On Contreras' first offering, Garciaparra hit a slider squarely and fortuitously, for it flew into the roaring gust above Yankee Stadium and kept carrying away from Bernie Williams in center. After hitting the wall, the ball caromed to Hideki Matsui. The Yankee left fielder whirled in the general direction of third base and fired, hoping to catch Garciaparra, who was digging for a triple. But the ball never came anywhere near Aaron Boone, and Garciaparra trotted home with the most shocking run of the whole series. Now it was 6–5. Now, in places like the Boston Beer Works and the Cask 'n' Flagon and Tequila Rain, Red Sox fans rose from their drink-to-forget comas and started screaming at television screens again. Now, inside Yankee Stadium, an uneasy buzz finally started to descend on 55,000 people who just seconds before had been planning pennant parties.

Now, in his offices at the American Broadcasting Company over in Manhattan, Peter Cipriano heard the fellow in the next office over, a Red Sox fan, scream crazily, his muffled roars bleeding through the wall. A half hour earlier, he would have ignored the noise. Now, a most unsettling prospect filled Cipriano's thoughts: *The Yankees might really lose this game.*

Contreras came back with another slider, to Manny Ramirez. Ramirez hacked away at that one, too, and for a brief second it looked like it might sail over the fence for a game-tying home run; this time, the wind blessed the Yankees, and the ball merely struck the wall's blue padding. Ramirez eased into second amid a hailstorm of boos.

Now, with the tying run in scoring position, Contreras returned to the heat. But his first pitch to David Ortiz caught way too much of the plate. Ortiz drilled a line drive that hugged the first-base line and actually bounced off the bag. Ramirez sprinted home.

Tie game, 6–6. Yankee Stadium was too stunned to boo.

And it got worse. After a Kevin Millar strikeout, Bill Mueller, who had struggled all series long, clubbed a single that finally chased El Titan de Bronze, and Contreras left covered in hoots and catcalls. Still, when Felix Heredia arrived from the bullpen to blow strike three past Trot Nixon, there rose in the bleachers a hopeful stir.

Then Heredia issued four straight balls to Varitek, loading the bases.

And four more balls to Damon, forcing in Ortiz.

It was 7–6, Red Sox. The momentum had officially changed hands. It would end 9–6. The losing pitcher was Jose Contreras. This appalled Yankees fans, who sulked out of Yankee Stadium, knowing that in less than twenty-four hours, they'd have to face an all-or-nothing game seven. The Yankees . . . well, they *never* lost games like this, to the Red Sox, at Yankee Stadium, in October. Right? Hadn't it all been set up perfectly, with Contreras—the emblem of the Yankees' superior off-season prowess—pinning one final indignity on the Red Sox?

Contreras was just the latest man to don a Yankees jersey and instantly morph into the very picture of baseball evil to the faithful parishioners of Red Sox Nation. There had been Carl Mays, the John the Baptist of this Red Sox–Yankees relationship, the submarine-style star pitcher whose trade from Boston to New York during the 1919 season had opened the diplomatic door through which Babe Ruth would follow five months later. There was Ruth himself, of course.

It's possible, though, that no one player represented the Yankees-inspired fear and loathing lurking inside of every Red Sox fan better than a man named Charles Herbert Ruffing, nicknamed Red, a pitcher who, as a youngster, had lost four toes on his left foot in a mine accident. That hastened his transition from outfield prospect to pitching prospect, but in his first six-plus years as a big leaguer, he'd struggled, assembling a 39–96 record for some of the worst teams Boston—and baseball in general—had ever seen. On May 6, 1930, with his record already 0–3 on the year, coming off back-to-back twenty-loss seasons, the Red Sox were delighted to unload Ruffing on the Yankees in exchange for $50,000 and a shopworn outfielder named Cedric Durst.

What happened next was almost comical.

Ruffing took to the pinstripes immediately, winning fifteen of the twenty decisions he compiled for the Yankees that year, soon blossoming, as if by magic, into one of the finest right-handed pitchers of the 1930s, the anchor of Yankees teams that enjoyed a then-unprecedented run of four straight world championships from 1936 to 1939. As a Yankee, Ruffing would pile up a 234–129 record, win seven World Series games, and gain admission to the Hall of Fame in 1967. Durst? For their efforts, the Red Sox received exactly one home run and twenty-four runs batted in from him before he called it a career at season's end.

And that trade doesn't stand alone as the worst player-for-player transaction in the teams' shared history. Forty-two years later, the Red Sox and Yankees got together for a deal that may have been even more disastrous, given the immediate ramifications.

On March 20, 1972, a Red Sox relief pitcher named Sparky Lyle was given a rare inning of work by his manager, Eddie Kasko. This set off warning flares in Lyle's head, since he'd long since earned a permanent place on Kasko's shit list for, among other things, reporting for camp overweight and generally grousing about his diminishing role in the Sox' plans. Though he'd been a steady bullpen presence for the Sox since making the club in 1967, they never seemed to fully appreciate his potential. So Lyle had been wallowing for much of the spring. The sudden burst of work perked his antennae.

"A year ago, I figured out I should laugh every time I get traded in the papers, especially in the spring," Lyle said afterward. "But I'm fully prepared. I went out this winter and bought 23 new hats—one for each of the other major league teams—so I'll be equipped when I go."

That very night, Lyle went to a nearby racetrack with fellow pitcher Ray Culp, and they ran into Kasko, coach Eddie Popowski, and trainer Buddy LeRoux. None of the men said a word to Lyle, which was all the evidence he needed. He was gone. He had a clue where he was going, though. Earlier that spring, Yankees manager Ralph Houk had approached Lyle before an exhibition game.

"Don't let them hurt that arm, now," Houk had said in a conspiratorial whisper. "It's your bread and butter."

Lyle's instincts were right. Two days later, the Red Sox announced they had dealt Lyle to the Yankees in exchange for Danny Cater and a player to be named later. To listen to Kasko, it sounded as if the Sox truly believed the sale of Babe Ruth had finally been avenged fifty-two years later.

"Cater was right at the top of our list," Kasko said. "I hated to trade a pitcher of Sparky's quality, but we felt we had to do it. A right-handed player with power like Cater [who'd hit exactly fifty-two career home runs in eight full major-league seasons] is just what we need to compete for a championship this year."

Added Cater, who clearly believed Yankee Stadium was responsible for his dearth of gaudy power numbers: "I dream every night of playing eighty-one games a year at Fenway Park."

Cater's dream season of 1972 yielded eight more home runs, thirty-nine RBIs, a .237 average. Lyle, meanwhile, became the most dominating relief pitcher in baseball and an instant icon in New York City. The Yankees began playing "Pomp and Circumstance" whenever he entered a game, usually late, usually with runners on base, and Lyle delivered with a 9–5 record, thirty-five saves, and a 1.92 ERA. He was among the first building blocks of what would become a fresh generation of Yankees champions. And that vexed the Red Sox, who finished exactly one-half game behind the Detroit Tigers for the 1972 American League East pennant, and whose entire pitching staff accounted for only twenty-five saves that season.

By 1977, Lyle would win the Cy Young Award for his 13–5 record and twenty-six saves, the first relief pitcher to be so honored in the American League. Lyle, as much as anyone, fueled the Yankees to their first World Series victory since 1962, a fifteen-year drought that felt like a century to the gluttonous baseball fans of New York City.

It is unknown if anyone in Boston—which in 1977 enjoyed its sixtieth straight season without a title—sent along any congratulatory communiqués commemorating the conclusion of New York's trek through the baseball desert. Although it's doubtful.

Lou Merloni, the Boston utility man who'd grown up a Red Sox fan in Framingham, Massachusetts, understood what was coming better than anyone.

"Tomorrow will probably be a useless day of work for a lot of people in Boston," he said after game six. "It's all about this game. It's going to mean everything to the fans, especially to the city of Boston. It's going to be one for the ages."

In both clubhouses, that was a universal truth.

"Pedro vs. Clemens, this time at Yankee Stadium," Red Sox reliever Scott Williamson said, shaking his head. "This is what the baseball gods demanded."

"I'm going to relax, have a couple cocktails, and be ready to take on the Babe and the rest of the Yankees," Johnny Damon said. "It's balls-to-the-walls time now."

"I guess it was supposed to come down to seven games, as much as you hate to think about it," Yankees manager Joe Torre said.

There was no greater hint of that than the fact that the normally hushed Martinez agreed to an impromptu question-and-answer session in front of his locker—something Clemens had skillfully avoided by heading home once it became apparent his services would be needed the next day. A team spokesman reported that Clemens had said as he reached the door: "I'll be here tomorrow." That was that.

Pedro was asked if he was starting to feel some butterflies.

"I gotta wait for the game tomorrow," he said. "Maybe I'll feel nervous then."

He smiled, excused himself, headed for the door.

"This isn't the World Series," he said, "but it is close."

Actually, back home in Boston, it might have been construed as a little *too* close. The evidence reached Yankee Stadium a couple of hours before the first pitch of game seven, and initially it was greeted with snickers and disbelief. This had to be a hoax, right? Surely, the wire photographs had to be a gag. There's no way that workers were really allowed onto the Fenway Park field that afternoon to take paintbrushes to the sod behind home plate, to stencil a 2003 World Series logo there, right?

Right?

"I saw that," Red Sox fan John Miller says, "and I wanted to vomit."

Hadn't they learned? Hadn't they heard Bernie Mac's premature celebration just two nights before? Hadn't they realized that baseball's Star Chamber of mystical justice, for whatever reason, had frowned upon the Red Sox for eighty-five straight years, always on the lookout for just this hint of hubris? Wasn't anybody paying attention?

And yet there it was, a bright color picture, snapped hours before the two teams would even report to work 250 miles away, at Yankee Stadium. There was the logo: 2003 WORLD SERIES. There were the workers, doing their duty under the bright New England sun. Taunting the fates. Sneering at them, jeering at them, mocking them, scoffing at them, as if to say: *We don't believe in the C-word, dammit. And this proves it. This proves it once and forever.*

Months later, another Red Sox fan named Mike Carey would lament, "They couldn't wait another day, right? Couldn't wait until we actually *won* the stupid *game*, right?" And a Yankees fan named Pete Trinkle would say, merrily and gratefully: "That may have been the all-time best bulletin-board message in the history of sports."

It's doubtful either team realized that such an ethereal gauntlet had been thrown down. For many of the players, just arriving at the ballpark had been enough of an adventure. A water main had burst in upper Manhattan, dumping twenty million gallons of water onto the streets near the eastern terminus of the George Washington Bridge.

Jason Giambi, for one, was in big trouble. It was already nearing the 5 P.M. deadline for regulars to report to the clubhouse when he placed a frantic call to the Yankees' offices, saying he was stuck in the hopeless gridlock and wasn't moving.

"Look for the nearest police vehicle you can find," he was told.

He spotted a van at 145th Street; the driver recognized Giambi and immediately threw his flashing lights on, sounded his siren, and was joined by a cadre of cops from the 32nd Precinct. If passing motorists were at first furious about the special treatment given this gleaming Porsche, all it took was a peek inside the driver's-side window for the resentment to subside.

"Kick some ass tonight, Jason!" one such marooned driver screamed. His words were still ringing in Giambi's ears when he finally pulled into the players' parking lot at Yankee Stadium forty-eight minutes late.

Outwardly, Giambi took all this in stride. "It wasn't moving," Giambi said of the traffic. "There were all kinds of accidents because everyone was so pissed about the traffic. They were cutting each other off."

Giambi's interesting day took an even more curious detour when he was summoned to Joe Torre's office after getting settled in.

"I'm shuffling the lineup," Torre said. "I'm moving Nick [Johnson] up to the number-two hole. And I'm gonna put you in the seven spot." Torre let the announcement hang in the air for a second as he studied Giambi's reaction. Then he said, "Are you OK with that?"

"It isn't about me," Giambi told his manager. "I haven't been doing shit. Let's see how this lineup does." Later, Giambi would admit, "I was so scared about playing a game seven in this series, I don't even know if the words registered. I just wanted the damn game to hurry up and come. Waiting for it was torture."

Around New York, and around New England, hundreds of thousands of ordinary citizens were feeling exactly the same way. These are the games that define not only the careers of athletes, but also, in many ways, the most zealous of their fans, too. Every fan has a ritual. Every fan has game-day rites. And every fan believes, deep in the pit of their soul, that if they want something bad enough, if they truly yearn for something strong enough, they can affect what'll happen in a game like this. Logic doesn't apply to a fan's devotion. It never does. It never has.

Throughout New York City on this bright but chilly Thursday, baseball dominated every conversation. Much of it revolved around the Yankees and the Red Sox, of course, but if the folks wanted a breather from that, they could always dredge up the dear departed Cubbies, who'd completed their epic fall the night before, losing to the Marlins, sending all of Chicago into a deep, numbing funk. Many office workers with game-seven tickets took off early, the better to deal with their nerves and the massive traffic jams that had already begun to strangle most of the city's main arteries.

In Boston, the reactions were varied. The newly installed archbishop, Sean O'Malley, got into the act quickly, reporting in the morning, "The first request I received from a Boston priest was that the new arch-bishop make sure that the Red Sox would win this year. So I'm working on it." Not content with this spiritual injection, and unwilling to spend their night in a bar, dozens of Red Sox fans set up shop outside Fenway Park, fighting biting winds and dipping temperatures, filling the Yawkey Way sidewalk outside Gate A with a colorful array of lawn chairs, beach blankets, and comforters. Officially, they were first in line in the event World Series tickets went on sale the next morning, but in reality they were hoping to snag something else, an invisible slice of history.

"When they finally beat the Yankees and end this nonsense about a curse," carpenter Bill Millette said, "I want to be *here*, even if the team isn't."

Everywhere else, fans reported to their bunkers. In Manhattan, the telephone rang inside Pete Cipriano's office. Cipriano, like so many other Yankees fans, had been staring at the clock in his office all day, waiting for quitting time. He figured he'd be watching the game at home later on, in the privacy of his living room.

The phone call changed that. It was Jim Frasch.

"Hey," he said. "I have an extra ticket. You want to go?"

Cipriano barely let Frasch finish the sentence. He was going. Together, they climbed to Tier Box 26, near the left-field foul pole. Both men were delighted, because there are some events when a true believer needs the company of another true believer in order to survive four quarters, three periods, nine innings.

And sometimes you want to be left alone.

In Dudley, Massachusetts, a town that straddles the Connecticut border, Tony Zannotti wanted to be left alone. As game time neared, Zannotti descended to his basement, which for him is the best place imaginable to watch the truly important games of his life. He calls it his "sports shrine"; one of the walls is devoted entirely to the Red Sox, another to the Boston Bruins, and a third to auto racing. There is a panoramic picture of Fenway Park taken on the day Derek Lowe pitched his no-hitter. There are two newspaper articles written the day

Ted Williams died, along with a laminated full page of the *Boston Globe*. There's the eleven-by-sixteen collage that the Red Sox handed out at Fenway on the day they retired Carl Yastrzemski's number 8.

And there was his couch.

"Not for sitting," Zannotti says. "For pacing around."

There would be a lot of that this night. In bullpens. In dugouts. In clubhouses. In saloons. In restaurants. In living rooms. In dens. Everywhere. What was it that Johnny Damon had said the night before?

"It's balls-to-the-walls time."

Indeed it was.

The Yankees' most reliable good-luck charm approached Joe Torre in the clubhouse a few hours before he would throw out game seven's ceremonial first pitch, wearing a blue and gray varsity-style Yankees jacket and one of his classic deadpan expressions.

"Joe," Yogi Berra said, "I've got a problem."

Torre's nerves were already frayed, thanks to six previous stomach-churning games and the one that would be getting under way in about an hour. What he didn't need to hear was that something was wrong with his designated talisman.

"What is it, Yogi?" the Yankees manager asked.

"You keep sendin' me out to the mound on short rest, game after game after game," Berra said, keeping the straight face as long as he could. "My arm's gettin' sore."

Both men laughed. Ever since Joe DiMaggio's death in 1999, Berra had become something of an honorary greeter at Yankee Stadium. Whenever there was a big game, a special occasion, whenever a Yankee presence was needed, the phone would ring inside Berra's home in Montclair, New Jersey, or inside the museum that bears his name on the campus of Montclair State University (which sits adjacent to the minor-league baseball stadium that also bears his name). And Berra, enjoying the role as most beloved living Yankee, would throw on the varsity jacket, drive to the stadium, trot out onto the mound just before the opening pitch, and try to wake up the echoes. Sometimes he did it alongside his old battery mate Whitey Ford. Sometimes he shared the duty with his old business partner and New Jersey neighbor, Phil Rizzuto.

Sometimes, like this time, he flew solo.

"I wish I was about fifty years younger, so I could play in this game," Berra said during the endless pregame countdown.

"I wish you were fifty years younger, too," Torre said. "We could use an extra lefty swinger against Pedro."

"You know, on second thought, maybe I'll just watch this one," Berra said, winking. "My reflexes aren't so good anymore. I may have to jump out of the way of one of them fastballs of his."

In all the years they'd been playing big games at Yankee Stadium, all the heavyweight boxing matches, all the championship football games, there had never been a buzz pulsing through the big ballyard like the one before this game. People like Yogi Berra, who first made the trip to the Bronx in 1942, a brief visit before he joined the wartime Navy, were stunned by what they encountered when they arrived. There was a sharp crackle of excitement piercing the crisp autumn night, a genuine blanket of anticipation that cloaked the old stadium for a good ninety minutes leading up to the game. Nobody chanted; what good would that do? Besides, deep down, Yankees fans understood that Boston certainly did *not* suck. After six nerve-fraying games, the Sox had proven as much. They'd teamed with the Yankees to deliver a series for the ages already.

And, for history buffs, there was this bonus: This would be the first game seven of any kind played within Yankee Stadium's walls since 1957. Forty-six years New York had been waiting for a game like this, on a stage like this.

And when Roger Clemens fired a ninety-three-mile-per-hour fastball over the plate, parallel with Johnny Damon's knees, the place went berserk.

"The loudest I've ever heard it here," Torre would say later.

The Red Sox knew there was one way to solve the dilemma of the din: score runs. Get a lead. Knock Clemens out of the box. Turn the cauldron of sound that is Yankee Stadium in on itself.

They did that. They scored three times in the second inning, two on a home run by Trot Nixon, one on an error by Enrique Wilson, playing third base in favor of Aaron Boone because of his career numbers against Martinez (ten for twenty lifetime, seven for eight during the 2003 season). They scored another in the fourth, on a home run by Kevin Millar, and sent Clemens to the showers shortly thereafter. It was 4–0, and hardly anyone noticed when Mike Mussina walked into the ball game inheriting a first-and-third, nobody-out mess from Clemens, then proceeded to strike out Jason Varitek on three pitches and induce Damon to bounce into a double play. Why should anyone notice? When was the last time anyone had ever seen Pedro Martinez blow a four-run lead? With the World Series on the line, no less?

Yankee Stadium sounded like study hall.

Giambi, of all people, was the one who tried to awaken the faithful. Hidden down in the seven hole, he twice swatted solo home runs off Martinez, in the fifth and in the seventh, cutting the lead in half, rousing the fans ever so slightly. But the Yankees scratched out only four other hits in the first seven innings, and Martinez was showing more and more confidence with his fastball.

Then David Wells chugged in from the bullpen in the top of the eighth, threw one pitch to David Ortiz, and watched Ortiz make it disappear into the upper deck in right field. It was 5–2. Suddenly, an unsettling reality blanketed the 56,277 people inside Yankee Stadium. The Yankees were three runs down. They had only six outs left in their season. The mood in the bleachers and the grandstand, the loge and the mezzanine, was neatly summed up by Wells' reaction the moment Ortiz connected with his slow hanging curveball, a rejoinder easily audible throughout the hushed stadium: *"Fuuuuuck!"*

Up in Tier Box 26, Pete Cipriano had seen enough. After quietly watching Ortiz circle the bases, he turned to his friend, Jim Frasch.

"I can't take any more of this," Cipriano said. "I'm not gonna sit here and watch them celebrate on this field."

Frasch shook his head.

"Do yourself a favor," he said. "Wait awhile. Wait through the bottom of the eighth. If nothing happens by then, I'll run out the door with you. It's the Yankees and the Red Sox, man. You know as well as I do that a lot of crazy things can happen between now and the end of the night."

What happened next, soon enough, would contain the cruel tinge of inevitability. For months, it would inhabit nightmares across New England, and happy saloon talk across New York, and fascinated debate in every other American baseball precinct.

It was impossible to know that as it unfolded, of course. Pedro Martinez had thrown exactly one hundred pitches through seven innings; rare were the days when he would push his arm much further than that. Grady Little already had his two most reliable middle relievers, Alan Embree and Mike Timlin, warming up. If he could get through the eighth with Martinez and still have a three-run lead, that would be ideal. If Martinez stumbled, the Red Sox bullpen, maligned all year, had been virtually unhittable in the postseason. If Pedro found trouble, the posse would be eager to ride to the rescue.

Nick Johnson worked the count full on Martinez, then fouled off a pitch, then popped a ball straight up. Nomar Garciaparra easily gloved it.

Five outs to go.

Up in Tier Box 26, Pete Cipriano turned again to Jim Frasch and said, "I really think I'm going to be sick."

Frasch was running out of excuses to keep his friend planted in his seat; in fact, *he* was starting to feel a little queasy, too. Just then, a woman sitting in front of them turned and offered a bag full of Swee-Tarts. Not that either man believed in such nonsense, of course, but she'd done the same thing twice before; both times, Jason Giambi smoked a home run a few seconds later. Frasch and Cipriano looked at each other with expressions that said: *What the hell?* And they reached for the candies.

Elsewhere, Yankees fans tried to fight off feelings of resignation. In New Jersey, Frank Russo shut off the television early, after the Sox grabbed their 4–0 lead, and clicked on the radio. "That way," he reasoned, "I'd hear the Yankees announcers doing the play-by-play. It was better than hearing [Joe] Buck and [Tim] McCarver do it." It wasn't working, though. So just after Johnson's pop-up, Russo climbed the stairs from his basement room to join his mother, watching the game on the living room TV upstairs. "She's an even bigger Yankees fan than me," Russo said. "And it was *really* driving her crazy." In Boston, Yankees fan Pete Trinkle tried not to let the swirling mania growing outside his window affect him too much. He reached for a Don Mattingly model bat and started pacing his living room, waiting for a miracle. His was a calm port insulated from a burgeoning storm.

The rest of New England, quite naturally, felt like it was about to burst.

In Dudley, Massachusetts, Tony Zannotti stared at his Yaz poster, stared at the rest of the shrine wall, tried not to let his mind jump too far ahead of the proceedings. Inside Tequila Rain, a bar on Lansdowne Street right across from the Fenway Park bleachers, Steve Silva was lost in a room stuffed with revelers as they readied for a historic countdown. On the television, Martinez threw a blazing fastball that Derek Jeter never came close to catching up with, for strike one. In his living room in Queens, Mike Carey found himself wrestling his brain, refusing to think ahead any farther than the next pitch, even as Jeter fouled off a pitch for strike two. In Grafton, Massachusetts, John Miller had no such luck. Sitting by himself in his living room, he actually started thinking of the Florida Marlins. *Pudge Rodriguez is tough,* he figured. *They have some damn good pitching,* he reasoned. *But we get the extra game at home in the World Series this year, and—*

Martinez slung a ninety-three-mile-per-hour fastball toward the plate, and Jeter sent a rocket out toward right field. Maybe, with a better break on the ball, Trot Nixon could have flagged it down. But he didn't. The ball barely cleared his head, and it bounced against the wall. Jeter sauntered into second with a double.

At that exact instant, in Dudley and in Grafton, in Queens and in Tequila Rain and in every saloon and living room in the United States of America, the same notion flashed through millions of minds: *That's all for Pedro.* Even in Tier Box 26, Jim Frasch looked at Pete Cipriano and said, "Well, he pitched a hell of a game. Maybe we can take our chances with the bullpen."

But Grady Little never even left his seat in the third-base dugout. A curious move, maybe. But the tying run was still in the on-deck circle. Martinez was still clear of danger. And his fastball was still in the low nineties. The big clock at Yankee Stadium clicked to eleven o'clock. Martinez got ahead of Bernie Williams, 1 and 2, and unleashed a fast-ball that tipped the radar gun at ninety-five. Williams ripped it for a single. Jeter scored. It was 5–3, and Hideki Matsui, a left-hander, was due up, the potential tying run, and now there was no question what would happen, especially when Little hopped out of the dugout. He ambled to the mound. He did not motion with his left arm, which would have signaled Embree, a left-hander, into the game. Instead, he started to chat with Pedro.

"What the *hell* is he doing?" Mike Carey yelled at his TV.

They kept talking. Little patted Pedro on the shoulder. Inside Yankee Stadium, a buzz of disbelief began to grow. Inside Tequila Rain, some-one shouted, "Are you *shitting* me, Grady?" Martinez nodded. Catcher Jason Varitek nodded. Little turned on his heels.

And left Pedro Martinez in the game.

Baseball fans of all stripes immediately thought that was quite a gamble. Red Sox fans immediately believed Little had gone truly insane.

"Red Sox fans like me have this conversation a lot," John Miller would explain months later. "During a game, it's so obvious when Pedro has passed the point where he's *Pedro* anymore. Anyone who pays attention can tell. His overall demeanor changes. His body language. He's almost screaming: *I'm done for the day! Take me out!* And he was screaming it loud and clear at Grady. Grady just didn't hear him."

Still, Martinez came back with two quick strikes against Matsui. And the third pitch looked perfect: It was fast, it had bite, it was in on Matsui's hands. Martinez had busted a thousand big-league bats with that riding fastball. Only this time, at the last instant, the ball tailed back over the plate. Matsui jumped on it, yanked it down the right-field line. It landed a foot fair. Williams scored. A fan touched the ball, so Matsui was held at second with a ground-rule double. It was 5–4. Matsui, suddenly, ridiculously, impossibly, represented the tying run, and he was in scoring position.

Bill Lee, driving home to Craftsbury, Vermont, from a television studio in Boston, had listened to most of the previous two and a half hours on the radio. The old Yankee-killer had taken great delight in hearing the Red Sox pummel the Yankees for seven and a half innings. Now he heard himself saying in the car, "Well, Grady, you waited a batter too long." Lee couldn't see Martinez on his car stereo, much as he tried, but he could clearly hear Pedro hollering, ever so silently: *I'm done for the day! Take me out!*

Grady Little never left his seat in the dugout. He never stirred. He was paralyzed. Even Yankee Stadium seemed perplexed; the crowd was waiting for the manager to pull Pedro so they could assault him with boos and jeers and catcalls and worse. Yet Little never did. He never moved. Jorge Posada stepped up to the plate. Martinez suddenly looked very, very small, much frailer than five foot eleven, 170 pounds.

In his car, Bill Lee leaned his head back and said, "Shit. Shit. Shit. Shit. Shit."

Martinez was working carefully now. Posada was, too. The count reached 2 and 2, and Martinez threw his 123rd pitch of the night, another good pitch, right on Posada's fists. It was too good, in truth. What flew off his bat was a flare that fell softly into the no-man's-land between Garciaparra, Todd Walker, and Johnny Damon. Matsui roared around third and scored the tying run. With both Garciaparra and Walker away from second, Posada dashed to the unoccupied base. It was 5–5. The lead was gone. The Stadium was apoplectic. Yankees fans struggled to come to grips with what they'd just seen. Jim Frasch would call it "the most religious, overjoyed, ecstatic, euphoric, incredible experience of my life."

Red Sox fans?

Red Sox fans watched Grady Little trudge to the mound and finally take the ball out of Martinez' hands. And all of them, bonded through a lifetime of torture and passion and suffering and angst, understood precisely what Steve Silva was thinking as he watched all of this unfold.

"Once a game like that is tied, it's over," he said. "We just know these things."

Midnight came. Midnight passed. October 16 had become October 17. Seven games, it turned out, weren't enough to contain all that this American League Championship Series had to offer. Amazingly, it was going to spill over into the tenth inning, into the eleventh inning, who knew how long? Mariano Rivera had come on to start the ninth inning for the Yankees, and he'd told Joe Torre he would be willing to pitch until his arm became numb. Earlier in the year, thanks to a bullpen Torre only occasionally trusted, Rivera had added the six-out save to his bag of tricks; Yankees fans debated the wisdom of this all summer long, especially since Rivera was given to more spasms of injury and ineffectiveness than at any other time in his eight full years as a Yankee. Rivera hadn't gone more than two innings in more than three and a half years; Torre didn't want to think that far ahead.

Soon he would have to. With each pitch carrying dire ramifications, the Red Sox and Yankees spent two innings shadowing each other like two exhausted fifteenth-round club fighters barely able to lift their arms any longer. The Red Sox did scratch a pair of hits off Rivera, a single by Varitek in the ninth and a double by Ortiz in the tenth. But they couldn't push either man across. Meanwhile, the Yankees' bats went back into hibernation. Mike Timlin retired them in order in the bottom of the ninth, and Tim Wakefield—yes, Wakefield—did the same in the tenth.

The fact that Wakefield was anywhere near this game at this juncture was, in the eyes of many Red Sox fans, the final indictment of Grady Little as a manager. Yes, Wakefield had shut the Yankees down twice before in this series. Yes, Wakefield had made it quite clear that if he was needed, "my spikes will always be on." But he was a knuckleball special- ist. Even in a knuckleballer's best games, he is going to throw a handful of balls that don't knuckle, don't dance, don't spin and flutter and bounce. Sometimes those flat medicine balls land in outfielders' gloves. More often, they land in parking lots. Now, with the season on the line, with his closer, Scott Williamson, rested and ready to throw all night long if necessary, Little picked Wakefield.

"Having a knuckleballer in a sudden-death game on the road is a death wish," Steve Silva said. "I mean, we all know Wakefield is always one pitch away from a three-run home run, even when no one is on base."

"That's not the pitcher you bring in when you're one swing away from disaster," Tony Zannotti said. "I mean, anyone can get lucky against a knuckleball and just crush it. Wakefield had been great twice in the series. Why press your luck there? Why?"

Of course, most Sox fans had already begun preparations for dealing with the inevitable, whenever the inevitable arrived. Mike Carey turned to his computer to keep himself occupied, to keep from going mad, but every few moments he kept looking over his shoulder at the television screen, "kind of like when you're driving your car and you have to look at an accident. I was waiting for the worst to happen." Silva hung around Tequila Rain for a couple of innings after the Yankees tied it up, the way you hang around a funeral parlor longer than you'd like out of a sense of duty to the bereaved. "Then," he said, "I found myself leaving the bar, walking to my car, driving home, putting on the radio. And waiting for whatever calamity was next." Bill Lee, making the lonely drive up I-93 toward northern Vermont, heard himself yelling at the radio: "A knuckleballer? *Now?*"

Nobody had any such compunction about Mariano Rivera. Pitching a third inning for the first time since April 2000, he blew away the Sox in the top of the eleventh inning, his forty-eighth pitch of the night a dazzling cut fastball that Doug Mirabelli waved at for strike three.

Wakefield walked out for his second inning of work. Aaron Boone, who'd been benched for the game in favor of Enrique Wilson, whose enfeebled bat had earned him growing derision from the throatier Yankee Stadium denizens, stood in the on-deck circle. As he watched Wakefield complete his warm-up tosses, Joe Torre's voice was still fresh in Boone's ear. Just before he'd left the dugout, Torre called Boone aside.

"I noticed when Aaron hit against Wakefield before, his left shoulder was flying open so bad, he was pulling everything foul," Torre would explain a few days later. "So I told him, 'Think about hitting the ball to right field. That doesn't mean you won't hit it out of the ballpark, but it will help you keep it fair.'"

This echoed something another wise old hitter had told Torre, decades before, when Torre was a kid catcher playing for the Milwaukee Braves, struggling with his own swing. "You're hitting a lot of ground balls to shortstop, right? Well, try hitting a line drive right at the second baseman. It doesn't mean you'll hit it there, but it'll keep your swing right."

Ted Williams had offered that simple tip to Joe Torre.

Now Torre offered it to Aaron Boone, who walked to the plate, dug in, saw Wakefield's knuckler arch toward him. In his mind he heard the manager's Brooklyn voice, advising him to lay back. *Wait on it. Think about hitting the ball to right field.* He held back a fraction, watched the ball inch closer. Swung.

Up in Tier Box 26, Pete Cipriano and Jim Frasch had just popped another mouthful of the lucky SweeTarts when they heard the unmistakable thwack of a ball soundly meeting the sweet spot of a bat. What they saw next was an unmistakable, majestic sight: The baseball was heading right toward them. It got bigger and bigger the closer and closer it came, before soaring right past them, disappearing into a tangle of arms and legs, into a dense kettle of bliss.

Boone had taken two steps out of the batter's box before it hit him what he'd done. He threw his bat aside, raised his arms in triumph, and began the sweetest 360-foot jog of his life. Mariano Rivera didn't even wait for the ball to disappear before sprinting to the mound and collapsing, hugging the dirt, lying prostrate in a most holy place.

The celebration that followed was the most raucous of any that Yankee Stadium had ever seen, the tensions and anxieties of the past nine days bursting like a champagne cork, flooding every available corner. Roger Clemens, David Wells, and Mel Stottlemyre each lugged bottles of champagne out to Monument Park, beyond the left-field fence, where they offered a toast to Babe Ruth's plaque. "He's shining on us. He's looking down on us," Wells crowed. "Why not give him a toast, man? He's the one that got us here. From 1918 until now, the curse lives!" Outside the ballpark, on his way to his chauffeured sedan, a jubilant George Steinbrenner filled reporters' notebooks with glee, and added this exclamation: "The curse still lives. I sure do believe it now!"

Right now, in the immediate aftermath, even the most fervent opponents of the C-word had a hard time mustering enough energy for a rebuttal.

The two men who shared the moment understood immediately that from now on, they would be locked in a slow dance of history, the same way Mike Torrez and Bucky Dent had been tied for twenty-five years, the same way Ralph Branca and Bobby Thomson had been attached since 1951.

"To be in that spot, to get the chance, it's humbling," Aaron Boone said. "This game humbles you all the time in good ways and bad ways. It's been humbling a little bit lately for me in a bad way, and this is just the same. It's humbling. It's a humbling game, and right now, I feel that way."

Wakefield, his voice quaking in the solemn silence of the loser's locker room, was feeling the full gale force of baseball's humbling power.

"When he hit it," Wakefield whispered, "I knew it was gone. It hurts. All I can say is I'm sorry." He took a deep breath. "I was trying to get ahead . . ." His voice trailed off.

Over in another corner, Red Sox general manager Theo Epstein was saying, "Tim didn't lose this game. There's not a single loser in this clubhouse." But Wakefield wasn't buying his boss' cup of kindness.

"I feel like I let everybody down," he said.

Actually, there wasn't a soul in all of New England who blamed Wakefield. The co-conspirators had different surnames: Little and Martinez. They tried to offer excuses.

"Pedro Martinez has been our man all year long and in situations like that, he's the one we want on the mound over anybody we can bring in out of that bullpen," Little said. "He had enough left in his tank to finish off Posada. He made some good pitches to him, squeezed his ball out over the infield and there's nothing we can do about it now. Pedro wanted to stay in there. He wanted to get the job done, just as he has many times for us all season long, and he's the man we all wanted on the mound."

Said Martinez: "I'm the ace of the team and you have to trust me. That is no time to say I'm tired. This is no time to blame Grady. If somebody wants to point the finger, point it at me. I'm the one pitching. The fans in Boston right now have to be sad like we are, heartbroken like we are. But we battled. Even though we lost the game, we gave our best. Grady asked me if I had enough bullets in my tank to get them out, and I said yes. I would never say no. I tried hard and I did whatever I could do to win this ball game."

All across the victorious expanse of New York City, the parties lasted all night, some until dawn, sporadic spasms of unbridled relief. All across the hurting landscape of New England, fathers were forced to explain to their sons about the shared scars of suffering, a new generation freshly christened to the agonies of their ancestors. Fans deal with their pain in different ways.

Bill Lee, for instance, was fifteen minutes from his house—"close enough to see my driveway," he said—when Wakefield delivered his knuckler. Fourteen years as a big leaguer had trained Lee's ears precisely; he could tell when he heard the contact on the radio that Boone had gotten all of it. Lee clicked off the broadcast before the announcers could confirm his suspicions. A familiar stain of regret slowly crawled into his heart until he opened the door of his house. A surprise was waiting for him.

"I'd been trying to catch this Norwegian rat all summer," Lee said. "He'd been shitting in my fridge, and he ate a hole through my kitchen wall, and I gave him the only appropriate name I could think of: Billy Martin. Well, I'd put a live trap out that morning, cheese with peanut butter on it. And damned if that wasn't the day I finally caught the little son of a bitch."

Lee chuckled.

"Killing Billy Martin," he said, "made me feel a little better."

CHAPTER

7

JUST ADD ONE MORE GHOST TO THE LIST

I would always hear people talking about something that happened in
some game in 1946 or 1949 or 1967. I'd go up Boylston Street to get a
cup of coffee almost every day, and I'd hear people talking crazy.
It would be the last week in April, and they'd come up to me and say,
"That was a devastating loss last night." I'd look at them and say,
"Just relax. We've got 140 more to play." —*Grady Little, March 3, 2004*

These guys haven't been able to beat us for eighty years. They ain't
gonna start now. —*Yogi Berra, October 9, 2003*

He remembered fragments, mostly: the unyielding noise, the deafening din, the waves of joy crashing all around him. He remembered making the long, endless journey from pitcher's mound to
dugout and from dugout to clubhouse, but after that, he admitted, it
was awfully fuzzy, a terrible blur of tears and angst and anger, twenty-
five men holding an instant Irish wake for themselves within seconds of
a most public demise. What Tim Wakefield recalled best of all was the
dull ache that filled him in those seconds immediately after the knuckleball left his hand, fat and flat, as it danced so invitingly toward Aaron
Boone's bat. Wakefield had thrown thousands of knuckleballs in his
career. He knew what a bad one felt like.

"You live with that as a knuckleballer, throwing one that doesn't do what it should," he said. "It's just better when you throw one of them in the top of the fourth, not the bottom of the eleventh."

Wakefield laughed. He was able to do that now, at the start of an extraordinary journey, exactly four months and three days after the conclusion of another. Wakefield's voice echoed softly inside another quiet clubhouse this late-February morning, this one in the middle of the Red Sox' minor-league complex in Fort Myers, Florida. Soon enough, the room would fill with the bursting bustle of baseball life, Red Sox pitchers and catchers reporting for their first day of work. For now, Wakefield spoke softly, spat tobacco juice into a nearby garbage can, and checked out the basketball scores in a morning newspaper.

"You have to take things like a man," Wakefield said. "That's the way I was always taught. You give up the game-winning home run, you take responsibility for it. And then you have to deal with it. You have no choice. Eventually, you move on, but it's like a process. In some ways, it's like dealing with a death in the family."

Wakefield couldn't escape the grieving that consumed New England. In the days and weeks after Boone's blast landed in the left-field stands, he could barely step into a room without seeing a television filled with the image of that flat knuckleball and that soaring drive. But Wakefield was fortunate. Spending a few extra days in Boston before driving to his off-season home in Melbourne, Florida, he mixed with the townsfolk, and the funniest thing happened: They never talked about the home run ball. Not once. They thanked him for his part in the best baseball season Boston had known in a long time. They offered to buy him drinks to celebrate the two wins he'd posted earlier in the series. Red Sox fans, apparently, had come a long way since the days when they chased Bill Buckner all the way to Idaho after he let a ground ball drizzle through his legs.

"I'm a fan on the days I'm not pitching," Wakefield said, "so I know the emotional roller coaster you go on watching the kinds of games we played last October. All they said was they just couldn't wait until spring training, so we could get after it again. And so we could reengage with the Yankees."

On his drive from Melbourne to Fort Myers a few days earlier, Wakefield had suddenly noticed a car pulling up alongside him. The folks inside wore Red Sox caps, and they brandished a sign: GO RED SOX! YANKEES SUCK!

"I have tinted windows," Wakefield said. "I have no idea how they knew it was me. I guess that tells you something about the Red Sox fans, though, right? And about the rivalry, too."

Four months and three days after the lowest moment of his professional life, Tim Wakefield spat another stream of tobacco juice into the garbage can, grinned, and pounded his mitt. "I can't wait for us to play again," he said. "Can you?"

That answer was palpable all across New York and New England, but as the sun rose over the 2004 baseball season, it had also grown to include the greater baseball constituency at large, a populace plainly divided into its own sets of red states and blue states. The Red Sox' appeal had exploded, and the Olde Towne Team had, in many ways, gone national: Sox fans sprang up seemingly overnight in every corner of the country. And, of course, the Yankees were still the original America's Team, appealing to millions of people who appreciated the relentless excellence the Yankees had displayed, almost uninterrupted, for the better part of a century.

In an election year that would, quite appropriately, bring national political conventions to both Boston and New York City during the summer, it seemed only right that the nation's baseball attention be focused on those two metropolises, too. There was no off-season. While the Yankees were losing to the Florida Marlins in six decidedly anticlimactic World Series games, the Red Sox had already begun to crank their engines for another run up Sisyphus' hill. And it started in the one place it had to start. Even Grady Little understood this. From the moment he'd decided to leave Pedro Martinez in too long in game seven, from the moment he watched in horror as that faith was brutally betrayed, from the moment Aaron Boone's home run sealed it as one of the most second-guessable decisions in baseball history, Little realized one thing: He was a goner. He would be the scapegoat, the severed head fed to the greedy, grieving masses.

During the World Series, Little had told Gordon Edes of the *Boston Globe*: "I'm prepared for the likelihood [that I'll be fired]. I'm not sure that I want to manage that team. That's how I felt when I drove out of town. If they don't want me, fine, they don't want me. If they want me to come back, then we'll talk and see if I want to come back up there. That's the way I feel about it. Right now I'm disappointed that evidently some people are judging me on the results of one decision I made—not the decision, but the results of the decision. Twenty-four hours before, those same people were hugging and kissing me. If that's the way they operate, I'm not sure I want to be part of it.

"Just add one more ghost to the list if I'm not there, because there *are* ghosts," Little added. "That's certainly evident when you're a player in that uniform."

Little's farewell address would have sealed his fate, but the truth was there had been whispers about Little's future even before game seven. He'd nearly been let go in late August, and only a late-season Sox surge had spared him then. The Pedro decision may well have been the perfect prism through which to explain why he wouldn't be retained, but satisfying the bloodthirsty mob was only a small fraction of the reason. If anything, Little's refusal to pull Pedro underlined who he was as a manager: He worked by instinct, not numerical mandate. He followed his gut, not computer printouts. When his decisions worked, his *Moneyball*-influenced bosses could live with them. When they didn't . . .

"It's fair to say," Larry Lucchino said, "that there were some misgivings expressed in the last month of the season as we began to examine the prospect of a longer-term extension for Grady."

Six weeks later, on December 4, Terry Francona would be introduced as Little's successor, and at first it seemed an odd choice. Francona had already logged four undistinguished years as the manager of the

Philadelphia Phillies; saddled with some terrible teams, he hadn't made them much better, winning only 44 percent of his games. At his own introductory press conference, Francona had joked, "I've been released by six teams, fired as manager, I've got no hair, and my nose is bigger than it should be. So I think my skin's pretty thick."

But Francona's thick skin wasn't the ace he held up his sleeve.

It was the ace up his sleeve that was the real ace up his sleeve.

Because if Francona hadn't won many ball games during his tenure in Philadelphia, he had earned the loyalty and respect of Curt Schilling, who during his own hitch at Veterans Stadium had seemed destined to play out his days in relative obscurity, pitching very well for teams too often shoved helplessly out of the playoff hunt by Memorial Day. But that changed forever in 2001. Traded to the Arizona Diamondbacks, Schilling blossomed, winning twenty-two games during the regular season and four more during the playoffs, teaming with Randy Johnson to form the most intimidating one-two, lefty-righty punch since Don Drysdale and Sandy Koufax were dominating the National League with the Dodgers in the early and middle '60s. He'd won twenty-three more games in 2002, and though he'd suffered through an injury-plagued 2003, there was one thing about Schilling that interested every contending team in baseball: He was invariably at his best during the biggest games, and his numbers reflected that. In eleven postseason starts, he was 5–1 with a 1.66 ERA, with ninety-one strikeouts (and only seventeen walks) in eighty-six and two-thirds innings. Those were staggering figures.

Best of all, Curt Schilling was *available.*

Naturally, since Schilling carried a price tag for the 2004 season in the amount of $12 million, the Yankees were the first team to jump into the mix. And the Diamondbacks, eager to rein in their payroll and more willing to start trading their big-ticket stars for more reasonably priced younger players, grasped that the Yankees stood to be their most likely dance partner. This was more complicated than it sounded, given the long-simmering feud between the Diamondbacks' chairman and CEO,

Jerry Colangelo, and George Steinbrenner. The two men had clashed for years over Buck Showalter (whom Colangelo hired to be the Diamondbacks' first manager within hours after his contract with the Yankees expired in 1995), Bernie Williams (whom Arizona wooed as a free agent in 1998), and David Wells (who broke a handshake agreement with Colangelo after Steinbrenner offered a sweeter deal in 2001—not long after Colangelo's Diamondbacks had defeated Steinbrenner's Yankees in an epic seven-game World Series). Still, the Yankees had the deepest pockets in baseball. And business was business. So it came as little surprise when Schilling—who'd expressed a desire to end his career either in Phoenix, his hometown, or in Philadelphia, where he'd become a star—told Ed Price of the *East Valley Tribune* on November 11 that he'd expanded his list.

"They asked me if I would be willing to talk to the Yankees," Schilling told the reporter. "It's something I thought about for a while. I went back to them and said yes."

There was one hitch: The Diamondbacks were demanding the Yankees' two best bargaining chips in return, Alfonso Soriano and Nick Johnson. And they wouldn't budge. If Colangelo was going to feed the Yankee machine, it would come at a premium. Plus, if Schilling stayed in Arizona, his value would only increase by the July 31 trading deadline. He stood firm. The Yankees turned their attention to Montreal's Javier Vazquez—nearly a decade younger than Schilling and available for much less. By December 4, Vazquez would be a Yankee, traded for Johnson and outfielder Juan Rivera.

And by then, Schilling had officially signed up with the enemy.

It took a marathon session of negotiation, the details of which would make Steinbrenner squirm. For starters, the Diamondbacks were willing to take far less than the ransom they'd demanded from the Yankees—pitchers Casey Fossum, Brandon Lyon, and Jorge de la Rosa and minor-league outfielder Michael Goss. Then, with Schilling willing to listen—and with his friend Francona all but guaranteed the manager's job—he invited Lucchino, Theo Epstein, and Boston's assistant director of baseball operations, Jed Hoyer, to visit his Paradise Valley, Arizona, home. Major League Baseball granted the Red Sox a seventy-two-hour window to negotiate the two-year extension that would lock up the deal, then extended the deadline by a few hours after a Thanksgiving dinner session between Schilling and Epstein brought them ever closer.

By the next day, it was done.

"I want to be a part of bringing the first World Series in modern history to Boston," Schilling said. "I guess I hate the Yankees now."

Suddenly, forty-nine days after Aaron Boone, the Red Sox had thrown a counterpunch, and it floored Steinbrenner, who suddenly saw an immediate shift in the balance of power atop the American League. Schilling was on board. The Red Sox were already engaged in a full-court press with free-agent relief pitcher Keith Foulke, officially abandoning the bullpen-by-committee strategy in favor of one of baseball's top closers.

Meanwhile, the Yankees were in a serious state of flux. Against the wishes of his own general manager, Steinbrenner handed a two-year deal to aging speedster Kenny Lofton, an obvious panic reaction to the emergence of Johnny Damon as a classic leadoff man for the Red Sox. He personally handled negotiations with free-agent slugger Gary Sheffield, then watched with horror and anger when Sheffield—a long-time favorite of Steinbrenner thanks to his Tampa roots—backed out of the deal at the last moment. (Sheffield would later reconsider, but only after Steinbrenner began a dalliance with Vladimir Guerrero.) And the Yankees' pitching staff, long its impenetrable strength, was suddenly quite vulnerable: Roger Clemens had retired. David Wells, after initially agreeing to a make-good minor-league contract, bailed on that when the San Diego Padres offered guaranteed money. Most shocking of all, Andy Pettitte had decided to accept a free-agent contract with the Houston Astros, meaning 60 percent of the Yankees' rotation had vaporized.

Pettitte had long been a symbol of how very well things tended to go for the Yankees through the years, even when they weren't trying.

"Take nothing away from the Yankees, they're great and they deserve respect," said Johnny Pesky, who's had a front-row seat to this feud for fifty-five years as a player, broadcaster, coach, and manager, and who just happened to be born on September 27, 1919—the last day Babe Ruth ever wore a Red Sox uniform. "But they are also the luckiest fucking baseball team in the history of mankind."

Pesky was referring to the way the Yankees nearly let Pettitte go for a song as a rookie. This was 1995, and the Yankees coveted an Anaheim Angels veteran left-hander named Mark Langston. To showcase Pettitte, whom the Angels expressed an interest in, the Yankees started him in the exhibition game that would christen Denver's Coors Field. It didn't work. In three innings, Pettitte allowed seven hits and three runs, and the Angels' scouts didn't even wait to get back to California before informing the Yankees they weren't interested.

That day would come to summarize in a neat bundle all the good Yankee fortune that drove Red Sox fans crazy for so many years. Think of it: What if Pettitte had thrown a tidy five-hitter that day? What if anyone had known what a graveyard for pitchers Coors Field would turn out to be? Remember, this was the *first game* ever played there; soon enough, scouts would know that seven hits in three innings at Coors' mile-high altitude wasn't such a dreadful pitching line at all, but more like the norm. And of course, there is this: Pettitte would win 149 games across the next nine years and compile an especially crucial 13–5 mark against the Red Sox. Langston, for whom the Yankees so desperately pined, won exactly twenty-eight more games the rest of his career.

"Stuff like that," Johnny Pesky said in February 2004. "That's what I'm talking about. How great would it be to have taken Pettitte away from that team the last nine years? But that's what happens. The Yankees are like Ali. We're Joe Frazier. We look good in the ring together. But damned if they don't always look a little bit better."

That was all about to change, though.

Back on November 11, the first whispers began to emerge that the Red Sox, Texas Rangers, and Angels were in preliminary discussions for a blockbuster three-way trade. The principals: Manny Ramirez, whom the Red Sox had placed on unconditional waivers two weeks before, hoping someone would take Ramirez' flighty attitude and his $20 million annual salary off their hands (though no team took the bait). And Alex Rodriguez, the consensus choice as baseball's single greatest talent. "That's baseless," Theo Epstein said. "It's totally false."

But the rumors never evaporated. Six days later, on a conference call where he was announced as the American League's Most Valuable Player, Rodriguez spent most of the call addressing speculation he would be moved. Six days after *that*, Arn Tellem, the agent for Nomar Garciaparra, felt compelled to issue a statement insisting Garciaparra wanted very much "to stay in Boston, his baseball home." Soon, Jeff Moorad, Ramirez' agent, released a similar testimonial on *his* client's behalf. Clearly, someone was talking to somebody about *something*.

On December 6, the walls of denial came tumbling down at last. Word leaked to several media outlets that John Henry had, in fact, already met with Rodriguez to gauge his interest in coming to Boston, a summit that had been cleared through commissioner Bud Selig to avoid the appearance of tampering. Now, with the story out in the open, emotions flared everywhere. A furious George Steinbrenner called up Brian Cashman and wanted to know why the Yankees hadn't been informed of Rodriguez' availability—never mind the fact that there really wasn't anywhere for A-Rod to play on the Yankees, unless he wanted to try his hand as a starting pitcher. Garciaparra, married the previous weekend to soccer star Mia Hamm, actually called from his honeymoon to reaffirm his affinity for the Red Sox: "It's been the only uniform I know and it's the only uniform I want to know my entire career," to which the Red Sox responded by revealing Garciaparra had turned down a four-year, $60 million extension the previous spring.

By December 15, the city of Boston was fully immersed in A-Rod mania, and slowly the details of a purported deal were surfacing. The Red Sox and Rangers would swap Rodriguez and Ramirez, exchanging the two biggest contracts in baseball history. The Red Sox would then ship Garciaparra to the Chicago White Sox in exchange for Magglio

Ordonez, a hard-hitting outfielder who would, like Garciaparra, be eligible for free agency after the season. Yankees fans, including the number one Yankees fan sitting in the owner's office at Legends Field in Tampa, were numb. Every few days, the Red Sox were getting stronger. Every few days, it seemed, the Red Sox were inching a few lengths ahead of the Yankees. And they were powerless to stop it.

"After a while, you wanted to remind him that, you know, we'd actually beaten these guys on the field a few months before," one Yankee employee would say. "But that wouldn't have done any good."

The momentum seemed unstoppable.

Except, at the last possible moment, it not only stopped, it backtracked, and it wound up wiping the trade out completely.

On December 16, Henry, Rodriguez, and agent Scott Boras met in New York to try to hammer out the deal's final details. A growing sense of inevitability had already attached itself to these proceedings, and speculation about Steinbrenner's possible countermoves was already electric on the city's streets.

But it was here that the dimensions of Rodriguez' contract—ten years and $252 million, the fattest deal in the history of American team sports—seemed finally to weigh heavily on Henry's shoulders.

The Red Sox, Henry said, would need Rodriguez to restructure the contract, and offered a deferred-payment solution that would reduce Boston's burden by $28 million over the life of the contract. Rodriguez, desperate to escape last place, authorized Boras to agree, and even Boras, the most ruthless agent ever born, understood the wisdom of agreeing to the deal.

But Gene Orza, the deputy director of the Players Association, did not. And he was willing to play the bad guy in all of this, saying that the last thing Alex Rodriguez should consider doing was setting such a precedent, although he did suggest a counterplan by which the Red Sox would get relief of some $16 million. Rodriguez could have ignored Orza's advice, no matter how strong, a point Red Sox fans would emphasize in the months ahead. He did not. And the Red Sox, refusing to pay the extra $12 million in the Orza plan, finally pulled the cord.

"The deal," Larry Lucchino announced on December 17, "is dead."

With that, everything seemed settled on a path toward relative normalcy. The teams completed some quiet transactions—the Red Sox adding infielders Mark Bellhorn and Pokey Reese, the Yankees welcoming reserves Miguel Cairo and Tony Clark, and strengthening their bullpen by signing Tom Gordon and Paul Quantrill. By Valentine's Day, both teams were eager to shift their operations south and get on with the business of baseball again.

That was the plan, anyway

Except that morning, on the back pages of *Newsday* and the *New York Post*, there landed on doorsteps all across New York the news that would rock baseball—and Boston—to its core in a way that would make Aaron Boone's home run seem like a routine groundout to shortstop.

The Yankees and the Rangers were talking about a trade.

For Alex Rodriguez.

One longtime observer of the Yankees–Red Sox relationship would later summarize the feelings of an entire baseball region when he described his first reaction to that little piece of news.

"Holy shit," Johnny Pesky said.

The Yankees' motivation to pay top dollar for Babe Ruth as 1919 folded into 1920 was precisely the same as the impetus that would land Alex Rodriguez in pinstripes eight and a half decades later: They were stars, *superstars*, the brightest and boldest in the baseball firmament. New York City has long been a place where stars find their constituency, a city that lionizes the famous and shepherds them to a level of eminence unknown anywhere else in the world. That ditty they play at the end of every contemporary Yankees game, the one that boasts that if you can make it there, you'll make it anywhere? Fred Ebb and John Kander wrote that lyric in 1976. But the attitude that inspired that catchy libretto was born decades before.

The Red Sox of the early twentieth century, like the Yankees a hundred years later, always had a surplus of stars. Cy Young propelled the earliest Boston champions; Smokey Joe Wood and Tris Speaker drove the teams that dominated baseball in 1912 and 1915. And, of course, there was Ruth, whose left arm helped fuel the franchise's last two championships, in 1916 and 1918. So vast was Boston's stockpile of talent, in fact, that it led to a serious—and ultimately devastating—case of hubris. Young was unceremoniously dumped before the 1909 season, when he still had thirty-three wins left in his right arm. Speaker held out before the 1916 season when, despite leading the Sox to a World Series title the year before, Boston owner Joseph Lannin decided to slash Speaker's $18,000 salary in half.

Lannin let it be known his best player was available, and the Yankees' colorful new owner, Colonel Jacob Ruppert, desperate to find a name to post on the Polo Grounds marquee, offered an open checkbook and any name presently on his roster. Speaker wound up with the Cleveland Indians. Only later was it revealed that Ban Johnson, president of the American League, had a financial stake in the Cleveland team. Ruppert swore revenge, both on the president whose unethical double-dealing had cost him a star and on the franchise that played along with the ruse.

He would score on both fronts soon enough.

Boston would go eighty-five consecutive years without flying a World Series pennant from the Fenway Park flagpole in the days dating from December 26, 1919, when Ruth was shipped to New York. But just as significantly, the Red Sox rarely approached the Yankees in terms of star power. The Yankees always had more toys, always had more stars, whether the calendar read 1923 or 1953 or 2003. This may explain why Red Sox fans tend to attach their fevered devotions so completely to their stars of the moment. Pedro Martinez, therefore, is not just the best pitcher in baseball; because he belongs to Boston, his powers are practically mystical. And because in 2003, he would have a natural foil in Roger Clemens—the excommunicated idol—his mission was practically sacred.

Nomar Garciaparra was the other Red Sox player who understood this frame of reference. At the end of the 2003 season, almost everyone in baseball—Garciaparra included—would surely have agreed that the best shortstop in the game was Alex Rodriguez. In most of those same well-trained eyes, you would encounter little resistance if you labeled Garciaparra the sport's second-best shortstop. His numbers, through the first seven full seasons of his career, were fast-track Hall of Fame figures: a .323 batting average and power figures that worked out to roughly twenty-eight homers and 108 runs batted in per season. Other than Rodriguez himself, no shortstop had ever maintained numbers like that for so long in the whole history of baseball.

And yet . . .

"I don't worry myself with things I can't control," Garciaparra said during spring training of 2004. "And one of the things I can't control is the way people compare me with other players. It's natural that they want to compare me with Derek Jeter. It's natural, and yet it's totally irrelevant to me."

To him, maybe.

But to Red Sox fans, the question had long bordered on mania. Derek Jeter had become the clear favorite among many factions annoying to New England: teenyboppers, talking heads, media outside New England. And, of course, Yankees fans.

"If you think Jeter is the better player," Red Sox fan Mike Carey said, "you're proving how little you know about baseball."

Yankees fans, of course, find statements like that perfectly ludicrous.

"My guy has four rings, and by rights he should have five or six," Frank Russo said. "How many rings does their guy have? How many rings have any of their shortstops had since 1918? Do any of them even know who the shortstop was the last time the Red Sox won the World Series? Does anyone?"

It's true, Jeter did have four World Series rings, and along with Mariano Rivera he was the acknowledged foundation around which the modern Yankee dynasty was built. That status was unchallenged. But his lifetime batting average *was* seven points lower than Nomar's. His twenty-four home runs in 1999, a career high, *were* four fewer than Garciaparra's *average* output, and he'd driven in one hundred runs exactly once, also in 1999. Jeter's lifetime fielding percentage of .972 was three points higher than Garciaparra's, but every scout with a working set of instincts would tell you Garciaparra's range, the standard point of comparison for shortstops, was far greater.

Yet none of this seemed to matter.

Not in New York City, certainly. Nor was it an incidental fact that Alex Rodriguez never agreed to play third base to accommodate Nomar Garciaparra, but in the first week of February 2004, he certainly did consent to the move out of respect to Derek Jeter, and that was the key to his becoming a Yankee.

"If Nomar and Pedro played in New York . . . ," Mike Carey said.

He didn't finish the thought.

He didn't have to. Red Sox fans always notice. They keep score. On a bright, sunny Sunday in July 2003, a twenty-eight-year-old paralegal named Harry Killian had woken up early, gone to nine o'clock Mass, proceeded directly to Fenway Park . . . and spent three straight hours "killing" Derek Jeter from his sniper's nest behind the Yankee dugout, along third base.

"Freaking Jeter," Killian said in between innings as he tried to salvage his voice. "He's young. He's good-looking. He wins all the time." Killian shook his head, fired off a "Jeter! You suuuuck!" and then pondered his quarry some more. "When you think about it," Killian said, "he *is* the Yankees. He makes me ill."

It is telling that the one Yankee to whom Derek Jeter was most often compared was Joe DiMaggio; it's equally significant that the last Red Sox player to earn the consistent praise of Ted Williams was Nomar Garciaparra.

Jeter's quiet elegance and dashing style easily summoned the young

DiMaggio. Both men relished their privacy while simultaneously enjoying their well-earned places as princes of the city. DiMaggio favored the Stork Club, or Toots Shor's saloon, where table 1 was always his for the asking; Jeter's preferred haunts included the Broome Street Bar and Veruka. Wherever they went, the night seemed to follow—as did a gaggle of starlets and showgirls, movie stars and photographers.

"I like what I see of this kid, Jeter," DiMaggio said in 1997, Jeter's second year as a big leaguer. "He reminds me of Phil Rizzuto. And I think he's just as valuable to this Yankees team as Rizzuto was to us, I really do."

"To even see my name in the same sentence as Joe DiMaggio," Jeter said in 1999, shortly after DiMaggio's death, "blows my mind."

Garciaparra, meanwhile, immediately captured the imagination of his franchise forebear. At the 1999 All-Star Game, held at Fenway Park, Garciaparra was one of the players whom Williams sought out, greeting him as he would a favored nephew. "He's as good a young player as anyone I've ever seen come into the big leagues," Williams said of Garciaparra. "He's tremendous. One of the very best young hitters I ever saw. He's a smart kid and he knows all about hitting."

"I can't imagine a higher compliment than that," a humbled Garciaparra said.

In their day, in their era, DiMaggio and Williams faced the same daily comparisons as Jeter and Garciaparra, Clemens and Martinez. In some ways, it was an easier grind—there was no such thing as twenty-four-hour sports talk radio in the 1940s and '50s, no Internet chat rooms, and relatively few newspaper reporters who believed in gathering quotes before and after every game. Yet, in its own way, the crush they faced was even more intense. Baseball was king in those simpler years. Only a championship prizefight or the occasional horse race could compete with baseball for the nation's less-addled attention span, and the public fascination with both men was enormous.

Especially since DiMaggio and Williams seemed to spend so much of their careers lurking within each other's shadow, performing their heroics in each other's company. During the ten years in which their careers overlapped—from 1939 to 1942, and from 1946 to 1951—the Yankees won seven pennants, the Red Sox won once, and in the other two years, 1940 and 1948, both teams were in the race until the very end of the season. DiMaggio's Yankees famously knocked Williams out of the World Series on the last weekend of the 1949 season; not nearly as well remembered is the fact that the Red Sox, thanks in large part to the greatest extended period of clutch hitting in Williams' career, had done exactly the same thing to the Yankees the year before. DiMaggio was named most valuable player of the American League three times; Williams earned the award twice and easily could have won it—probably *should* have won it—three other times.

"Playing on the same field with those two was like playing with a couple of gods," Johnny Pesky said in the spring of 2004. "They were larger than life. They were larger than the game. Sometimes, you would look at DiMaggio, and you would look at Williams, and you would wonder, 'What in the hell do I possibly have in common with these two?' The rest of us, we were playing baseball. Those two, they played some other kind of game, on some other kind of level."

Said Phil Rizzuto: "You couldn't take your eyes off either one of them."

The first time they met, April 20, 1939, opening day, there were ten future Hall of Famers on the field at Yankee Stadium, five on each side. For Williams' first-ever major-league game, he would share a lineup with Lefty Grove, Jimmie Foxx, Bobby Doerr, and Joe Cronin; in the other dugout, there were DiMaggio, Lou Gehrig, Bill Dickey, Red Ruffing, and Lefty Gomez. Babe Ruth was in the stands, sitting near the Yankees' dugout, and the pregame ceremonies were held up fifteen minutes because the iconic emblems of both teams had been delayed by traffic. It was a heady place to start a remarkable career.

"There they were," Williams later wrote of seeing the Yankees on that first day on the job. "A hell of a lineup. I'm watching them, studying them all, and I remember so distinctly, I said to myself, 'I *know* I can hit as good as these guys.'"

When Williams stepped to the plate for the first time in the top of the second inning, Ruffing, the former Red Sox, was waiting for him. Ruffing was squarely in his prime, soon to produce a fourth consecutive twenty-win season, and he started off with a whistling fastball that Williams barely fouled back. He followed with a curveball, which Williams also fouled off. And when Ruffing put Williams away with another curve, completely overmatching the nervous newbie, Williams trudged back to the dugout, still steamed that he hadn't caught up with the fastball. Jack Wilson, a veteran Red Sox pitcher, approached the red-faced rookie, who'd stunned so many of his teammates in spring training with his brash approach and his swaggering gait.

"What do you think of this league now, Bush?" Wilson asked, taunting the kid soon to be nicknamed the Kid.

"Fuck you," Williams replied. "That's one guy I *know* I'm going to hit. If he puts that fucking pitch in the same place again, I'm riding it out of here."

He nearly did, too. In the fourth, Ruffing again tried to sneak a high fastball past the kid's bat. Not this time. Williams lashed a low line drive that smashed off the 407-foot sign in right-center field, and he pulled into second with the first of his 2,654 major-league hits, the first of 1,117 that would go for extra bases. He still wasn't happy.

"Two feet higher," he griped later, "and that's out of here."

More than the hit, Williams would remember the game as the only time he stood on the same field with Lou Gehrig, who grounded meekly into a pair of double plays but, in his third time up, hit a screaming line drive straight at Williams in right field. Later in the month, a three-game series between the teams was washed out at Fenway Park, and it was a few days after *that* when Gehrig finally took himself out of the lineup, in Detroit, ending a streak in which he'd played in 2,130 consecutive games.

"He was already sick when we played them in New York," Williams would recall years later, "and nobody knew it."

Williams and DiMaggio would spend a large portion of their careers shadow-boxing each other, constantly fueled by the continuous com-

parisons. Never would they be so closely aligned in the national conversation than throughout the schizophrenic summer of 1941, when the
country badly needed a diversion, something to blunt the unending
torrent of troublesome headlines and news bulletins arriving from
across the sea. During the baseball season alone, Adolf Hitler pulled off
a stunning aerial attack on Crete; the Luftwaffe pounded London, striking Westminster Abbey; the German army invaded Russia, the most
ambitious military campaign ever launched; and the leaders of imperial
Japan began piecing together a diabolical plan intended to crush the
slumbering U.S. Navy, much of which was anchored in a Hawaiian base
unknown to most American citizens, an exotic-sounding quay called
Pearl Harbor.

"You read the sports section a lot," Phil Rizzuto said, "because you
were afraid of what you'd see in the other parts of the paper."

It was against this baleful backdrop that Joe DiMaggio and Ted
Williams co-authored the most remarkable baseball summer of all
time. On May 30, Memorial Day, the two converged at Fenway Park,
where the teams met for a doubleheader that drew 34,500 people to the
cramped confines, while another 25,000 were turned away at the gate.
This happened again and again that summer, in ballparks and theaters,
in restaurants and amusement parks, people flocking to their recre-
ational pursuits in record numbers, as if everyone understood this
would be a final, fleeting flavor of normalcy for a long time.

On this day, the Red Sox fans who squeezed their way inside Fenway
saw a split decision: The Yankees won the opener, 4–3, while the Sox
exacted revenge with a 13–0 throttling in the nightcap. DiMaggio had
hits in both games, extending a modest hitting streak to sixteen consecutive games; more noteworthy were the six hits Williams collected during the twin bill, lifting his average to .429 on the season, sparking the
first public debates about whether he could maintain that average
across the long season and become the first big leaguer since Bill Terry
in 1930 to hit .400 or better.

Soon enough, of course, it would be DiMaggio who would generate all the attention, as his hitting streak grew from sixteen to twenty-five, from thirty to forty-two, which broke George Sisler's modern-day record of forty-one. Before long, the final impediment separating DiMaggio from eternal acclaim was Wee Willie Keeler, the 140-pound wisp of an outfielder who once plied his trade for the New York Highlanders but before that, in 1897, had hit in forty-four consecutive games as a member of the National League's old Baltimore Orioles.

DiMaggio was sitting on forty-two when the Red Sox paid a visit to Yankee Stadium for a July 1 doubleheader. Despite temperatures that inched near one hundred degrees, the games drew a midweek gathering of 53,832. And while the Yankees delighted these customers by sweeping the Sox and stretching their lead atop the American League to two and a half games over Cleveland, what sent them into their loudest spasms of euphoria were the two hits DiMaggio collected in the first game, extending his streak to forty-three games, and the first-inning single off Williams' old friend Jack Wilson that drew him even with Keeler, at forty-four, in the second game. The next day, DiMaggio reached uncharted territory in the fifth inning, smoking his eighteenth home run of the year off Dick Newsome.

That ball sailed high and far over the head of the Red Sox left fielder, who gamely gave chase until he saw it disappear into a tangle of arms ten rows behind the fence. The cowed witness shook his head with wonder later on as he described what the Yankee Clipper had done.

"I really wish I could hit like that guy DiMaggio," Ted Williams gushed. "I'm being honest. Joe's big and strong and he can club that ball without any effort. These hot days I wear myself out laying into it, and I lose seven or eight pounds out there. When it's hot, I lose my snap or something. But not Joe."

That humility would serve Williams well a few months later, when the votes for the league's Most Valuable Player Award were tabulated, DiMaggio receiving 291 votes to Williams' 254. DiMaggio's hitting streak reached fifty-six, a number that has earned a permanent place in the sport's mythology. The fact that Williams had seven more home runs and just five fewer RBIs—playing on a much weaker team—didn't sway voters, nor did the fact that he famously went six for eight on the season's final day to raise his batting average from .3995 to .406. No player in the sixty-three years since has come within sixteen points of that number.

Williams would soon grow uncomfortably used to these postseason snubs. The next year, the MVP inexplicably went to Yankees second baseman Joe Gordon, who may have been only the third most valuable player *on his own team.* And in 1947, DiMaggio again earned the nod of the baseball writers, who deemed his season (.315, twenty home runs, ninety-seven RBIs) superior to that of Williams (.343, thirty-two, and 114), a referendum reached thanks to one writer from Detroit (*not* from Boston, a fable that has long been advanced) who failed to list Williams on his ballot at all. Even a tenth-place vote would have put Williams over the top.

"I guess you could argue that the team that wins the pennant ought to have the MVP on their side," mused Pesky, Williams' longtime friend. "I guess you could argue that Teddy wasn't as friendly with the writers as he could have been, didn't curry their favor, and that bit him in the ass time and time again. But if you're asking me if the fact he played in Boston instead of New York had anything to do with it? I won't argue the point with you."

Of course, you could always argue that DiMaggio was simply the better player. Williams was perfectly willing to concede that years later, when he wrote, "Joe was a better fielder than I was. A better thrower. Everything he did was stylish. He ran gracefully, he fielded gracefully, he hit with authority and style. Even when Joe missed he looked good. It is also true, of course, that in his thirteen years with the Yankees they won the pennant ten times. That has to be a factor."

DiMaggio himself, though he would never say the words exactly, surely believed it. Asked once, in 1950, what he thought about Williams, DiMaggio said, "I think that Ted is the greatest left-handed hitter of all time."

"Fine," the interrogator asked. "But what about Williams as an all-round player?"

DiMaggio let a beat pass by, smiled a wry smile.

"I think," he said, "that Ted is the greatest left-handed hitter of all time."

The Williams-DiMaggio rivalry nearly reached a staggering climax twice within the space of three months in late 1946. On the eve of that year's World Series between the Cardinals and the Red Sox—the only fall classic in which Ted Williams would ever compete—word leaked through the Boston newspapers that Red Sox owner Tom Yawkey was pondering an unthinkable deal for the coming off-season, regardless of how the Series played out: Williams for DiMaggio, straight up. Everyone quickly denied it, and whether the rumors bothered Williams—he would hit only .200 in the Series, a failure over which he despaired the rest of his life—he never admitted as much. That time, it was likely the product of the fertile imagination of Boston's always provocative fourth estate.

Two months later, it was an entirely different story. And a legitimate one.

Sometime in mid-December, Larry MacPhail, one-third of the Yankees' ownership group and the one primarily charged with procuring player personnel, invited Yawkey, his friend and rival, out to dinner during one of Yawkey's frequent stops in New York. They went to Toots Shor's, the most famous sports saloon of its time, a place where poets and politicians, wiseguys and writers, judges and jurors all gathered to swap lies and put the world to bed through the endless New York night. Both MacPhail and Yawkey were drinkers of some renown, so they ordered one round, then another, then some steaks, and then another round. They exchanged small talk. They told jokes. MacPhail told tall tales of his service in both world wars; Yawkey spoke in aggrieved tones about the recent integration of baseball, how it pained his Old South soul to its core (the Red Sox would be the last team to dissolve the color barrier, in 1959, some *twelve years* after Jackie Robinson). They ordered another round. And another. Yawkey was getting drunker and drunker and didn't seem to notice that MacPhail, whenever he repaired to the bathroom, was taking *his* drink with him and dumping it in the toilet.

MacPhail had serious business to discuss and wanted to remain clear-eyed.

Along around two in the morning, he finally made his pitch.

"Let's do it, Tom," he said. "Let's make the deal."

"What deal?" Yawkey asked.

"DiMaggio for Williams. Let's make it happen."

They talked it through, and even Yawkey had to admit it made perfect sense in a lot of daring ways. Yawkey would get DiMaggio, who was already an icon to millions of Italian-American New Yorkers and who would surely be similarly adopted by Boston's sizable Italian population. DiMaggio's brother Dominic was already there. And the idea of DiMaggio taking aim at the left-field wall, 315 feet away, was almost enough to bring tears to an owner's eyes. How many DiMaggio home runs through the years had been swallowed whole by Yankee Stadium's left-field power alley, Death Valley, 457 feet from home plate? This would even his ledger, and then some.

MacPhail? He wanted the deal in the first place because he figured Williams would slaughter Babe Ruth's home run record the very first year he had seventy-seven games to fire away at Yankee Stadium's short right-field porch, only 296 feet down the right-field line. Williams was also four years younger than DiMaggio. And MacPhail had already spent much of 1946 convincing himself that the best of DiMaggio had been left behind on wartime exhibition fields. He'd even proposed a trade of DiMaggio for Washington's Mickey Vernon, and the Senators, remarkably, had turned it down. But that was Mickey Vernon. This was *Ted Williams*.

"Deal!" Yawkey said. They shook on it. They had one more for the road. They toasted their new stars.

And then morning arrived.

Sleepy, thick-tongued, his head still heavy with drink, Tom Yawkey called Larry MacPhail at his Yankee Stadium office. MacPhail was already preparing how he would spin the news, how he would make the newspapers see the wisdom of this seismic shift.

"I can't do it," Yawkey said. "I'll get run out of town if I give the Yankees Babe Ruth all over again."

"We had a deal!" MacPhail protested.

"We'll still have one if you throw in the kid catcher from Newark."

"You're out of your mind, Tom."

"Sorry, Larry," Yawkey rasped. "Can't do it."

The two men hung up. Williams kept his red socks. DiMaggio stayed a Yankee. And so did the kid catcher from Newark, a prospect off the St. Louis sandlots named Yogi Berra.

Williams would describe the near-trade years later.

"I knew New York was one town I did *not* want to play in," he wrote. "I didn't like Yankee Stadium. A bad background in center field when the crowd is big, and all that smoke hanging in there. It's not a conventional park. As an outfielder, you had to get used to it. I remember when Gehrig hit the first ball ever hit to me in Yankee Stadium my rookie year, he didn't really rip it, just a mediocre line drive, and I staggered around and staggered around and finally caught it right where I had started. I always felt jacked up in Yankee Stadium because of the crowds, but I never wanted to play there."

Remarkably, years later, he had one last opportunity to change his mind.

A few weeks after Williams played his final game for the Red Sox—September 28, 1960, when Williams fatefully said farewell to Boston with a home run off Baltimore's Jack Fisher in his final Fenway Park plate appearance—Williams' business manager, Fred Corcoran, got a call from Dan Topping, co-owner of the Yankees. They met at the Savoy Plaza in New York, and Topping got right to the point.

"Would Williams play one year for the Yankees, strictly as a pinch hitter, for $125,000?" Topping asked.

Corcoran was intrigued. Williams was still technically the property of the Red Sox, even in retirement, thanks to the old reserve clause that was standard in every player contract until 1975 and bound a player to his team in perpetuity. But Corcoran knew Tom Yawkey well enough to be aware that if Williams wanted to take the Yankees up on their golden parachute, the Boston owner wouldn't stand in anyone's way. So Corcoran called Williams. Who told him to forget it.

"What does New York have to offer?" Williams asked. "Just a lot of bad air. And a lot of bad traffic jams."

Sixteen years later, another Boston star would have this to say about Fun City: "You know what they should do with New York? Clear all the people out and drop a hydrogen bomb on it. That's what I think of New York. I get a terrible headache every time we fly in there. I mean, we're flying in, and I look out the window and the headache begins. It doesn't leave until we're flying out. That's New York. I don't have that headache anywhere else in the country, but I get it in New York."

The speaker was Carlton Fisk.

And Fisk made up one-half of the other great positional debate that occupied the obsessions of Red Sox and Yankees fans between the dusk of the Williams-DiMaggio era and the dawning of Jeter-Garciaparra. Fisk and Thurman Munson, the Yankees' fireplug, firebrand catcher, lit up much of the 1970s with their snarling competitions and their ferocious ambitions. Each man won a Rookie of the Year Award in the American League (Munson in 1970, Fisk two years later). Each played an integral role on pennant-winning teams and made the most of October's defining glare (Fisk's home run to win game six of the '75 World Series, and the body English he employed trying to will the ball fair, is among the most famous images in baseball history; Munson hit .357 in thirty postseason games). Munson made seven appearances in the All-Star game between 1971 and '78; Fisk made six.

Better still, they disliked each other intensely.

Best of all, unlike the subtle simmering that marked the Williams-DiMaggio relationship of a generation before, they made no pretense any other way.

The rivalry was grounded in ego. Munson had made the first big splash in 1970 and seemed certain to roam unchallenged as the American League's catcher of the 1970s, the junior circuit's answer to Johnny Bench. But when Fisk emerged in 1972, leading the Sox to within a half game of a division title, he immediately surpassed Munson in the public's fancy. Fisk was big, strong, and handsome, Paul Bunyan with a chest protector, New England to his bones, born in Vermont, raised in New Hampshire, now performing exquisitely for the Olde Towne Team in Massachusetts. Munson was short, boxy, from the decidedly unpoetic city of Canton, Ohio, his Fu Manchu mustache seemingly always draped around a scowl.

In 1971, during a late September call-up, Fisk had unwittingly fanned the first embers of this feud by unintentionally embarrassing Munson. In the middle of a meaningless game between two teams already eliminated from the playoffs, with a runner on first, Munson hit a bouncing ball wide of the first-base bag. The first baseman easily pegged the lead runner at second but was so out of position that Munson figured there was no way he'd be doubled up. But Fisk was charging right behind and nearly beat Munson to the bag for an inconceivable 3-6-2 double play.

Red Sox fans were devoted to Fisk.

But Yankees fans were virtual acolytes in the cult of Thurman.

"I used to add fuel to that fire," said Gene Michael, a longtime Munson teammate, now a Yankees front-office executive. "Munson was my roommate. I'd get a picture of a magazine with Fisk in it, I'd gather these magazines and clippings and stuff, and I'd always stick it in Thurman's locker. He didn't know who was doing it, and nobody gave me up as the guy who was doing it.

"Finally, one day, they'd been piling up the stuff I'd put in it; he came running out of that locker and screamed, 'What the hell, do you guys think this is funny or something? This ain't funny anymore!' He was a very prideful guy and I guess it bothered him the way he'd be overlooked. He wasn't the glamorous-looking guy; Thurman always felt a little slighted, but he was an outstanding player. They were both outstanding players."

Whatever tensions may have lurked under the surface exploded one sunny afternoon in Boston, August 1, 1973, which, coincidence or not, also happened to be a week that featured Carlton Fisk on the cover of *Sports Illustrated.* In a 2–2 game, Munson led off the top of the ninth inning with a double, advanced to third on a Graig Nettles groundout, and then, after a walk to Felipe Alou, charged home on the front end of a suicide squeeze play. Michael was batting. He never got the bunt down. Munson kept charging anyway, on and through Fisk, who held on to the ball and flipped Munson onto his head for good measure. Munson responded with a straight right hand to Fisk's chin, and the benches emptied.

"He flipped me over with his feet after the play was over," Munson said. "That's what made me sore. I don't know why he did that. We said a few things and I hit him. He kicked me off him with his feet pretty good. What a fucking shame. I only wish I could have had another chance at him."

Munson, always more of a hothead than a bad guy, tried to make amends the next day, when Fisk stepped to the plate for the first time. "How's your eye?" he asked. Fisk ignored him, and later explained, "I wasn't ready to forgive and let live. I'm not going to be bought off with kind words."

They never did become as close as frat brothers, but eventually the two best catchers in the American League established détente and formed something of a mutual admiration society. Fisk conceded that Munson's quick-strike throws to second base were as close to artistry as the position allows. Munson marveled at Fisk's durability and at his power stroke—although he did allow, late in the 1978 season, "I wouldn't mind switching ballparks with that son of a bitch for one year, see who hits more home runs."

It was a wonderful duel that, like DiMaggio-Williams, seemed destined to end up in the corridors of Cooperstown. But on August 2, 1979—six years and one day after their ugly collision at home plate—Munson clipped a treetop and crashed his private Cessna Citation jet near a runway at the Akron-Canton Regional Airport. Munson, a novice pilot, was practicing takeoffs and landings on an off day. Fisk and Mike Torrez were getting off the Red Sox' bus at Milwaukee's County Stadium later that afternoon, and as they walked into the clubhouse door, a couple of kids approached.

"Hey, Pudge, you hear?" they yelped. "Munson died."

Torrez, a former Munson teammate, immediately felt chills. Fisk wanted to run after the "sick little smart-ass" at first, but realized nobody would joke about something like that. Later, in front of his locker, he fought a losing battle with his emotions.

"We both thought for a while that we were the two best catchers in the American League, and we tried to prove to one another that each of us was better than the other," Fisk said, choking back tears. "That was for three, four, five years. But we really got to respect one another the last three years, personally. I talked to him more than anyone else when we played them. We'd talk about catching, about how we hurt . . ."

Fisk's voice trailed off.

"I'll really miss him."

The depth of dislike that colored the Fisk-Munson rivalry hadn't been reached, or even approached, until now. Suddenly, in the middle of February 2004, Alex Rodriguez had emerged as a singular lightning rod, available for both sides of the Great Divide, accessible to all the passions and energies that drive both sets of fans. What was most incredible—or appalling, depending on your viewpoint—about this deal was the swiftness with which it was accomplished, and the irony that kick-started it into action. Aaron Boone—*Aaron Fucking Boone*—had been playing basketball in early January when he fell hard to the court and heard a pop in his left knee. This was in direct violation of the standard player contract, which routinely forbids such off-season activities as skiing, surfing, or basketball playing. The Yankees were furious and immediately talked of terminating Boone's contract, regardless of what he'd helped them do a few months before. A more pressing concern was this: Who would play third base now?

Brian Cashman pondered the possibilities. Miguel Cairo? Enrique Wilson? Move Alfonso Soriano to third and find another second baseman? He chewed on all of these. And then he dialed the phone, using the 817 area code for Arlington, Texas, and asked John Hart, the Rangers' general manager, a simple question.

"Is A-Rod still available?"

Two weeks later, Rodriguez was standing in front of a bank of microphones, a Yankees cap on his head, a pinstriped number 13 jersey (in honor of Dan Marino, his idol as a kid growing up in Miami) on his back. Not only had Rodriguez been available, he'd been willing to think about giving up his position. Rodriguez had won the last two AL Gold Gloves for shortstops. He was universally acclaimed as the game's slickest fielder at that spot and was well on his way to becoming the greatest two-way shortstop who ever lived. Yet in deference to Derek Jeter, Rodriguez agreed to switch to third base. That possibility had never even been broached with the Red Sox.

As Rodriguez charmed the New York media during his introductory press conference on February 17, an interested bystander watched from the wings.

"This could have been happening in Boston, but somebody fell down," Reggie Jackson said, watching a scene eerily reminiscent of the one when he joined the Yankees twenty-seven years before. "They had a greater need [for the player] than money. . . . Twelve million is huge for normal people but not the people running baseball, especially when it comes to arguably the best player in the game."

But Jackson wasn't there simply to take Boston to task for what it had lost; he was also willing to provide Rodriguez with a first lesson for what *he* had bought into, too.

"It's not about winning 112 or 114 regular-season games around here, it's about winning eleven games in the postseason," Jackson said. "You need guys that will help you win the last eleven games. We were the only team in baseball with the balls to pull this off and take the chance."

A few days later, when the Red Sox migrated to Fort Myers and the Yankees settled in Tampa, it already felt like the middle of September. Both teams were already feisty. Rodriguez showed up a few days early so he could work with Graig Nettles as he took a crash course in learning to play third base, and he virtually gushed at the "gift" that had been bestowed upon him. "I was eliminated from contention in early May or late April the last couple of years," he said. "I've had enough of last place." Then, showing that he'd already taken Jackson's warnings to heart, he had this to say about the prospect of playing his home games at Yankee Stadium: "Well, I'm hoping to play over ninety games there next year." He knew perfectly well that a regular-season schedule includes only eighty-one of them. The extras come in October, if everything goes according to plan. Rodriguez winked. He understood exactly what he was talking about.

The Red Sox, for their part, carried on with their own business, even Kevin Millar, who'd gone on ESPN during the height of A-Rod mania in December and nearly thrown a wedge into the Red Sox clubhouse. Asked by SportsCenter host Dan Patrick if he'd rather have Rodriguez or current teammates Ramirez and Garciaparra, Millar replied: "I'm taking Alex Rodriguez, Schilling, and Foulke." Patrick asked why Millar was "quick to get rid of Nomar and Manny," and Millar kept charging.

"I'm not quick to get rid of them. I mean, it's a tough situation. . . . Nomar Garciaparra is a two-time batting title champion. Manny Ramirez is one of the greatest hitters in the league, but when you're looking at an all-around great player who can hit fifty home runs, drive in 140, and possibly, obviously, win a batting title . . . With his defense, A-Rod is the best in the game. . . . I'm not saying that we'll be better without those two and better with A-Rod. But when you're talking about the greatest player in baseball, I'll take my chances with that."

Oops.

"Don't worry about me, and don't worry about us," Millar effused as he walked into the Fort Myers sunshine for the first time. "I honestly believe that we're going to win the World Series this year."

Garciaparra wasn't quite so happy. "I'm definitely hurt by what happened this winter and I probably feel like anyone else would who spent their whole career in one organization and had to find out you'd been traded, or pretty much gone, over the television," he said upon his arrival. "How would you feel if you were in that situation? I thought their priorities were obviously not for me. They were for somebody else [Rodriguez], and that was pretty evident throughout the whole winter."

That same day, Pedro Martinez said he admired George Steinbrenner for signing Rodriguez "because it shows he'll do anything to win."

That very subject, however, provided the grist for the spring's most surreal showdown. It was a giddy George Steinbrenner who fired the first salvo when reporters caught up with his blue BMW as it exited the Yankees offices in Tampa on February 17, the day of Rodriguez' introductory press conference. Asked about the notion that trading for A-Rod was the equivalent of purchasing a pennant, the Yankees owner began to crow.

"We didn't buy it!" Steinbrenner roared. "[Critics] don't know their math. They don't know what the costs were or were not. We didn't go out and buy him. Texas got a very good deal. I hated to lose Soriano. He'll do great in Texas, given the time. He'll be a great player out there. But you look at the finances before you make that statement. It is a good day for the Yankees, yeah, a very good day. But we haven't won anything yet. It'll be a big spring. It'll determine a lot of things.

"Besides," Steinbrenner went on, "we're not the favorites. The American League East is the toughest division in baseball. I've said it for many years, and every year everybody gets better. Boston is probably the favorite."

John Henry, formerly a limited partner with the Yankees, wasn't buying that last bit, nor was he terribly convinced by Steinbrenner's contention that his baseball people had merely engineered a sound baseball transaction in order to acquire Rodriguez. At precisely 6:04 A.M. the next morning, Henry pushed a button on his laptop computer and sent a stinging rebuttal into the e-mail bins of several newspaper reporters. And his message instantly rocketed the entire notion of this Red Sox–Yankees relationship into a whole different stratosphere.

"We have a spending limit and the Yankees apparently don't," Henry wrote. "Baseball doesn't have an answer for the Yankees. Revenue sharing can only accomplish so much. At some point it becomes confiscation. It has not and it will not solve what is a very obvious problem." A salary cap, Henry noted, "may be the only fair way to deal with a team that has gone so insanely far beyond the resources of all the other teams."

Interestingly, Henry found little sympathy for his claims, probably because, while the Yankees were slated to start the season with a $187 million payroll, Boston's own payroll was creeping past $125 million. The Red Sox were hardly the ideal candidates to be singing the small-market blues. And Steinbrenner immediately called Henry on it.

"We understand John Henry must be embarrassed, frustrated, and disappointed by his failure in this transaction," Steinbrenner said in a prepared statement. "Unlike the Yankees, he chose not to go the extra distance for his fans in Boston. It is understandable, but wrong, that he would try to deflect the accountability for his mistakes on to others and to a system for which he voted in favor. It is time to get on with life and forget the sour grapes."

At this, a worried Bud Selig stepped in and urged both owners to shut up. They did that . . . for three whole days.

On February 21, Henry held court for a few New York reporters at the Sox' training facility and defended the contents of his e-mail rant. "Don't you think it's more compelling if it's a large-market team that's complaining?" Henry asked. "Hypocritical? You think it's hypocritical if you have a high payroll? I mean, people have their own opinions on what happened. There has never been any animosity between George and me. I don't take anything he said personally. He's a guy who takes everything personally. That's one of the differences between us."

And then Henry added this small coda: "I don't mean to equate

[Steinbrenner] with Don Rickles, but if Don Rickles insults you, it's funny. I don't mean that in a negative way. It's just when someone does that all the time . . . I've always laughed at the bellowing."

Steinbrenner, of course, rarely lets anyone get in the last word. And so before Selig could fly to Florida and manually duct-tape the two owners' mouths shut, the Yankees' owner fired off one last parting shot.

"I consider it a great compliment because Rickles is somebody I really like," Steinbrenner said. "Rickles is funny and a warm and caring person. As far as Henry is concerned, he reminds me of Ray Bolger, the scarecrow in the *Wizard of Oz*."

Who needed the season to start? How could it possibly be more fun than this?

8

WE DON'T THROW AT
.260 HITTERS

Obviously, anybody who gets hit isn't too happy. Then things got out of
hand. You lose your emotions sometimes. It's not a good thing for
our sport. You work on yourself for those things not to happen,
but sometimes it happens. —*Jason Varitek, July 24, 2004*

It already was the biggest rivalry long before the Championship Series
ended the way it did last year, before all the off-season moves and
countermoves. I actually think this is going to be on a different level than
even the experienced people in this series have known. Why? Because we
have A-Rod when they thought they had A-Rod and we have A-Rod
because the guy who beat them in game seven blew out his knee.
—*Mike Mussina, April 14, 2004*

Fenway Park is one of the true jewels of American sports, proof that
a stadium needn't be overrun with trendy modern amenities to
satisfy its customers. The seats are too narrow, constructed to fit
the bodies of early-twentieth-century immigrants, who were, on average, three inches shorter and thirty pounds lighter than their great-
grandchildren. The capacity is too small; holding 36,298 (including
standing room), it's easily the tiniest venue in the major leagues, some
20,000 smaller than Yankee Stadium. The unobstructed sightlines are
too few; posts abound, and the odd, antiquated configuration of the

grandstand means that the seats down the right-field line are pointed, more or less, in the vicinity of left field. You have to crane your neck for nine innings to see home plate. A modern architect would lose his license if he came up with such a setup today.

And yet, through the decades, whenever the Red Sox have started making noise about campaigning for a new place to play, the very same people who would benefit most from a modern park crawling with contemporary creature comforts—Red Sox Nation itself—threaten to revolt. No other ballpark has the same physical quirks as Fenway, and no other fan base so completely consumes itself with the physical plant that houses its team. Much of the charm of cheering for the Red Sox, in truth, lies in cheering for them *at* Fenway Park, with its thirty-seven-foot wall in left field, with its manual scoreboard (providing an inning-by-inning account of out-of-town scores, too, a perquisite that vanished from Yankee Stadium for a few weeks early in 2004, before public outrage reversed the omission), with the "Pesky Pole" sitting but 302 feet down the right-field line, so named after Johnny Pesky curled a long fly just inside the pole for one of the six home runs he hit at Fenway during seven full seasons as a Red Sox.

Moving the Red Sox from Fenway to anywhere else—even if it's an exact replica down the block—would be, Boston fans believe, the equivalent of moving Laverne and Shirley from Milwaukee to Los Angeles. And it would constitute a similar jump-the-shark violation.

"Part of the character of this club is the park in which we play our games," Red Sox CEO Larry Lucchino said when the Yankees were in town for a three-game series at the end of July 2003. "People think of the Red Sox and they think of Fenway Park together. Look, nobody is going to tell you this place will stand forever. It's ninety-one years old, for goodness' sake. Even the Roman Coliseum couldn't remain state-of-the-art forever. But as long as it's standing, we're committed to making it what it's always been: the best place on earth to watch a baseball game."

It's funny, too; every time an owner grows restless for the wrecking ball, something akin to baseball providence tends to wrap its protective arms around the brick palace that Roger Clemens mistook for a warehouse all those years ago. After all, within weeks of Tom Yawkey's vow in the summer of 1967 that he'd be playing in either a new ballpark or a new city within five years, the Red Sox recaptured the hearts and souls of New England's baseball fans with a march to the American League pennant that was every bit as theatrical as it was improbable. Yawkey lived nine more years after the end of that gallant pennant push, and never once did he revisit that pledge. Similarly, just as the talk of putting up a note-for-note, brick-for-brick facsimile of Fenway began to gather momentum in the late 1990s and early 2000s, the Red Sox were sold to a group led by John Henry that went against the tide of so many new-age sports owners who lust after brand-new, billion-dollar baseball basilicas. Why, even in New York, George Steinbrenner had spent many hours deriding Yankee Stadium—memorialized in poetry and prose for more than eighty years by awestruck pilgrims—criticizing everything from its physical infrastructure and the dearth of local access roads to a lack of luxury boxes. So strident were his pleas that before the Yankees' championship renaissance in 1996, many wondered: *If the owner doesn't think it makes sense to make a trek to the South Bronx, why should* we?

Henry, Lucchino, and other members of the Sox' top brass went another way. They listened to their fans. Sure, they would never say no to a new ballpark, but getting that done in the city of the Big Dig would take years, perhaps decades, of delicate negotiation. In the meantime, the Red Sox decided to commission architectural Valentines for their ballpark. They constructed "Monster Seats," which were built atop the Wall in left field and were crafted with such care for the overall ballpark experience that once they were in place, in time for the 2003 season, it was difficult to remember what Fenway Park had looked like without them. Similarly, when seats were built on top of the roof in right field, the finished product looked as if it had been in place since April 20, 1912, the day the Red Sox christened their sparkling new ball field with a 7–6 victory over the Yankees.

That, for sure, remains a big part of Fenway Park's relentless charm. You can take your ten-year-old kid there, buy a box seat, and look out on a baseball diamond that looks almost identical to the way it looked when Tris Speaker played here, when Babe Ruth broke in here, when Jimmie Foxx and Ted Williams and Jim Rice slugged here, when Mel Parnell and Jim Lonborg and Roger Clemens hurled here.

"Fenway Park," Red Sox fan Steve Silva said, "was always bigger than life."

Silva is like every other Red Sox fan ever born: He remembers exactly what his first visit to Fenway Park looked like, felt like, sounded like, smelled like. For him, it was June 30, 1975, a doubleheader between the Red Sox and Orioles. In the ninth inning of the opener, a young Sox pitcher named Dick Pole was trying to close out a complete-game shutout. The bases were loaded with one out when Pole threw a fastball to Baltimore's Tony Muser, and Muser sent a screaming line drive back through the box that nearly killed Pole, stealing 90 percent of the vision from his right eye. It's hard to erase a memory like that. Yet that was only one reason why Silva remembered it so well.

"As a kid, you take every mental snapshot you can; everything is totally seared into your memory," he said. "I can still close my eyes and remember everything from that day. The Sox split the doubleheader [maintaining a one-game lead over the second-place Yankees]. We did that a lot when I was a kid. My dad was a cop, and he'd take me and a couple of my friends to a few games each year, we'd make the drive, and stop at Simco's for foot-long hot dogs. It was a big deal going to Boston from Fall River."

Mike Carey's first game was also extraordinary: October 2, 1983. Earlier that season, when Carl Yastrzemski announced his retirement, Carey's older brother, Ed, had bought tickets for the season finale, knowing that would be the last time they'd ever get to watch the great Yaz. The Red Sox had honored Yastrzemski with an emotional ceremony the day before, a hedge against bad weather, but both games that weekend were played in perfect conditions. As a fitting fare-thee-well,

Sox manager Ralph Houk had Yastrzemski play left field that afternoon, where as a kid twenty-two years before he'd started mastering all the quirky bounces and caroms the Wall created, elevating the position to art. The most popular Red Sox player of all didn't get a hit that Sunday afternoon, didn't end his career quite the way Ted Williams had, with a home run in his final at-bat. Nobody in the place cared. Certainly not eleven-year-old Mike Carey.

"I remember that day like I remember my wedding and the birth of my daughter," he said. "We had seats in center field, as close to the Wall as you could get without—at that point, mind you—actually sitting *in* the Wall. I brought my Yaz button and a sixty-page paper I had written on him as the person I most admired in the world. Al Nipper pitched that game, and I remember Yaz waving to the crowd and thinking it was the coolest thing in the world. The lasting memory from that day is when we were leaving. I saw a line and thought, 'Maybe he's signing autographs.' It was a long drive back home to Albany, New York, so we couldn't stay and find out, but the next day, I read the *Boston Globe* and that was exactly what Yaz was doing. I thought Yaz was God. And that Fenway Park was what heaven looked like."

Sometimes, to outsiders, it seems Red Sox fans try to outdo themselves with the ethereal references and otherworldly devotions to their favorite team and their favorite ballpark. Except the more Red Sox fans you talk to, the more you realize this isn't shtick at all, but a very real, most tangible emotional bond.

"Baseball has been a part of Boston since the 1860s and 1870s," noted Bob Rutchik, a government worker who lives in Rockville, Maryland, but has been a Red Sox fan since the early 1960s. "The Red Sox have been around for over a hundred years, they were around long before you were born, they'll be around long after you die, they remind you that rooting for them makes you part of something much bigger than just the 30,000 other people in the park. It's a small ballpark, a smaller city geographically than most of the other 'big' cities. I think all of that makes the baseball more emotional, more passionate. I mean, this isn't Dodger Stadium, where you show up in the top of the third inning and leave in the bottom of the seventh. Fenway's been there a long time. And all the heartbreak tends to reinforce the devotion all the more."

Rutchik chuckled.

"And as everyone knows," he added, "there's always next year."

There is a flip side to this Valhalla, of course. There always is.

For all its charms, for all its hidden nooks and secular naves, Fenway Park has never provided the all-consuming home-field advantage you would think it should. Yes, the Sox have long built their teams around right-handed sluggers who take dead aim at the Wall, which sits only 315 feet from home plate. Yes, there have been many left-handed swingers, from Ted Williams to Carl Yastrzemski, from Fred Lynn to Wade Boggs, Mo Vaughn to David Ortiz, who discovered just how perfectly the contours of the park befit a smart southpaw, since they can practically reach out and touch the Wall with the tips of their bats. For years, that inviting target has been all the incentive they've needed to abandon the power hitter's instinct to pull the ball. Thousands of dents pockmark the wall, the scars leaving a loving testament to a century's worth of line drives.

You would think the Sox would be all but unbeatable here.

"You would think that, wouldn't you?" Bill Lee asked. "But that place holds more broken hearts than a cemetery."

The truth is, across nine decades of residence, the Red Sox have been bitten here far more often than you'd ever think possible. The American League has conducted three one-game playoffs in its history to determine the winners of pennant races that finished in dead heats; twice, the Red Sox were involved, each time at home, at Fenway, and each time they lost those heartrending playoffs, in 1948 to the Indians and in 1978 to the Yankees. Bob Gibson came into Fenway and pitched a three-hitter in game seven of the 1967 World Series, ending the Sox' "impossible dream" season. Eight years later, one night after Carlton Fisk's epic twelfth-inning home run had rescued them in game six of the 1975 World Series, the Sox blew a 3–0 lead in game seven, watched Cincinnati's Joe Morgan scratch across a thoroughly anticlimactic run in the top of the ninth, and sent another moribund crowd home to a long and utterly disconsolate winter.

Now, on the morning of Saturday, July 24, 2004, there was a distinctly somber pall covering Fenway Park. Part of that was due to the weather: gray, miserable, rain falling steadily. Part of that was anticipation and a divided attention span: not only were the Yankees in town for a three-game series, but the Democratic Party was gathering in the city's North End to nominate Massachusetts' own John Kerry for president the following week.

Mostly, though, it was the result of a baseball season gone horribly wrong. The night before, the Yankees had battered Curt Schilling, hammering him for seven runs in less than six innings. They'd won the game in the ninth inning when Alex Rodriguez, of all people, had roped an RBI single off the Wall, pinning the loss on Keith Foulke, and when Mariano Rivera closed the game out in the bottom of the inning the Yankees increased their lead over the Red Sox in the American League's Eastern Division to nine and a half games. What had begun in Boston as a season of triumph—the Red Sox beat the Yankees six out of seven times the teams had played in April, including a three-game sweep in the Bronx, and bolted out to a 15–6 record after twenty-one games—had lapsed into a mud pit of mediocrity. Since the hot start, they'd gone 37–38 and allowed the Yankees to practically lap them.

And all the brazen confidence that had imbued them in the spring, all their trademark bluster—it was nowhere to be seen. It had started to vaporize three weeks earlier, when the Sox went to Yankee Stadium and were swept in three games by the Yankees in a series that went about as badly as a series can go. Curt Schilling and Jason Varitek were overheard jawing at each other before the opener, an exchange that was either some extra-loud trash talk (the way the players later tried to spin it) or an angry conversation about Schilling—who wasn't scheduled to pitch in the series—blowing off the pre-series pitchers' meetings (the way almost everyone else privy to the dialogue described it). During the series, Scott Williamson, a key bullpen contributor, would go down with a season-ending arm injury. And the series finale was boldfaced by an extraordinary defensive play by Derek Jeter, who dashed after a late-inning foul pop and dove headfirst into the stands, coming away with some serious cuts and bruises on his cover-boy face. More than the play itself came an instant, and unflattering, comparison: Nomar Garciaparra, sidelined much of the season already with a bad Achilles tendon, hadn't played in the game, hadn't made himself available for late-inning duty, and never even ventured off the dugout bench during what became a thrilling 5–4, thirteen-inning Yankees win. The disparity between the fearless Jeter and the pouting Garciaparra became an instant hot point around the Red Sox.

But it wasn't until the day before the Yankees arrived at Fenway Park that things truly began to scrape bottom in Boston. The Red Sox lost a dispiriting game at Fenway Park to the moribund Baltimore Orioles at almost exactly the same moment that Ruben Sierra was hitting a bottom-of-the-ninth home run to give the Yankees a 1–0 win over the Toronto Blue Jays in New York. Afterward, the mood in the Sox clubhouse, which normally resembled a freshman dorm room on Friday night, was somber, almost macabre. It had been a long fall from "cowboy up."

"Semi-lifeless" was the sobering term reserve outfielder Gabe Kapler used.

"This team is gonna find its way into the playoffs, and when we do we'll be as tough to beat as anyone," said Kevin Millar, which would have been more comforting if not for his unabashed guarantee of World Series glory just four months before.

But it was Johnny Damon who captured the mood best. Damon had become the hirsute face of this team from the moment he showed up in spring training with hair that hadn't seen a pair of scissors in a year, and a beard that made him look, in Millar's estimation, "like a cross between Charles Manson and Jesus." Damon had trimmed his beard for charity a few weeks back, but he never spared his thoughts on any subject related to the Red Sox. He was honest to a fault. And this was his take:

"We're still seven or eight games above .500. But it sort of feels like we're twenty games back."

This was a team in need of a spark.

And as everyone gathered at Fenway Park this dreary morning, it seemed this was the last place on earth to find one. The grounds had absorbed two inches of rain overnight. The outfield looked like an Irish bog. Red Sox officials toured the field, looking grim. Finally, two hours before the game, they visited the Yankees, who had just arrived and were getting dressed in the cramped visitors' clubhouse behind third base.

"Nothing official," they were told, "but it doesn't look like we're playing baseball today."

The Yankees shrugged and began to think of ways to fill the unexpected gift of an off day in Boston. They took off their uniforms. Some players showered. Joe Torre took out a yellow legal pad and began to fiddle with the names of his starting pitchers. As much as players hate doubleheaders, especially September doubleheaders (which is when this game would have to be rescheduled), what could you do? Rain was rain. Baseball games have been washed away for a hundred years.

A few hundred paces away, in the Red Sox clubhouse, a similar piece of news arrived: *Soaked field. Gray skies. Don't plan on playing. Makeup date to follow.*

This time, the message wasn't greeted with such passive acceptance. A few of the Boston players had just returned from the field. No, they protested, it wasn't ideal. But the skies were clearing in the distance. The Fenway Park ground crew had performed miracles before. Why not give them a chance—just an hour, why not?—to see if they could make things playable?

As Johnny Damon would explain, weeks later, "The last thing we wanted to do was sit around another freakin' day and feel sorry for ourselves and stare at each other and think about how horseshit we were. We had to play some baseball."

"We gathered as a team and said we want to play, no doubt about it," Kevin Millar said. "We didn't want anybody to make decisions for us. Ultimately, it should be the players' decision. We wanted to play regardless. This is a battling clubhouse."

The Red Sox abided by their players' wishes. They relayed the information to the Yankees, who were annoyed at the sudden flipflop but started to get back into their uniforms without incident. The ground crew grabbed rakes and wheelbarrows, sawdust and clay and squeegees, and took to the field. The Fox first-team baseball crew, which would televise the game nationally, began to get ready for their broadcast.

And Dropkick Murphys walked out to the field to do a sound check.

This was a small part of the pregame ritual, overlooked by everyone at the time. But Dropkick Murphys, a local Irish punk/rock band, was scheduled to perform before the game, where they would debut an important new song. Actually, it was a modern interpretation of a very, very *old* song: "Tessie," the very same rallying melody that the Royal Rooters used to employ a hundred years before, the song that so annoyed the Pirates during the 1903 World Series and the Highlanders (and their fans) during that epic chase to the 1904 American League pennant.

It was back in spring training that Charles Steinberg, the Red Sox' executive vice president, had offhandedly remarked that someone should think about dusting off the old ditty that used to fuel so many Pilgrims and Red Sox victories. Jeff Horrigan, who covered the Red Sox for the *Boston Herald*, was intrigued enough to e-mail Ken Casey, Dropkick's lead singer, and Casey was intrigued enough to ask Horrigan to send him a copy of the original. And the idea nearly ended there. Remember, the song's lyrics were considered excruciating for 1904 ("Tessie, you know I love you madly / Babe, my heart weighs about a pound"), and in 2004, they were practically nauseating. The melody wasn't exactly "Rhapsody in Blue," either.

Still, an idea had been hatched. Casey and his bandmates enlisted Horrigan's help, and together they rewrote the lyrics and composed a new melody that included a "hint" of the original. The new song told the story of the old Red Sox, including references to Nuf Ced McGreevy, Cy Young, and Big Bill Dineen, and it was ridiculously catchy, and from the moment the first chords filled Fenway Park that afternoon, it found a place inside the eardrums of Red Sox fans. And so did the chorus:

> *"Tessie," Nuf Ced McGreevy shouted*
> *"We're not here to mess around*
> *Boston, you know we love you madly*
> *Hear the crowd roar to your sound*
> *Don't blame us if we ever doubt you*
> *You know we couldn't live without you*
> *Tessie, you are the only, only, only!"*

The 34,501 folks in the crowd appreciated the song. But they treasured what came next, during the game, even more.

Not at first. The Yankees were already up 3–0 with two outs in the third inning when Bronson Arroyo plunked Alex Rodriguez on the elbow with a sinker. Was it a message pitch? Was it a nervous pitcher grown rattled? There seemed little reason for debate. Rodriguez wasn't hurt. The crowd got a little charge out of watching him writhe when the ball hit him, but they were as dead as the Red Sox' pennant hopes. This wasn't Pedro Martinez throwing a ball at someone's head, after all.

Only Alex Rodriguez didn't see it that way. Maybe it was the pressures of his first season in New York finally reaching the surface. Maybe it was the relentless slander that fell in sheets out of the grandstand. Maybe it was the fact that an early-season slump still affected A-Rod's mood, and he had a hard time getting used to seeing a number like .278

next to his name on the scoreboard, after a lifetime hitting north of .300. Maybe it was a little of all of that that came together when the baseball ticked his elbow.

What Rodriguez did was take a small step toward Arroyo, as if to say, *I know what you did.*

Jason Varitek, standing in full catcher's regalia behind Rodriguez, didn't care for the implication. "Hey," he said, loud enough for only Rodriguez' ears. "We don't throw at .260 hitters. Shut up and take your base."

Archduke Francis Ferdinand had just been assassinated.

Rodriguez spun on his heels.

"Go fuck yourself!" he screamed at Varitek.

"Go fuck *yourself!*" Varitek screamed back.

And in one shocking, remarkable heartbeat, they were upon each other, their hands at each other's throats, Varitek looking like Darth Vader in his catcher's mask, Rodriguez holding his ground, grabbing Varitek's chest protector. What followed was a familiar dance: Here came the dugouts. Here came the bullpens. Here came Fenway Park, the crowd rising as one to witness another amazing installment of this angry serial, sounding more alive than it had since early April.

Here, unbelievably, came Tanyon Sturtze, son of a Worcester cop who used to bring his boy to Fenway every year for opening day, who on this day was the starting pitcher for the hated Yankees; dashing across the field, Sturtze grabbed Gabe Kapler by the neck ("To get him off our guys," he insisted later, although there wasn't a Yankee uniform spotted anywhere near Kapler) before getting buried under a pile of Red Sox, Kapler and David Ortiz and Trot Nixon. Blood spurted from his face. The pinky on his pitching hand got bent back. Finally someone led him away from the mob. It was almost too much to believe. But here it was, all over the Fenway Park turf.

You half expected to see ring-card girls between innings.

Calm was restored. Varitek, Rodriguez, Kapler, and Kenny Lofton were ejected. The Red Sox came back against Sturtze and seized a 4–3 lead. The Yankees exploded for six runs in the sixth inning, expanded the lead to 9–4, and took a 10–8 cushion into the ninth inning with Mariano Rivera again on the mound. For all the drama, all the passion, all the noise and fury generated earlier, it looked like just another Yankees–Red Sox game that would end with Rivera shaking hands with Jorge Posada. Hadn't seen *that* before, right?

Then Nomar Garciaparra led off with a double to left center. Trot Nixon moved him to third with a long fly ball to right that looked like a certain game-tying home run before the wind knocked it down. And Millar singled to right center, his fourth hit of the day, scoring Garciaparra, shaving the lead to 10–9.

Up stepped Bill Mueller, the Boston third baseman. As he stood there on the mound, Rivera had converted twenty-three consecutive save opportunities. He was considered an early favorite to win his first Cy Young Award. Free of any nagging arm worries, he was as reliable and as dominant as he'd ever been. But that didn't sway the Red Sox at all. They have had success against Rivera through the years, more than any other team, mostly because they've had more opportunities to face him given the nineteen times they play the Yankees each year. "You have to be patient against him," Mueller would say later. "You have to wait for him to make a mistake, even though he doesn't make many of them. And when he does, you'd better pounce."

Mueller waited. He waded through four pitches, worked the count to 3 and 1. Now Rivera needed to throw a strike, not wanting to put the winning run on base. He threw a cutter, his signature pitch. But he left it up and over the fat part of the plate. And Bill Mueller knew exactly what to do with it.

The Red Sox didn't even wait until the ball landed in their bullpen before exploding out of the dugout. They knew. They gathered around home plate, mobbing their third baseman, and every one of the 34,501 people who remained began whooping and howling and, of course, chanting.

"Yankees suck!"

"Yankees suck!"

"Yankees suck!"

During the course of the long season, every once in a while you get a game that you know, as soon as it ends, that you'll remember long after the season is over. Mueller was still on the field, still celebrating with his teammates, and all across the Great Divide fans started pondering the significance of such a seminal win.

On Cape Cod, writer Pete Trinkle, a Yankees fan trapped living in downtown Boston, was staying with his wife at a friend's house. The next morning, Trinkle's hosts, knowing well of his pinstriped affiliation, went to the local candy store and bought several copies of the *Boston Globe*, specifically to make sure Trinkle wouldn't have to miss a single word about the Red Sox' glorious triumph. They placed them strategically along the side of the driveway.

"I ran them over," Trinkle reported proudly.

In Dudley, near the Connecticut border, Tony Zannotti was at a neighbor's thirtieth-birthday party. Normally, of course, the Red Sox–Yankees game would be everywhere. At nine and a half games back, though, it was limited to the living-room television, which guests of the party were visiting only infrequently. Zannotti happened by the screen just as the brawl was breaking up. He sat, transfixed by the highlights.

"You won't believe what just happened," he reported back to the other guests.

Later, it was his great privilege to witness Mueller's home run and report *that* piece of news, too. "That," he said, "made a good party even better."

That was the sentiment that echoed throughout the Red Sox clubhouse. Yes, they still trailed by eight and a half games. No, one game didn't make up for four months of underachievement. But, man, for one day at least, it sure was good to be a member of the Boston Red Sox.

"I hope we look back on this a few months from now and say, 'You know what, that really turned us around,'" Terry Francona said.

"You don't want to wake a sleeping dog," Millar crowed. "All I know is, the Boston Red Sox came to play today."

Someone asked Alex Rodriguez if this first look of the rivalry's dark underbelly had provided him a glimpse of how much the teams disliked each other.

"Put it this way," he said with a smile, "it isn't love."

The Sox won the next day, too, taking a few parting whacks at Jose Contreras, whom the Yankees were days away from shipping to the White Sox. For one of the few times in their history, it truly seemed the Red Sox might really be able to cash in on what always should have been one of the great home-field advantages in all of sports.

Finally.

Of all the haunting ironies that filled the pages of Red Sox history, perhaps the grandest one was this: As much as the Yankees have owned Fenway Park through the years, winning one important game after another within those hostile walls, the Yankees, for a time, actually *owned* Fenway Park. Literally. And were a couple of stubborn shenanigans away from becoming . . . gulp . . . the *Boston Yankees.*

It's true. In 1920, when their Polo Grounds landlords, the Giants, first began playing hardball with them, threatening not to renew the Yankees' lease, it grew increasingly likely that the Yanks might not have a place to play the 1921 season. That was a delicious possibility for the team's small but growing list of enemies, which included not only the imperious Giants but also the American League itself, in the person of league founder Ban Johnson, who was determined to crack up the Boston–Chicago–New York coalition that had split his league into warring factions.

Harry Frazee had narrowly, and shrewdly, avoided Johnson's sinister wrath on May 3, 1920, when he'd purchased Fenway Park. It had been widely assumed that the ballpark had been part of the deal when Frazee bought the Red Sox three years before, but in fact Charles Taylor had retained ownership rights when he'd sold the club in 1911, leasing it to subsequent owners like Frazee for a $30,000 annual fee. When Johnson discovered this, he had tried to beat Frazee to the deed, figuring if a Johnson loyalist could buy Fenway, then demand outrageous rent on the park, it would all but drive Frazee out of the league. When Frazee outraced Johnson to the property, the league president was furious.

Then Frazee upped the ante on him.

Twenty-two days after buying Fenway Park, Frazee and Jacob Ruppert consummated the "other" financial arrangement that had first been discussed as part of the Babe Ruth deal: a personal loan, at a favorable interest rate, somewhere between $300,000 and $350,000. Frazee had the perfect asset to put up as collateral: the title to Fenway Park itself. For years, mythologists have pointed to this, among many other things, to show just what a Ruppert bobo Frazee really was. In actuality, it was a brilliant scheme hatched by both men to circumvent Ban Johnson, who continued to try to undermine Frazee, searching for ways to revoke his franchise license and install another owner in Boston. But when the Giants—with Johnson's secret endorsement—nearly evicted the Yankees, Ruppert simply shrugged. His team, after all, already had an alternative place to play: Fenway Park.

Johnson had been outflanked. Nobody would be happy with a Boston Yankees situation: not the American League, which would have two teams crowding one market; not Giants owner Charles Stoneham, who would lose out on some serious rent money; certainly not Johnson, who had long hoped to have a star like Babe Ruth in New York and who with such a move would suddenly see him shuffled back to Boston after only a teasing glimpse in the league's signature market. Stoneham backed down. The Yankees broke ground on Yankee Stadium. Frazee ultimately repaid the loan in full, and Fenway Park's deed was returned to its rightful place. The Yankees never did get to own Fenway Park outright.

They simply spent most of the next eighty-three years figuratively buying it back, piece by piece, brick by brick, heartache by heartache. The first notable balloon payment arrived during one three-game blitz during late June of 1949, in the middle of the last peaceful, baseball-mad summer before Korea, when the postwar bliss that covered the nation would vanish forever. For this was when Joe DiMaggio rose from his sickbed and completed his transition from superstar baseball player to transcendent American mythmaker.

On March 2, the first day of spring training, DiMaggio had pulled up in pain during a running drill. The first reports were of a "stretched adhesion" in his left heel, one of the exotic-sounding maladies that regularly litter spring medical reports. But this was Joe DiMaggio, the most famous baseball player in the world, idol to millions of boys, and a $100,000 investment for the New York Yankees. Plus, DiMaggio had undergone an operation on that same heel the previous November, just the latest in a series of injuries that had knocked him out of so many springs in the past. The Yankees took no chances. They sent DiMaggio to Johns Hopkins Hospital to visit his surgeon, Dr. George S. Bennett. Bennett's words were reassuring: "Joe is now paying the penalty for having trained too hard the first day of spring training."

DiMaggio himself was less optimistic. "Dr. Bennett told me there was thickening where the spurs had been removed," he explained when he returned to the Yankees' camp at St. Petersburg, Florida. "This is not good. Maybe the trouble is returning. I can't take another year like 1948. I got the worst charley horse of my life. My ankles swelled. If the spur is pretty bad, and all this happened, I just don't see how I could go on playing."

It was already the most difficult spring of DiMaggio's career. For the first time, he could feel the tug of age, even though he wouldn't turn thirty-five until November. Eight years had passed since the mystical summer of 1941; to DiMaggio, it felt much, much longer. Even as a young man, he'd had difficulty avoiding the pulls and sprains and strains of the baseball craftsman, mostly because he insisted on playing so hard every day. But now, the pain emanating from his left foot told him something else.

"There's nothing worse," he would say forty-six years later, sitting in the Yankees clubhouse during an Old-Timers' Day celebration, "than an athlete watching his body grow old and brittle."

There were other issues. For the first time in his career, he was playing for a manager he didn't hold in especially high regard. From Joe McCarthy to Bill Dickey to Bucky Harris, DiMaggio had always respected the men he'd played for; the previous winter, when the Yankees had hired Casey Stengel, DiMaggio had called a friendly reporter and asked, "That's got to be a mistake, right? I've never seen a guy who looked so bewildered." Stengel had been an abject failure as a manager with the Brooklyn Dodgers and Boston Braves, compiling a record of 581–742, and had most recently been expelled to Oakland, managing the Class AAA Oaks. After the Yankees made the official announcement in an elaborate press conference at "21" on October 12, 1948, Dave Egan, the acerbic columnist for the Boston *Record* best known for his bloody newsprint feuds with Ted Williams, mused, "The Yankees have been mathematically eliminated from the 1949 pennant race."

Stengel himself understood fully the furor surrounding his appointment. When most of the preseason prognosticators picked the Yankees no higher than third in the American League, behind the Red Sox and Indians, he'd quipped, "Third? Third ain't so bad. I never finished there before. That's pretty high up."

Each day, the dispatches from spring training brought fresh updates about DiMaggio's condition. On March 4, he invited photographers to take pictures of him taking treatment in a diathermy machine. Nine days later, he stepped to the plate to take his first official at-bat of the spring, a pinch-hitting assignment against a twenty-one-year-old pitcher for the St. Louis Cardinals named Jackie Collum, who struck DiMaggio out on three pitches.

DiMaggio tried to speak hopefully of his recovery, but it was difficult. On March 17, he invited his closest friend among the writers, Jimmy Cannon of the *New York Post*, to lunch, and as he munched on a chicken sandwich and sipped from a glass of milk, DiMaggio poured his heart out to Cannon.

"Even with the pad in my shoe it hurts me as much as it did last year before the operation," DiMaggio conceded. "You've got to run to get strong and I can't run on it with it hurting me that way. If I ran hard to second base now I would fall down. How can I be in shape if I can't run? The heel has to come along gradually, the doctors say. I know that. I'm going along with the doctors. I'm going to give it a lot of time. But I hate to do nothing. I like to be active. I hate sitting and looking like a bump on a log. It would be nice to have two good feet to run on. I don't think about it when I go up to hit. But wouldn't it be nice to have two good feet to run the bases on? I forget what it feels like to have two healthy feet. How good will I be when I do play?"

It wasn't until March 29 that DiMaggio finally told Stengel to put him in the lineup, against the Cincinnati Reds. He grounded out twice, flied out once, handled all his defensive chances flawlessly, and declared at game's end, "I feel OK," a message that was gleefully transmitted to all eleven New York newspapers the next day.

But he wasn't OK. He played forty-three innings in eight exhibition games, came to bat thirty-one times, scratched out seven hits, and never once looked comfortable at the plate or running after fly balls with a slight but perceptible limp. He tried anything to ease the discomfort: new shoes, new spikes, removing spikes near the inflamed area of his heel, adding extra spikes there. The doctors diagnosed a "hardening" of the heel.

"They tell me one day I'll wake up and the pain will be gone," he'd told a small group of reporters while drinking coffee in a diner in Montgomery, Alabama, on April 8. "All I know is, there's no use kidding anyone anymore. My heel still hurts. It's no better and no worse than when I started."

Within a couple of days, he wouldn't be playing at all, which is when the waves of depression would finally overtake DiMaggio and a city overrun with his fans. On April 9, in Beaumont, Texas, DiMaggio ran hard from first to third on a single into the outfield, and when he slid into third the pain became instantly unbearable; he had to be helped off the field. The next day, in Greenville, Texas, he tried gritting his way through the sting—the opener was only nine days away, he figured, he'd have to get used to living with it—but after lumbering home from second base on a single, he knew he had to shut it down. While the Yankees moved on to Terre Haute, Indiana, the next destination on their northbound whistle-stop exhibition tour, DiMaggio was bound for Johns Hopkins again, where he was given a different diagnosis: "immature calcium deposits" in the tissue adjacent to the heel bone. The prognosis was exactly the same: He'd be out until the pain went away. That could be a week, a month, four months. Nobody knew.

"We don't think he'll be gone for the entire year," Yankees general manager George Weiss said, although that *was* very much a possibility. Weiss also eschewed the disabled list, since in that era it meant a minimum of sixty days, "and we believe Joe will be back before then."

The patient wasn't so sure. All around him, rumors of a pending retirement swirled like dust on a minor-league infield. "I certainly am not going to retire from baseball. That's just talk from people who want to see me retire. There are some of those people around, you know."

Presumably, some of those people resided in Boston, Massachusetts, although the Red Sox themselves, always fond of Dominic's older brother, were sad to see Joe limp into the background. "If I know Joe at all," Ted Williams declared, in a bit of unknowing prophecy, "he'll get himself well just in time to knock the ball around against us."

DiMaggio did show for opening day on April 19, flying up from Baltimore on owner Del Webb's private plane. He decided to shift his daily treatment to New York, where he lived out of the well-appointed Hotel Elysée on Fifty-fourth Street between Park and Madison Avenues. DiMaggio had always spent his baseball seasons quartered at a hotel, ever since arriving in New York thirteen years before and taking a room (and later a suite) at the Edison Hotel on Forty-seventh and Broadway. But now, even the luxury of the Elysée escaped him; in his room, he saw imaginary prison bars, and sank into a deeper and deeper depression, repeating the same heartbreaking task every morning. He would rise before the alarm, fling his feet over the bed, wait a couple of seconds, and then put pressure on the heel. Sometimes the resulting throb would make him yelp in fright and agony; sometimes it was just a dull ache; always, there was a reminder that he was not yet well. And another wasted baseball day would be upon him.

He'd kept a low profile when he showed up at Yankee Stadium that afternoon, observing from a safe corner of the Yankee dugout, sullenly sipping coffee, chain-smoking cigarettes. It was exactly how he'd taken to spending many of his days at the Elysée, except instead of listening to the close-up chatter of a baseball game, his daily companion was a soundtrack of jazz records, stacked high on his turntable as he waited for the pain to go away.

"I stayed close to the stairs," DiMaggio said of his game-day activity, following the Yankees' 3–2 win over the Washington Senators. "I don't want to be too active. I'm in my street clothes and the umpires might not like it. I'll bet you I drank a gallon of water sitting on the bench. It got uncomfortable sitting in one spot and I came into the clubhouse every few innings so I could smoke my cigarette."

Surprisingly, the Yankees took to Stengel immediately, flourishing with his platoon system of constant righty-lefty match-ups. They started quickly, winning ten of their first twelve. Stengel made Jerry Coleman, a twenty-four-year-old rookie, his everyday second baseman. He used a five-man outfield, somehow finding enough at-bats to keep them all relatively happy. The Yankees took over first place on opening day and wouldn't be displaced for five months. Better, their two chief rivals were struggling badly. As late as June 12, the defending world champion Indians were languishing under .500 and had already fallen nine games behind the Yankees. And the Red Sox, inexplicably, were even worse; they would hover around .500 deep into July, and would fall as many as twelve games behind New York.

The Yankees' hot start only darkened DiMaggio's mood. He received few visitors, granted no interviews. What was there to say? Every night he went to bed, waited for sleep to overtake him, and hoped the morning would bring relief. Every morning brought that same sad ritual, waiting for the pain to arrive.

Until the morning of June 19, when he arose, stepped on the floor . . . *And it was gone.*

It was just as the doctors had predicted. DiMaggio put pressure on the heel, felt nothing. He walked around his suite. Nothing. He jumped, ever so cautiously, on the offending foot. Nothing!

For the first time in months, his mood lifted. He made two calls: one to Al Schacht, who made his living as a baseball clown but was a perfect batting practice pitcher—threw hard, threw strikes—and the other to Gus Niarhos, the Yankees' bullpen catcher. Each day, before his teammates arrived at the ballpark, before the inquisitive crowd of writers and the prying masses of fans would flock to Yankee Stadium, the three men arrived early, just as the broiling June sun began its ascent in the South Bronx sky, Schacht throwing BP to DiMaggio until the hitter's palms oozed red.

"I don't care about my hands," DiMaggio told his workout partners, "as long as my feet feel good." By June 27, he felt good enough to try his luck against the real thing. That afternoon's *New York Post* back-page headline spelled out the giddy news for a city overrun with DiMaggio curiosity: "DiMag May Test Heel Against Giants Tonight."

The annual Mayor's Trophy exhibition game against the Giants had fallen at a most fortuitous time, an off day between a home game against the Tigers and a three-game series at Fenway Park against the Red Sox. DiMaggio figured he was close, but he wanted to use the Giants' pitching as a sparring partner. In the home-run-hitting contest beforehand, he knocked one out, much to the delight of the 37,537 at Yankee Stadium; it proved to be the hardest he hit a ball all night, as he popped out four straight times. But he played all nine innings and jogged off the field without incident, and though he made no promises about joining the Yankees in Boston the next night, he was noticeably upbeat. "I'll think about it," he said. "I'm not worried about my hitting. That'll come."

But he *was* concerned with his hitting, because he understood as well as anybody that when he did come back, the people would scrutinize what they could see most clearly. Did he look like the Joe D. of old, roping line drives, scorching the baseball with his bat speed, generating staggering power out of a surprisingly modest leg stride? The next morning, while the rest of the Yankees boarded a morning shuttle for Boston, DiMaggio headed to the Stadium for a solitary session of batting practice. There, he finally felt the old magic enliven his bat. He felt his rhythm. He showered and hopped a cab across the Harlem River to Toots Shor's saloon on West Fifty-first Street for lunch.

"So, crumb-bum, you gonna get back to work anytime soon?" Shor asked, using his favorite appellation as he stopped by DiMaggio's regular spot, table number 1.

DiMaggio just smiled. He hadn't yet made up his mind to play, but his morning workout had inspired him to get out of the city for a couple of days. He finished his meal, went back to the Elysée, packed a few things, and hailed a taxi for Idlewild Airport, in time to take the 3:15 flight to Boston, where baseball fever had officially seized the Hub. The Sox had won ten out of eleven and now found themselves within striking distance of the Yankees, only five and a half games back with more than three months to go. All over town, people wondered if Ted Williams' prediction would come true, if DiMaggio would pick Fenway Park on this Tuesday night to parachute back into the baseball season.

A thick pile of baseball writers surely wanted to know as they crowded around Casey Stengel in the small visitors' clubhouse. Across the room, DiMaggio dressed slowly. He hadn't spoken to his manager yet, so Stengel didn't know what to tell them. "It's his decision," Stengel said. So the crowd scurried over to DiMaggio's locker to get the verdict from him. DiMaggio looked over to Stengel and nodded. And Stengel immediately stenciled the name "J. DiMaggio" on his lineup card, in the customary number-four spot. The writers flew upstairs to the press box to alert their offices.

DiMaggio's first at-bat of the season came leading off the top of the second inning against lefty Mickey McDermott, and the two men engaged in an instant epic. McDermott got ahead of DiMaggio, 0 and 2, then tried to nick the outside corner with fastballs, figuring there was no way even Joe DiMaggio could keep up with a barrage of heat after not facing real pitching in almost nine months. Six times he tried that. Six times DiMaggio fouled the pitches off. It was like a condensed version of spring training right there, DiMaggio coming closer and closer to each pitch until finally, on the ninth pitch of the at-bat, the seventh straight outside fastball, DiMaggio not only made solid contact, he pulled the ball ten feet over Junior Stephens' head at short for a clean single. Even Fenway Park had to concede that it was a hell of a battle.

An inning later, after Phil Rizzuto led off with a single, DiMaggio came up again, and this time there was no classic duel. McDermott threw one pitch, a fastball that got a little too much of the plate—the kind of mistake pitch DiMaggio had feasted on since he was sixteen years old.

"As soon as you heard the ball hit the bat, you could just tell it was gone, and I just watched in amazement as it soared over that big wall," Rizzuto recalled more than fifty years later. "Just thinking of that sound gives me goose pimples, all these years later. Holy cow. It's still hard to believe he could do something like that after sitting out the whole season."

But DiMaggio wasn't done. Prior to the game, in Joe McCarthy's presence, a couple of Red Sox surmised that DiMaggio wouldn't be able to run at top speed yet, probably wouldn't feel a hundred percent in his legs for a few weeks at least. McCarthy stiffened; you didn't ever talk about Joe DiMaggio like that, not as long as he was in earshot. He shook his head ruefully.

"You don't know him," McCarthy muttered. "You watch him the first time there's a chance for an infield hit. You watch how he runs."

All of Fenway was watching in the bottom of the eighth. With DiMaggio on first base after drawing a walk, Yogi Berra followed with a sharp grounder to Bobby Doerr at second, a tailor-made double-play ball. Doerr fielded the ball cleanly and quick-flipped to Stephens, who wound up eating a mouthful of base path dirt, courtesy of a vicious takeout slide by the guy with the bum wheel.

"Junior wound up ass over elbows," Johnny Pesky, playing third that night, remembered with a smile. "I wanted to see DiMaggio's X-rays after that play."

When it was over, after DiMaggio had provided one final curtain call by running down Ted Williams' long fly ball to the deepest cranny of center field for the final out, DiMaggio looked giddier than he'd seemed in years.

"It went all right, didn't it?" he asked. "I certainly was glad the first game wasn't tied in the ninth and sent into overtime because I would have been forced to quit. The leg would not have carried me into the tenth."

It carried him well enough the next night, after the Red Sox jumped out to a 7–1 lead behind Ellis Kinder, who would win twenty-three games that season. In the fifth inning, Rizzuto and first baseman Tommy Henrich both walked, bringing DiMaggio up. Kinder, angry at himself for issuing free passes with a six-run lead, reached back and threw a high, smoking fastball that crossed the plate a shade north of the "New York" on DiMaggio's gray flannel road uniform, an almost impossible pitch for anyone to drive. But DiMaggio caught it clean, crushed it, watched it soar over the Wall in left center. Suddenly, it was 7–4. Fenway Park wasn't cheering Joe DiMaggio anymore.

"If you'd have told us then that Joe could walk on water," Henrich said years later, "we wouldn't have given you an argument."

By the eighth, the Yankees had pulled even at 7–7, they'd chased Kinder, and now Earl Johnson, a thirty-year-old left-hander, inexplicably tried to get cute with DiMaggio, serving up a big, slow curveball. To DiMaggio, by now, every pitch looked as big as a beach ball. Another swing. Another vicious crack of the bat. And another baseball soared high into the night, finally settling into the screen behind the Wall. As he crossed home plate, DiMaggio was greeted not only by a platoon of exuberant teammates, but also by Stengel, who began bowing with a "we're-not-worthy" flair.

"Nothing hurts," DiMaggio conceded after the Yankees' 9–7 comeback was complete, "when you play like this."

And still he wasn't completely satisfied.

"I've hit four balls pretty good, but the others I've been behind the pitch. I'm still a little off in my timing."

Said Cliff Mapes, speaking on behalf of the mortal members of the Yankees: "Just once, I'd like to be that off in *my* timing."

That night, Jimmy Cannon, who hadn't made the trip to Boston, reached his exhausted friend in his hotel room.

"What's doin'?" the columnist asked.

"What have *you* been doing?" DiMaggio replied, chiding Cannon for finding a better place to spend his week than Fenway Park. "I just took in a picture. I'm in bed. I'm a little tired."

"You really broke out."

"A couple of balls dropped in for me."

"The stories I read said they were well hit."

"I like this park."

"How does the heel feel?"

"It's a little swollen, but pretty good."

"You sound like a new guy," Cannon said, and DiMaggio pondered that.

"I got lucky," he said. "I got hold of a couple."

The next night, just after the first pitch, a small plane glided over Fenway Park carrying a simple message in its wake: THE GREAT DIMAGGIO. More remarkable, after all he'd already done, DiMaggio found himself at the plate at the biggest moment of a splendid pitcher's duel between Boston's Mel Parnell and New York's Vic Raschi, the Yankees clinging to a 3–2 lead. It was the top of the seventh, two outs and two on, and with a base open, almost everyone expected McCarthy to walk DiMaggio intentionally. Except McCarthy. He ordered Parnell to pitch to DiMaggio, who worked the count to 2 and 2. Parnell had to come in with a strike now, which he did, and which DiMaggio promptly deposited over the Wall, over the screen, clear over Lansdowne Street, his longest blast of the week. The score was 6–2, the Yankees' lead was now eight and a half games, and the Fenway crowd, defeated, gave DiMaggio a long ovation, a sporting tribute for what they'd just witnessed.

"What do you think the other contenders will think of Joe's return?" Stengel crowed in the clubhouse. "They probably won't like it too much. Babe Ruth alone could match Joe's flair for drama, for responding to an occasion. And not even Babe Ruth would have put on the kind of demonstration DiMaggio staged here. Eight workouts, and then socko! Four home runs!"

Down the hall, in the Red Sox clubhouse, another interested onlooker expressed his bittersweet emotions.

"How do you like how my big brother broke in? He sure broke in with a bang against us," Dominic DiMaggio marveled.

A day later, with all of America buzzing about DiMaggio's remarkable return, four home runs and nine RBIs in three forever games, DiMaggio conceded to Cannon that he could never script his own life as perfectly as it often turned out on its own.

"At one time, I thought I was all through for the year," DiMaggio said. "I felt I'd be lucky if I was able to do some part-time work, some pinch-hitting. I was really down for a while. I came into Boston very cool and collected. I was cooler than I thought I'd be. I didn't expect so much of myself, but I was cool as hell. The worst part about this whole thing was people constantly asking me about the heel. People were trying to be nice, but they had me crazy. They had me out of my mind. I'd be up at six, seven in the morning. What was I going to do? I just sat there and smoked."

As difficult as those three games may have been for the most faithful Fenway flock to fathom, they weren't the most agonizing hours ever spent watching a Yankee run roughshod on their beloved lawns. No, across four unbelievable Boston days and nights in September 1978, the Yankees would forever emblazon their dark footprint on the imaginations and the memories of Red Sox fans. Forget any other games these two teams have ever played. The four that would forever be known as "The Boston Massacre" live on, and will continue to live on, as a permanent symbol of what this rivalry was for eighty-five long summers. The Yankees walked into Fenway Park and rifled the place, robbing Boston of a pennant that had been all but ceded to them months earlier.

On July 19, 1978, the Red Sox throttled the Milwaukee Brewers, 6–2, moving their record to 62–28, easily the best record in baseball, nine games clear of the second-place Brewers and fully fourteen games ahead of the Yankees, languishing in fourth place. Unbeknownst to them, the Red Sox had already suffered an enormous bad break when a Fenway Park date with the Yankees was washed out on July 4. The Yankees' pitching staff was decimated with injuries, and they literally had no one to throw against the hardest-hitting team in baseball. New York manager Billy Martin had summoned Paul Semall, pitching at Class AA West Haven at the time (and destined to never throw even one inning in the major leagues).

"If he looks good," Martin said, "we may start him." Rain made those emergency plans obsolete. The game was rescheduled for September 7, a Thursday night, a mutual off night before a three-game Yankees–Red Sox series that looked sure to be meaningless. As Reggie Jackson had said the previous day, after the Red Sox had smashed the Yankees 9–5: "The way the Red Sox are going, not even Affirmed [that summer's winner of horse racing's Triple Crown] can catch them."

Even Reggie, with his perfect-pitch understanding of what makes for terrific melodrama, could have no inkling of what was to come, a blur of improbabilities and impossibilities that will forever brand 1978 as the American League's most unforgettable summer. On July 17, Jackson earned himself a five-game suspension and a $12,500 fine for defying Martin's orders not to bunt in the tenth inning of a 9–7 loss to the Royals. It was the latest and the ugliest flare-up between two ego-driven behemoths, and it seemed to provide a fitting epitaph for the Yankees' one-year reign as world champions. When Jackson returned on July 23 in Chicago, he delivered the most memorable sound bite in a career overrun with them: "The magnitude of it all is incredible. *The magnitude of me.* The magnitude of the incident. The magnitude of New York. It's uncomfortable. And it's miserable."

The next day, Martin finally reached his boiling point and resigned, after issuing his own priceless statement duty-bound for a future baseball edition of *Bartlett's.* "They deserve each other," Martin had told three writers after having a few drinks in a bar at O'Hare Airport, referring to Reggie Jackson, his chatty star, and George Steinbrenner, his owner, who'd once pleaded guilty to making illegal contributions to Richard Nixon's 1972 presidential campaign and had earned a one-year suspension from baseball for it. "One's a born liar, and the other's convicted."

The next day, in a tearstained press conference, Martin resigned. Later, he apologized to Steinbrenner, who always reserved a soft spot in his heart for his troubled manager. Within a week, he would rehire Martin, effective at the start of the 1980 season. Steinbrenner did this during Old-Timers' Day ceremonies at the Stadium, and it brought the house down. Around those Yankees, in those years, anything was possible.

When news of this madness reached Boston, manager Don Zimmer was forced to smile. "I know George Steinbrenner, and I know Billy Martin, and I hope they'll both be happy together forever. But I'm glad to be where I am, here in Boston. Where it's sane."

A funny thing had happened amid all that insanity, however. The Yankees won the last five games they played under Martin. They kept winning under Bob Lemon, his ultra-low-key successor. And the Red Sox, out of nowhere, stopped winning, dropping nine out of eleven. The Yankees were still in fourth place. But they suddenly had reason to believe maybe they weren't destined to be Alydar, who'd spent that summer fruitlessly pursuing Affirmed the same way the Yankees were now chasing the Red Sox.

"I notice Milwaukee, and I see what Baltimore's doing every day,"

Carlton Fisk said in early August. "But I always keep my eye on what the Yankees are doing. We can't rest until those guys are dead and buried."

The Yankees wouldn't die, but neither would the Red Sox fold, as so many Yankees fans expected they would. Over the next six weeks, the Yankees began to play more like the team that had won the 1977 World Series. They started to hit, started to get terrific pitching, had baseball's best one-two bullpen tandem in Goose Gossage and Sparky Lyle, yet they couldn't eat into the Red Sox' lead. They passed the Orioles. They passed the Brewers. By August 29, they were alone in second place, but still seven and a half games behind. After six weeks of splendid baseball, they'd gained exactly half a game. That four-game series at Fenway Park still loomed large, but what good would it do if they were still so far behind? The Yankees kept staring at the out-of-town scoreboard, waiting for a little help. They had grown obsessed with the Red Sox.

"I can tell you when the meat of their order is up, just looking at the scoreboard," Jackson said. "The meat comes up in the second inning and in the fourth and fifth, and in the seventh. If they score runs, I can tell you who batted in the inning. There are those who watch the scoreboard and those who lie about it."

Added pitcher Eddie Figueroa, ruefully: "They always win."

But between August 30 and September 7, the Yankees went 7–2 while the Red Sox lost five out of eight. Yankees shortstop Fred Stanley, talking about the pressures of a pennant race, spoke for all fifty players on both clubs when he said, "You go out there and play, and just hope you don't screw up." Fred Lynn concurred: "Every day, it feels like you walk in from the field and you drop six tons of bricks off your back. It's exhausting, every day."

In New York—all but muted thanks to a citywide newspaper strike that had kept the Yankees out of the news for more than a month—there came the curious tale of Paul Mitchell, a pitcher for the woeful Seattle Mariners, who on September 1 shut the Yankees out 3–0, one of thirty-two games he would win as a major leaguer, the only game the Yankees would lose in an eleven-game stretch against Western Division opponents. After the game, Mitchell allowed that even though he had been born and raised in Worcester, Massachusetts—squarely in the heart of Red Sox Nation—he had grown up, inexplicably, unforgivably, *a Yankees fan.* And with a straight face that night, Mitchell actually said, "It hurt me a little bit, beating the Yankees. Especially with the Red Sox losing tonight."

But the Yanks kept charging. On September 5, the Yankees beat Detroit while the Sox were losing to Baltimore. Four games was where it would stand after both teams won on September 6, with four games in Fenway afoot.

"They've got to hear us breathing," Gossage said. "You bet they do. We're playing good ball right now. And I'm not sure the Red Sox are."

By the sixth inning of the first game, Gossage had his answer. By then, the Yankees were already up 13–2, and passions were so muffled that even when Sox pitcher Dick Drago drilled Thurman Munson's forehead with a fastball in the sixth, there was no incident. The Sox simply couldn't do anything right. The final score was 15–3, with the Yankees banging out twenty-one hits, and now New York was within three. There were 34,119 people jammed into Fenway at the start, maybe a few hundred after the seventh.

"I really didn't notice," Yastrzemski quipped. "I left early, too."

Zimmer tried to absorb the bludgeoning with as much good humor as he could muster. "The only good thing is that this is only one game," he said. "Maybe we tired them out. They had scheduled extra hitting practice tomorrow afternoon. They called in the fifth inning and canceled it."

The Yankees really could have done without regulation batting practice on Friday, too, because an armada of Red Sox pitchers kept serving BP-worthy pitches once the game started. The assault continued: seventeen hits, thirteen runs, *seven* Red Sox errors, a 13–2 butchering that was so one-sided that Mickey Rivers, the Yankees' leadoff hitter, came to bat three times before George Scott, the Red Sox' number eight hitter, hit once.

Nobody could believe what was happening.

"I've never seen the Red Sox get blown out two nights in a row in a pennant race before," Carlton Fisk said. "I never saw us play as listlessly. To me, it's the reverse of pennant pressure. You try to relax and end up over-relaxing. It's not a case of complacency. We know who we're playing."

A quarter century later, Graig Nettles still smiled when he thought of those first two games.

"I mean, we were up by about six runs those first two nights before anyone in the building had even sat down," he said. "In the days leading up to the game, we'd hear guys like Yogi or Scooter fool around and say, 'You know, in the old days, all we had to do was show up against the Red Sox and they wouldn't want to play us.' We thought it was funny, some old-timers telling stories. And then that's exactly what happened. We just murdered them. It was almost too much. It was almost embarrassing."

Yastrzemski, the Red Sox' captain, tried desperately to scribble a happy face on his team's dire circumstances, saying, "I think people are losing sight of the fact that we are still in first place," but now that lead was only two games, and it was the Yankees who walked with the unapologetic swagger the Sox had carried themselves with through most of the summer.

And it was the Yankees who now seized on every opportunity, who picked at every Red Sox scab and exploited every Boston weakness. Saturday afternoon was sunny but windy, and it pitted the teams' two best pitchers, Ron Guidry and Dennis Eckersley, and for one day, the pitchers dominated, keeping runs off the board in seventeen of the game's eighteen half innings.

Of course, the Yankees did scratch seven runs across in the top of the fourth.

"I remember walking through the press room that afternoon," says Phil Rizzuto, then in his twenty-first year as a Yankee broadcaster. "I ran into a Red Sox employee I knew and he said, 'Well, if we lose today, it's over.' And I thought, over? Forget that no matter what happens, there's still three weeks to go. I mean, even if they lost, they would still be in first place! But that's how demoralized everyone was."

The Red Sox kept looking for bad things to happen, because when things go wrong in a pennant race, it *all* goes wrong. Yastrzemski, who had called a team meeting before the game, made a terrific defensive play in that fourth inning, racing all the way from left center toward the left-field line to snare a wind-mangled fly off the bat of Reggie Jackson, then firing it back to the infield in time to double Munson off first, exactly the kind of play that's supposed to pick a team up. Chris Chambliss followed with a double and Zimmer ordered Nettles intentionally walked, but when Lou Piniella popped up on the very first pitch he saw, it seemed Eckersley would emerge with his shutout intact. But the ball got tangled up in the swirling thirty-three-mile-per-hour winds high above Fenway's infield, and it began to draft. Frank Duffy, the Red Sox' second baseman, was settled under the ball one minute; the next it was landing at his feet, in the middle of five different Red Sox, for a devastating double. Bucky Dent, warming up for a bigger stage and another day, followed with a two-run hit, and the door was officially opened.

By the time the Red Sox came to bat again, the score was 7–0.

On NBC-TV's telecast, Tony Kubek was saying, "This is the first time I've ever seen a first-place team chasing a second-place team."

Up in the press box, Joe Gergen was tapping out a lead to his column for *Newsday*—one of only two papers regularly covering the Yankees that wasn't on strike—that would still be remembered twenty-five years later: "The Yankees are a game behind and drawing away."

Downstairs, after Guidry went the distance to pick up his twenty-first victory in twenty-three decisions, Frank Duffy tried to explain what had happened: "I saw it go out to the outfield. Then the wind blew it back toward the right-field line. Then I lost it in the sun. The sun bothered me more than the wind. I lost it about the time it blew back." Said Eckersley: "The ball must have moved a hundred feet easily. But that didn't beat us. What beat us was Dent's hit."

Actually, Dent spent a lot of time beating the Red Sox that weekend, collecting seven RBIs in all, or one less than the entire Red Sox team. He would only drive in forty runs all year, hitting out of the number-nine hole in the Yankee order; if you add the three runs he would drive in with one fateful swing of the bat three weeks later, Dent accounted for one-quarter of his entire season total in his final five appearances at Fenway Park.

The finale was less one-sided if you just look at the 7–4 score, but it was just as devastating to the psyche of the Red Sox and their Nation. Zimmer steadfastly refused to pitch Bill Lee, who was perfectly healthy but buried on Zimmer's shit list. He refused to pitch Luis Tiant on short rest, even though Tiant's reputation as a Yankee-killer was second in baseball only to Lee's.

"An intractable bastard" is how Lee puts it, all these years later.

"Inexcusable" is the word Tiant uses.

Instead, Zimmer decided this would be the perfect time to throw a twenty-two-year-old rookie named Bobby Sprowl into this bubbling cauldron of a pennant race. In explaining his decision, Zimmer said, "Everyone tells me this kid has ice water in his veins," which was an odd depiction since Sprowl's Triple-A manager at Pawtucket, Joe Morgan, had described him just a few weeks earlier this way: "He's kind of a jittery kid." Sprowl's day lasted exactly six hitters: He walked Rivers and Willie Randolph, induced Munson to hit into a double play, surrendered a run-scoring single to Jackson, then walked Piniella and Chambliss to load the bases. Zimmer came to get him, and Sprowl walked off the field into obscurity, an instant footnote in the bibliography of Red Sox misery, the ice in his veins presumably well thawed.

Bob Stanley was summoned; he gave up a two-run single to Nettles. Another day in the sun had rapidly devolved into the third ring of hell for the Red Sox, who had been alone in first place since May 22. Now, for the first time in 111 days, they had a roommate atop the AL East. And they started to sound like a team that was already beaten.

George Scott: "When I left home today, I hoped it would rain."

Carlton Fisk: "I think if the Yankees win the pennant, they'll remember us rather than them. We had a consistent nine- or ten-game lead most of the season and they made it up in about ten days. I hope they would get a little credit. But you never know."

"Some home-field advantage," Bill Lee said years later. "Fenway Park sure scared the hell out of the damn Yankees."

Twenty-six years later, the Red Sox were still seven and a half games out when the Yankees left town on July 25, and the deficit would grow by another game before the week was out and the July 31 trading deadline would arrive. That 11–9 game made for great theater, but the Red Sox still needed some help. And Theo Epstein knew it.

The Yankees, meanwhile, had also circled July 31 in bright red ink. The biggest fish available was also the tallest man playing in the major leagues, the six-foot-ten Randy Johnson. There was one problem, of course: Johnson toiled for the Arizona Diamondbacks, a team destined to lose 111 games, and was still in the employ of Jerry Colangelo, though the Arizona owner would soon be squeezed out by his partners. And Colangelo wasn't any more inclined to help the Yankees in July than he had been in November. But it wasn't just spite that impeded the deal. Though Johnson had made it perfectly clear that he desired a trade and that the Yankees were his preferred destination, the Yankees were hamstrung by a farm system devoid of prospects, one that had been bankrupted by past deadline transactions, including the one that had landed Aaron Boone the previous summer.

"If they had anything that interested us, that would be helpful," a Diamondbacks source told the *New York Post* on July 30. "But the fact is, they don't."

Around the country, baseball fans rejoiced at the evidence that there really were some deals even the Yankees couldn't get done. Critics had assailed the idea of Johnson joining the Yankees and jacking the team's payroll well north of $200 million. They called Johnson a luxury that a team $60 million clear of anyone else's ledger simply shouldn't need, arguments that surely warmed John Henry's heart. But Brian Cashman, the Yankees' GM, knew differently. This is what he saw when he looked at his pitching rotation: one reliable ace (Mike Mussina) who was struggling through his most difficult season; one moody former ace (Kevin Brown) who was battling an intestinal parasite; one former twenty-game winner (Jon Lieber) who was slowly pitching his way back into shape after a two-year layoff; one young right-hander (Javier Vazquez) who was supposed to be the ace of the future but who, after the All-Star break, suddenly couldn't get anyone out; and one old flame (Jose Contreras) who had made it plain he would never succeed in New York, and whom Cashman was now desperately trying to unload.

"People who think we couldn't use a little help," Cashman said late in that trading-deadline week, "aren't looking at the same roster I'm looking at."

Cashman would receive no sympathy; in the end, the Yankees would receive no Johnson, either, since the Diamondbacks held on to their most valuable commodity. The Yankees' lone transaction of note as the 4 P.M. deadline passed that Saturday was to dump Contreras on the White Sox in exchange for another talented pitcher with issues, Esteban Loaiza. That announcement was greeted with a loud, expansive yawn, and then something else entirely, as word filtered in from Boston that Epstein had been quite busy indeed over the last few hours.

As Johnny Pesky might have said: *Holy shit.*

CHAPTER

9

WE'RE A BUNCH OF IDIOTS, BUT WE'RE GROWN-UP IDIOTS

What can I say? I just tip my hat and call the Yankees my daddy.
I can't find a way to beat them at this point. You just have to give them
credit and say, "Hey, you guys beat me, *not my team." I wish they would*
fucking disappear and never come back. —Pedro Martinez,
September 24, 2004

Don't try and get me to say anything about winning right now.
The Red Sox are going to be tough. Heck, the Red Sox are always tough.
If we wind up winning this thing, we're gonna know we beat the very
best to get there. And if they win, they're gonna know the same
damn thing. —Tommy Henrich, September 26, 1949

The money issue always bothered George Steinbrenner. It always bothered Brian Cashman. Neither man ever apologized for the Yankees' seemingly bottomless storehouse of wealth, their boundless resources, their open-checkbook policies. But neither were they proud of it. Whenever a story about the Yankees appeared, invariably there was talk of their $187 million payroll. Whenever a feature on the Yankees aired on television, inevitably the phrase "the best team money could buy" would sneak its way into the script. What the rest of the world saw as gluttony, the Yankees saw as smart business practice. And the disparity in perception would drive them to distraction.

"If spending the most money guaranteed you anything, then we wouldn't all be nervous wrecks every year in October, would we?" Cashman said later in the 2004 season. "All you have to do is look at the recent past. Look at how much money the Dodgers have spent; how many championships do they have? Look at the Mets; how many championships do they have? When the Orioles had a huge payroll, why didn't every story mention that? And it isn't like the Red Sox are playing with a bunch of underpaid players, right? But all people want to talk about with the Yankees is how much money we spend. I don't understand the relevance. You still have to win on the field."

What the Yankees top brass never admitted—what was probably too difficult to concede—was that the best Yankees teams of recent vintage were rarely criticized for their fiscal munificence. Those Yankees, who won four championships in the five years spanning 1996 to 2000, were powered by players who'd been acquired, in almost every instance, by traditional means, by time-tested baseball methods approved by people who believed in old-fashioned baseball values.

There was a home-grown core of players who'd come up through the Yankees farm system—Derek Jeter, Bernie Williams, Andy Pettitte, Jorge Posada, Mariano Rivera. There were key players who'd arrived through trades—Paul O'Neill, Chuck Knoblauch, Scott Brosius, Roger Clemens, Tino Martinez. There were some key deadline acquisitions—Cecil Fielder, David Justice, David Cone. There were fruits of the Yankees' growing international presence—Alfonso Soriano, Orlando Hernandez, Hideki Irabu. And there were several key free-agent imports, too, notably Wade Boggs, Jimmy Key, and David Wells. Yes, as the Yankees won more and more titles, their payroll swelled accordingly, and by the time the Yankees knocked off the Mets in the 2000 World Series, they were paying out $113 million in player salaries. But even their most ardent critics had little argument with this. Essentially, the Yankees were rewarding players who'd already won for them. They were taking care of their own. They hadn't gotten where they'd gotten by gobbling up every glitzy star on the board.

"That reflected why people like me loved those teams so much," Yankees fan Frank Russo said late in the 2004 season. "We didn't have a huge superstar, like Barry Bonds. We were a *team*. Every night, someone else was the hero. And the best example of that was the way we beat the Mets in the last game of that World Series. Luis Sojo got the game-winning hit in the ninth inning, and that was exactly how it should be. Other teams might say, 'Who the hell is Luis Sojo?' And we'd say, 'He's exactly the kind of player who belongs on the Yankees. He's a winner.'"

The irony was stark, too, for after that 2000 World Series, the Yankees picked up at least one marquee superstar in every off-season: Mike Mussina in 2000, Jason Giambi in 2001, Hideki Matsui in 2002, and Gary Sheffield and Alex Rodriguez in 2003. Those five players alone represented in excess of $520 million in total salary. Only the Yankees could foot that bill. And yet the Yankees had gone three years without a title, while the Diamondbacks, Angels, and Marlins won World Series using much the same blueprint the Yankees had always used: strong pitching mixed with a surplus of role players (Tony Womack, David Eckstein, Alex Gonzalez) who saved the very best of themselves for October's brightest lights. All around baseball, people emulated the Yankee Way of winning championships—with the notable exception of the Yankees themselves.

That included the Boston Red Sox.

So it was that Theo Epstein got to work on the morning of July 31. Two-thirds of the way through what was supposed to be a magnificent season, the Red Sox led the league in offense, boasted the strongest front of the rotation in baseball, had a gaggle of crowd-pleasing sluggers in the lineup every night. And they were in serious danger of not even copping the American League's wild-card berth.

Before the Sox would take the field in Minneapolis that day, their thirty-year-old general manager would put his career squarely on the line and give Boston the kind of baseball jolt it hadn't felt in generations. First, he acquired speedster Dave Roberts from the Dodgers. But that was just the appetizer. Because just after the 4 P.M. deadline passed, the first wisps of a blockbuster four-team trade involving the Red Sox, Cubs, Expos, and Twins started to surface. The Red Sox' imports would be significant: Gold Glove first baseman Doug Mientkiewicz from Minnesota and Gold Glove shortstop Orlando Cabrera from Montreal. Teamed with Roberts, the Red Sox had, in a few hours, gone from a thin, plodding, station-to-station team that had difficulty catching the ball to a deep, quick, potentially well-above-average defensive team.

There was one hitch. That, too, was more than a little significant.

Nomar Garciaparra was going away. To Chicago. To play for the Cubs.

The impact was startling, and it was immediate.

"We just traded away Mr. Boston, a guy that meant so much to the city, and just like that, he's gone," a stunned Johnny Damon said.

"They can take the shirt off my back, but they can't take away the memories I got," a melancholy Garciaparra said before he left the Metrodome. "They can't take away the standing ovation that I got when I came back this season when I walked up to the plate. Or when I hit three home runs on my birthday [in 2002]. Every time I stepped up to the plate, the fans cheered for me. When I went deep in the hole to make a play, they'll never be able to take away that. What it's meant to me, they all know that every single day I went out there and I was proud to put that uniform on and what it represented."

The city of Boston was horrified. Nomar? Gone? *To the Cubs?* Garciaparra might well have been the best everyday player to come up through the Red Sox system since Ted Williams. Teddy Ballgame himself had regularly gushed about Garciaparra's talents, his grace, his baseball instincts. "By the time he's done," Williams had said in 1999, "this is going to be one of the all-time great players Boston's ever seen."

For weeks, Epstein literally had to worry every time he emerged from his office, for fear of encountering an outraged Nomar devotee. The trade's immediate fallout was ugly, too. Garciaparra claimed he'd essentially become persona non grata in the Sox organization, ostracized by John Henry; the Sox fired back that Garciaparra had all but forced their hand by hinting he might need more time to recuperate from his foot woes. For his part, though, Epstein never wavered from his belief that the deals had to be made.

"I liked the club the way it was," Epstein said the day the trade was made. "The safe thing to do would have been to play it out. The safe thing to do would have been not to touch it. But in my mind, we were not going to win the World Series as we were."

The thing is, even through their anger, Red Sox fans ultimately came to understand the need to do *something*, even if it had to involve their beloved Nomar. John Miller was at his girlfriend's graduation party in Worcester when Michael Dube, his roommate, called to tell him of the trade.

"I called him back in immediate disbelief," Miller said. "I had somewhat of an uneasy feeling in my stomach. I asked him who we got in return . . . and that actually made me laugh a bit. That was the emotional reaction. But when you started to think about it, and the fact that Nomar was unhappy, and likely to leave at season's end . . ."

"I was happy, even immediately," Tony Zannotti insisted. "It was almost like Nomar had done what he could here. Deep down, I knew he wouldn't be back, anyway, based on what happened at Yankee Stadium. I'd lost a little respect for him after that. If we could get something in return that could help, I was all for it."

Maybe at the start, that was a minority opinion.

But within a few weeks, you couldn't find a dissenting voice anywhere within the giddy boundaries of Red Sox Nation. The new Sox took about a week to find their sea legs, losing three of their first five games together, falling ten and a half games behind the Yankees on August 6, a night when they also went to bed two full games out of the wild-card lead. But the next day, Pedro Martinez won his twelfth game of the season, beating the Detroit Tigers 7–4. And from then on, the Red Sox very nearly forgot how to lose. From August 7 through the end

of the season, their record would be 40–15. During one almost unbelievable stretch from August 16 to September 8, the Red Sox won
twenty out of twenty-two games. They built a five-game lead in the
wild-card standings. And, more deliciously, they threw a legitimate
scare into the Yankees, too, slicing the distance between them from ten
games to two in what felt like fifteen seconds.

The Yankees noticed, too. You know how you could tell they noticed?
Because the Yankees insisted they *didn't* notice.

"I only worry about the Red Sox when we're playing them," Derek
Jeter said on September 19. "They've been on my mind all weekend.
They'll be on my mind next weekend. Now we have other teams to
worry about."

This was at the conclusion of a three-game series at Yankee Stadium
that had halted the Sox' momentum and reaffirmed the Yankees' place
atop the Eastern Division, however tenuously. In the series opener on
Friday night, Mariano Rivera had failed in another ninth-inning save
situation (he blew only three all year, two to the Sox), and the Red Sox
seemed intent on ending their six-year run of second-place finishes.
But the Yankees responded with a pair of resounding thumpings, 14–4
on Saturday and 11–1 on Sunday (battering Pedro Martinez), to
reestablish their first-place foothold. And it was another victory over
Martinez five nights later, in the opener of a three-game series at Fenway, that virtually locked up the division for the Yankees and inspired a
frustrated Martinez to verbalize what had been brewing inside him for
months.

"What can I say?" the exasperated erstwhile ace said. "I just tip my
hat and call the Yankees my daddy. I can't find a way to beat them at this
point."

Both teams still had playoff series to worry about—the Yankees drew
the Twins, the Red Sox would get the Angels—but if they could both
somehow survive, it wasn't difficult to imagine hearing that sentence
quoted back to Martinez some night soon by the throats of 55,000 most
appreciative Yankees fans.

Pedro Martinez was an exception to almost everything the Yankees and the Red Sox had represented for so many years, because he was the single most polarizing element ever injected into this feud's ever-combustible cocktail. He was the first player on either side to be so singled out for scorn, partly because of his excellence, mostly because of his willingness to shave Yankees players with well-placed fastballs. Even the contempt Red Sox fans regularly showered upon Derek Jeter—and it could be as vile as anything you ever heard anywhere in the world—was tinged, at its base, with respect. Jeter killed the Red Sox time and again in his career. Red Sox fans hated him for that. But they also respected the fact that he *made* them hate him for that.

Mostly, though, for all the outbursts and firefights that have splintered so much of the Yankees–Red Sox relationship through the years, there has almost always been an underlying mutual respect, too, one that tends to grow deeper and fonder with time. Even after fifteen years with the Yankees, Babe Ruth longingly referred to Fenway Park as "my old home" and the Red Sox as "my old friends." Carlton Fisk and Thurman Munson, sworn enemies on the field, eventually grew to admire each other, since each could appreciate just how much the other contributed to the success of his team.

Joe DiMaggio was almost never booed at Fenway Park and was often cheered by the large number of Italian-American fans who flocked to the Fens whenever he was in town. The Red Sox certainly admired him, even as they feared him for what he was capable of doing to them, and all but adopted him thanks to the presence of his kid brother Dominic on the great Red Sox teams of the 1940s and early '50s.

But never was there a deeper, more affectionate relationship between these two sworn enemies than the one that existed between Ted Williams and the Yankees. Williams was a man who could talk baseball all day long, who would dispense advice and opinions to anyone who would listen, no matter what flannel vestments you might wear on a baseball diamond. And the Yankees of Williams' era were men who weren't too proud to listen to such counsel, especially when it was delivered by someone who may have crammed more knowledge into his brain regarding the science of hitting than any man who ever lived.

"One time I was in a batting slump and I talked to Ted Williams about it," former Yankees first baseman Bill "Moose" Skowron told Dom Amore of the *Hartford Courant* shortly after Williams' death in the summer of 2002. "And he said, 'Moose, you're trying to pull everything. Try to hit the ball to the opposite field.' The next day I hit two home runs into the bleachers in right-center field at Fenway Park. After the game, Ted called me. He said, 'Don't tell the writers I told you how to hit the ball.'"

Yes, despite living in a time when fraternizing with opponents was the most capital of all baseball offenses, Williams couldn't help himself, even if it meant helping out the Red Sox' sworn enemy. Of course, sometimes he never had to open his mouth to dispense the wisdom. Williams was such a craftsman in the batting cage that if you were paying attention, just watching him swing during batting practice could be a valuable study tool.

"When he took BP," said Hank Bauer, a Yankee outfielder from 1948 to 1959, "we all stopped what we were doing to watch. We soaked it all up. And later on, he paid us quite a compliment. He said, 'If we had Bauer and Moose on our team, we would have won all those titles.' He helped a lot of young ballplayers."

And one time, reciprocating the favor, Skowron lent Williams one of his bats; Williams promptly hit a home run, one of thirty he'd hit at Yankee Stadium in his career. When Casey Stengel later learned of his first baseman's largesse, he nearly popped an artery; it makes you wonder how he would have responded if he'd ever had to manage the man he always called "Mr. Williams." Still, Stengel—who'd seen up close every great hitter from Wee Willie Keeler to Ty Cobb to Honus Wagner to Rogers Hornsby and studied them all—may have been intimidated by Williams' gifts more than anyone.

"We used to have team meetings before we played the Red Sox," said

Charlie Silvera, a catcher who backed up Yogi Berra from 1948 to 1956. "Dom DiMaggio was leading off, Casey would say, 'Fastball hitter.' Then Johnny Pesky was second, and he'd say, 'High-ball hitter.' Then he'd get to Ted Williams, and say, 'Next hitter.'"

But the most famous of all the Yankee friendships Williams developed was with Phil Rizzuto, the Yankees shortstop, whose candidacy for the Hall of Fame Williams would tirelessly champion as the years flew past and it seemed that Scooter would never receive enough support from the Veterans' Committee to gain enshrinement (which he finally did, in 1994). On many occasions, Williams spoke just as highly of Rizzuto as he had of Skowron and Bauer, never more eloquently than the August morning in 1985 when the Yankees retired Rizzuto's number 10. "Johnny Pesky is one of my dearest friends in life, and I always loved playing with Junior Stephens," Williams said that day. "But I have to say that if Phil Rizzuto was the Red Sox shortstop all those years, I think history would have gone a little differently."

If they seemed an odd couple, it was genuine warmth they shared. Williams first struck up a conversation with Rizzuto in Rizzuto's rookie year, 1941, the season Williams hit .406 and almost always seemed to be finding his way to second base, in Rizzuto's neighborhood. After one double, he told Rizzuto, "You play hard. I love this game, and you better love it too."

So touched was Rizzuto by Williams' words that when his manager, Joe McCarthy, later ordered Rizzuto to jump and wave in the field while Williams was hitting, in a bush-league attempt to distract the great hitter, Rizzuto refused, admitting, "I felt funny doing that."

One day, Rizzuto learned that Williams' lectures weren't confined merely to other baseball players, either, as he recalled to Amore.

"One time, my wife was up in Boston, and she was at this hospital getting some tests done," Rizzuto said. "Ted hit a double, and when he got to second base, he said, 'Where are you eating tonight? Why don't you and Cora join me?' I told him she was in the hospital getting tests and, holy cow, he was at that hospital after the game before I was. I

came in, and Ted had a broomstick in his hand, showing her some hitting tips. Cora was scared to death."

Rizzuto laughed.

"Actually," he said, "she was like the rest of us. She liked Ted."

The 2004 playoffs began amid an odd sense of inevitability. Yes,
the Yankees still needed to win three games off the Twins, and they
would prove three difficult wins to get. After dropping game one, the
Yankees were behind by a run in the twelfth inning of game two, but
rallied thanks to a clutch double by Alex Rodriguez. They were also four
runs behind in the eighth inning of game four, before storming back for
another extra-inning win, the big blast a three-run home run by thirty-
nine-year-old Ruben Sierra that tied the game in the eighth. Rodriguez,
flexing his October muscle, capped that comeback by doubling in the
eleventh, stealing third, and scoring the winning run on a wild pitch.

And the Red Sox still needed to dispatch the Angels, which looked
like it would be a routine task until Anaheim's Vladimir Guerrero
blasted a grand slam that capped a five-run rally and tied game three at
6–6 in the top of the seventh inning. In other years, with other teams,
this would have forced a funereal pall to descend upon the Fenway Park
grandstand, as everyone waited for the Red Sox to lose this game—and
the next two, for kicks—in the most hideous fashion possible. But if
anyone remained who didn't believe that a different karma had taken
root in Boston, all they had to do was close their eyes and listen as soon
as David Ortiz made contact with a hanging curveball from Jarrod
Washburn: the percussion of ball hitting sweet spot; the crushing roar
of a crowd witnessing its first series-clinching in eighteen years; the
immediate, joyous melody of "Dirty Water" by the Standells, the Sox'
victory anthem all year long; capped, at last, by the first few notes of
"Tessie," with almost every one of 35,537 hoarse voices singing along
with Ken Casey and the other members of Dropkick Murphys.

And suddenly, it was real. It was tangible. It was upon us. From the moment Aaron Boone's ball disappeared into the New York night fifty-one weeks before, there had been an instant sense that an encore was essential, that another Red Sox–Yankees Championship Series would be the highest-quality sequel since *The Godfather, Part II.*

"I guess it was supposed to come down to this," Joe Torre would say a few minutes after the Yankees eliminated the Twins. "Every single game we've played takes on a life of its own. I think it's going to be electric again."

"I never thought," Sheffield said, "that I'd love to see Boston so much."

The Red Sox were just as anxious. Inside their foamy, exultant clubhouse, the Red Sox passed around a twenty-eight-inch-tall Dominican actor named Nelson de la Rosa, a friend of Pedro Martinez' who'd become something of a good-luck charm for them, as he'd shown up in the Boston clubhouse the first time on the day after Pedro's "the Yankees are my daddy" monologue. The scene was certainly surreal, and it absolutely captured everything about the Red Sox' charm, their passion, and their quirky energy.

"It's a frat house," Johnny Damon said, laughing, shaking his head, sipping from a green bottle of champagne. "We have no rules. We're playing cards. We're playing our PlayStations. We don't stretch. We show up two or three minutes before the game on the field and play."

A few weeks earlier, Damon had teamed with Kevin Millar—the man who'd invented "cowboy up" in 2003—to provide the perfect handle for this new collection of long-haired baseball insurgents. It was Millar who had first hinted at it, early in September, when he'd described the Red Sox thusly: "We make sure guys run out the ground balls and play the game the right way. We don't care about the little things. We're unique. We're a bunch of idiots. Theo's done a good job bringing in character guys. Some teams are built on the draft, on potential, on radar guns. People around here got some hair growing or something or bad bodies. That's what you have on this club. But we grind you to death out there."

Damon had echoed those same thoughts a few weeks later, on the day after the Red Sox had celebrated their wild-card berth at Tropicana Field in St. Petersburg: "Our team was a lot more professional about clinching a playoff berth than a few of us probably thought. We're a bunch of idiots, but we're grown-up idiots now. We celebrated the right way for a little bit and that was it." This time, the name stuck.

Now, they would meet again, the idiots from Boston and the emperors from New York. Twenty-nine years earlier, Muhammad Ali and Joe Frazier had met for the third time in an epic boxing match in Manila, and one ringside observer, Larry Merchant, had been so moved by what he saw that night he said the two fighters fought "for the championship of the heavyweight division. And of each other."

The Red Sox and the Yankees understood. The analogy Johnny Pesky had used back in February, likening the Yankees to Ali and the Red Sox to Frazier, was right on the mark. It wasn't fair to call the Red Sox the Yankees' sparring partners, even after the way so many of their encounters had gone through the years, even with the extensive bruising Red Sox fans have endured for so many years. Sparring partners aren't supposed to hit back, after all, not with the venomous rage of a near-equal. And regardless of the ultimate outcomes each year since 1918, there was no denying the competitive equality that now defined this relationship.

It wasn't always so. The Yankees and the Red Sox kept running into each other in the years and the decades after the Ruth transaction; sometimes it was even a happy day for Boston. On September 12, 1979, for instance, Carl Yastrzemski stroked a single off Yankees pitcher Jim Beattie for the 3,000th hit of his career. On April 14, 1967, Red Sox rookie Billy Rohr, making his major-league debut, threw a no-hitter in Yankee Stadium for eight and two-thirds innings, a gem that wasn't besmirched until Elston Howard laced a single with two out in the ninth. Seven days later, Rohr dominated the Yankees again, 6–1. They would be the only two games Billy Rohr would ever win as a major leaguer. In early July of 1939, the Red Sox walked into Yankee Stadium and swept a five-game series from the best team Joe McCarthy ever assembled, a team that would lose only forty-five games all season long and win the pennant by seventeen games.

Mostly, though, the Red Sox were ideal travel partners for their New York rival, which finally dropped its "Highlanders" nickname in 1913 in favor of the more headline-friendly "Yankees" that the New York newspapers had been using for years. Through the years, almost every time the Yankees did something to add to their growing legacy, the Red Sox were right there to get a good, up-close look at it. It was against the Red Sox on May 1, 1920, after all, that Ruth hit his first home run in a Yankees uniform, a titanic blast that cleared the Polo Grounds' right-field roof, helped the Yankees to a 6–0 thrashing of the Red Sox, and, most important, ended speculation that Harry Frazee had been right, that Ruth's twenty-nine homers the year before had been a fluke. Ruth had suffered through eleven games' worth of nagging injuries and unmet expectations, without once clearing the fence. Worse, the Red Sox had started the season 10–2, some five and a half games better than the Yankees when they took the field that day in Manhattan. But as Ruth swung, as soon as the ball soared high into the cloudless Harlem sky, those sentiments were never even whispered ever again. The Babe had arrived. He hit eleven more before the end of the month and finished the season by obliterating his own record with fifty-four, by which time Frazee was already beginning to seek out potential buyers.

Three years later, New York unveiled Yankee Stadium, the most magnificent baseball park ever built. Triple-tiered, topped by a gothic façade—and, not coincidentally, highlighted by a right field that stood only 296 feet from home plate to foul pole. The Yankees, who'd become the Giants' Polo Grounds tenants in 1913, wore out their welcome soon after Ruth joined the team, outdrawing their landlords by over 700,000 across the 1920, '21, and '22 seasons, a number made even more galling by the fact that the Giants had beaten the Yankees in the World Series those last two seasons. So the Yankees found a plot of farmland in the South Bronx wilderness and built themselves a palatial baseball estate, and on April 18, 1923, they opened the doors and 74,217 people flooded inside, to fill all 62,000 seats and all of the available standing room.

In a wonderful quirk of scheduling serendipity, the opponent that day was Boston, the perfect patsy, soon to finish under .500 for the fifth time in a woeful fifteen-year streak of futility. It was also a measure of payback. On April 20, 1912—with the morning newspapers still filled with ominous headlines describing the sinking of the *Titanic*—the Red Sox had opened Fenway Park by tripping the Yankees, 9–7, in extra innings.

When the Yankees took the field for batting practice eleven years later, inside their own brand-new basilica of a ballpark, Ruth peered out to the inviting right-field porch (already dubbed "Ruthville") and shook his bat.

"To hit one in this building, against this team on this day," he told a gathering crowd of reporters, "I would give up my eyeteeth."

Whether that transaction was necessary or not, Ruth did connect with a slow Howard Ehmke curveball in the third.

"Governors, generals, colonels, politicians, and baseball officials gathered together solemnly yesterday to dedicate the biggest stadium in baseball, but it was a ball player who did the real dedicating," the *New York Times* burbled the next morning. "In the third inning with two team mates on the base lines, Babe Ruth smashed a savage home run into the right field bleachers, and that was the real baptism of the new Yankee Stadium. That also won the game for the Yankees, and all the ceremony which had gone before was only a trifling preliminary."

And the Red Sox, by this point, were merely a trifling footnote in the Yankees' world. By the time they won their first World Series five and a half months later, the Yankees would have eleven former Red Sox on their roster. History has unfairly labeled this as still another sure sign of Frazee's compliance with the Yankees, but the truth is, he had little other choice. He knew his team was awful; he had to do something to shake up the roster; the other five members of the American League were still aligned with Ban Johnson, unwilling to trade with him; his only other potential trading partner, Charles Comiskey, had his own problems, having had his own roster gutted of eight top-flight players following the Black Sox catastrophe.

One of the few members of the Yankees who reported to work at Fenway Park on September 27, 1923, with no ancestral tie to the Red Sox was a young first baseman recently called up from Hartford. His name was Lou Gehrig, and he wasn't expected to play in this final series of the year between the two clubs, but when Wally Pipp, the regular first baseman, injured his ankle while stepping off the train, Yankees manager Miller Huggins opted to replace him with the kid, Gehrig (a pattern Pipp, much to his eternal chagrin, would famously repeat two years later; he wouldn't ever get back into the lineup after that one). Gehrig had gotten some late-season at-bats after being called up from the bushes, since Huggins wanted to rest his regulars before the postseason. Given the chance to get a full day's work in, Gehrig responded by hitting the first home run of his career into the right-field bleachers off a right-handed Californian named Wild Bill Piercy, driving in Ruth, who had earlier tripled. Gehrig also walked twice in an 8–3 Yankees win.

Together, Ruth and Gehrig would get fat the rest of their careers on Red Sox pitching, never more so than during their epic home run battle of 1927. Eleven of the sixty home runs Ruth swatted during that most celebrated of all his extraordinary seasons came at the expense of Red Sox pitching. In fact, it was against his hapless former team that Ruth finally shook off Gehrig in their season-long one-on-one battle to surpass Ruth's existing home run record (fifty-nine, set in 1921) and put on the most astonishing display of concentrated power anyone had ever seen.

By 1927, the brutalization of the Red Sox, once the proudest of all baseball franchises, was complete. The year before, they had lost 107 games. In 1927, they would improve to 51–103, yet finish a staggering *fifty-nine* games behind the Yankees, who beat them in eighteen of their twenty-two meetings. By the afternoon of September 5, the Red Sox were officially playing out the string and the Yankees were marking time to the World Series, but there was still a greater issue to be settled: Both Ruth and Gehrig entered the game with forty-four home runs (no other player in the American League would hit more than eighteen). They were already the greatest power tandem the game had ever known; how far could they go, and who would reach higher?

Gehrig answered first, in the opener of a doubleheader, drilling his forty-fifth homer of the season in the fifth inning off Tony Welzer, a line shot into the right-field bleachers. The Boston crowd, some 20,000 strong, roared for Gehrig. But they nearly blew the roof off an inning later when Ruth, suddenly trailing his unassuming teammate, sized up another Welzer fastball and blasted it to deep center field, long over the distant fence, a shot instantly declared the longest ever hit at Fenway Park.

The Babe, he was warmed up now.

In the seventh, with poor Tony Welzer still serving up meatballs, Ruth smoked a towering drive to right that barely cleared the wall but delivered the crowd into an equally shattering tizzy. And in the ninth inning of the nightcap, Ruth added his third home run of the day, a prodigious wallop far over the right-field wall. Challenged, Ruth had roared back and seized the lead clear away from Gehrig, forty-seven to forty-five. By the next day, he was into a full gallop after clubbing two more homers, one off Danny McFayden (a shot over the Wall in left field, one of the few times he ever cleared that baseball landmark in his many Fenway Park games), and one off Slim Harriss, to dead center. He was up to forty-nine.

"For the first time," Ruth would remember years later, "I thought I had a chance at breaking my record. Those two games in Boston made me feel anything was possible. I always felt good whenever I visited Boston."

All these years later, you can still hear the fair citizens of Boston gritting their teeth as they hear of that hospitality. *It was nothing, Babe. Really. Nothing.*

The Red Sox arrived for a workout at Fenway Park on Sunday, October 10, 2004, amid the grandest civic party Boston had seen in quite some time, the excitement enough to dwarf even the Super Bowl merriment the Patriots had generated eight months earlier. And why not? The Red Sox were in a most unfamiliar position: near-unanimous favorites to unseat the Yankees, to beat them head to head, to end the near-constant spell their ancient rivals held over them. Las Vegas said so. So did most media prognosticators. And even the most rabid Yankees fans had a hard time making a case for their team.

"I won't watch the games," a distraught Frank Russo said. "Isn't it enough for me to admit that they're the better team? OK, I admit it. It's the Red Sox' year. But that doesn't mean I have to watch it happen, OK? I'll watch the World Series. But I don't want to watch them destruct my team."

That was just fine with the fans who came to Fenway on that Sunday, who stood in the encroaching autumn chill to try to steal a glimpse of one of their Sox and who stomped their feet and started screaming madly as Manny Ramirez steered his silver 2003 Chrysler 300 Hemi C around Van Ness Street and onto Yawkey Way.

"They keep saying, 'This is the year,' and I believe them," Johnny Damon said of these faithful baseball pilgrims as he sat in a clubhouse dominated by a bulletin board that defiantly declared: SPORTS COATS OPTIONAL. "And I've believed it more and more this year. I think we're the better team. We enjoy the fact that we're going up against history. Nobody is scared of it. Everybody wants to take it."

They wanted this. They all did. The fans. The players. Even the Boston newspapers had begun openly rooting for the Yankees after the Sox had secured their own place in the Championship Series, reflecting a public belief that if the Red Sox were going to end their eighty-six-year World Series drought, they first would have to go through the New York cauldron of nightmares. This was non-negotiable.

"It was like the way it used to be with the Celtics and the Lakers in basketball," Tony Zannotti explained. "When the Celtics beat the Rockets in the finals in 1981 and 1986, it was sweet. We weren't gonna give those titles back. But when we beat the Lakers in 1984 . . . man, that was just the best. Indescribable."

Said Mike Carey: "I want to win a World Series so bad, I could give a shit if we beat the Tampa Bay Devil Rays to get there. But if we have to go through the Yankees to win it? That would be the best thing I could ever dream of. I mean, ever."

That kind of attitude was so infectious, it swept through the Red Sox clubhouse, touching even those players who'd barely had enough time in Boston to catch their breath. "If you make one good play, get one big swing, you'll be a hero for the rest of your life," said Doug Mientkiewicz, a superb summation for someone who'd played his entire career in Minnesota until nine weeks before.

It was Terry Francona who tried to pierce this ever-expanding Yankees–Red Sox bubble when he leaned on an old John Henry maxim, one the Sox' owner had used more than once when asked during the season if he wanted to play the Yankees in October.

"I want to play a National League team in October," Francona said.

For that to happen, for the Red Sox to actually make it to the World Series for the first time in eighteen years, for them to beat the Yankees when it really, truly mattered for the first time in exactly one hundred years, they would need their first-year manager to be at his very best. Francona understood that pressure. He could feel it. And he could read. In all the pre-series match-ups, the Red Sox were given strong advantages in almost every category: offense, starting pitching, bench depth. The Yankees had checkmarks next to their name in only two categories. One was the bullpen, and that was mostly because of the presence of the peerless Mariano Rivera.

And the other was the manager.

Joe Torre, in his ninth year at the Yankees' helm, had already cinched himself a place in the Hall of Fame whenever he decided to retire, and since he'd signed a three-year, $19.2 million extension in April, that wouldn't be for a few more years yet. Torre was in many ways the modern incarnation of Casey Stengel. Both men enjoyed excellent playing careers that landed just shy of Cooperstown's doorstep. Both had suffered through the early stages of their managing careers, bouncing from one bad team to another, Stengel going 581–742 in nine years with the Boston Braves and Brooklyn Dodgers, Torre amassing an 894–1,003 mark in parts of fourteen seasons with the Mets, Atlanta Braves, and St. Louis Cardinals. And both had seemed dubious choices for the Yankees: Stengel's hiring in late 1948 alienated Joe DiMaggio and was ridiculed widely in the baseball press, and when the Yankees tapped Torre, the New York *Daily News* famously proclaimed him "Clueless Joe."

How long ago that now seemed.

"There's never been a manager alive who's been able to win without good players," Torre said in the summer of 2004. "The trick is, once you get players good enough to win with, you have to get them there. A good manager can't do much with a bad team. But a bad manager sure can screw up a good team."

Torre's gift had always been in his gut. He was instinctively able to calm the strongest clubhouse storms, and had enough power that a conflict usually resulted either in complete capitulation by the offending player or in the player's outright exile. Similarly, though many of Torre's in-game strategies tended to be by the book, he'd often gone against the grain when either his sixth sense or Don Zimmer, his longtime bench coach, told him to. During the Yankees' run of four titles in five years, those weapons almost never failed him. Zimmer was no longer in the picture, having sought asylum in St. Petersburg with Lou Piniella and the hapless Devil Rays. But for the ninth straight year, Torre was here. Game one of the ALCS would be Torre's 103rd playoff game as a manager.

It would be Francona's fourth.

"I'm learning quickly," he said. "But let's be honest, I have no other choice."

Francona had earned his players' affection quickly, but his acceptance by the Red Sox public at large had been slower in arriving. Some viewed him as a stooge to his stars; in his very first game, he'd done nothing when Pedro Martinez left Baltimore's Camden Yards before the game was finished, even though he'd pitched that night, a naked breach of protocol that Francona shrugged off with a wave and the lame explanation that "maybe he didn't know the rule." His strategies were dissected every night, even more than Little's had been, even though his first team would win ninety-eight games, more than any Red Sox team had won in twenty-six years. But then, this should have been of little surprise to anyone, because the job Francona presently occupied had long been the most thankless one in American sports. Don Zimmer, whose ghostly image still shadowed this rivalry, certainly understood that. And so did Joe McCarthy, maybe the greatest manager who ever lived. No two men ever born could better empathize with Francona and more thoroughly understand Torre, for no two men spent more time on either side of this great schism.

McCarthy managed the Yankees from 1931 to 1946 and the Red Sox from 1948 to the middle of 1950. Zimmer never managed the Yankees (save for a brief tour while Torre convalesced from prostate cancer in 1999), although as Torre's bench coach from 1996 to 2003, he was a faithful first lieutenant, relied upon for his fertile strategic mind and his loyalty. But he *was* the Red Sox' manager from 1976 to 1980. So he presided on one side during the combustible 1970s and was a devoted deputy on the other side during the explosive first years of the twenty-first century. Both men became beloved figures in New York. Both men had to skip out of the way of insults in Boston, even though they came as close as anyone to delivering New England out of its empty October wilderness.

Since Ed Barrow guided the Red Sox to the 1918 title, thirty-three men occupied the manager's office inside the home team clubhouse at Fenway Park. Joe Cronin, Dick Williams, Darrell Johnson, and John McNamara all led the Sox to game seven of the World Series in 1946, 1967, 1975, and 1986. Yet even those teams, all of which came within nine innings of baseball's grandest prize, don't tantalize the memory banks of Bostonians the way Joe McCarthy's teams did, the way Don Zimmer's teams did. Because those teams both had the whiff of dynasty about them—and somehow, some way, never even made the World Series.

Meanwhile, the men who ran those squads each collected multiple rings . . . *with the Yankees.* McCarthy won seven. Zimmer won four, to go along with the one he earned as a player on the '55 Dodgers.

"What other example do you need of how unfair life is," former Red Sox pitcher Bill Lee asked, "than the fact that Don Zimmer has four World Series rings with the Yankees? Where is the justice in that? Tell me, please. Tell me."

Lee remains the man who harbors the most resentment toward Zimmer, bitter that he never was allowed to pitch any meaningful games while the Red Sox squandered every ounce of an American League East Division lead that stood at fourteen games over the Yankees on the morning of July 20, 1978. Lee and Zimmer were never going to be great friends, anyway. Zimmer was a throwback to the crewcut-and-a-chew era of the 1950s, while Lee was very much a spawn of the '60s, often eager to speak out on social issues, always willing to speak out on Red Sox issues. The two men clashed. Zimmer pulled Lee from the rotation even though he was a bona fide Yankee-killer, his 12–5 lifetime mark against New York the third best record by a Yankee opponent in history. Even though he was perfectly healthy.

Lee called Zimmer a "gerbil."

Zimmer buried Lee even deeper.

The lead continued to melt. The Red Sox' pitching staff was reduced to Jell-O. In the last meeting of the famous four-game sweep in early September that came to be known forever as "the Boston Massacre,"

Zimmer bypassed Lee, whose arm, he said, was "so rested, it was practically snoring on cue." Instead, Zimmer went with a petrified rookie named Bobby Sprowl, who lasted four batters into the top of the first inning before being pulled from the game, one of only four he would ever start as a major leaguer.

"And Zimmer's earthly reward," Lee said, "is a fat, cushy job with the Yankees."

But Lee wasn't the only critic. And Lee's absence from any meaningful late-season games in 1978 wasn't the only piece of evidence still held against Zimmer, more than a quarter century after the fall. Carlton Fisk, for example, caught 154 games, an ungodly number. By comparison, Jason Varitek, the Red Sox' rugged, durable first-string catcher in 2003, only caught 119. Zimmer kept Fisk in the lineup even though Fisk would admit by late August, "I feel like I've got a knife stuck in my side," thanks to a cracked rib, even though his various knee and elbow injuries begged for a day off a week.

"My glove needs stitches," Fisk said as he wheezed through September, "and my knees do, too. My legs are gone. I'll tell you, we had an off day on Monday and I went home to New Hampshire for the first time since April and I didn't want to come back."

Nor would Zimmer take Butch Hobson, the slugging third baseman, out of the lineup, even after floating bone chips in Hobson's elbow got so bad he would rearrange them in between pitches, much to the regular horror of his teammates; Hobson finished with an astonishing total of forty-three errors.

During a game in Baltimore in early September, Orioles first-base coach Jim Frey chatted up George Scott, the Red Sox first baseman, who was rolling grounders to his infield mates before the start of an inning.

"Jesus, Boomer," Frey said. "You had this huge lead. What the hell's going on with you guys?"

Scott looked left, looked right, then peered right at Zimmer in the Red Sox dugout before giving his answer: "Some of these guys are choking, man."

"I'm not kidding," Lee said. "I think one of the reasons Joe Torre kept Zimmer around so long was because he saw how he botched every big decision in 1978. He'd ask, 'Hey, Zim, what would you do here?' Zim would tell him. And then Torre would do exactly the opposite. Come to think of it, maybe he did earn all those rings after all."

Zimmer wound up getting three full seasons on the Red Sox bench. He won ninety-seven, ninety-nine, and ninety-one games, a winning percentage of .593. Between 1917 and 2003, the Red Sox had won ninety-plus games three years in a row exactly twice. Zimmer, for all the grief he continues to absorb, was the last to do it, until the 2002–04 Sox of Grady Little and Terry Francona. Before that, you have to go back to 1948, '49, and '50. The manager then was Joe McCarthy.

McCarthy had been the man who had reinvigorated the Yankees' burgeoning dynasty. By the time he took over the club in 1931, for all the attention twelve years' worth of Babe Ruth had brought them, the Yankees had still won only three world championships—two fewer than the Red Sox and Philadelphia Athletics, exactly the same as the crosstown Giants. Ruth was getting old. The Yankees, many believed, had wasted the era. McCarthy was hired away from the Chicago Cubs as much to tweak Ruth—who badly wanted the manager's job—as to manage him. McCarthy was told he would get three years to produce a fourth championship.

He did it in two.

And added six more before he was through.

"Joe McCarthy is the best manager I ever saw when it came to handling young ballplayers," Ed Barrow, the man who hired him, said many years later. "He had great patience with them and had a way which was unmatched in giving young fellows confidence. That was one of Miller Huggins' failings. The Mighty Mite ranked with the great managers of all time. He belongs with any group that includes Joe McCarthy and Connie Mack. But in dealing with young talent, McCarthy never had an equal."

He also made them dress, in his own words, "the way Yankees are

supposed to dress." Coats and ties were required at all times, no excep-
tions. Clubhouse card games were out. So were golf outings on the
road. McCarthy's own demons were often on display—he had a weakness for White Horse scotch, which sometimes exploded into full-
blown, week-long benders. When he was lucid, he may well have been
the best manager who ever lived, playing hunches and guesses with
stunning success, playing percentages in his head that managers seventy
years later would study on computer spreadsheets for hours.

But when he wasn't . . .

By 1946, McCarthy had already grown disillusioned with the "modern" player, many of whom had spent four years in places like Anzio
and Iwo Jima and Normandy and weren't inclined to let a baseball
manager give them even one ounce of shit more than their drill
sergeants had handed out. That first postwar Yankees team had started
out sluggishly, and by May 21, after dropping two straight at Cleveland,
they already trailed the Red Sox by six games, which was all the excuse
McCarthy needed to seek solace in his flask. By the time the team
boarded their chartered flight to Detroit, McCarthy was already drunk,
and he was looking for a fight. At 30,000 feet, the manager wandered
over to pitcher Joe Page, a big, hard-throwing Pennsylvanian who'd
waded through nine minor-league seasons before making the Yankees.
McCarthy's chief complaint—ironic, given his present state—was that
Page had squandered his talent chasing too many late nights and too
many last calls. He began to lecture Page, and his slurred message grew
louder and more uncomfortable the longer he looked at his pitcher.

"You know what I oughta do with your bush-league ass?" McCarthy
blathered. "I oughta send you back to Newark, see how you like making
$400 a month there."

Page, finally, had enough.

"So do it!" Page yelled. "Maybe I'll be better off there!"

By the time the plane landed, McCarthy disappeared, off to confront
his demons during an epic three-day drunk. He failed to show up for
either of the games in Detroit (both won by the Yankees), and instead of

following the team to Boston, he flew back to his farmhouse in Amherst, New York, a suburb of Buffalo, and resigned by telegram. He figured he was done with baseball for good.

But two years later, Joe Cronin decided to shed his managerial duties and focus on his front-office work. Almost from the moment McCarthy quit the Yankees, Cronin had tried to convince him to reconsider retirement. Cronin, a fine manager himself, knew he finally had the deepest assemblage of talent in the American League, and for years he'd seen, up close, what McCarthy could do when he had the horses. "It's against the man's beliefs," Cronin once joked, "to finish in second place."

Alas, it was McCarthy's fate—and Boston's—that that's exactly where the Red Sox would finish in both 1948 and '49, his two full seasons with the Red Sox. McCarthy may have left behind his share of hard feelings in New York—in spring training of '49, after the Sox had beaten Page, the pitcher snapped, "He's a great manager and that's all. I don't like him and I never will. I'd like to beat his brains out, and his whole club, too"—but his new players adored him. Many wondered how Ted Williams, notoriously anti-necktie, would respond to McCarthy's rigidity; McCarthy answered that the first day of spring training by showing up wearing an open-collared shirt, declaring, "If I can't get along with a .400 hitter, they ought to fire me right now."

The Red Sox put together a familiar pattern under McCarthy, starting slow, gaining speed, and coming on like a locomotive through August and September. The Red Sox hadn't enjoyed such consistent excellence in thirty years. But it didn't matter. Despite all those regular-season victories, McCarthy would be remembered forever for two ill-fated personnel decisions. In 1948, after outdueling the Yankees down the stretch, he started Denny Galehouse in a one-game playoff with Cleveland to determine the American League champion, with Mel Parnell and Ellis Kinder both available. Galehouse was shelled in the last game he would ever start in the major leagues, and all these years later the name Galehouse can stop a saloon cold anywhere in New England. A year later, with Kinder pitching his heart out and losing, 1–0, on the last day of the season at Yankee Stadium, in a win-or-go-home showdown, McCarthy lifted his twenty-three-game winner in favor of Parnell, who'd gone the day before. Parnell allowed four Yankees runs to seal the pennant, and a furious Kinder unloaded a profane, alcohol-fueled tirade on McCarthy on the team train back to Boston later that day. The manager had little choice but to absorb the diatribe in silence. Kinder was right.

Unfortunately for McCarthy, his departure in Boston was just as unsightly as it had been in New York. On June 21, 1950, after a dreadful 10–2 Father's Day beating in Detroit the day before, with the Red Sox loitering in fourth place, eight and a half games off the pace, McCarthy didn't show up for work at Chicago's Comiskey Park amid press reports that he'd suffered an attack of "pleurisy and influenza." Immediately, knowing reporters read through the euphemisms and understood: McCarthy was drinking again. Rumors quickly circulated that McCarthy was quitting, this time for good. The next morning, McCarthy issued a statement denying those claims.

"Sure I'll be back with the Red Sox," the manager said. "These reports that I'm resigning are really too silly. You can bet your last dollar that as soon as I am well enough, I'll be back. I still believe my team will win the pennant."

But the decision was no longer his to make. Cronin could see that McCarthy had never recovered from the strategic collapses of 1948 and 1949, that McCarthy's own unshakable self-confidence, buoyed through so many pennants in New York, had been destroyed. Cronin told McCarthy they would honor the rest of his contract if he walked away quietly, went back to Buffalo, and "rested." Hours after his denials, Joe McCarthy issued the final sentences he would ever speak as a major-league manager, after 3,487 games and 2,125 wins.

"I've resigned," he said. "It's final. What became apparent is I just can't seem to do anything right for the ballclub. I finally reached the decision. I don't have a single regret, unless it was my failure to do the job that everyone expected me to do—win a pennant."

To the end, the Red Sox adored McCarthy. "I'm awfully sorry to hear the news," a visibly distraught Ted Williams said. "Joe was always great to me and we never had a hard word. I'm sorry I couldn't be more of a help to him, and you know I wouldn't say it if I didn't mean it. Perhaps it's for the best that he retired. You could see that our lack of success was killing him."

Added Dominic DiMaggio: "He was tops in my book."

In the lore of Red Sox Nation, he remains something less than that. Right alongside Don Zimmer.

If any of this bothered Terry Francona, he wouldn't admit to it.

"I just gotta stay out of the way," he said on October 11, the day before hostilities would officially resume. "Red Sox–Yankees, that's a pretty big deal all its own, without my help. I think both teams are ready to get this thing started."

They weren't the only ones, by any stretch of the imagination.

CHAPTER

10

AS BIG A HOLE AS YOU COULD DIG YOURSELF IN

The Red Sox are a walking disaster. They act like they're tough, how they care so much about winning, but it's all a front. They're just a bunch of characters. They know what we're all about. We can still beat them, and they know it. Let's see what they do this time when it counts.
—*Gary Sheffield, October 13, 2004*

It was definitely an ass-whupping. They're doing exactly what we thought we would be doing in this series. We felt we'd be up 3–0 right now, but those guys have found another switch. —*Johnny Damon, October 16, 2004*

There was something eerie about walking into Yankee Stadium late in the afternoon of Tuesday, October 12, a tangible sense of déjà vu. Three hundred and sixty-one days had passed since the last time these baseball teams had gathered here to contest a playoff game. Quite a few of the major characters who'd enlivened that game seven would be absent from this series, from Roger Clemens (whose short-lived retirement ended when he was lured back by his hometown Astros, still alive in the National League playoffs) to Jason Giambi (sidelined most of the prior three months with a benign tumor), from Aaron Boone (who'd signed a contract with the Cleveland Indians after the Yankees terminated his contract in March) to Todd Walker and Nomar

Garciaparra (teammates now on the Cubs, who suffered through a staggering final-week swoon to match any Red Sox heartbreak, knocking them out of playoff contention, ensuring a ninety-sixth consecutive title-free season on Chicago's North Side).

But there were plenty of holdovers, too, on both sides, players who could still recite every detail of that epic confrontation that had begun the previous October 16 and ended October 17, that had wrenched their emotions and drained them dry and exhausted them and ultimately made them all appreciate the great gift they'd all been given to take part in a rivalry so extraordinary, so emotional, so . . . *meaningful.*

"I hate that we lost the game," Jason Varitek said. "But I'm proud to have played in it. People will talk about that game forever. And I think they'll remember us kindly."

And even those who had been nowhere near Yankee Stadium fifty-one weeks earlier could feel the residual energy still swirling within the Stadium's corridors.

"I remember seeing that game," Gary Sheffield said earlier in the year, "and saying to myself, '*That's* the reason you want to play baseball.' I knew right there that if one of those teams wanted me, that's where I wanted to play this year."

"I wanted to jump through my TV screen," Alex Rodriguez said of sitting in his Miami living room and watching the Yankees' eighth-inning comeback against Pedro Martinez.

"An astonishing game," Curt Schilling called it. "Just astonishing."

As always, though, the players were merely the temporary caretakers of those memories. One year later, after the nineteen regular-season preliminaries, after the exhibition game in Fort Myers that had set eBay bids for tickets flying sky-high, after enduring a relentless assault of hype and hyperbole from a baseball media grown completely enamored with this rivalry, fans across New York and New England were eager to put their souls on the block one more time. Yankees fans were clinging to their historical talismans, fervent in their belief that the natural order of the universe would eternally dictate these plot lines. Red

Sox fans? Once again, there flowed an inordinate amount of stress among the populace. In the oft-repeated vow of Jeffrey Lyons, the fine movie critic for WNBC-TV in New York and one of the most famously tortured Red Sox souls on earth, his tombstone would read like those of so many other true Boston believers: CAUSE OF DEATH: BOSTON RED SOX.

"They are going to put me in my grave one of these days," Lyons had said earlier in the year. "And I figured the 2003 team was as good a candidate as any. They didn't quite finish me off. I'm not sure what this team will do to me."

You could forgive Red Sox fans their skepticism; you could also forgive the Yankees fans their haughtiness. Both sets had seen plenty of treatments of this same script. New Englanders were hoping to step out of the way of the onrushing Yankee bull; Yankees fans were simply waiting for their team to slam the trunk on Red Sox Nation's collective fingers.

"You cannot deny that there is an extra level of excitement when the two teams play that you just don't get with other match-ups," Yankees fan Peter Cipriano said. "No Yankee fan likes losing to the Red Sox. Yankee fans just don't obsess about it all year the way Red Sox fans do, I guess."

Cipriano laughed. "One of the new wrinkles to this is the recent attitude in Boston that's spread from the fans to the team itself like some sort of demented SARS virus," he said. "These days, if *anything* bad happens to the Sox, it's now blamed *directly* on the Yankees. Sox didn't get A-Rod? Blame the Yankees. Sox lost 1–0 to the Blue Jays? Blame the Yankees. Beer at the concession stand is too warm? Blame the Yankees. The whole franchise is starting to sound like a younger brother that whines to Mom and Dad because big brother gets whatever he wants and they get nothing. The only thing Boston needs to see where all their problems come from is a *mirror*—but it's always easier to blame someone else than to actually fix your problems."

Pete Trinkle, Boston resident and Yankees fan, had a unique take on the matter, given his front-row seat within the enemy camp all season. "The thing that I still can't understand was the level of hatred on the

Red Sox side," he said. "Local news programs routinely refer to the Yankees as the 'Evil Empire.' People take it to another level here. They don't just hate the Yankees—they hate New York and anything from it. They enjoy watching New York teams lose, even when they aren't playing New England teams. I had one person explain to me that Boston Common was better than Central Park, and he was serious.

"New Yorkers are born with a sense of superiority: If you can make it here, you can make it anywhere. I guess we don't bother to compare ourselves with other parts of the country; we just sort of ignore them. Boston views New York as the enemy and wants to beat it at anything."

Sox fan Mike Carey, who is Trinkle's mirror opposite—a Red Sox fan living in New York—had a simple response to these observations, and the many similar ones with which he was assaulted every day.

"Please spare me," Carey said. "And please shut up."

Curt Schilling was bringing similar tidings into this series. The man around whom so many Red Sox dreams had been constructed was spotted limping into Yankee Stadium on Monday, the official workout day, and there was much talk that the ankle he'd injured during his game one start against the Angels in the Division Series was actually much worse than he was letting on. But Schilling refused to harp on it, even though the ankle in question—the right—was the one he used to push off on. And power pitchers like Schilling need their legs in working order every bit as much as their arms.

"A nonissue," he said.

What was very much an issue was Schilling's presence in this series. George Steinbrenner had done little to disguise how badly he'd wanted Schilling in pinstripes the previous November, saying that it had been Brian Cashman, among others, who'd pushed hardest for Javier Vazquez, whose psyche was so damaged he wasn't even scheduled to start at all in this series. Each of the twenty-two victories Schilling collected in 2004 stabbed the Yankees' owner like a miniature dagger. And he wasn't wont to share that pain in solitude.

Schilling understood his role and played it perfectly.

"This is what I had envisioned when I agreed to come here last year, to be part of games like this," Schilling said. "I don't know that I've ever pitched in a game that will have the atmosphere that this game has. In Arizona during the 2001 World Series, it was electric. But I think the Yankees and the Red Sox is a step above everything else."

He was just getting revved up. Schilling recalled a chat he had with Terry Mulholland when the two anchored the Philadelphia Phillies' rotation during the 1993 playoffs. "He said the awesome thing about being a starting pitcher is you have the ability to make 55,000 people shut up when you're on the road," Schilling said.

He smiled, and paused for maximum impact.

"I'm not sure of any scenario more enjoyable than making 55,000 people from New York shut up," he said.

Schilling was asking for it now. He might well have spared the middleman and pinned those words onto bulletin boards in every office, living room, and bar in the five boroughs. It's one thing to provide motivational material for another team, but for an entire fan base? New York had laughed along with Schilling in 2001 when, before the start of the World Series, someone had asked him about the prospect of pitching against the Yankees, with their vast history of playoff success.

"When you use the words 'mystique' and 'aura,'" Schilling had famously quipped, "those are dancers in a nightclub. Those are not things we concern ourselves with on the ball field." Schilling had made Yankees fans chuckle and Yankees bats crumble. That was one thing.

This was something else entirely.

So it was with great delight that the vast majority of the 56,135 people lucky enough to score tickets rose with rancor in their voices and revulsion in their hearts when Schilling took the mound in the bottom of the first inning of game one, after Mike Mussina retired the side in order in the top. And it was with an almost supernatural degree of glee that every one of them noticed right away that Schilling looked nothing like himself, right from the start, even as he induced the Yankees' first two hitters, Derek Jeter and Alex Rodriguez, to fly out to right field.

Gary Sheffield smacked a hard line drive to left for a long double, and Hideki Matsui followed with a double to deep right field, driving in the first run. When Bernie Williams added an RBI single, the Yankees had a 2–0 lead, and everyone could see that Schilling wasn't even scraping ninety miles per hour with his pitches. He was hurting, and the Yankees were feasting.

They scored four more times in the third inning, chasing Schilling, who could barely put any weight at all on his right ankle. They pushed the lead to 8–0 in the sixth, by which point everyone inside Yankee Stadium had stopped wondering if the Yankees could compete with the Red Sox and instead started pondering something else: Could Mike Mussina throw a perfect game?

Mussina had come achingly close to doing that once before, on September 2, 2001, when he'd engaged with David Cone (by then pitching for the Red Sox) in an unforgettable pitchers' duel. Mussina would win the game, 1–0, but he would lose his perfect game when pinch hitter Carl Everett singled with two outs and two strikes in the bottom of the ninth. But that had been a most pedestrian Red Sox team; this was one of the hardest-hitting teams of all time. Yet when Johnny Damon struck out feebly to lead off the seventh, Mussina stood only eight outs from throwing the second perfect game in postseason history. He hadn't looked this sharp, this unhittable, all year; he was in command of every pitch, shaving every corner, fooling every Boston hitter he faced.

Until Mark Bellhorn.

Maybe Hideki Matsui could have caught up with the Sox' second baseman's drive if he'd gotten a better jump, and perhaps he still could have nabbed the ball had it not gotten caught up in the swirling winds high above Yankee Stadium. But the point was moot. The ball landed against the left-field fence for a double, and Yankee Stadium rose to salute Mussina, now that the one remaining mystery of this blowout baseball game was out of the way. When he induced Manny Ramirez to ground to second for the second out of the inning, a fair segment of fans began filing out of the ballpark.

By now, they should have known better.

David Ortiz singled. Kevin Millar doubled in two runs. Trot Nixon singled in another, and that was all for Mussina, who left to a standing ovation, though his lead was now only 8–3. Tanyon Sturtze, who'd evolved into one of the most reliable members of Joe Torre's bullpen in the final weeks of the season and whose stature on the team had grown significantly after he'd taken such an active role in the July brawl precipitated by the Jason Varitek–Alex Rodriguez grappling match, came in to quell the Sox rally. Instead, he poured kerosene on it, surrendering a mammoth home run to Varitek that cut the Yankees' advantage to 8–5 and stemmed the exodus of Yankees fans to the Major Deegan Expressway. This was a ball game now.

An inning later, it officially became a nail-biter.

Tom Gordon, so valuable all year as Mariano Rivera's chief setup man, received the ball to start the eighth. Gordon had once been the Red Sox' closer, effective enough that he saved forty-six games and made the All-Star team in 1998, popular enough that rabid Red Sox fan Stephen King once wrote a book entitled *The Girl Who Loved Tom Gordon*. But Gordon, whose presence had helped reduce Mariano Rivera's workload significantly by limiting the number of times Rivera had to ride to an eighth-inning rescue, had himself thrown eighty-nine and two-thirds innings, the most work he'd put on his surgically repaired right arm since 1997, when he was still a starter; he'd been spotty during the Division Series win over Minnesota. He'd also been hit in the eye with a champagne cork during the clubhouse celebration in Minneapolis. He clearly wasn't in top form, but after allowing an infield single to Bill Mueller leading off the inning, he promptly struck out Damon and coaxed Bellhorn to fly out easily to left.

Manny Ramirez singled to left, pushing the tying run to the plate.

And David Ortiz nearly ripped the heart out of Yankee Stadium with one swing of his bat. Ortiz, who thought he'd put game seven out of reach with his eighth-inning homer off David Wells almost exactly one year before, caught a Gordon fastball flush and sent it on a beautiful arc toward left-center field, and the moment he made contact a sickening silence filled Yankee Stadium.

Were the Yankees *really* about to blow an eight-run lead to the Red Sox?

As it turns out, no: Ortiz had sent the ball to the patch of earth formerly referred to as Death Valley. It was no longer 457 feet out there, just 399, but it was just enough to keep Ortiz in the ballpark, halt him at third base, and maintain the Yankees' lead, ever so tenuously, at 8–7. As Joe Torre walked slowly from the dugout, a surreal silence descended on the Stadium—a nervous shroud that threatened to swallow the Yankees whole.

Metallica changed that with a set of lyrics as ominous as "Tessie's" were trite.

> *Say your prayers little one*
> *Don't forget, my son*
> *To include everyone*
> *Tuck you in, warm within*
> *Keep you free from sin*
> *Till the sandman comes*
> *Sleep with one eye open*
> *Gripping your pillow tight*

If Mariano Rivera, a devout Christian, ever bothered to listen to his theme song's lyrics, he might be horrified by what he discovered. But then Yankee Stadium would be denied one of its great theatrical moments: the instant the bullpen gate swings open and Rivera, the greatest reliever of his generation—probably of *any* generation—comes jogging in to save another one for the local nine.

The Yankees had hoped they wouldn't need Rivera on this night. For one thing, it's never a positive development when a game that had been 8–0 at one point requires a closer's presence—in the eighth inning, no less. But that was only an asterisk compared to the broader issue at war in Rivera's soul. For that very morning, in Puerto Caimito, Panama, Rivera had buried two close family members: Victor Avila, his wife's cousin, and Avila's fourteen-year-old son, also named Victor. Three days earlier—while the Yankees were closing out the Twins in Minnesota, aided by Rivera's one-two-three shift in the bottom of the eleventh—both Avilas had been killed in a pool at Rivera's house. Rivera kept the water electrified to keep his dogs out; when the younger Avila jumped in, he'd been instantly electrocuted, and his helpless father had dived in after him. The funeral in Panama was scheduled for Tuesday morning; Rivera told the Yankees he would do his best to get back in time for the game.

His return was delayed when his car got snarled in traffic on the way from his house to the airport in Panama City; thanks to a police escort, he was able to get in the air by about 2:30 New York time. The Yankees had arranged for a customs agent to greet his plane when it landed at Teterboro Airport in northern New Jersey, to expedite his paperwork. With that done, he stepped into the back of a dark blue Cadillac and received a police escort for the twelve-mile drive from the airport to Yankee Stadium. He arrived at 8:49 P.M. to a warm cheer from the small coterie of fans still standing outside the players' entrance, and then headed to the Yankees clubhouse, where a small floral arrangement had been placed in front of his locker.

Mel Stottlemyre, hearing Rivera was back, came into the clubhouse to greet him.

"How are you?" the pitching coach asked.

"Hurting," Rivera said. "But I'm here to pitch if you need me."

Now they needed him. The tying run was ninety feet away, and Kevin Millar was digging in, knowing that right-handed hitters traditionally have had more success against Rivera's signature cut fastball than lefties. Even when Rivera is at his best, he's susceptible to giving up flare hits and infield scratch hits. Millar would have taken one of those, easily. He passed on ball one, then got a good look at Rivera's second pitch—"Dang, it was *right* there," he said, "and then the sonofabitch hopped"—and popped it up high over the infield. Derek Jeter settled under it, squeezed the ball, and that was that. The Yankees tacked on a pair of insurance runs in the bottom of the inning, and Rivera ended matters for good in the ninth when he started a 1-6-3 double play. The final score was 10–7. The Yankees weren't sure whether to be relieved or exultant, but they didn't care.

"I don't think I've ever trusted anybody more than I trust Mariano," Joe Torre said. "When he says he's OK, he's OK."

Rivera himself conceded to being emotionally spent. "It was tough, coming on that plane alone," he said. "I was thinking, just tears coming out of my eyes. It was tough. It wasn't easy, almost five hours on a plane. But I was coming here to pitch. I would have been upset if I didn't pitch today."

He pitched again the next night, too, this time to protect a 3–1 cushion handed him by Jon Lieber and Tom Gordon. The Yankees had jumped out to another quick first-inning lead, as Pedro Martinez tried to tend to his business while the ubiquitous chant "Who's your daddy?" kept raining on him, but first baseman John Olerud had finally reached him for a two-run homer in the sixth, and Lieber was brilliant, his best performance as a Yankee coming at the absolute perfect moment.

When it was over, Yankees fans were jubilant over their 2–0 lead, and the New York tabloids began speculating about a sweep, the *Post* splashing a picture on its back page of Gary Sheffield, substituting a broom where Sheffield's bat should have been. Even Martinez, a loser to the Yankees again, seemed upbeat.

"I actually realized that I was somebody important tonight, because I caught the attention of sixty thousand people, plus the whole world, watching a guy that if you reverse the time back fifteen years ago, I was sitting under a mango tree without fifty cents to actually pay for a bus," Martinez said. "And today, I was the center of attention of the whole city of New York. The chanting about 'Who's your daddy,' well, my biggest daddy is the one that put me out there and the one that brought me over from the mango tree to the biggest stage in the world."

One thing was certain as the series switched venues: You really could set your watch by the Yankees and the Red Sox. No matter what, when you threw the two of them in the same building, *something* was going to happen. Because something always did.

In 1977, for the first time in a very long time, the Red Sox and the Yankees shared a summer in which they were both very good, in which they both played exceedingly well. As early as May, there was much talk of a rivalry renewed, something that put New York City in a very good mood for the first time in a very long time.

And New York needed the boost, because 1977 was turning into a long year in the metropolis formerly known as Fun City. A killer, later dubbed "Son of Sam," stalked parked cars on lover's lanes throughout the outer boroughs, leaving citywide terror and paranoia in his wake. A blackout plunged the city into darkness on July 13, sparking rampant looting. The city coffers were still scraping bankruptcy. Across town, on June 15, the Mets had officially declared themselves dead, trading future Hall of Famer Tom Seaver and slugging outfielder Dave Kingman, their only drawing cards, their only stars, for a batch of nameless and faceless players, none of whom would ever capture the city's fertile baseball imagination.

The Yankees needed a foil. New York was a one-team town again, for all practical purposes. The Mets were out of the baseball conversation and would stay that way for years. New York yearned for a villain.

They found one wearing a familiar uniform.

The Yankees–Red Sox relationship had so cooled that the only memorable moments the series yielded from the early '50s to the mid-'70s were compliments of beanball wars, bench-clearing fights, and other on-field ugliness.

On October 1, 1961, the two teams did share one of the most memorable moments in baseball history, although it was more a product of sheer scheduling luck than any leftover juice. The Red Sox happened to be in town on the last weekend of the season, which meant they provided the last opportunity for Roger Maris to hit a home run and shatter one of the most cherished records in baseball history, the single-season mark of sixty held by a former Boston pitcher named Babe Ruth. Despite the prospect of witnessing history, and despite the presence of the Yankees' oldest foe, only 23,154 fans made their way to Yankee Stadium on that Sunday afternoon. Many of them were clumped together in the lower right-field stands. One of them was a nineteen-year-old, $75-a-week truck driver from Coney Island named Sal Durante, sitting in Section 33, Box 163D, Seat 4.

When Maris stepped to the plate in the bottom of the fourth inning of a tie game, he peered at the pitcher, a green, twenty-four-year-old Virginian named Tracy Stallard who was completing a 2–7 season and would compile a lifetime mark of 30–57 and a career ERA of 4.17 in seven seasons with the Red Sox, Mets, and Cardinals. Maris had nearly gotten the record in the most unconventional way possible three innings earlier, when he'd drilled a sinking line drive to left field, where rookie Carl Yastrzemski had made a diving catch. Had Yaz not gloved the ball, it would have rolled forever in Death Valley, and Maris' record breaker may well have come on an inside-the-parker, and there wouldn't have been enough asterisks in creation to describe *that* feat for posterity.

Instead, Maris was still stuck on sixty. Stallard started off with two balls, but they didn't miss by much. The Red Sox pitcher had already determined that he wouldn't pitch around Maris.

"I was just trying to get him out," Stallard said. "Just like I want to get everyone else out. I got behind Roger and came in with a fastball. I didn't know just where about over the plate it was headed, but it would have been a strike if he hadn't hit it."

But Maris did hit it. Lou Clinton gave it chase in right field before slowing to a trot, watching it sail into a chaotic stack of arms, two of which belonged to Sal Durante. Durante, with Maris' blessing, would sell the ball for $5,000 to a Sacramento businessman named Sam Gordon and would use the money to marry his girlfriend, Rosemarie Calabrese.

Forty years later, Durante would tell a newspaper reporter: "One of the nice bonuses, looking back, was that Roger did it against the Red Sox. I think there's some historical poetry in that."

Stallard, too, would earn a permanent place in the memory of this rivalry.

"I don't feel bad about it at all," he said that afternoon. "Why should I? The guy hit sixty home runs off a bunch of other pitchers in the league before he got me today. This was the third time I pitched to him this year and the first hit he got off me. I knew he hit the shit out of it, but I didn't think it was going to be a home run. I turned around then saw the thing going way up and it came down farther back than I thought it would. I gave him what I feel was my best fastball and he hit it. That's all there was to it."

And for the next thirteen years, that was all there was to this alleged rivalry, with the exception of the on-field encounters in 1967 and 1973. The closest they'd come to chasing each other in the standings was the final grisly days of the 1966 season, when both teams were trying to avoid last place in the American League; that was one time the Red Sox did prevail in the end, finishing a half game ahead of the Yankees (helped by the fact they played three more games than the Yankees), even though New York tried to nullify even *that* small victory by winning five out of six from the Sox down the stretch.

Quite suddenly, and quite unexpectedly, the enmity crashed out of its decades-long stupor in the final six weeks of the 1974 season. Neither the Red Sox nor the Yankees were quite ready to make a championship run yet, though both had been quietly putting the pieces in place for several years, biding their time while the Baltimore Orioles dominated the American League East for the early portion of the 1970s. For much of the summer, the Red Sox had taken on a similar look to the 1967 "Impossible Dream" Red Sox, so much so that beginning in late August, as the Red Sox surged to a seven-game lead over the rest of the field, the *Boston Globe* began running day-by-day, game-by-game comparisons between the two seasons.

But a funny thing happened.

The Sox, who hadn't played in the postseason in seven years, promptly lost eight in a row, and twenty out of twenty-eight, just as August was melting into September. And the Yankees, deep into their tenth year without a taste of October, were finally reacclimating themselves to the special pressures of autumn baseball. As recently as the morning of the Fourth of July, the Yankees had been seven games under .500. As recently as July 16, they were still toiling in last place in the AL East, and Yankees fans, forced to watch their team play at Shea Stadium in Queens while Yankee Stadium underwent a two-year renovation, settled into what they assumed would be another in a seemingly endless list of moribund seasons.

Then the Red Sox began to tumble.

The Yankees, remarkably, went the other way, winning eighteen out of twenty-four in late August and early September. By the time they made their way into Boston on September 9 for a two-game series with the Red Sox, the teams were in a flat-footed tie, at 74–65, one game ahead of the stubborn Orioles. It was the closest they'd been at the top of the standings since September 19, 1950, when the Sox had been within a half game of the Yankees with twelve games to play in that season. Though the Sox were in free fall, they were actually pleased to see New York come to town since they'd beaten the Yankees eleven straight times at Fenway Park, going back to the day Munson and Fisk had first become entangled at home plate more than thirteen months earlier, the day Gene Michael had hit Fisk with his "purse."

But as Boston fans would discover often enough, the Yankees' ancient spell in meaningful October games hadn't been stricken, even if the rivalry itself had lain dormant for more than twenty years. The Yankees won both games, 6–3 and 2–1, and left the Red Sox for dead on the way to first place, seemingly on the brink of sneaking into October as their own lead grew to one and a half games with a week and a half left in the schedule.

But the Red Sox would get a small consolation prize out of their tortured stretch run. On September 24, they arrived in Flushing for a twinight doubleheader against the Yankees, whose cushion over fast-charging Baltimore had been reduced to a single game. Boston had plummeted helplessly out of the race, and the New York newspapers were stuffed with hopeful stories that if the Yankees could carry on where they'd left off in Boston and sweep the Sox, they would be able to start calculating magic numbers. There were 46,488 people waiting for the Sox at Shea, which has always been an edgier, uglier venue than any of New York's other baseball stadiums.

"Our fans are passionate," Yankees center fielder Bobby Murcer said heading into the game, "but they aren't as bad as Boston fans. In Fenway last week, they started throwing darts at us. Darts! What the *hell* is that?"

Sox fans had also adopted the customs that would last for the rest of the decade, the rest of the century, and on into the next millennium, unfurling anti-Yankees banners in the bleachers, hawking anti-Yankees T-shirts out on Jersey Street (soon to be renamed Yawkey Way). And for the first time, the profane anthem of angry Red Sox fans—"Yankees suck!"—began to echo around the ballpark. So in many ways, Shea Stadium was the perfect place for Yankees fans to answer back, to rekindle a renaissance of anti-Boston sentiment. The last years of Yankee Stadium hadn't been kind to the great rivalry, apathy and the abject Stadium conditions teaming up to suck so much of the life out of those games. Often those who did show up were Red Sox fans. Sometimes the cheers for Carl Yastrzemski were louder than the ones for Thurman Munson.

Starting this night, that would never be the case ever again.

"I was hit with three or four apple cores and I threw them back in the crowd," said Don Zimmer, who spent all eighteen innings coaching third base that night. "I didn't think much of it, but then I was hit in the back of the neck by a whole apple. I said, the hell with it, and got a batting helmet, and wore that for the last five innings."

Said Yastrzemski: "I saw two kids kick the shit out of each other. One of them was really bloody. Next thing I know, they're both yelling, 'Let's go Yankees!' What a crazy, crazy night."

It was also the last night the Yankees would spend in first place the rest of the season. The Red Sox won both games, 4–0 and 4–2, and even though the Yankees won the next day, 1–0, and in fact won five of their last six games, it wasn't enough to hold off the Orioles, who ended the season winning their final nine games, and thirteen out of fourteen. It was the final spasm of glory for a proud old Baltimore team, because the next four years would belong to the Red Sox and the Yankees. The Red Sox won handily in 1975 and came within one game of knocking off the favored Cincinnati Reds in the World Series; the Yankees dominated the rest of the AL East in 1976, finally ending a twelve-year post-season drought, and then, after knocking off Kansas City in an American League Championship Series that wasn't decided until Chris Chambliss' home run in the last inning of the last game, the Yankees were steamrolled by the Reds in four straight.

Still, both teams had been officially reloaded, and both teams had absorbed the necessary cuts and bruises that toughen all championship teams. Both were ready to make the next step. But only one of them would.

By 1977, the Red Sox had bolstered their lineup with an array of young sluggers: Fred Lynn, Jim Rice, Dwight Evans, Butch Hobson. They'd developed an All-Star shortstop in Rick Burleson. Their five-man rotation included four pitchers (Dennis Eckersley, Bill Lee, Luis Tiant, and Ferguson Jenkins) who'd been named to All-Star teams. Their first foray into the nascent free-agent pool yielded Bill Campbell, who would lead the league with thirty-one saves in 1977.

But the Yankees were also blessed with a wealth of talent, including a once or future All-Star at catcher (Munson) and at every infield position (Chambliss, Willie Randolph, Bucky Dent, Graig Nettles). Mickey Rivers was baseball's most feared leadoff hitter, Sparky Lyle its most reliable closer. Billy Martin, the manager, had lived through dozens of Yankees–Red Sox wars, some of his own creation. But the most combustible component of this wicked brew was the new right fielder, Reggie Jackson, the most coveted of all the first-time free agents. As he so enthusiastically volunteered in his very first moments as a Yankee, he hadn't come to New York to become a star; he'd brought his star with him. He'd already won an MVP award, already won three World Series rings with the Oakland A's, already driven in a hundred or more runs on three different occasions (in an era when only a couple of players per season reached that plateau), already slugged 281 home runs on the way to 563 for his career.

His impact on the Red Sox–Yankees saga was immediate and, true to the way he lived his life and managed his career, dramatic. Although both teams had broken from the gate slowly (the Yankees actually losing eight of their first ten games, initiating the first of dozens of Billy Martin watches through the years, introducing the world to just how impatient George Steinbrenner really was), the Yankees and Red Sox entered their first meeting of the 1977 season tied with each other in second place, a half game behind the Orioles. On the night of May 23, when Bill Lee made his dramatic New York City comeback almost a year to the day after tearing up his left arm in a Yankee Stadium brawl, Jackson launched a game-tying home run in the seventh inning that brought the capacity crowd to its feet. It should have been the first magic moment for Jackson in pinstripes, suitable for framing.

Only it was anything but.

After crossing home plate, instead of heading toward the right side of the Yankee dugout, where all his teammates had clustered to greet him with backslaps and handshakes, Jackson veered away and walked to the extreme left side of the bench, where he sat down alone.

It was a stunning display, one few people who were at the game could understand.

But to the Yankees, and to Jackson, it made perfect sense. That day, the first advance copies of the new issue of *Sport* magazine found their way into the Yankees clubhouse, and they caused an instant sensation. Included in a long piece written by freelance writer Roger Ward was one of the most famous quotes ever attributed to a baseball player.

"I'm the straw that stirs the drink," Jackson said in the article. "It all comes back to me. Maybe I should say me and Munson, but really he doesn't enter into it. Munson thinks he can be the straw that stirs the drink, but he can only stir it bad."

And in the fifteen or twenty seconds it took twenty-four other sets of eyes to read those sentences, Jackson had gone from messiah to pariah in his own clubhouse. Munson, the Yankees captain, was a beloved figure, the most respected Yankee in the room, the only player who'd stood up to the Reds in the previous year's World Series, hitting .529. The rest of the Yankees, white and black, starter and reserve, pitcher and hitter, took their cues from Munson. And Munson was beside himself after he read the story.

"For a man to think that Thurman Munson is jealous of anyone, that guy has got to be ignorant and an imbecile," he fumed. "I don't need material things to make me jealous of anyone. I've never done anything but try to make Reggie feel at home."

Jackson felt the icy dagger stares from the moment he'd walked in the clubhouse, and he'd absorbed the silent contempt all through batting practice. He'd already seen more than enough of Martin to know he would never be able to get along with the fiery manager. Now he was an outcast among his peers, too. But he was also a stubborn man. So even in a moment of great communal triumph, Jackson drifted off to a lonely corner of the dugout to celebrate his blast.

"I had a bad hand" was the reason he gave reporters later on for not wanting to engage his teammates.

"He hurt his hand?" Munson crowed. "He's a fucking liar. How's that for a quote?"

But Munson wasn't alone in his outrage. Veteran outfielder Jimmy Wynn said, "It was strange. I'd call it unsportsmanlike. I think he's got to realize the guys are rooting for him and want to congratulate him."

And Paul Blair, another longtime outfielder, added, "It wasn't called for. It didn't help at all. We're trying to put things together and you hate to see that."

Even long after the game, Munson was still apoplectic.

"You know, I've had some people talk to me lately, trying to sway me to keep my mouth shut," Munson said. "They don't want me to open up. I'll kiss your ass if there's anyone on this club who wants to play more than me. Nettles, Chambliss, they like to play. Roy White, Blair, they like to play. Fucking Catfish, [Don] Gullett, all those guys . . . don't get me started."

Someone told Munson that Jackson's interview with Ward had taken place nearly four months earlier, before he'd really grown comfortable as a Yankee. The captain was unmoved.

"I don't care if he said it four fuckin' years ago," he said before excusing himself, rolling up his dog-eared copy of *Sport* and sticking it in his back pocket. On his way out, he finally smiled as he said, "I'm going home to read it again."

The Yankees were in turmoil, but they were also about to put on display a rare baseball gift: That assemblage of players, personalities, and performers actually managed to play *better* when they were trapped in the middle of a buzzing shit storm. They won the next night, splitting the series. They split another two-game set in Fenway Park the following week. They gradually began playing better. They gradually began talking to Jackson again, and Reggie tried his best over the next month to fall into line, be a regular guy, even though he silently stewed that Martin refused to bat him fourth, the cleanup slot in the batting order traditionally reserved for a team's biggest bat.

"We got to the World Series with Chambliss hitting there," Martin insisted, and so he hit Jackson fifth, sixth, seventh, everywhere but fourth. But the Yankees were winning, feasting on the Western Division, so it wasn't an issue. Besides, there was another baseball calamity obscuring the discomfort in the Bronx: Across town, Seaver was demanding that the Mets trade him. Just before midnight on June 15, the team granted him his wish, shipping him to Cincinnati for a slew of young players. Minutes later, the Mets also exiled Kingman, their other prominent drawing card, sending him to San Diego for, among others, Bobby Valentine, who would be a fine manager someday but was a no-impact player. The Yankees had slowly been regaining prominence as the dominant team in the New York market anyway, a title they'd fully ceded during the Mets' improbable run to the world championship in 1969. But this midnight massacre crippled the Mets for years, and once the smoke and the outrage cleared away, there would be no other baseball distractions for New York City. The Yankees were it.

"Some kids," Graig Nettles would famously quip a few years later, "want to grow up and join the circus. And some kids want to grow up and be a baseball player. I got to do both."

The great Yankee circus arrived in Boston on a Friday night, June 17, leading the Red Sox by a half game in the standings, and it was promptly buried under an avalanche of eye-popping Red Sox power. Catfish Hunter allowed four first-inning home runs, the Sox hit six in all, and that might have gone down as the Yankees' low point in New England for the year if not for the wicked situation comedy that played itself out on national television the next afternoon. Funny as it may sound, Yankees–Red Sox wasn't the primary baseball story on New York's mind that afternoon, even a Yankees–Red Sox game with first place on the line. For in Montreal that day, Seaver made the first appearance in his career in a uniform other than the Mets' orange and blue; Mets fans already experiencing the worst week of their lives were forced to watch the new Cincinnati ace throw a three-hit shutout at the Expos on NBC-TV's Game of the Week, and they sank into an even deeper depression.

Within a few hours, Yankees fans would join them on that couch. Because in the sixth inning of another lost afternoon, in what would become a 10–4 Red Sox drubbing, Jim Rice lofted a lazy fly ball in the general vicinity of right field. Jackson had difficulty picking up the ball off Rice's bat in the hazy sky, and when he did finally see it he approached it with great trepidation, as if it contained a live explosive. By the time the ball found its way back to the infield, Rice was on second base, and Billy Martin was practically in orbit.

"I have had enough of this bullshit!" he fumed in the dugout, and before storming out to remove pitcher Mike Torrez, he practically grabbed Paul Blair and threw him toward right field. It was a surreal sight. The manager of the New York Yankees was publicly humiliating his highest-profile player. Jackson was draped along the outfield fence, shooting the shit with the boys in the bullpen, when he saw Blair running toward him, pointing.

"Who?" Jackson asked, disbelieving.

"You, Reggie," Blair said sheepishly.

"Me? Why?"

"Take it up with Billy, Reggie," Blair said. "Take it up with him."

Reggie didn't have to be asked twice. He stormed to the dugout. He marched right over to Martin.

"You never liked me and I never liked you!" Reggie said.

"You don't play hard!" Martin screeched back.

"You're a son of a bitch, nothing but an old motherfucker," Reggie roared. "You're too old. You want to fight me?"

"You want to fight *me*?" Martin asked.

They never got the chance. Elston Howard and Yogi Berra, coaches now, throwbacks to a time when the Yankees focused their anger in Fenway Park on the *other* side of the field, restrained Martin. Jackson was led off to the clubhouse. He wound up walking, alone, back to the Sheraton Hotel, convinced he'd just played his last inning as a Yankee. Truth be told, that would have been Martin's greatest wish, too.

"I only ask one thing of my players," Martin seethed afterward. "Hustle. If they hustle for me, they can play for me. I told them in spring training, I had a meeting, told them you only play one way, to win. You play hard and give me 100 percent. If you don't hustle I don't accept it. If a player shows up the club, I show up the player."

Later that night, Jackson invited a handful of reporters to his room and issued his own form of rebuttal.

"I'm a good ballplayer and a good Christian and I've got an IQ of 160, but I'm a nigger and I won't be subservient," he said. "The Yankee pinstripes are Ruth and Gehrig and DiMaggio and Mantle. They've never had a nigger like me before and they treat me like shit."

The next day, the Red Sox completed their three-day butchering of the Yankees, manhandling them 11–1. The Yankees left town two and a half games out of first, staggered, splintered, shattered. The Red Sox were flying.

"I think they'll remember this weekend," Carlton Fisk said.

He was right. They did. And they paid the Red Sox back exactly one week later, pulling off their own three-game sweep, minus the theatrics.

"Most teams, they go into disarray and, you know, they really *go into disarray*," Jim Rice would lament more than a quarter century later. "The Yankees would be at each other's throats and that's when they were *really* tough to beat. I could never understand that."

The Red Sox did play terrific baseball across most of that summer. On August 16, their record stood at 70–44, the best in the American League, four and a half games clear of the Yankees, six up in the loss column. Barring a collapse, they were set for a wonderful September pennant dash.

Barring a collapse.

On August 19, in Kansas City, the Royals handed the Red Sox a 9–3 beating. That was the turning point. The Red Sox didn't win for a week, dropping seven straight while the Yankees were in an epic groove that reached eight straight victories and, at its peak, twenty-four wins out of twenty-seven games. They passed the Red Sox on August 23, and the Sox were forced to point, in desperation, to the five games the teams still had left to play with each other. By the time they reconvened at Yankee Stadium on September 13, the Yankees' lead was only a game and a half, yet the Red Sox sounded defeated already. They were certainly spooked at the prospect of having to play such a meaningful series in a ballpark that completely disagreed with their right-handed-heavy lineup.

"We're supposed to play baseball in a ballpark, not the Grand Canyon," Jim Rice said before the first game.

"This is a park for giants and rabbits," Fisk added. "You've got to be a giant to hit it out and a rabbit to catch it."

When those comments made their way back to the Yankees manager's office, Billy Martin could barely contain his glee.

"This ballpark used to beat the Dodgers in the World Series, too," Martin crowed. "They had all those right-handed hitters and they'd smash the ball 400 feet and make a right turn at first, back to the dugout."

The Red Sox did a lot of that the next two nights. Ron Guidry suffocated them in game one, 4–2, and the Red Sox were heard audibly grumbling about the Stadium's unfriendly dimensions. But they weren't the only ones feeling melancholy. Jackson, who'd been on fire since Martin finally broke down and slotted him in the four hole in late August, had struck out three times in four at-bats during the night, belying his big-game reputation, and he was feeling a little depressed. An invitation to P. J. Clarke's on Third Avenue and Fifty-fifth Street picked him up mightily.

"You know what's gonna happen tomorrow night, right?" George Steinbrenner asked his emotional employee over a burger and a beer at the owner's favorite New York watering hole.

"I don't, George. What's going to happen?"

"You're going to hit a home run to beat those sons of bitches." Steinbrenner reached for the $30 tab, handed it to a waiter. "Consider this your reward, in advance."

The next night, Munson led off the bottom of the ninth of a scoreless tie with a single. Martin flashed third-base coach Dick Howser a batch of signs, which Howser relayed to Jackson. Jackson, confused, called time to consult with Howser.

"Dick," Jackson said, "I didn't catch the sign."

"It's a bunt, Reggie," Howser said. "Where do you like to bunt it?"

Jackson paused. It was an interesting question. A few months earlier, if Billy Martin had flashed him a bunt sign, there was a good chance that Jackson would have ignored the sign and tried to hit a screaming line drive right at Martin's head instead. Not now. Not in a pennant race. But Jackson still didn't have a good answer for Howser.

"I have no idea, Dick," Jackson said. "I don't do this too often."

Howser laughed.

"Just do the best you can, Reggie."

He didn't have to. Reggie Cleveland's first pitch was a ball, so Martin took the bunt off. Jackson fouled off the second pitch, so Martin put the bunt back on; another ball took the bunt off for good. Jackson worked the count to 3 and 2. Cleveland was determined not to give in to Jackson, not to give him a fat pitch over the heart of the plate. And he didn't.

"I threw ball four, is what I did," Cleveland would say later. "Low and outside. If he hits it, it's supposed to be a ground ball."

Jackson didn't hit a ground ball. Somehow, he turned on it, sent it soaring high and far toward the seats in right field, and Reggie, who knew a home run when he felt one, gazed lovingly at it as it made its journey toward the distant seats. The Stadium was sheer bedlam. So was home plate by the time Jackson was done taking his leisurely stroll around the bases, filled with teammates he certainly wasn't about to ignore. Not this time. Not after everything they'd been through. Jackson, with one swing, had just earned his pinstripes, against the one team against whom that always meant the most. He would never again consider himself subservient to anyone. Certainly not the Red Sox.

"You can feel everyone loving you and everyone being very appreciative," Jackson said later. "It makes me feel good that people want to share in the joy of the home run, and the excitement. Tonight, they got something back from me. This is my most satisfying moment as a Yankee. I'm not Joe DiMaggio. I'm not Mickey Mantle. I'm not Lou Gehrig. I never will be."

For once in his life, Reggie Jackson had undersold himself.

For the first time in too long, people on both sides of the Red Sox–Yankees schism could understand what a real summer-long pennant race tasted like.

What they wouldn't have believed, even if you'd told them, was that it was merely an appetizer.

Wait until they got a look at the main course.

It was a hell of a way to celebrate an anniversary.

Game three of the 2004 American League Championship Series was washed away by torrential rains, meaning the series would resume on Saturday, October 16—one year to the day after the game seven mini-classic for which the '03 ALCS was bound to be forever remembered. This game, too, was destined to bleed past midnight and usher everyone from October 16 to October 17. But there was one little difference.

By midnight, the Yankees had a nine–run lead.

By 12:30, it was an eleven-run lead.

And that's how it ended: Yankees 19, Red Sox 8. Numerologists could have a field day with that: 19–8. It could be a score. Or the hyphen could represent a missing digit. And if Red Sox fans really wanted to torture themselves, they could make that digit a one, make that number 1918, and there's no telling how many sleepless nights that could produce.

But why would Red Sox fans want *additional* torture? What was the point? Hadn't they just seen the Yankees pound out twenty-two hits? Hadn't they seen a procession of pitchers get pulverized by Yankees boasting batting averages so high as to be almost obscene? Hadn't Hideki Matsui and Bernie Williams just tied a postseason record by scoring five runs . . . *apiece*? And worst of all, weren't the Sox now in a three-games-to-none hole in this best-of-seven series?

Jesus. Weren't the Sox about to get swept by the Yankees?

Or, as so many Red Sox fans had come to call them, the MFYs? (Use your imagination to figure out what the initials stand for.)

"This is as big a hole as you could dig yourself in," said Bronson Arroyo, Boston's young starting pitcher, who'd been brutalized in the most important game of his young career. "At crunch time, to have a football score up there like that is definitely embarrassing."

The bad news had been arriving in waves, almost from the start of the series. First Schilling had gotten bombed. Then he revealed that his ankle was, in fact, as bad as it looked to be. His arm had been perfect for Game One; it was his legs that robbed him of his velocity. Immediately after the game, Schilling himself had admitted, "If I can't go out there with something better than what I had today, I'm not going back out there. This isn't about me braving through something. This is about us and winning the championship, and if I can't give them better than I had, I won't take the ball again."

A day later, Red Sox physician Dr. William Morgan had expanded on the grisly nature of Schilling's ankle, describing it as "a subluxation, or a tear, on one of the tendons in his ankle, the sheath that houses the tendons themselves, so now the tendon is snapping over the bone. We've been working on ways of making modifications for that so that he'll be able to continue to pitch."

Morgan had pitched the notion that Schilling might be ready for a game five; Terry Francona saw game six as a far more realistic possibility.

And now the most likely scenario was Fort Myers, next February.

That's how depressing the night had been. The Yankees were up 3–0 in an eye blink, smoking everything Arroyo was throwing at them. The Red Sox came back against Kevin Brown, who'd only recently been allowed to see the sun again after spending almost six weeks deep on Torre's shit list for breaking his left (nonthrowing) hand when he punched a clubhouse wall at Yankee Stadium. But Alex Rodriguez hit a breathtaking home run over the screen in left field in the third to tie the game immediately, and Sheffield hit a backbreaking three-run job to give the Yankees the lead for good one inning later, and it was off to the races from there.

Or, if you lived in Boston and rooted for the Red Sox, off to a long, restless, sleepless night. Or a bar. It was that bad.

"You know what? It doesn't matter," Francona said. "Tomorrow is going to come real quick, and we've got to try to win tomorrow. I mean, I sat in that dugout for a lot of wins this year and took the smiles and the laughs and everything. You have to sit through a night like tonight, I can't wait—I won't bail on those guys. We'll show up tomorrow and play. It was disappointing for everybody, but we're not done. I fully expect we'll come out tomorrow and play our asses off."

It's what the manager was supposed to say, but it sounded like so much vacant happy talk. So did this message from Johnny Damon, uttered in a voice so quiet it barely registered: "I still think we can do it."

Yeah. Right. Sure they could. In the entire history of playoff baseball, dating to 1903, no team had ever come back from an 0–3 hole to win a seven-game series. In the entire history of American team sports, exactly two teams had done it—both times in hockey. The Red Sox could reverse all of that now? *Against the Yankees?*

Yeah.

Right.

Sure they could.

HERE WE GO AGAIN

Last year was last year. —*Tim Wakefield, October 18, 2004*

They're tough sons of bitches. We're tough sons of bitches. When we play
it's like it's always been. It's the Red Sox and the Yankees, the Yankees and
the Red Sox, and we're gonna try and kick each other's asses until only
one of us is standing. —*Lou Piniella, September 29, 1978*

For decades, Red Sox fans had watched with a blend of wonder and
wariness as the Yankees pulled one personnel coup after another
out of the sky. This was the hardest reality to accept if you pulled
against the Yankees, and if New England may not have been the only
anti-Yankee district in baseball America, it was certainly the most fervent. It's easy, after all, to dismiss the Yankees as bullies who overwhelm
you with their bottomless bottom line. As much as the Yankees' financial might has been a boon to them over the years, it has also provided
aid and comfort to their on-field enemies, too, in the form of a built-in
excuse. *We can't spend with them,* the masses scream. *How can we beat
them?*

The problem with that logic is that it was never always the brass-
plated names that beat the Red Sox over the years in so many games.
Yes, Reggie Jackson hit a home run in that fabled 1978 playoff game,
but it was Bucky Dent's blast that everyone remembers, especially since
he hit only thirty-nine others in his entire twelve-year career. Ron

Guidry, who won twenty-four games that year and single-handedly kept the Yankees in the race that summer? The Yankees tried to include him in almost every trade they consummated from 1974 through 1977, didn't, and backed into an ace instead—a tale eerily similar to the way the Yankees were forced to keep Andy Pettitte in the fold for so many years. Joe DiMaggio was the star of the 1949 Yankees, but it was Johnny Lindell (seventy-two lifetime long balls) who hit the home run on the final weekend in 1949 that kept the Yankees alive in *that* race. On and on, through the years, it has been the humble Yankees, the unnoticed pickups, who have shone as brightly as the stars. Scott Brosius hit .203 as an Oakland Athletic in 1997; traded to the Yankees a year later, he hit .300 out of the number nine slot in the batting order and was named World Series MVP. Chad Curtis hit a key home run in the 1999 World Series; Luis Sojo contributed the hit that won the championship in 2000.

"It's like magic," Derek Jeter had marveled in 2001. "Guys come here, they wear pinstripes, and they start doing things they never did before. Magic."

The Red Sox never knew such magic. Not until January 22, 2003, that is. That was the day they completed a little-heralded deal, one of the many minor midwinter pickups that litter the transactions lists of newspaper agate pages. For the relatively modest sum of $1.25 million for the 2003 season, the Sox added some left-handed pop to their lineup by signing a six-foot-four, 240-pound first baseman/designated hitter named David Americo Ortiz Arias. In 2002, Ortiz had helped lead the Minnesota Twins to the American League Championship Series, hitting .272 with twenty home runs and seventy-five runs batted in. He was an enormously popular clubhouse presence with the Twins, earning the nickname "Cookie Monster" for his affable personality and his affinity for junk food. He was twenty-seven years old, and with three years of big-league service time under his belt, he was eligible for salary arbitration, which meant a jump from the $950,000 the Twins had paid him in '02 to something in the $2 million range. And the Twins, who sang the small-market blues louder than anyone else even though their owner, Carl Pohlad, had more personal wealth than any other owner in baseball, didn't want to cough up that kind of money. So on December 16, 2002, they released Ortiz.

"This isn't an easy decision," Twins general manager Terry Ryan said at the time. "But when you're in our shoes, sometimes you have to make tough decisions."

When you are in Theo Epstein's shoes, sometimes you have to size up such a gross miscalculation, see it as manna from heaven, and seize it. There was only one other team that showed any credible interest in Ortiz. One man, specifically. George Steinbrenner called Brian Cashman when he saw Ortiz was available, and asked his general manager if he thought Ortiz was a player worth pursuing.

"I've always liked him," Steinbrenner said.

But Cashman assured his boss the Yankees were already crowded with first basemen. Jason Giambi was coming off forty-one homers and 122 RBIs in 2002. Nick Johnson, the Yankees' brightest young prospect, also played the position, and he'd be given plenty of work there in 2003. Cashman saw Ortiz as a luxury the Yankees didn't need. Steinbrenner reluctantly acceded, although he told his general manager that he reserved the right to remind Cashman of this down the road. Cashman understood.

Ortiz signed on with the Sox.

"We think, all the scouts think, he has a very high ceiling," Epstein said. "You're looking at a player with the potential to be a middle-of-the-lineup bat. We're comfortable with him defensively, and more than comfortable with him offensively."

But even the Red Sox had little idea what they'd obtained. By the time Ortiz reported to spring training, he found himself behind Jeremy Giambi on the Sox' first-base depth chart, and there would be a lot of players clamoring for at-bats as designated hitter. Ortiz had instantly become as much of a cheery presence in the Sox' clubhouse as he had in the Twins', and he picked up another nickname, this one a term of high affection bestowed by the Sox' Latin players: "Papi." Still, he stewed as he waited for a chance to play every day. "That's all I've ever wanted," he said in April 2003. "Just let me prove myself."

Players always say that when they want more at-bats. But Ortiz did something else: Once Giambi started breaking down and Grady Little started penciling him into the lineup every day, he did exactly what he swore he'd do given the opening. He hit .288. He slammed thirty-one homers, often taking advantage of the Wall with a powerful opposite-field stroke. He drove in 101 runs. Best of all, he had some of his grandest moments against the Yankees, which allowed the Sox a measure of satisfaction in the aftermath of the Contreras mess, and afforded Steinbrenner many opportunities to browbeat his general manager. In 2004, he was even better: forty-one home runs, a .301 batting average, 139 RBIs. He was, unquestionably, one of the five most dangerous offensive players in all of baseball, and teamed with Manny Ramirez to form the most feared heart of any batting order. Better, he brought the promise of something special every time he walked to the plate. The Angels surely found that out in the Division Series, which Ortiz ended with his shot over the Wall.

Now Ortiz had another opportunity. It was the bottom of the twelfth inning, game four of the 2004 American League Championship Series, October 17, 2004. The Red Sox and Yankees were tied 4–4. Manny Ramirez stood on first base. Paul Quantrill, the fifth Yankee pitcher of the night, stood on the mound. And 34,826 people were coiled like springs, ready to detonate, only hours after they'd half expected to see their baseball team lie in state in the last Fenway Park game of the year. As Ortiz stepped to the plate, the game passed the five-hour mark, already the longest in the thirty-five-year history of the American League Championship Series.

"Every inning was torture," Red Sox fan John Miller said.

"Every pitch made me want to throw up," Mike Carey said.

Still, with Ortiz at the plate, an odd serenity filled Fenway Park. Somehow, this onetime afterthought had become the most trusted man in Red Sox history.

"One thing I knew," Carey said. "Papi wasn't gonna pop up. Not while he was on the amazing run he was on. No way. No how. Not in this season."

What was truly amazing was that there was any season at all left for Ortiz to save, that the Sox and their fans weren't already far away from the Fens at 1:20 in the morning, that the Yankees hadn't already dried the champagne out of their hair and gotten on with the business of trying to win a twenty-seventh World Series.

Because less than two hours earlier, the Red Sox had been—no need to use any euphemisms here—dead. They were trailing 3–0 in games in this best-of-seven series. They were losing 4–3 in the bottom of the ninth inning, with Mariano Rivera on the mound. Since Rivera became the Yankees' closer in 1997, he had pitched in fifty-five postseason games. He had blown exactly three saves. In nine postseason games against the Red Sox—the team that had long given him the most trouble during the regular season—he'd been virtually untouchable: nine games, fifteen and one-third innings, thirteen hits, one run. Six saves in six chances. Fenway had already accepted what it was about to see, even if the thought of the MFYs celebrating on its home turf made the entire city sick to its collective stomach.

Kevin Millar led off the inning. Prior to the game, he'd fired off one last hopeful rejoinder to the avalanche of negativity swirling around New England, simultaneously triggering what sure seemed like an empty warning shot in the Yankees' direction: "Don't let us win tonight. This is a big game. They've got to win because if we win we've got Pedro coming back tomorrow and then Schilling will pitch game six and then you can take that fraud stuff and put it to bed. *Don't let the Sox win this game.*"

If it sounded like one final quality sound bite concluding a two-year run in which Millar had become one of the greatest go-to guys in the history of sportswriting, Millar decided to do something about it now: He drew a walk. Ball four caused Rivera to kick the dirt on the pitcher's mound, understandable since his memory was rewinding a few weeks, to the Friday night in Yankee Stadium when the Sox had reached him for the second time. That rally had also begun with a leadoff walk. That time, it had been Trot Nixon, but the real trouble began when Dave Roberts—one of Epstein's deadline pickups—had pinch-run for Nixon, stolen second, and set the comeback up on a tee.

Now here came Roberts again, replacing Millar at first base.

And up stepped Bill Mueller, the *other* principal player in the *other* game Rivera had lost to the Red Sox, all the way back in July.

Rivera remembered. He kept throwing over to first, trying to keep Roberts close while still trying to keep his mind on Mueller. Roberts kept diving back safely. Nothing stirred inside Fenway Park. This was the whole season.

In the first-base dugout, Terry Francona faced the first officially urgent moment of his managerial career. He'd never been in this position before, where one decision could end seven months of work. He'd never been in an elimination game before, unless you counted all those years in Philadelphia when someone would report after a game in early September that his team had officially been mathematically eliminated from the playoff chase. This was different. Boston had eyed him suspiciously all season long. One time, in a game against the Yankees in late September, he'd actually charged from the dugout with the intention of getting thrown out of the game, hoping to provide a spark for his team, and when it finally happened he was booed all the way back to the clubhouse. Now, Red Sox fans wondered, would Francona have the sack to send Roberts? There was no right answer in this situation. If Roberts made it, it was the right choice. If he didn't, Francona would have officially put himself on the firing line. Fun job.

"I think Dave is one of the few runners in the league that you can put him in a situation like that, give him the green light, and he can go ahead and steal a base when they are trying to hold him, trying not to let him steal," Francona would explain later. "He's done that a few times and directly led to wins for us."

Roberts did it this time, too, and got an extraordinary jump. Jorge

Posada made a strong throw but never had a chance. Advantage, Francona. And now Fenway was electric. For the first time all night, it didn't feel like the faithful were watching a sad death march, but rather a baseball team that hadn't yet given up on its season, which was backing up all of its brave words with action.

Then Mueller singled up the middle.

And Roberts came racing home.

And the look of horror on Mariano Rivera's face said it all to Red Sox fans: *This really isn't over.* A sacrifice by Doug Mientkiewicz moved Mueller to second, and an error by Tony Clark on a routine Johnny Damon grounder moved the winning run to third with one out, and suddenly you could see the Fenway Park grandstand literally shake with gleeful tremors. But this is where Rivera turned back into Rivera. He blew three strikes past Orlando Cabrera. And he induced Manny Ramirez to pop up.

Fenway didn't care. Even if this was just one more excruciating taunting by the gods, they'd seen Mariano Rivera surrender the pennant, however temporarily. That was something, right?

Now, much later, with Ortiz at the plate, they had the chance for something more, something even better. Quantrill threw two balls. He threw one strike. Each pitch seemed to bump the tension a few degrees higher. Quantrill threw a fastball. Ortiz swung.

The crowd thought he got it right away, then started to wonder as Gary Sheffield started running after the ball, looking as if he might have a play. But then he slowed, and finally he stopped altogether. That's when Ortiz finally raised his arms in recognition and started his gallop, while the rest of his teammates crowded around home plate waiting for him to finish his magnificent journey. Some players play their whole careers and never get a moment like this, a walk-off homer to win a playoff game; Ortiz had gotten two of them in the space of ten days.

"We're alive," Papi said. "We got more baseball to play."

Suddenly, that idea energized Red Sox fans in a way they hadn't believed possible until this very moment. The lateness of the game meant that the subways were closed; thousands of fans had no way of getting home, so they simply hung around and packed the streets surrounding Fenway Park, staying long into the morning.

"Sox in seven!" went the chant.

"Sox in seven!" came the chorus.

They were loud but peaceful. "They're just excited," one cop said. "They aren't bothering anyone. Believe me, the neighbors don't mind."

Those who weren't there started to let their imaginations run wild. Mike Carey, watching from his home in Queens, got on the phone with his brother, Liam, in California and started speaking in tongues as soon as he heard "Hello."

"Look," he said, "we have Pedro going tonight, at home, and you just *know* he's due to have a big game against these guys. All we have to do is win this one, then we got Schilling going in game six, and I don't care if they have to amputate afterward, there's no way he's gonna lose that. Then we're tied. And at that point, I'll take our chances in a seventh game. . . ."

If that call had been placed even two hours earlier, Liam Carey might have suggested the name of a good therapist for his kid brother. Not now. Suddenly, anything seemed possible.

Besides, as any Red Sox fan with any sense of history could have told you, despite popular belief, the Red Sox hadn't always lain down before the Yankees' scepter.

"Not that anyone ever wants to remember this, of course," Johnny Pesky said. "But we beat those sons of bitches a bunch of big games." The old infielder shook his head sadly, tilting his blue cap to shield himself from the sun, and maybe from a lifetime of hearing how he could never lick the Yankees. "A *bunch* of big games."

The fact is, for the longest time, it was the Red Sox who held sway over the Yankees. There was 1904, of course, when the Red Sox were the Pilgrims and the Yankees were the Highlanders, and they'd chased each other to the final Monday of the season before Boston reestablished supremacy. Then there were four and a half decades of dormancy before the Yankees and the Red Sox could ever figure a way to field championship-caliber teams at the same time.

But in the heady first few years after World War II, there was little doubt in anyone's mind that the Red Sox and the Yankees had blossomed into the two most powerful teams in baseball. The Red Sox won 104 games in 1946, finished twelve games clear of the rest of the American League (seventeen ahead of the Yankees), and came within a game of winning their first World Series in twenty-eight years; the Yankees had followed with ninety-seven victories in 1947, twelve ahead of Detroit and fourteen in front of the Red Sox, capped by a seven-game World Series win over the Dodgers, their first championship in four years.

By 1948, the Red Sox had Joe McCarthy managing, they had pitching, they had a lineup that would average nearly six runs a game. The Yankees were getting older and grayer, but they still had DiMaggio in his prime and a kid catcher named Yogi Berra on the rise, they were still the defending champions, and they were still, of course, *the Yankees.* And into the mix stepped an unlikely third-party candidate, the Indians, who hadn't finished within double digits of first place in eight years, hadn't won a pennant in twenty-eight, but were now led by a thirty-year-old player-manager named Lou Boudreau, who was about to embark on a fairy-tale season.

It was a wild, unpredictable ride for all three teams. The Indians jumped out quickest, and after sweeping a doubleheader from the Yankees on June 12, they were three and a half games ahead of the field but, more notably, six games in front of the Yankees and a full eleven games ahead of the staggering Red Sox; they wouldn't be going away anytime soon. But neither were the other two teams. The Yankees won fourteen of their next twenty, and by the Fourth of July they'd pulled to within a game and a half of the top. By then, the Red Sox were also lurking, having finally figured out McCarthy's quirks and odd quibbles, playing better ball, edging to within eight games of Cleveland. Then things *really* heated up. The Sox swept three from the Yankees at Fenway, and suddenly they were in a full swagger. Between July 4 and July 31, the Sox went 25–5, winning twelve in a row at one point and seventeen out of nineteen, and by the end of the month the Red Sox found themselves, quite improbably, in first place by two games.

The Red Sox, in fact, were the only one of the three contenders that made even the slightest pretense that they were capable of running away from the others. On one absurd day, in fact—August 3, 1948—there were four teams (the A's being the fourth) that were locked in a virtual tie for first place, but as August segued into September, the Red Sox embarked on another nine-game winning streak that culminated when they took the first two of a three-game series with the Yankees on September 9.

At the close of business that day, the Red Sox had won sixty-nine of their previous ninety-three games since June 3, an almost inhuman .742 pace. They led the Yankees by three and a half, the Indians by four and a half, and seemed primed to run away with the American League. The city of Boston was in a full-blown frenzy, because unlike the Red Sox' easy pennant glide two years earlier, this time the Yankees were still very much in play; that three-game series at Fenway Park marked the first time in forty-four years that the two teams met so late in a season with direct playoff implications for both participants.

"I was young, and I hadn't seen too much yet," Yogi Berra remembered more than half a century later. "But I'll never forget how excited Boston was when we showed up those three games. First time I ever played with goose bumps."

This, in essence, was the postwar coming-out party for what would become the defining rivalry in all of baseball. Remember, at this point, the Yankees hadn't yet been forced to defend their decades-long dominance over Boston on the field. There was no baggage yet weighing down the collective mind-set of the Red Sox, or their devotees. In each of the first two games of this seminal collision, in fact, it was the Yankees who stormed to big early leads, only to see the Red Sox calmly rally back and sprint past them, 10-6 in the first game and 9-4 in the second. Newspaper reporters in both cities cautiously wondered if they weren't finally witnessing a shifting of power, from New York to Boston, reversing the winds that had swept the two franchises in different directions almost thirty years earlier.

These feelings were nearly fortified in the finale, with the Red Sox poised to bury New York for good. The Yankees again jumped out to a 6–2 advantage, and again they squandered every ounce of it, the Red Sox forcing extra innings and driving a full Fenway Park to the brink of its wits. The Yankees did load the bases with one out in the top of the tenth inning against forty-three-year-old right-hander Earl Caldwell, but the cagey veteran struck out the normally reliable Hank Bauer. Up stepped Joe DiMaggio, whose heel was starting to scream at him, who had played much of the second half of the season with a throbbing charley horse, who nevertheless, at age thirty-three, was putting together the last truly great season (.320, thirty-nine homers, 155 RBIs) of his life.

"The man had trouble walking most of the last two months of that season," Johnny Pesky said. "And yet, against us, he always managed to walk on nails, or through a bed of hot coals, anything he had to do to beat us."

Caldwell quickly got ahead of DiMaggio, although the second strike was a mammoth drive that barely curved outside the left-field foul pole before settling into the screen. Shaken, Caldwell threw two straight balls, and Fenway filled with a nervous buzz; no player ever petrified them more than DiMaggio, and with good reason. On Caldwell's fifth pitch, DiMaggio connected, a rocket shot that soared high above his brother's head in center field, clearing the 379-foot sign, settling ten rows deep in the bleachers. Fenway fell silent. The Yankees won, 11–6. They were still very much alive.

But so were the Indians. And so, despite that deflating loss, were the Red Sox. On the morning of September 25, all three teams were knotted once again, with 91–54 records, but the Indians, who would win twenty of the twenty-six games they played in September, inched ever so slightly ahead. By the time the Yankees and Red Sox reconvened at Fenway Park on the afternoon of Saturday, October 2, they were both a game behind the Indians. There was no wiggle space, no margin for error, on either side.

And when word reached Boston that the Indians had clinched at least a tie for the pennant by beating the Tigers before more than 80,000 pennant-fevered fans in Cleveland, there was suddenly *no* room. The loser of this game would be immediately eliminated; the winner would still need some help from the Tigers on Sunday and would have to win themselves that day, too, in order to force a one-game playoff. On so many autumn days and nights in so many years to come, the blueprint for what would happen at Fenway would seem inevitable, almost preordained.

But on this day, it was the *Yankees* who blinked first. And it wasn't close. Ted Williams—who would spend so much of his career defending his performances in big games—seized this one by the throat, drilling a two-run home run in the first inning, kick-starting a final weekend in which he would come to bat ten times and deliver eight hits. This delighted the gathering of 32,118 anxious fans that grew quiet every time DiMaggio walked to the plate, waiting for him to do *something* to ruin their weekend. But that never happened. He did crack a double in the seventh, but by then the Red Sox were comfortably ahead, 5–1. It ended that way, and afterward, Joe McCarthy, for maybe the only time in his tempestuous two-and-a-half-year reign as Red Sox manager, looked the part he was hired to play: the swaggering Hall of Famer who would find a way to drag even the Red Sox to the finish.

"Stay with me, boys!" McCarthy crowed in the gleeful Red Sox clubhouse to his giddy players. "Cleveland's gonna get knocked off by Detroit tomorrow, and we're taking the Yankees! That's the ending, boys. That's my dream."

Joe DiMaggio would spend that night at his brother's house in suburban Wellesley, where much of the DiMaggio clan had gathered in anticipation of Dominic's impending wedding, to Emily Frederick. Before Saturday's game, Dominic had confided to a Boston reporter, "This is a special time for all of us, not just because of the wedding. This is the first time our parents have ever seen Joe and me play against each other."

Joe's heel was killing him the next morning, everyone in the family could see that, but Dominic knew his brother too well to think he would sit out this game, even if it was now completely meaningless to the Yankees. "It meant everything to us and to Cleveland," Dom would explain many years later. "And so it meant everything to him, too." As they drove in together for the Sunday finale after attending morning Mass, the brothers rode mostly in silence. As they neared the park, Joe suddenly piped up.

"You got us yesterday, but we'll take you out today. I'll see to it personally."

"I may have something to say about that," Dom replied. "I'll be out there, too."

"I'm gonna get my fortieth homer," Joe predicted.

"I don't think you will," Dom answered. "But I'm gonna get my ninth."

Dominic, it tuned out, proved the prophet on both counts. He did hit his ninth home run, and it helped the Red Sox win the game, 10–5, ending the Yankees' season on a sour note but buying Boston another day, since the Indians had proved true to McCarthy's prediction, losing to the Tigers, forcing a one-game playoff the next day at Fenway Park.

Of course, the Yankees—specifically, Joe DiMaggio—did find a way to faintly foil what would have been the wildest baseball party in Boston's history. The Braves had already wrapped up the National League pennant, meaning the Hub was now one win away from a first-ever all-Boston World Series. Caught up in their excitement, dreaming about all the possibilities the coming week could hold, many Red Sox fans failed to notice how DiMaggio was helping to lay the foundation for a looming Boston calamity. He had doubled in the first inning, driving in a run and staking the Yankees to a fleeting lead. In the fifth, with the Red Sox now holding a 5–2 advantage, the mule-stubborn McCarthy opted to pitch to DiMaggio with two outs and two on, and the Yankee Clipper promptly doubled to cut the Sox' lead to 5–4. With that, something snapped inside McCarthy. Boston rebuilt its lead, finally to 10–5, but McCarthy, paranoid now that DiMaggio was on a single-minded quest to destroy his team, ordered a thirty-six-year-old journeyman right-hander named Denny Galehouse to warm up, and keep warming up, in the event that McCarthy needed a righty pitcher to neutralize the righty-swinging DiMaggio late in a tight game.

DiMaggio did finish the game four for five, enduring all of it in excruciating pain, and when he singled in the ninth inning, Yankees manager Bucky Harris gave him a fitting curtain call by sending little-used infielder Steve Souchock in to run for him. The crowd of 31,306 gave DiMaggio a protracted standing ovation as he limped off the field, and he responded by tipping his cap—something no amount of Fenway Park adoration could ever coax out of Ted Williams. It was only then, with DiMaggio officially out, that McCarthy sent word to the bullpen that Galehouse could sit down. He'd been warming up for nearly five innings. There is no telling how many meaningless pitches he threw.

"He pitched the equivalent of a whole game there in the bullpen," one of his teammates would later grumble anonymously to the Boston *Post*. So when McCarthy stunned the world by giving the ball to Galehouse the next day in the one-game playoff against Cleveland—bypassing Mel Parnell, among others—he was handing it not just to a surprised pitcher, but to a tired one. Galehouse, famously, was slaughtered, and the Sox lost out on the pennant. And while the Red Sox may have eliminated the Yankees from the pennant, so, too, had the Yankees indirectly done the same thing to the Sox.

Still, the Red Sox' late-season dominance of the Yankees had inspired the Boston *Post*, in an unsigned editorial, to report on the season's final day: "Today ends an era in sport—the end of the Yankees' dominance of the American League."

A year later, DiMaggio would test that theory to its limits with his welcome-back explosion at Fenway Park at the end of June. But as dire as Boston's circumstances would look that early in the summer—following a Fourth of July sweep at Yankee Stadium, the Red Sox stood at 35–36, twelve full games behind the Yankees—they would spend the rest of the season on a historic roll, putting together two separate seven-game winning streaks, an eight-game run, and an eleven-game tear. By the time the Yankees and Red Sox split a two-game series at Yankee Stadium in early September, the Sox were within a game of first place, and both teams eagerly looked forward to the five games they had left with each other: two at Fenway Park on the next-to-last weekend of the season; one immediately following at Yankee Stadium, a makeup date for an earlier rainout; and then two more at the Stadium on the season's final weekend.

"We don't have to win all five from the Yankees, or even four," Ted Williams said. "I've said that all along we could do it even when we were twelve games out. After what happened last year when we caught Cleveland on the day before the season ended, I'm convinced anything can happen."

Anything *did* happen, and it was a devastating blow to the Yankees. On September 18, after taking batting practice at Yankee Stadium before a game with the Indians, DiMaggio started to feel ill. Yankees team doctor Jacques Fischl called it "grippe" and said DiMaggio would only miss a few days and would surely be back in time for the first showdown with Boston, beginning in six days. That turned out to be a terribly optimistic diagnosis. In fact, DiMaggio had viral pneumonia, and it weakened him so completely he found himself back where he'd been in the spring, unable to get out of his bed at the Elysee. On September 21, although Dr. Fischl announced, "He was better last evening, and there is every indication he should be up and around within a week," it was also announced that DiMaggio wouldn't be available for the key "pennant series" coming up against the Red Sox.

Stengel, so close to his first-ever pennant that he could taste it, lamented, "They told me he'd be laid up for two days, and now it's four, pretty soon it'll be a week, and then in another week the season will be over."

As hot as the Red Sox were playing, that didn't sound so outlandish, either. When the Yankees arrived at Fenway Park on September 24, they'd managed to win four of the six games DiMaggio had already missed, but the Red Sox came in with a seven-game winning streak, and though the Yankees' cushion stood at two games, both teams understood a Red Sox sweep not only would topple the Yankees out of first place for the first time all season, it could demoralize the Yankees so much they might never recover.

McCarthy, hardly chastened from his premature bluster of the year before, said on the eve of the series, "You bet we feel good. We don't intend to get out of first place once we've gotten there."

Added Ellis Kinder: "They have to remember what we did to them when it counted last year. That has to be in their minds."

Kinder would be starting the first game of the series against the Yankees that Saturday afternoon at Fenway, and the evening before, Ralph Houk, the Yankees' backup catcher, tried to take one for the team by going out on the town with his old friend, who knew his way around most of Boston's essential nightspots. Houk and Kinder, who'd been battery mates in the minor leagues at Binghamton, New York, stayed out all night, and neither man was drinking ginger ale, and while this was technically a bold violation of curfew, Stengel privately commended his catcher.

"Mr. Houk did his part for the cause," Stengel said years later.

Mr. Houk, nursing an epic hangover, reported for work a few hours after finally calling it a morning and told his teammates, "You should be OK. Believe me, the other guy looks worse than I do."

Houk tucked himself into a corner of the Yankees' bullpen and listened to his head pound. From there, he watched Kinder throw a six-hit shutout, maybe the most magnificent performance of Kinder's career, which spanned twelve years and 102 victories. Only one Yankee reached third base all day. Ted Williams continued his September mastery of the

Yankees, blasting a 400-foot home run. Scalpers reported brisk sales; general-admission seats that normally went for $1.80 were fetching as much as $5, while you could peddle a $9 box seat for as high as $25. Everyone in Boston wanted in; 34,515 managed to get there. The Sox were within a game, thanks to their twentieth straight win at Fenway and ninth straight overall, thanks to Kinder's thirteenth victory in a row, his career-best twenty-third of the season.

A day later, Parnell was even stingier, winning his twenty-fifth game with a four-hitter, 4–1. Pesky cracked the ice with a two-run single in the second inning, while Williams put the game away with his forty-third homer in the seventh. Not incidentally, on four separate occasions, the Yankees had runners on base when the number four slot in the batting order—DiMaggio's spot—came up, and all four times the Yankees failed to get the runners in. They were staggering, and with the loss yielded sole possession of first place for the first time since the fourth day of the season.

"At this point, I don't know that I've ever been part of a team that's played this well," said McCarthy, who had won seven titles with the Yankees, all of them in breezes. "You have to play almost perfect baseball to beat us."

McCarthy's hubris was contagious; his players enjoyed a most enjoyable train ride to New York to play the makeup game Monday afternoon. The Yankees, arriving at Grand Central Terminal Sunday night suddenly locked in a first-place tie, were greeted by a modest mob of fans that included Babe Ruth's widow. But those last strands of optimism would be tested the next afternoon. First, the Red Sox cuffed around Yankees starter Tommy Byrnes, scoring three times and knocking out Byrnes before he could record even one out.

But the Red Sox had something far more sinister in mind. At the beginning, they would watch the Yankees score six unanswered runs, which could have been nine unanswered runs but for a miraculous catch by right fielder Al Zarilla, who robbed Johnny Lindell of a three-run homer in the second inning. Stengel handed the ball to Joe Page, who was having the best year of his career, and all was well until the eighth inning, when Boston's Birdie Tebbets led off with a single and pinch hitter Lou Stringer followed with a walk. Dominic DiMaggio then ripped a scorching line drive right at Phil Rizzuto at short.

"I didn't even have to move," Rizzuto recalled. "It went straight into my glove."

It would have been an easy triple play, an early entry into the log of Red Sox hard luck, and it would have sent a jolt through Yankee Stadium that would *still* have been felt more than half a century later. Only there was one problem. The ball was hit so hard, it didn't just hit Rizzuto's glove. It bored its way *through* the mitt.

"Tore the webbing right off," Rizzuto said. "Only time I ever saw that happen. Ever. It was like a bad movie."

The ball rolled away from Rizzuto, Tebbets scored, and suddenly the Red Sox were very much in business. Pesky then sliced a ball to second base, where George Stirnweiss booted it for an error, scoring Stringer and trimming the lead to 6–5. Stirnweiss tried to make immediate amends, gloving a whistling shot by Ted Williams, but a shaken Page never covered first. Now it was bases loaded, nobody out, and Yankee Stadium was filled with a sickening silence. The quiet grew even eerier a few moments later when Junior Stephens lofted a sacrifice fly that scored the tying run and moved Pesky to third with the go-ahead run.

This is when the fabled 1949 pennant race *really* started to get interesting.

Bobby Doerr laid down a splendid bunt, trying to squeeze Pesky across the plate, but Tommy Henrich, playing first base and listening to his sixth sense, anticipated that, charged the ball, and fired home to Houk, who was blocking the plate. It was a heads-up play befitting a man known to Yankees fans as "Ol' Reliable"; pictures of the play would later show clearly that Houk cradled the ball, flush against the dirt, as Pesky slid into it. But umpire Bill Grieve wasn't studying a replay. What he saw was Pesky sneaking his foot under Houk's glove.

What followed was the wildest on-field argument Yankee Stadium ever saw. Houk was purple with rage, nearly swallowing his chaw of tobacco, spitting his fury all over Grieve's uniform. Stengel, feisty as hell at age fifty-nine, sprinted out of the dugout and bumped Grieve, then bumped him again. Amazingly, neither man was thrown out. The Red Sox had their 7–6 lead and it stood up, and now the Red Sox Express was really jubilant. For the first time all year, the Yankees weren't in first place. The Sox had won ten in a row. They were one game up with five to play.

"We thought," Pesky says, "that we might never lose another game, ever."

Better, the Yankees were ensnared by chaos, furious at the call they believed cost them the game and maybe the pennant. Cliff Mapes, a reserve outfielder who'd run out of the dugout with Stengel (and also, inexplicably, wasn't ejected), confronted Grieve after the game.

"How much you got on the game, you son of a bitch?" Mapes screamed.

Grieve, known throughout his career as an umpire who gave as good as he got, shot back: "There have been ballplayers found guilty of betting on games, but never an umpire. Remember that!"

Mapes wasn't the only angry Yankee. Even Henrich, normally genteel win or lose, exploded: "Anyone in the league will tell you that Grieve is the worst umpire in the game."

Pesky argued afterward, even after studying the seemingly damning photographic evidence, "I was safe. He tagged me over here, on my side. The ball beat me but Houk seemed to freeze. He didn't even block the plate. I beat him. I know I did." Fifty-five years later, he smiled, winked, and said, "The umpire called me safe. I was safe."

Grieve, by now, was also enraged. "I'm including this in my report to [American League president] Will Harridge. I'll explain about Mapes and also how I was pushed by Houk and the manager. I left Houk in because he was the only catcher they have left. Otherwise, he would have been out of there. I called it right. Pesky's legs were on the plate and Houk did not have the plate blocked. Pesky got around him."

In the jubilant Red Sox clubhouse, nobody much wanted to discuss the play. They were in first place now, and just as they'd done a year before, they'd beaten the Yankees when they had to. "This is far from over," Dominic DiMaggio warned. "We've caught them and now it's a dogfight. They won't quit and neither will we. But there isn't any sense popping off until we get around to next Sunday. Then we'll know what happened."

For the Yankees, the lone piece of good news came from Dr. Fischl regarding Dominic's big brother. "DiMaggio's temperature is down to normal," the doctor said. "He will be permitted to get out of bed today and should be able to work out soon." Back in the Elysee, DiMaggio enjoyed his biggest and best meal in days: roast beef, baked potato, string beans, rice pudding, a head of lettuce with dressing, and a bottle of milk.

The Yankees said he might be ready to play in a few days, when the Red Sox returned to Yankee Stadium for the season's final two games. They could only hope they would still be meaningful games. And even if they were, would it really matter?

It was clear the Red Sox could beat them anytime they really needed to.

Fifty-five years later, the Yankees had been three outs from the World Series, with their best pitcher on the mound. They'd been flattened by an emotional steamroller, and their buses had to weave a path through streets clogged with ecstatic Red Sox fans just to make it back to the Ritz-Carlton by two-thirty in the morning. But they weren't feeling bad.

"Up one, three outs to go," Joe Torre said before game five of the 2004 ALCS, which was scheduled for a first pitch less than fifteen hours after the last pitch of game four. "If you let me sign up for that again tonight, I'll take it."

The gods weren't that generous. He wouldn't get that again. Instead, he'd get a two-run lead with six outs to go.

It could have been more, too, *should* have been more. And if it had been, there's a very good chance the Red Sox would have had a job listing seeking a new manager before the next morning's newspapers were published. But Terry Francona, having rolled a 7 the night before with Dave Roberts, decided to see how long his supply of pixie dust would last him.

The Red Sox jumped to a 2–0 lead, but that was all they were going to get off Mike Mussina. Bernie Williams homered in the third inning to cut the Sox' lead in half, and while Pedro Martinez was setting Yankees down with little further incident, his pitch count was growing. By the sixth, he was clearly laboring, and he loaded the bases by issuing two soft hits and plunking Miguel Cairo. That brought up Derek Jeter, the only Yankee who hadn't been able to get his bat out of mothballs during the series. But these were precisely the moments where Jeter has shone brightest in his career, and after Martinez threw him a ball and a strike, Jeter laced a fastball over first base, into the right-field corner. While Nixon, a below-average fielder, chased the ball, the bases emptied. Jeter wound up on third. The Yankees were suddenly ahead 4–2, and Martinez was clearly through.

That's when an astonishing thing happened: Francona kept Martinez in the game.

He did this despite the pleas of Fenway fans who'd seen this movie before, who'd watched Grady Little pour lighter fluid all over game seven—all over his own career, for that matter—for making this exact same mistake exactly one year and two days earlier. Martinez plunked Alex Rodriguez on the elbow . . . and Francona *still* stayed where he was. The booing got uglier. Martinez walked Gary Sheffield on five pitches. He'd now thrown 107 pitches, his fastball was gone, his arm shot. The booing had become begging.

Francona never moved.

Ball one to Hideki Matsui, hitting just under .500 for the series, the hottest baseball player on the planet right now. Ball *two* to Matsui. The anger circulating through Fenway was palpable. They were watching a hideous train wreck, powerless to stop it. Matsui, taking all the way, let an 84-mile-per-hour fastball creak past, then laid into the next offering, another 2-and-1 fastball, the 111th pitch Pedro Martinez would throw this night.

Matsui sent a rocket out toward right field. The only significant question was where it would land: in front of Nixon, in which case only two runs would score, or past him, in which case at least three would come merrily marching in. The only other question was this: When the game was over, and the season with it, would Francona go to Kinko's or Mailboxes Etc. to update his résumé?

Only a funny thing happened.

Nixon dived. He reached out his glove.

And the ball stuck there.

"If that ball drops," said Jeremy Perelman, a hedge fund analyst and a Red Sox fan who, like Carey, lives in New York, "then all we talk about until the end of time is how Terry Francona is the second coming of Grady Little."

Matsui looked on with a smile. The Yankees were stunned. Nixon was such an ordinary defender, he regularly left games in the late innings in favor of Gabe Kapler. Now, with his glove, he'd helped extend the Sox series every bit as much as Ortiz had done with his bat the night before.

Ortiz?

Leading off the eighth inning, facing Tom Gordon, he sent a mammoth drive up and over the Wall in left field, cutting the lead to 4–3. Now it was Millar's turn again. Millar's bat had been quiet most of the series, but less than twenty-four hours earlier, he'd drawn the biggest base on balls of his life, against Mariano Rivera. After swinging at and missing Gordon's first two pitches, he decided to force Gordon to throw strike three. Gordon couldn't do that. Ball. Ball. Ball. Ball. Millar was back on first base. Soon enough, Dave Roberts was back there, too, pinch-running.

And Gordon wasn't going to let Roberts steal on him. He threw over once, twice, three times before delivering strike one to Trot Nixon. He threw over twice more. Ball one. Ball two. By this time, it was clear that Gordon was so obsessed with Roberts he couldn't concentrate on Nixon. Ball three. Fenway could smell blood. So could Francona. He sent Roberts with Gordon's fifth pitch, and this time Gordon couldn't have hand-delivered a straighter, more beautiful-looking fastball to Nixon, who drilled it for a single, sending Roberts scurrying to third.

Torre had a problem. He really had wanted to avoid using Mariano Rivera in the eighth inning this game, after extending him two innings in game four. Now he would ask him to do the impossible: get six outs for this save, the first three of which would come with the tying run dancing off third base, only ninety feet away. That was too much even for Rivera; Jason Varitek drove his first pitch to medium center field, a routine out but deep enough to plate Roberts with the tying run. Rivera would have little trouble with the five other hitters he'd face, but the damage was already done. Rivera had blown only three saves in eight years as a closer; now he'd blown two within the space of twenty-one hours.

They were even again. They would head into extra innings again, and toward uncharted playoff waters again. Both bullpens sent a flurry of little-used pitchers into the teeth of a game where the pressure multiplied by the inning; somehow, the likes of Felix Heredia and Mike Myers and Bronson Arroyo and Esteban Loaiza were equal to the task. Then, in the twelfth inning, Terry Francona did something that might have been considered cruel and unusual if it didn't seem so wickedly defiant.

He brought Tim Wakefield into the game.

Wakefield, with the unpredictable knuckleball. Wakefield, who had begun his baseball life in 1988 with the Pittsburgh Pirates, drafted out of Florida Tech as a hard-hitting first baseman, who soon discovered the difference between small-college ball and the low minor leagues when he hit all of .189 for Watertown of the New York–Penn League. The Pirates instantly scratched him off their lists of short- and long-term prospects; he would be kept around only as long as they needed live bodies to fill out their farm-system rosters. Except one day, Woody

Huyke, Wakefield's manager at Watertown, saw him goofing around on the side throwing a knuckleball that all but laughed at whoever Wakefield was having a catch with. If it was that hard to catch, Huyke figured, it would *really* be a bitch to try and hit.

"Son," Huyke said, "I've looked at you swing a bat. You might want to try doing this full time."

Wakefield did that. He became an All-Star. He was now the longest-tenured member of the Red Sox, and he'd pitched wonderfully in the 2003 Championship Series in his two starts. But then Grady Little had given him the ball in the last of the eleventh, and it was like Wakefield himself had said in the spring: Knuckleballs sometimes don't knuckle as they should. You just hope that happens in the fourth inning, not the eleventh.

Or the twelfth, which is when Francona handed him the ball this time.

"I just wanted to keep us in it as long as possible," he would admit later.

It was obvious from the moment he threw the first floater, to Tony Clark, that he'd brought his best stuff in from the bullpen. He did allow a one-out single to Miguel Cairo that Manny Ramirez misplayed, allowing Cairo to reach second with one out. But then he retired both Derek Jeter and Alex Rodriguez on lazy fly balls. He didn't have to worry about the Yankees hitting the knuckler, not on this night.

No, it was his own *catcher* who had the most trouble with that.

Jason Varitek was, by almost every account, the guts and the grit behind the Red Sox grunge. Kevin Millar could be glib, and Johnny Damon could talk about how little the Red Sox took themselves seriously, and Manny Ramirez and David Ortiz could laugh and joke and clown around and keep everyone loose, but it was Varitek who made sure they all played professional baseball. It was Varitek who refused to take shit even from Curt Schilling, who'd loudly confronted Schilling when the staff ace had missed a pitchers' meeting before the Yankees series in late June. In many ways, he was a custom-tailored catcher:

smart, tough, impossible to dislodge while blocking the plate, an able handler of pitchers and their fragile egos, and a reliable switch-hitter to boot. But he didn't have the greatest throwing arm in baseball (no regular American League catcher had a worse percentage throwing out base stealers in 2004 than Varitek).

And he never caught Wakefield's knuckleball.

Every fifth day during the regular season, when Wakefield took his regular turn in the Red Sox rotation, the catching assignment fell to Doug Mirabelli, whose bat wasn't as dangerous as Varitek's but who was far more proficient in making sure that even Wakefield's wildest floaters wound up in his mitt. Francona toyed with the idea of inserting Mirabelli along with Wakefield in the twelfth but decided against it. Varitek could easily end matters with one swing of his bat. That was the greater value to Francona.

Wakefield struck out Gary Sheffield leading off the thirteenth, and as badly as the knuckleball fooled Sheffield on the way past, it handcuffed Varitek even worse, slithering past, allowing Sheffield to take first base on the passed ball. Wakefield stiffened, getting Matsui to ground into a force play and Bernie Williams to fly to right. But on a 1-and-1 pitch to Jorge Posada, another wobbly knuckler skipped past Varitek, and now the go-ahead run, Matsui, advanced into scoring position at second. Francona ordered Posada walked, opting to let free-swinging Ruben Sierra have a go at the knuckler; on a 1-and-2 pitch, though, Varitek allowed still *another* ball to squeeze through to the backstop, and for a couple of heartbeats, it all became perfectly clear to the 35,120 still crammed into Fenway. *This* was how the Sox were going to break their hearts this time, with a barrage of passed balls. Of course.

Sierra swung through strike three. Fenway released something that sounded like a 35,120-voice-strong sigh of relief. Wakefield lived to see another inning. And this time, in the top of the fourteenth, it would be a one-two-three inning, and Varitek would catch every single pitch.

Now it was the Red Sox' turn.

Esteban Loiaza came on for his fourth inning of work in the bottom of the fourteenth, and this may have been the biggest upset of a night overstuffed with them. Loaiza had come to the Yankees from the Chicago White Sox for Jose Contreras at the trading deadline and had been, in a word, dreadful. A twenty-game winner in 2003 for the White Sox, Loaiza had been awful as a Yankee. His ERA in ten games was 8.50, he allowed a home run every four innings or so, and toward the end his confidence was so shot, he'd barely been able to compete. But his arm *was* fresh thanks to the fact that Torre couldn't bear to put him in a meaningful game, and he'd shut the Red Sox down in these three most pressure-packed innings of the season.

Torre had no one else up. Loaiza was his man. And Loaiza struck out Mark Bellhorn leading off the fourteenth, just as it was announced that this had officially entered the record books as the longest postseason game ever played. Loaiza walked Johnny Damon, struck out Orlando Cabrera, and tried to pitch too carefully to Manny Ramirez, losing him on a full-count fastball that pushed Damon up to second base . . . and brought up David Ortiz.

It almost seemed unfair: Every time Ortiz had swung the bat the past few weeks, something magical happened, and every time Loaiza had thrown a baseball, it seemed, something dreadful occurred. It seemed like a horrible mismatch. Only Loaiza jumped out in front of Ortiz, 1 and 2, challenging him with fastballs. He did that two more times; Ortiz barely fouled off both, then took ball two. Three more times Loaiza threw the fastball; three more times Ortiz fought it off. It was almost too much for the people inside the ballpark to bear.

So Ortiz took them out of their misery.

He lasered the tenth pitch of the at-bat into center field. Bernie Williams picked the ball up on a hop and threw in but knew he had no chance to beat Damon, who raced home, threw his helmet into the air, and jumped into yet another joyous pile of Red Sox. Once Damon touched the plate, making it official, the pile moved quickly toward Ortiz, who by now was in such a rarefied place that his teammates fully believed he was capable of anything.

"What he's doing," Gabe Kapler said a few minutes later, back in the Red Sox' clubhouse, pointing a few feet away at Ortiz' empty locker, "is Jordanesque."

Someone told that to Ortiz, who dismissed the very notion with a smile and a wave of his hand.

"That's basketball, man," he said. "One guy can do it in basketball. This is baseball. You need more than one guy."

If these Red Sox had proven anything the last few days, it was that they needed every man available on the roster. They'd played nearly fifteen hours of baseball over the past three days. They'd used six pitchers in game three, six in game four, *seven* in game five. They'd given Tim Wakefield an opportunity to redeem himself. And the dean of the Red Sox pitching staff had responded with three of the guttiest, grittiest innings of his life.

"He was running on fumes after two innings," pitching coach Dave Wallace marveled. "I mean, he had *nothing* left, strength-wise. And I said, 'You think there's any chance we can get one more inning out of you?' And he said, 'Just give me the ball.'" And then he made that ball dance.

"You saw Varitek trying to catch it," Derek Jeter said, shaking his head in wonder. "Nobody knows where it's going to go. It's no fun trying to hit it, either."

Somehow, they would be bringing this traveling passion play back to New York for a game six. Somehow, the Sox still had a season, and they had Curt Schilling ready to take the ball again, and when Schilling was asked if he was planning on doing anything out of the ordinary to get his battered ankle ready, he coyly replied, "I'm not ready to talk about that right now."

Everyone else was talking—and then some. That night, a Yankees fan named Julio Rodriguez was driving in a van on Interstate 93 with five friends—all of them Red Sox fans—after watching all fourteen innings on television at bars in Boston and Lynn, Massachusetts. An argument broke out over the game. A shot was fired. And a thirty-three-year-old man named Jose Rivera wound up dead, while two others were injured.

"They were arguing over the Red Sox game," one source familiar with the investigation told the *Boston Herald*. "The shooter was a Yankees fan."

Almost everywhere else, the passions were confined to the usual excitements and anxieties all fans carry when difficult series grow long. After all this time, after these two years that were unprecedented even in the long and colorful history of this long and colorful rivalry, there would be another game six, at Yankee Stadium, with the very real possibility of another game seven, at Yankee Stadium. A sequel for the ages. An encore for all time.

"Here we go again," Derek Jeter said.

CHAPTER

12

ALL EMPIRES FALL

Tonight, God did something amazing for me. I tried to be as tough
as I could, and do it my way, in game one, and I think we all saw how
that turned out. I knew that I wasn't going to be able to do this alone.
And I prayed as hard as I could. I didn't pray to get a win or to make
great pitches. I just prayed for the strength to go out there tonight
and compete, and he gave me that. I can't explain to you what
a feeling it was to be out there and to feel what I felt. —*Curt Schilling,*
October 19, 2004

They didn't want to get beat. They kept playing the way we used to play,
kept playing the small game, around the cornerstones like Manny
and Johnny, and the rest of the team was nothing but tough outs.
It's taken them a long time to be in this position they are right now. It
feels weird to be at the other end of the coin. —*Bernie Williams,*
October 20, 2004

The first close-ups were astonishing. They focused in on Curt
Schilling's right foot, on white sanitary hose stained a rich, dark
red. Schilling had spoken cryptically the night before about having to have a few things done in order to get himself out to the pitcher's
mound at Yankee Stadium on Tuesday, October 19, 2004, but most
folks assumed it would be the usual stuff: an ice bucket, some tape and
gauze, maybe some extra-strength Tylenol, perhaps a painkilling needle.

Anyone who's ever suffered an ankle injury knows how relentless the pain can be, but you don't ever see blood.

But now, all of America could plainly see the blood.

"It looked worse than it felt," Schilling would insist much later, and though it was hard to believe that, he *was* throwing the ball a hell of a lot harder than he had in game one, when his velocity barely escaped the high eighties.

This time, the first pitch he threw, to Derek Jeter, hit ninety-four. Jeter—the rare leadoff hitter who likes to feast on first-pitch fastballs, who has twice in his career led off critical playoff games with home runs and was no doubt trying to do the same here—flied out to right field. Alex Rodriguez battled Schilling through an eight-pitch at-bat, every fastball of that sequence registering between ninety-three and ninety-five, the last of which ended with Rodriguez lining out to Orlando Cabrera at short. Gary Sheffield popped out to first to end the inning, and while there was a slight limp to Schilling's step as he left the field, if you hadn't known he'd been hurt, you probably wouldn't have noticed it. He looked, by every indication, perfectly healthy. Cured, even.

The reality was something else, something so unimaginable it hardly seemed possible when it was explained much, much later. It was Epstein who had said after Schilling's painful game-one misadventures, "We will explore every medical technique under the sun to try to get his tendon stabilized." But even Epstein had no idea how great those lengths would be.

The Reebok athletic company was the first to try to save the day for Schilling, rush-delivering a pair of high-cut spikes the manufacturer believed could keep Schilling's tendon immobilized. Schilling tried them out the previous Friday, before the heavy rains came to wash away game three. Schilling looked like a modern-day Johnny Unitas in the shoes as he began tossing in the bullpen, but he threw only a few pitches in them before switching back to his regular-cut shoes. It didn't fit right. There would have to be another solution.

It was Dr. Bill Morgan, the Red Sox' medical director, who came up with one, and if it seemed perfectly ghoulish at first . . . well, that's because it *was* perfectly ghoulish. Morgan's suggestion was to suture the skin around the dislocated tendon down to the deep tissue, creating an artificial sheath that would seal the tendon in place.

The Red Sox training staff stared blankly. Epstein asked Morgan to repeat himself.

Morgan did that. He was serious. As soon as the others could stop squirming at the prospect of what Schilling would have to submit his ankle to, they could understand the reasoning.

"We were going to do it as a last-ditch scenario," Epstein said. "Although it seems extreme—we couldn't find a case of it ever having been done before—we thought it was almost a conservative approach in that it would be the best way for Curt to have his normal mechanics."

Now it was up to Morgan to make the procedure work, but there was one slight drawback: He'd never done it before. This made perfect sense, of course, because *nobody* had ever done it before. He was in absolute virgin territory here. And as much of a gamer as Schilling might well be, Morgan wasn't going to use the Red Sox' $12 million ace as a test dummy for his offbeat scheme. So he did what doctors always do when they need a little practice at their practice: He experimented on a cadaver's leg.

The cadaver didn't complain.

So Schilling was next.

"Curt understood what we wanted to do," Morgan said. "He wanted to give it a try."

That was Monday. While his teammates prepared to play game five, Schilling walked into a sterile back room at Fenway Park along with Morgan and three of his assistants. They applied a local anesthetic to the trouble zone, then quickly tended to their knitting.

Morgan worked as rapidly as he could. Several sutures were threaded through skin and tissue beneath the skin and placed between the groove and the loose tendon. This created a tiny wall of flesh that kept the tendon in place, about two centimeters outside its groove.

"We forced it to stay out of the groove so it wouldn't move around,"

Morgan explained. "It's going to stay out until his surgery, whenever that is."

Well. That certainly explained the blood.

What was less easy to clarify was the brilliance Schilling dragged back to the mound with him each inning. He kept the Yankees off the scoreboard entirely for six innings; Bernie Williams finally reached him in the seventh, drilling a home run into the seats in right. But he went right back to work after that, striking out Ruben Sierra to close out the seventh, the last batter he faced on a most extraordinary night of work.

And Schilling's courage was only part of what made it so extraordinary.

Yankee Stadium wasn't itself on this night. Something was amiss, although it wasn't difficult to see why. Yankees fans, born with an extra helping of hubris, outwardly scoffed at the notion that the Red Sox— the Red Sox, of all teams—would be the first team in baseball history to recover from an 0–3 hole in a seven-game series. Hell, they still needed to win twice in Yankee Stadium, the fans reasoned. The Sox needed every break along the way merely to avoid getting swept. Besides, wouldn't it be *just like* the Red Sox fans to get strung along this way, as their team worked the series all the way back to 3–2 (or even 3–3, for that matter), just to have the rug pulled out by the Yankees? Wouldn't that be perfect?

Inwardly, though . . .

"The moment Trot Nixon caught that ball in game five," Peter Cipriano would admit, "I really started to think the Yankees weren't going to win the series."

"A team that's three outs away, the way we were in game four, and can't finish it out," reasoned Pete Trinkle, "is just asking for bad things to happen."

It really was an amazing juxtaposition; Yankees fans were already sounding like the most stereotypically star-crossed of Red Sox fans, were already foreseeing their own doom and forecasting their own demise, *and their team was still ahead in the series three games to two!* It was staggering, hearing Yankees fans speak so fatalistically. Yet that might have explained why Yankee Stadium was so stunningly quiet during game six, a game that was scoreless through three innings and then took a serious turn for the surreal in the fourth.

Jon Lieber, suddenly (and quite surprisingly) the Yankees' most reliable starting pitcher, retired the first two hitters in the fourth before encountering trouble. Kevin Millar, tired of doing all of his damage by simply drawing walks, laced a double to deep left; after advancing to third on a wild pitch, he scored when Varitek smashed a single to center. Orlando Cabrera followed with a single, which brought Mark Bellhorn to the plate. Bellhorn was a *Moneyball*-blueprint player sprung to life—he struck out a lot (a league-leading 177 times in 2004) but also had an innate ability to get on base (his eighty-eight walks were ranked fourth, and were a staggering total given that he hit just above Manny Ramirez and David Ortiz all year long, so it follows that pitchers would rather do *anything* than put extra runners on base for those two, who combined for 269 RBIs). But Bellhorn had been brutalized in this series—his average stuck at .100, his fielding shaky—and all during the Boston phase of the series, fans had been loudly chanting for Pokey Reese, Bellhorn's sure-handed, light-hitting, but enormously popular backup.

Bellhorn understood. "If I were a fan," he said, "I'd boo the shit out of me, too."

His hitting woes followed him to New York. In the second inning, with the bases loaded and one out, Bellhorn had grounded into a rally-snuffing double play, and now Lieber quickly jumped ahead of him, 1 and 2. But on the fifth pitch of the at-bat, Bellhorn connected and sent a rocket soaring toward left field. It kept carrying and carrying, well over Matsui's head, well over the fence, where it hit a fan and bounced harmlessly back to the Yankee left fielder. Everyone in the ballpark could see it was a three-run homer, could see that the Red Sox were now up 4–0 on a night when Curt Schilling was sure to make that feel like a 40–0 lead.

Everyone but one man, that is. Left-field umpire Jim Joyce refused to twirl his right index finger to signal a home run. Somehow, to his eyes,

Bellhorn's blast had caromed off the wall and into Matsui's hands. Matsui, in a heads-up maneuver, had facilitated the ruse by throwing the ball back into the infield. Terry Francona stormed from the dugout to confront Joyce, but for the moment it seemed the Yankees had received a ridiculous break, the kind they'd been living off for decades.

While the umpires deliberated, Michael Appelbaum shook his head. If there was one person who could swear under oath that Bellhorn's ball had in fact cleared the fence, it was Appelbaum, sitting in the first row of Section 122, because the ball had hit Appelbaum, a Manhattan resident, on the chest. There was irony here: Mindful of not wanting to gain a dubious slice of fame, the way Jeffrey Maier had eight years earlier, or an even worse helping of infamy, as ill-fated Cubs fan Steve Bartman had the year before, Appelbaum, in an amazing display of restraint, had kept his arms at his side and let the ball hit him, not moving at all. That, it turns out, is what fooled Joyce.

"There shouldn't have been any controversy," Appelbaum later said. "I was surprised when there was."

Added his twelve-year-old daughter, Mia, in a corroborating confession: "I didn't want it to be a home run. But it was."

Remarkably, after conferring with each other, the other five umpires assured a stricken Joyce that they'd definitely seen the ball clear the fence, and rightly waved Bellhorn home. It really *was* 4–0. And the Yankees really *were* in a deep mess.

"It was the right call," Yankees fan Jim Frasch would admit. "But the fact is, it was the kind of call you never, ever saw go against the Yankees at Yankee Stadium. All these things start to add up. You start to wonder. I mean, how many times do you see umpires overrule the Yankees at home?"

Amazingly, the answer to that question would soon multiply.

Williams' homer, which sliced the Sox' lead to 4–1, was the only thing the Yankees could scratch off Schilling. But even Schilling knew he'd had enough. As he walked off the mound after striking out Sierra, Schilling shouted, "Good job!" at home plate umpire Joe West, who reciprocated the feeling. He knew he was done, that ninety-nine pitches on an ankle held together, literally by a string, would more than qualify as a full night's work. He'd hand the three-run lead over to his bullpen, beginning with Bronson Arroyo—a breathtaking transfer of power to Red Sox fans, given the pounding Arroyo had absorbed in game three.

There was something else, too.

Red Sox fans and Yankees fans alike still believed in the mystical qualities attached to this rivalry, for very different reasons, and to far different ends. It was therefore lost on no one that as the Yankees came to bat in the bottom of the eighth inning, they trailed by three runs— just as they had a year earlier, in game seven. In 2003, Pedro Martinez began the inning by retiring the Yankees first baseman, Nick Johnson; in 2004, Bronson Arroyo began his inning by retiring the Yankees first baseman, Tony Clark.

In 2003, Derek Jeter started it all with an opposite-field double to right field.

In 2004, with one out, Miguel Cairo doubled over Ortiz' head, into the right-field corner.

In 2003, Bernie Williams had followed with an RBI single, and for the first time all night it looked like the Yankees might really be in business.

In 2004, it was Jeter who followed with an RBI single, and for the first time all night it looked like the Yankees might really be in business. It was 4–2. Yankee Stadium, at long last, had been slapped in the face: the meat of the New York lineup was coming up, Arroyo looked completely shaken, the Red Sox bullpen was frantic with action, the small Red Sox rooting sections were sick with worry. It was impossible to ignore all the similarities between this eighth inning and the one that had preceded it by fifty-three weeks; it was also impossible to ignore the relentless tug of history.

And now, as if to tip a cap to all the ghosts standing sentry to the moment, up stepped Alex Rodriguez, the center of so much fury, the one-man eye of the storms that had brewed between these two teams for more than eleven months. A few days earlier, as rain fell on Fenway

Park, Reggie Jackson had been talking about Rodriguez, extolling his talents, saying he believed A-Rod could wind up being a great October player—greater, even, than the man who'd earned the nickname of "Mr. October." But the only way for that to happen, Jackson warned, was to perform when the brightest lights were shining.

"Some guys don't have the makeup for it," Jackson said of his favorite autumnal month. "You can't be a Yankee if you don't have the makeup. You have to have a certain makeup to perform and excel here."

This was A-Rod's moment. He took ball one, then watched two borderline pitches get called strikes, then watched ball two. Longtime A-Rod watchers were alarmed; when he was truly locked in, he rarely kept the bat on his shoulder. It was his aggressive nature teaming with his abundant talent that had made Rodriguez the greatest offensive player of his generation. He seemed too passive here. He fouled off a pitch. The tension inside Yankee Stadium grew to an almost unbearable level.

Arroyo's sixth pitch fooled Rodriguez. He swung, but managed only a sick dribbler down the first-base line. Arroyo fielded it just as Rodriguez was barreling toward him, didn't think he had enough time to turn and flip to Doug Mientkiewicz at first, so he tried to tag Rodriguez. But as they confronted each other, the ball went flying out of Arroyo's glove, rolling helplessly down the right-field line. Jeter roared around the bases, and Rodriguez steamed into second base, and suddenly it was 4–3, and the tying run was on second base, and Yankee Stadium felt like the inside of a jumbo jet engine.

So *this* was what manifest destiny looked like. And sounded like.

Only here came Terry Francona again, sprinting out of the dugout, his arms flailing. He pointed at first base. He was as calm and reasonable as an angry man who felt he'd just been grievously wronged could look. Television replays showed why Francona was so upset. Rodriguez hadn't simply collided with Arroyo; he'd actually *slapped* the ball out of his hands. And there was a rule forbidding such folly: Rule 7.08 states, in part, "Any runner is out when . . . he intentionally interferes with a thrown ball; or hinders a fielder attempting to make a play on a batted ball . . . if the umpire declares the batter, batter runner, or a runner out for interference, all other runners shall return to the last base that was in the judgment of the umpire, legally touched at the time of the interference."

Francona knew the rule. So did first-base umpire Randy Marsh. The problem was, Marsh had been partially screened on the play by Mientkiewicz; he'd never actually seen Rodriguez slap the ball out of Arroyo's hands. But West, the home plate umpire, had. Another umpires' conference commenced, and again they got it right: Rodriguez was called out, Jeter was returned to first, and the third Yankee run was taken off the scoreboard. Yankee Stadium howled in protest, and more than a few drunken cretins began tossing beer bottles onto the field, necessitating a ring of police around the dugouts for the next half hour or so. Calm ultimately was restored; the inevitable Yankee rally was not. Though Keith Foulke walked two men in the ninth, he struck out Tony Clark on a full-count pitch, and the Red Sox were officially even.

There really would be another game seven after all.

"We had the momentum early in this series," Joe Torre said, "and they have it now. But we have something I think both teams would want: We have the last game of the season in our building. And that still means something."

In the long course of this rivalry, it certainly had.

Fifty-five years earlier, the Red Sox had pulled into Grand Central Terminal on the Merchants Limited train on that final weekend of the regular season in 1949, needing only one victory in the final two games to complete a remarkable resurrection and deny Casey Stengel a pennant he so desperately needed for self-validation. The Sox arrived a self-assured bunch, having taken two out of three from the Senators while the Yankees took two of three from the A's in the penultimate series of the season. The mission ahead was clear: The Red Sox would enter these final two games at Yankee Stadium with a 96–56 record. The

Yankees stood at 95–57. All the Sox needed was a lousy split, and the pennant was theirs—this after having gone an astonishing 61–20 since the Fourth of July.

So confident was Red Sox owner Tom Yawkey that his team would do what it had done so regularly the past few years—knock off, and knock out, the Yankees when they needed to—that he ordered the Red Sox' wives to be on the ready to board their own train as soon as their boys had wrapped up the pennant, either on Saturday, October 1, or Sunday, October 2, so the entire Red Sox extended family could party in style in New York City. On enemy turf.

The Boston newspapers got into the act Saturday morning, as readers awakened to story after story regarding the Sox' World Series ticket plans. Some 22,000 tickets were to be made available in all, 5,500 for each of the four possible games that would take place in Boston. The plan was simple: If the Sox won Saturday, the tickets would go on sale Sunday at 1 P.M. If the Sox waited until Sunday to clinch, the box office would open at 6 P.M. Bob Belisle of Woonsocket was the first to queue up on Jersey Street, the avenue long since renamed Yawkey Way. Belisle arrived at 1 a.m. Saturday morning, thirty-six hours before the earliest possible ticket availability. He was taking no chances, and soon he was joined by a swollen throng of Sox fans, who brought food, drink, and radios to follow the games. Yankees were hung in effigy all along Jersey Street.

But the real-life Yankees had their own ace to play, quite literally.

Stengel seemed unaffected by the stakes in play for the weekend, which was odd for a man who'd never won a thing as a manager. Before Saturday's opener, he'd chirped to the writers, "We're going to win two, boys. We're going to keep you here all winter." Later, to his players, Stengel said, "Boys, did you ever win a doubleheader? Did you ever win two in a row? Well, let's do it now. Now is the time to do it. We've done it before. We can do it now."

Much of Stengel's courage surely came from the welcome sight of Joe DiMaggio, who finally had made his way back to the Stadium after battling pneumonia for two weeks. Of course, just having DiMaggio in the building would help little once the game started, and anyone who looked at DiMaggio was amazed he was able to walk without collapsing, much less play the most important baseball game of the season. In truth, the only reason DiMaggio came to the park at all was that the Yankees had scheduled a pregame celebration in his honor and had advertised it in all the city's newspapers for days—"A great day for a great Ball Player," the ad copy had read, under a caricature of DiMaggio's smiling face— and DiMaggio would be damned if he'd let that ceremony go on without him, especially since 69,551 had bought tickets for the day.

On the eve of Joe DiMaggio Day, Stengel had tried to strike an optimistic chord, saying, "If he feels a little better tomorrow than he did today, then I'll start Joe against the Red Sox. But if he'll be able to go, I don't know. It would be pretty hard for him to be a detriment to us in any condition, wouldn't it?"

DiMaggio best knew the answer to that question: If he tried to play in his condition, he'd be humiliated. And there was no greater crime in Joe DiMaggio's personal canon than to embarrass yourself on a baseball field. He could barely stand. During the ceremony, each of DiMaggio's family members was introduced, and when Dominic emerged from the Red Sox dugout to offer his hand, Joe kept it, and wrapped him in a hug.

"Dom," he said, "stand here with me. I'm afraid I might not make it."

Dom could feel Joe slacken against him. He wasn't going anywhere.

Mel Allen, the Yankees broadcaster, was the master of ceremonies, and when he was done with the preliminaries he finally said, "It's always best to be brief when you introduce a great guy. Ladies and gentlemen, Joe DiMaggio!"

The roar grew from the top of the stadium, swirling and building and finally spilling onto the neighboring streets. DiMaggio had heard a lot of cheers in this house for a lot of years. None compared to this, a mixture of thanks for all the years dating back to 1936 and hope that he could find his way into the batting order in a few minutes.

DiMaggio, knees quaking, arms shaking, stepped to the microphone.

"Thank you, ladies and gentlemen. First of all, I'd like to apologize to the people in the bleachers for having my back to them. I would like to thank the fans, my family, my manager, Casey Stengel, and my teammates, the gamest, fightingest bunch that ever lived. I'd also like to tell my former manager, Joe McCarthy, that if we can't do it, Joe, if we can't win the pennant, I'll be glad it's you. This is one of the few times in my career that I've choked up. Believe me, this is a big lump in my throat. Many years ago, a friend of mine named Lefty O'Doul told me when I came to New York not to let the big town scare me. This day proves New York City is the friendliest town in the world. In conclusion, I'd like to thank the good Lord for making me a Yankee."

That last sentence would become the second most famous line ever culled from a Yankee Stadium speech, trailing only the dying Lou Gehrig's insistence that he was the luckiest man on the face of the earth. The response buoyed him. So did the close to $50,000 in gifts he received from teammates, fans, the front office, and the team's sponsors. As he walked back into the dugout, he summoned his manager. "Casey," he said, "I think I can go three innings."

But by the third inning, he'd already struck out once and the Yankees were already down 4–0. Allie Reynolds had already been knocked out of the box and replaced by Joe Page. And Mel Parnell, seeking his twenty-sixth win, was untouchable. Still, DiMaggio, chain-smoking Chesterfields, figured he would have all winter to recuperate, and flashed five fingers to Stengel, telling him he'd play through five innings. Stengel was in no position to argue. He hoped for the best.

This was precisely what DiMaggio provided. In the fourth, with Parnell feeding him a strict diet of outside fastballs, DiMaggio decided to play along, drilling a line drive to right field that bounced over the fence. Ground-rule double. The entire yard was instantly revitalized, and the Yankee bench was electric. Stengel motioned to DiMaggio to see if he wanted a pinch runner. DiMaggio shook his head, then scored the Yankees' first run when Hank Bauer singled behind him. An inning later, after Phil Rizzuto, Tommy Henrich, and Yogi Berra singled in succession, cutting the Boston lead to 4–3, DiMaggio stepped up again. As always, McCarthy was spooked by No. 5. He went out to fetch his ace and brought in Joe Dobson, normally the Sox' number-three starter. DiMaggio connected on Dobson's first pitch, drilling one back through the box that would have taken the pitcher's head off had he not gotten his glove up. The Yankees had the bases loaded and no one out, and when Billy Johnson followed with a double play, Henrich scored the tying run.

Yankee Stadium was fully engaged now. Page was throwing pure, nasty gas. And when Johnny Lindell homered in the eighth—only his sixth of the year, one more than another light-hitting Yankee named Bucky Dent would collect twenty-nine years later—the Yankees finally had themselves a lead, 5–4. That's how it ended. Now both teams had identical 96–57 records. They would play the equivalent of a playoff game the next day. Nine innings for the pennant.

"I didn't expect to go all the way," a bone-weary DiMaggio said later on. "I'll need all the rest I can get tonight."

Added Dominic, inside the suddenly less boisterous Red Sox clubhouse: "I hope they give Joe the whole city of New York. All I want is the pennant."

That, suddenly, was a lot less promising possibility than it had seemed on the train ride in. Sixty-two thousand people would be at the Stadium Sunday afternoon, fewer than a handful backing the Red Sox. Those who would have cheered loudest, the Sox' wives, would gather at Back Bay Station in the early afternoon, still prepared to make the quick trip down in the event of a victory party. But their voices would be of little help so far away.

The equalizer, for the Red Sox, would be the limp, gray figure of Joe DiMaggio, who staggered onto the Yankee Stadium field for batting practice Sunday morning. Saturday's festivities had exhausted him, and he physically wore the strain of the day and of the pennant race, but when the writers approached him he waved them off with a firm wave of his hand and a direct message: "I'm playing."

The Yankees jumped out to a quick 1–0 lead when Rizzuto touched Ellis Kinder for a triple leading off the bottom of the first, followed by a Tommy Henrich ground ball to Bobby Doerr at second. But that was it. DiMaggio looked lifeless at the plate, but so did everyone else as Kinder (shooting for his twenty-fourth win) and Vic Raschi (gunning for his twenty-first) methodically muted the hitters' bats. Inning after inning, the two aces hung zeroes on the scoreboard, and the simmering tension inside Yankee Stadium boiled hotter and hotter.

In the eighth inning, the Red Sox flinched.

In the top of the inning, with the Yankees still nursing a slim 1–0 lead, Joe McCarthy made a strategic gaffe that ranks with his decision to start Denny Galehouse in the playoff game the year before: He lifted Kinder for a pinch hitter with two outs and nobody on. The percentage play, especially in an era when relief pitching was something of a frontier profession, was to stick with your best pitcher, assume he'd keep you close, and take your chances with the top of your lineup coming up in the ninth. Compounding the puzzling decision, McCarthy brought in Parnell, clearly running on fumes after pitching the day before. Henrich greeted Parnell with a home run. Then, after DiMaggio grounded into a double play, the Yankees busted the door down by loading the bases with two singles and a walk off Tex Hughson before rookie Jerry Coleman's seeing-eye triple cleared the bases. It was 5–0. In the Red Sox' clubhouse, Kinder started breaking everything in his path. The Red Sox' season lay in a heap alongside Kinder's rubble.

Or did it?

With one out in the ninth, Williams walked. Junior Stephens singled to center, DiMaggio hustling after the ball to keep Williams from taking third. Doerr then hit a long fly ball toward center that everyone in the ballpark keeping score quickly marked an "F-8," indicating a fly ball out to the center fielder, because DiMaggio had caught up with precisely that kind of drive in Death Valley's vast reaches thousands of times previously. But he hadn't been shaking off pneumonia those times. DiMaggio stumbled as he chased the ball, and it fell behind him for a triple. Now it was 5–2, the Sox had a man on third, and there was still only one out.

It was here that DiMaggio pulled one last shocking trick out of his bag. He raised his arm, trying to gain the attention of Charlie Berry, the second-base umpire. Puzzled, Berry granted time, then watched in disbelief along with everyone else as DiMaggio slowly trotted past him, past the pitcher's mound, and into the Yankees dugout. He was removing himself from the game. The fans, picking up on this, escorted him to the bench with one more girder-rattling standing ovation.

"If I'd let another one drop," he said afterward, "I'd never have forgiven myself the rest of my life. You can't give the Red Sox extra outs."

Raschi, himself tiring after throwing well over 130 pitches, got Al Zarilla to fly out to Cliff Mapes for the second out, but first baseman Bill Goodman singled in Doerr to make it 5–3 and bring Birdie Tebbets up as the tying run. Henrich walked to the mound to offer Raschi encouragement, but Raschi shot daggers at Henrich with his eyes.

"Get the hell back where you belong," he shouted. "I'll do my job. Do yours."

Henrich retreated. And a few seconds later he was drifting toward the stands abutting the first-base line, settling under a pop fly, gathering it in his glove.

Yankee Stadium was awash in elation. Of all the pennants the Yankees had won in the previous twenty-eight years—and this was the sixteenth—they'd never done it on the last day of the season, in this most famous of all baseball stadiums, certainly never against a rival as worthy and as bitter as the Red Sox.

"I've never gotten as much satisfaction out of winning before," DiMaggio said afterward, slumped on his stool, ecstatic and exhausted and exhilarated. "This is the one."

"This season," Charlie Keller declared, "couldn't have ended any other way."

Stengel, having finally shed his reputation as baseball's clown prince, its lifelong loser, was near tears in the Yankees clubhouse. "Just think!"

he exclaimed. "They pay me to manage these guys!" Later, he looked up and saw the glassy-eyed specter of Joe McCarthy looming over him, extending a hand in congratulation. Stengel was touched.

"Everything Joe DiMaggio said about you yesterday goes for me, too," Stengel told the Sox' crestfallen manager. "Men like you taught me all I know about the game, and if you'd won, we'd all be rooting for you in the World Series. You've won so many of these things; it was mighty nice of you to let me win just one."

McCarthy's own clubhouse was a chamber of silence. There were no tears, no emotional outbursts, just rows of slumped shoulders and shaken heads. A few Red Sox grumbled off the record about Rizzuto's triple, hinting that Ted Williams might have misplayed the ball. A few griped about McCarthy lifting Kinder. But the only voice that grew above a whisper belonged to Tom Yawkey, who groused, "If we can't win one out of two, then we don't deserve it." The Merchants Limited that mournfully chugged back to Boston was much the same, only snippets of chatter filling the long miles, until Ellis Kinder, fully fueled by liquid courage, confronted McCarthy and loudly offered his opinion of the manager's strategic acumen.

McCarthy, no stranger to the illuminating effect of whiskey, absorbed the verbal lashing in silence. What else could he do? Fighting back wouldn't bring the season back. After all, he wasn't the first manager to be second-guessed in a big game.

Nor would he be the last.

Joe Torre's tenure with the Yankees had earned him a Teflon shield, meriting the manager a place deep within the lasting affections of most Yankees fans. His players revered him, for the most part. Derek Jeter, nine years into his career, in the summer he turned thirty years old, still referred to his manager as "Mr. Torre." Mostly, Torre's reputation had been earned in October, where, for a magical five-year stretch from 1996 to 2000, every hunch he ever played worked to perfection.

Cynics scoffed that the notoriously demanding New York press had been soft on Torre, but the truth is he'd rarely given them any material with which to hang him.

Suddenly, in the 2004 American League Championship Series, that was no longer the case.

Suddenly, every move Torre made bore the distinct sound of a car backfiring.

In game four, he'd had the opportunity to start Mike Mussina on his normal rest day, and if he'd done that, Mussina might have been available for a couple of innings if a game seven became necessary; Torre opted to give Orlando Hernandez his first start in almost three weeks instead. In game five, after insisting Mariano Rivera would not be asked to get six outs, that's exactly what wound up happening—but not until the Red Sox already had men on the corners and no one out. If Rivera really *was* available for six outs, why not have him start the eighth inning? Later in that game, when Jason Varitek was having so much difficulty catching Tim Wakefield's knuckleball, Torre could have put in Kenny Lofton to pinch-run, knowing Varitek would have little chance of throwing him out off a knuckler; even without inserting Lofton, either Gary Sheffield or Hideki Matsui, both of whom spent time on first base that inning, probably could have stolen second without a throw, given all the difficulties Varitek was having just catching the ball. But Torre never sent them. He had pulled Lofton out of the lineup even after it was clear that Ruben Sierra, with whom Lofton shared the DH spot, was struggling. Surely, Yankees fans screamed, Lofton might have laid down a bunt or three against Curt Schilling in game six, made the pitcher field a ball on his gimpy ankle. But of the ninety-nine pitches Schilling threw that night, not one of them came back to him as a bunt. Not one.

Torre bristled at the criticism, knowing well what Francona had been discovering almost daily now: As a manager, the only bad moves you make are the ones that don't work out. There is no empirical formula. You're as smart as fortune determines you are.

"No manager ever goes into a game, or a situation, saying, 'Let's see how badly I can fuck this up for my team,'" Torre had said early in the season. "Sometimes things work out beautifully. And sometimes they don't. You move on."

Torre's options were shockingly limited now, heading into game seven, what some were calling the single most important of the 1,938 regular- and postseason games played between the two teams up to this point. The Yankees held a sizable 1,055–865 advantage in regular-season games, and an 11–7 lead in playoff games—and that wouldn't help the Yankees one bit on this night. Not in a one-game, winner-take-all game seven.

And not with Kevin Brown as the Yankees' starting pitcher.

Yankees fans had had difficulty warming up to Brown anyway, given his disagreeable manner, his sour disposition, and the fact that he clearly wasn't the same pitcher who'd dominated the National League in the late 1990s, who was once so coveted that in 1998 the Dodgers made him the first-ever $100 million pitcher, stuffing his contract with so many perks—the most famous of which required the club to provide twelve round trips on a private plane per year so his family could commute between California and Georgia—that he came to symbolize the very image of modern ballplayers as greedy mercenaries forever holding out their hands, demanding every penny.

One of those hands had collided with a Yankee Stadium clubhouse a few minutes after he was removed from a game on September 3; the punch broke a bone in Brown's nonpitching hand, sidelining him during a critical stretch of the season when the Yankees were desperately trying to hold off the Red Sox and infuriating Torre and Brian Cashman, who threatened a heavy fine. When Brown did return, paired with Schilling at Fenway Park in late September, he hadn't made it out of the first inning, and while he'd pitched well in a Division Series start against Minnesota, he'd once again been torched in Boston during game three of this series, the game the Yankees ultimately won 19–8 long after Brown had been sent to an early shower.

Yankees fans were horrified: a one-game season, and *this* was the best a $187 million payroll could produce? *Kevin Brown?*

The Red Sox, meanwhile, would start Derek Lowe, quite uncertain what they would be able to expect from him, but fully prepared to empty their bullpen at the first sign of trouble. Pedro Martinez vowed he would pitch, and even Schilling said that if they absolutely needed him, he'd be available, though it was unlikely that anything short of a thirty-inning game would compel Francona to take him up on that offer.

The Sox were a loose bunch before the game. Back home, the Fenway Park grounds crew opted to wait an extra day before painting any World Series logos on the field, but inside their own clubhouse, the swagger had most definitely returned, and in force. None of the Sox was especially shy in denouncing what Alex Rodriguez had done the night before, trying to slap the ball out of Bronson Arroyo's glove.

"What he did was completely unprofessional, and really hurt his team," said Kevin Millar, the same man who ten months earlier had gone on ESPN and publicly salivated at the prospect of A-Rod as a teammate. "It was an unprofessional play and he knows that. He has to brush his teeth and look at himself in the mirror in the morning."

"That was freakin' junior high school baseball right there, at its best," Schilling said in an interview with ESPN Radio's Dan Patrick on the afternoon of game seven. "Let me ask you something: Does Derek Jeter do that? You know for a fact he doesn't, because Derek Jeter is a class act and a freakin' professional, that's why."

Yes, it was a sign of how completely upside-down things had become that the Red Sox were officially ignoring the potential karmic consequences such brash statements could bring, while the Yankees were overturning every mystical rock they could find to try to reestablish order in their universe. Yogi Berra did his traditional turn on the field before the game, but he was asked not to throw the ceremonial first pitch, but to catch it.

From Bucky Dent, naturally.

Red Sox fans were able to laugh at that. And they were officially willing, twenty-six years later, to use the man's name without inserting his honorary middle name.

"Bucky Dent," Mike Carey huffed. "How desperate can they be?" That answer would arrive soon enough. Johnny Damon led the game off with a sharp single, then promptly stole second base. Brown was clearly laboring right from the start, and though he struck out Bellhorn, Ramirez followed with a single to left center that should have given the Sox a lead three hitters in. But an astonishing relay throw from Jeter to Jorge Posada cut down Damon at the plate. For the briefest of moments, Yankee Stadium was alive with the possibilities of big-play October.

Then David Ortiz stepped to the plate.

And it only took one Brown pitch for Papi to make the baseball disappear into the right-field stands, kicking the plug out of the wall at Yankee Stadium. It was 2–0, Red Sox, and by now, only the most fervent believers in history were willing to point out that it wasn't the first time the Red Sox had led by that score early in a do-or-die game with the Yankees.

Steve Palermo was still too caught up in the magic of the afternoon to have given any thought to the rawness of the pain that bled across the Commonwealth. On the afternoon of October 2, 1978, Palermo was umpiring third base at Fenway Park, a choice assignment given that the Red Sox were hosting the Yankees in a one-game playoff to determine the American League East Division championship. For Palermo, a native of Oxford, Massachusetts, this was especially poignant. Not only had he and his father, Vincent, attended many Red Sox games together, but Fenway had been the site of his first major-league game. Vincent had been at that game, and he was at this playoff game, too, courtesy of his son's tickets.

When Bucky Dent's home run cleared the left-field wall at Fenway Park in the top of the seventh inning, buckling Carl Yastrzemski's knees, cleaving a cloudless Boston afternoon, fraying the very fibers that bind Red Sox Nation together, Palermo had the best view of anybody. It was his job to track the ball from the moment it hit Dent's bat until it cleared the wall, making sure it soared inside the fair pole—which it did, easily, by a couple of yards. Palermo twirled his fingers in the air, signaling a home run. That's when Bucky Dent realized exactly what he'd done.

"I saw the umpire signal that it was a homer just as I got to second base," Dent said a quarter century later, "and I never touched the ground after that."

For Palermo, it was the first forever moment he'd ever been a part of on a major-league diamond, and he was still filled with the adrenaline of the day when he joined his father for the drive back to Oxford. Father and son drove in silence for many miles. Finally, Vincent could stand it no more. He turned to his son.

"How could you call that ball fair?" he demanded.

Steve was stunned.

"Dad," he said, "it was twenty feet from the line."

Vincent Palermo chewed on that for a few minutes, then shook his head.

"But how could you call that ball fair?"

That would be but one of a thousand difficult nights for Vincent Palermo and the millions of others who constitute Red Sox Nation. That was the game that throttled so many of them, ruining their optimism, forcing them to concede, at last, that some greater force might be at work—if not a curse, then . . . *something.* There had been difficult losses before that—Enos Slaughter dashing home all the way from first base on a single to beat the Sox in game seven of the 1946 World Series jumps instantly to mind, as does the blown 3–0 lead in game seven of the '75 Series. There would be bone-crushing defeats afterward, notably game six of the 1986 World Series, against the Mets, when the Sox had a two-run lead in the bottom of the tenth, and the Mets rallied for three runs after two men were out, down to their last strike three different times.

But nothing was worse than October 2, 1978. It was bad enough that the Sox had blown that huge late-summer lead. Bad enough that they'd been drubbed by the Yankees those four games in Boston in early September, and then in the first two of a three-game set in the Bronx the following week, meaning that a fourteen-game lead over the Yankees had become a three-and-a-half-game deficit in a mere fifty-nine days. No, this time the Red Sox *really* had something sinister in store.

Because over the last eight days of the season, the hottest team in baseball hadn't been the streaking Yankees. It was the rampaging Red Sox. Over eight straight days—knowing they had to win every game, knowing that one slip would be all the Yankees would need to wrap up the pennant in regulation time—the Red Sox won eight straight games. You can go through the whole history of baseball and not find another team who essentially had to play eight consecutive elimination games, and won them all. On September 23, the Red Sox crawled back to within a game of the Yankees, but for the next six consecutive days, the Red Sox and Yankees won every day, inspiring one of the most famous radio bits of all time. On September 28, during his 7:10 A.M. news briefing, WBCN-FM broadcaster Charles Laquidara led with this: "Pope dead, Sox still alive, details at eleven."

Still, as heroic as the Sox were, they needed the Yankees to stumble once; on Sunday, October 1, it finally happened. There was little pretense to what mattered at Fenway Park that afternoon, as only one out-of-town score was posted on the Wall: the Yankees-Indians game taking place in the Bronx. Beforehand, seldom-used Toronto reserve Sam Ewing had some fun with the early-arriving Fenway crowd, grabbing an 8 from the storage shed behind the wall and planting it next to the CLE on the scoreboard. It drew a big cheer. It also proved nearly prophetic. A Cleveland pitcher named Rick Waits threw a five-hitter at the Yankees, and the Tribe battered New York, 9–2. Red Sox reliever Bob Stanley, listening to the game on a transistor radio in the Boston bullpen, kept relaying the scores to the folks in the neighboring bleachers.

"Whenever we heard a cheer for no apparent reason," Fred Lynn said later, "we knew the Indians had scored another run."

Meanwhile, Luis Tiant was taking care of the Red Sox' business, shutting out the Blue Jays 5–0. Just as they'd done twenty-nine years before, the Red Sox and Yankees would play one last game, winner take all. Only this time, the Red Sox would have the home-field advantage.

"Had it been another year, I might have been worried about going up there," Graig Nettles said in the subdued Yankees clubhouse before they headed to the airport for the brief shuttle flight to Boston. "But we've shown we can win there. And that's got to help our confidence."

Nobody on either side could appreciate what would take place on that brilliant Monday afternoon better than Jerry Remy, the Red Sox second baseman who was born in Fall River, Massachusetts, and nourished on Red Sox baseball. On the last day of the 1967 season, when the Red Sox completed their impossible-dream dash with a win over Minnesota, fourteen-year-old Jerry Remy had been one of the thousands of fans who'd flooded Fenway's field. Now he would be playing in a game that was sure to be an equally unforgettable monument in the team's history, no matter how it turned out.

"I bet there's more interest in this one game," Remy said, "than there will be in the whole damned World Series."

It sure seemed that way. Some of the Yankees, after arriving in town Sunday evening, had headed over to Daisy Buchanan's, a joint near their hotel, to blow off steam and relax. It was there that the magnitude of what they were about to take part in started to hit. But it was the next morning, as the tiny ballpark quickly filled to its bursting point, that it really kicked in. The Yankees had threatened right away, getting their first two runners on in the first, and for a few minutes it seemed like a routine extension of the massacre that had taken place just weeks before. But Mike Torrez, the Boston ace who just a year before had started and won the World Series–clinching game six for the Yankees, settled down and retired the side.

The final out of that inning did provide a little uneasiness, however. Reggie Jackson smoked a ball high and deep to left field, but the wind in the first inning was blowing almost dead into the hitter's face. Jackson's ball died in the jet stream and dropped harmlessly to Carl Yastrzemski on the warning track. The Yankees had been warned beforehand that the Fenway winds in October were unpredictable and without pattern, that they could change at any moment. The paranoia stretched to the broadcast booth. As Jim Rice stepped to the plate in the bottom of the first, Phil Rizzuto, on WPIX-TV, announced that the wind had suddenly started reversing itself and was now blowing *out.* "Holy cow!" the Scooter cried on the telecast being beamed back to New York City. "The Red Sox even control the wind!"

It didn't matter there; Ron Guidry, seeking his twenty-fifth victory, blew strike three past the man who would edge him out for the league's Most Valuable Player Award. But an inning later, Yastrzemski, at thirty-eight still one of the most uncanny clutch hitters in baseball, turned on a Guidry heater and pulled it inside the right-field pole, just 302 feet away. The Sox had a 1–0 lead. They doubled it in the sixth, when Rice drove in his 139th run of the season, and should have had more. With two outs and two on, Fred Lynn got around on a hanging Guidry slider and pulled it down the right-field line for what Lynn, and everyone else, believed would be a two-run double that just might bury the Yankees for good. To his horror, something got in the way: Lou Piniella's glove.

"I'm a goddamned spray hitter," Lynn said. "I don't hit five balls all year to that spot of the park, especially not off a guy like Guidry, who throws gas. What the *hell* was he doing there?"

Twenty-five years later, sitting in the visitors' clubhouse at Yankee Stadium, Piniella asked himself that same question. "Guidry was working on three days' rest," he said. "His stuff that year was so overpowering, but Yaz had pulled that fastball earlier in the game. I was shading more to the line than usual. And, hell, I got lucky. He hit that thing right at me."

So instead of 4–0, it was 2–0 when the Yankees came to bat in the top of the seventh. Still, the way Torrez was throwing, 2–0 might as well have been 12–0.

"There were only a few other days my whole career where I felt better than I did that day," Torrez said years later. "Every pitch I threw after the first inning went exactly where I wanted it to go."

In the seventh, Graig Nettles led off with a lazy fly ball to right field, and now all around Fenway Park, the informal countdown began: eight outs to go. Chris Chambliss singled, and then Roy White followed with a base hit up the middle that was maybe half a foot away from being a 6-4-3 double play, just one of a thousand details that were forgotten soon thereafter. The Red Sox bullpen started to get busy, Bob Stanley and Andy Hassler warming up, but Torrez settled down and got pinch hitter Jim Spencer to lift an easy fly ball to left that Yastrzemski gloved.

Seven outs to go.

Up stepped Bucky Dent.

Dent was hitless in his previous thirteen at-bats, looking worse and worse with every swing. Under normal circumstances, Dent would never have come close to hitting in this situation. But in the season's final week, Yankees second baseman Willie Randolph injured his leg, and Yankees manager Bob Lemon couldn't afford to weaken his already depleted middle infield. So it was up to Dent, who took ball one, then fouled a ball straight off his left shoe. Yankees trainer Gene Monahan rushed out of the dugout to apply cold spray to Dent's throbbing foot. Third-base coach Dick Howser came over to make sure Dent could stay in the game.

And a bat boy approached with a new piece of lumber. Let Mickey Rivers—who was waiting on deck—explain why:

"Bucky and I used the same type of bat. The bats actually belonged to Roy White, but he didn't use them. I asked our clubhouse guy if he had any of the bats in his bag. The one I'd been using was a little chipped. He looked in the trunk and came up with a new one—a Max 44 model. It was the last one left in the bunch. I taped it up before the game the way we like it, and I told Bucky I had a new one ready for us. He said he was going to stick with the old chipped one. I was on him to change. I was even yelling to him from the on-deck circle that I had the bat with me. Finally, when the ball hit his foot and he was in big trouble, I grabbed the bat boy and told him to give Bucky the bat."

Play resumed. Torrez threw a fastball. Two innings earlier, he'd thrown an absolutely identical pitch: same speed, same spot, same movement. Dent had popped the ball up. He got it up in the air this time, too, and most of the Red Sox swore that when it left his bat, it didn't seem much different from the earlier ball.

"But it just kept carrying . . . ," Carlton Fisk said.

"It stayed in the air forever," Jerry Remy said.

"I thought I got the fastball in enough on him," Torrez said. "He kind of jerked it back and . . . Jesus, I never thought it would carry. Ever."

Dent: "When I hit it, I just hoped it would make the Wall. I put my head down and kept running . . . until I realized it was OK for me to slow down."

The floodgates opened after that. Torrez walked Rivers, Zimmer pulled him and inserted Stanley, and Munson scored Rivers on a pop-fly double. Now it was 4–2, Yankees. And an inning later, Reggie Jackson unloaded a drive that a hurricane wouldn't have been able to knock down, to dead center field. It was 5–2. The whole season had been reduced to one game, a perfect microcosm: Sox jump out fast, Yanks catch them, Yanks go ahead. All that was missing was the last-ditch, desperate Red Sox comeback.

It wasn't missing for long. The Sox scored twice off Goose Gossage in the eighth before the Yankees stopper retired Butch Hobson and George Scott with the tying and go-ahead runs on base, but Boston had replicated its desperate final-week stand now, in the season's final hours. It was 5–4, and the Yankees went meekly in the top of the ninth, and the tension now hung over Fenway Park the way cigarette smoke used to hang thick over old boxing arenas. It was virtually impossible to breathe.

"Every time my heart pounded," Gossage would admit years later, "I could feel my whole body rattle. That was pressure."

Gossage retired the first batter in the ninth inning, Dwight Evans, on an easy fly ball to left field. But that was the last easy thing about the ninth inning, for either team. Rick Burleson, the Red Sox shortstop who wore his heart on his sleeve always, who while the Sox were collapsing in September had muttered, "Every day you sit in front of your locker and ask God, 'What the hell is going on?'" drew a five-pitch walk from Gossage. Now the Red Sox had the tying run on base, the pennant-winning run at the plate, and the heart of the batting order coming up. And Fenway allowed itself to believe again. After everything that had happened—after the blown fourteen-game lead, after the massacre, after squandering the early 2–0 lead that afternoon thanks to Bucky Fucking Dent—the Red Sox were really going to find a way to make this right. Hell, they'd waited sixty years for a season like this; what were another few minutes of agony?

Gossage worked the count on Jerry Remy to 0 and 2. Remy—who'd been born in Fall River and raised in Somerset, who'd stormed the field in '67, who'd cried when the California Angels had traded him home the previous winter—fouled off one fastball. Gossage came in with another. And Remy jumped on this one, driving it sharply toward right, in the general vicinity of Lou Piniella. Burleson, on first base, tried to make a split-second judgment call. His head filled with questions: *Is Piniella gonna catch it? Can he? Should I run full speed, hope the ball falls at his feet so I can reach third base with only one out? What if I'm wrong, what if he makes the grab, what if I get doubled off?*

Piniella, meanwhile, had only one question: *Where the hell is the ball?*

The sun was at its worst angle now, and the ball was somewhere up there, camouflaged by the glare, invisible to him. Piniella was not blessed with grace or speed afoot, but the son of a bitch could think on his feet. He knew he had to try to keep Burleson from racing to third. The game depended on it. The pennant depended on it. So he pounded his glove, feigning confidence that he had a bead on the ball. Burleson froze ever so slightly, stopping ever so briefly. And so in that next instant, when it became apparent that Piniella truly had no idea where the ball was, he couldn't rev his engine back up again.

Piniella, of course, still had a bigger problem: He still had no clue where the ball was.

He had one hope: years of instinct. He thought he could guess where the ball might bounce, but he'd better be right. If it got by him,

Burleson would be able to walk home. And Remy, fueled by the passions of a million of his New England neighbors, just might be able to chase him there for an inside-the-park home run that would win the pennant for the Red Sox.

So Piniella turned into a hockey goalie. He stuck his glove out when he heard the thud of the ball against the turf. And damned if it didn't stick right in the pocket.

"Sure, I would have caught the ball if I'd have seen it," Piniella said. "But the way it was with the sun, so low, it could have hit me anyplace, in the stomach, in the chest, in the nuts, anywhere. You've just got to keep waiting, hoping you'll pick it up. You can't panic because then you'll let the runner know you're not catching the ball and he's going to go to third."

A quarter century later, a reporter from the *Tampa Tribune* popped a tape of the game into a VCR in Piniella's office at Tropicana Field. Piniella, by now the manager of the hapless Tampa Bay Devil Rays, would watch the whole thing: the ball jumping off Remy's bat, his confident pounding of the glove, then the clear terror in his mannerisms, then the ball bouncing and sticking in his glove.

"My God," Lou Piniella would exclaim all those years later. "That was close."

Burleson, watching all of this unfold, beat a hasty retreat to second base, from where he looked out at Piniella, shook his head, and yelled, "Holy *shit!*"

The Red Sox were still very much in business, of course, for up came Jim Rice, the most feared hitter in all of baseball in 1978: forty-six home runs, fifteen triples, 139 RBIs. He was a dead fastball hitter, facing one of the greatest fastball pitchers of that epoch. Gossage threw one by him for a strike. But Rice caught up with the next one, sending a rocket toward right field, toward Piniella, who was clearly destined to be in the middle of everything this day. A ball makes a different kind of noise when it hits the sweet spot of a bat; that's the noise Fenway Park heard now. Thirty-five thousand people rose as one, studied the flight of the ball . . . and then remembered. *The wind.* It had knocked Jackson's ball down in the first, then shifted to gently nudge Dent's fly ball in the seventh. The same wind that had been blowing toward right field for most of the day was now blowing in the opposite direction. It sank its teeth into Rice's ball and pushed it down. Piniella caught it. If Burleson had been on third base, he could have crawled home with the tying run. Instead, he raced from second to third. It wasn't the same thing. Rice returned to the dugout, put both hands on top, and dejectedly swung himself down.

Now it was Carl Yastrzemski's turn.

For many Boston fans, the truest of the true believers, this seemed incredibly poetic. Who better than Old Man Yaz to save them now? How often had he come through for them? He already had two hits today, including that icebreaking blast against Guidry. This was a moment tailor-made for him, wasn't it?

Gossage threw ball one. Later he said, "This is what I kept trying to think: 'The worst that can happen is that tomorrow, I'll be in Colorado. And would that really be so bad?'"

Gossage's next pitch at first made Yaz' eyes light up: a fastball, dead red, a shade inside, but very much in his wheelhouse. "All I wanted to do," Yastrzemski would later explain, "was get the bat out there and hit a ground ball through the hole and tie the score. I thought he would throw me a fastball, and when I saw it coming I thought: 'This is just what I wanted, right where I wanted it.'"

He paused.

"Then, all of a sudden," he said, "it jumped on me."

As Gossage's pitch found the slightest little tail, Yastrzemski swung, and the ball flew high above the Fenway Park infield. You could hear the final sounds of summer vanish from the Fenway Park grandstands, the place growing quieter and quieter as the ball reached its sad apex. Burleson and Remy chugged around the bases in the event someone would slip on a banana peel. But the ball had settled above Graig Nettles, the slickest-fielding third baseman in the game. He backed up, sidestepped into foul territory, squeezed the ball tight as it fell in his glove, then punched the sky with both hands.

The headline in the next morning's *Boston Globe* would sum it up perfectly: "Destiny 5, Red Sox 4."

Afterward, there was nothing but grace from both sets of exhausted warriors. Yastrzemski announced, "I'm rooting for the Yankees the rest of the way. I hope they win the World Series." Reggie Jackson slipped into the Red Sox clubhouse to seek out Yaz, found him, said, "We're the champs, and you're the champs." Even George Steinbrenner was overcome by the moment, knocking on Don Zimmer's door, extending his hand, shaking it warmly. Then he found Carlton Fisk.

"You did a hell of a job," the Yankees' owner told the Red Sox' catcher. "These are the two best teams in baseball, and it's a shame one of them had to lose. I thought we had you during the season, but you came back and caught us. Just a hell of a thing."

Dent, his legacy secure, was mobbed by teammates, fans, reporters. It was the high point of his baseball life. Twelve years later, Fenway's spirits would get a measure of revenge when Steinbrenner would pick Boston, of all cities, as the place where he would fire Dent as the Yankees' manager after a reign of eighty-nine desultory games. But that was a long, long way in the future.

"How did this happen?" Dent asked amid the madness, his words frosted with wonder. "How did this happen?"

As the people left the old ball yard that day, thousands of them were asking the same question. They didn't have any answers, either.

What Red Sox fans had long lamented about that game was how many chances the Sox had to bury the Yankees that day.

"We had Guidry on the ropes," Steve Silva said. "If you put the game out of reach early, then Bucky Dent's home run just makes it a closer game. It isn't a killer."

Twenty-six years later, another Red Sox team would take no such chance. What was most shocking about game seven was how relent-lessly anticlimactic it was. After Derek Lowe retired the Yankees one-two-three in the first, the Red Sox started piling on in the second, loading the bases with one man out on a single and two walks, and Torre had seen enough. Out came Brown. In came Javier Vazquez, the object of so much obsession the previous winter, the man the Yankees had decided they wanted instead of Curt Schilling, the man the Red Sox had abandoned once it became obvious they could get Schilling. Maybe it helped Torre's decision to see that Johnny Damon, the first man Vazquez would face, had hit only .167 against Vazquez in his career, only two hits in twelve lifetime at-bats. What might have been more helpful is if Torre had remembered that those two hits had come earlier in the year—and both of them were home runs.

Damon surely remembered.

"I was looking for one pitch," Damon would say, "and I got it right away."

And Damon knew exactly what to do with that pitch, a high fastball: He crushed it into the lower deck in right field, a monster shot that gave the Red Sox a 6–0 lead and started to make everyone understand that no amount of negative history, negative karma, or negative think-ing was going to change the tide now. Not even the remarkable decision by Terry Francona to bring Martinez into the game in the seventh inning—with the Red Sox up 8–1—could change that. Yankee Stadium had transformed into the world's largest mausoleum by this point. Fans were just itching for a reason to abandon the ballpark and head home, into a long and troubling winter, when in jogged Martinez, replacing Lowe (who'd responded in a big way for this choice assignment, throw-ing six innings of one-hit ball), and suddenly the Stadium was trans-formed. It was surreal. Here came the most feared, most intimidating pitcher of the last ten years, and yet inside Yankee Stadium, Martinez' arrival signaled an infusion of hope!

"*Who's your Daddy?*" came the chant.

"*Who's your Daddy?*"

And the thing was, they were right. The Yankees sprang back to life, nine outs from elimination. Hideki Matsui immediately doubled to deep right field. Bernie Williams followed with another double, also to deep right, scoring Matsui. Jorge Posada grounded out off his old nemesis, pushing Williams to third, but Kenny Lofton, liberated at last from deep on the Yankees' bench, delivered an RBI single, and everywhere inside Yankee Stadium, fans began to do mental calisthenics, trying to figure what it would take to get the tying run to the plate. Martinez stood impassively on the mound, his moment of triumph soured.

He recovered, though. He escaped the inning without further damage, and even the most cynical Red Sox fan had a hard time justifying concern with the Sox six outs from the World Series and five runs ahead. Just to make sure, though, Bellhorn hit another rocket into the upper deck in the eighth, pushing the lead to 9–3, and Cabrera added a sacrifice fly in the ninth, making it 10–3.

Not even the Red Sox were going to blow this.

And that reality started to make its way all across the many precincts of Red Sox Nation. At Yankee Stadium, Jeremy Perelman, the hedge-fund analyst, was busy making a perfect nuisance of himself, and there was little the Yankees fans surrounding him could do about it. Perelman admitted he'd been "walking on eggshells" all day long, calling his father, Steve, and his brother, Jonathan, as well as his buddy Don Bilson, as much for support and emotional reinforcement as anything else. To his surprise, they all believed the Red Sox were going to win. So did Jeremy. This wasn't in keeping with classic Sox fan pessimism, but Perelman wasn't going to argue.

And as the final outs of game seven melted away, Perelman couldn't help the glee that was pouring out of him, even in the growing quiet of Yankee doom.

"When Damon hit the grand slam, I don't know what I felt. It seemed like the ball was hit hard, and the next thing I knew Sheffield was looking up watching it go," Perelman said. "I could not believe my eyes, and didn't know if I could feel my feet. It was almost as though I was floating. Eighty-six years of futility were about to be erased in four days."

Tony Zannotti understood. He watched the game alone in his den, staring at his shrine wall, waiting for an apocalypse that never came. Periodically, his wife would visit, especially when it started getting late and he hadn't come to bed yet.

"She's from a family that always believes the worst will happen to the Sox," he said. "She was in bed, even with a six-run lead, thinking to herself, 'OK, but if they hit a grand slam, then it's only a two-run lead. . . .' She couldn't watch the ending."

Mike Carey understood.

"I was more nervous for game seven than I was for my wedding or the birth of my daughter," he said. "I couldn't do any work, I couldn't eat. It was just torture waiting for it. My in-laws had a birthday party for my nephew that day, and I told my wife she could take my daughter with her, but I wasn't going. I wasn't watching that game in front of anyone. I could watch it with her at home, but I could not go anywhere where other people would be watching it. I needed to be in my place.

"During games six and seven, when things got tense, I would get up, go to our bedroom, put the mute on the TV, turn the lights off, and get under the covers and watch out of the corner of my eye. Even in the ninth inning of game seven, I couldn't believe my eyes. I didn't even want to say out loud that they were going to win. I just couldn't believe it."

They could believe it. It was OK. Mike Timlin got the first two outs of the inning, sprinkled between a Matsui single and a Kenny Lofton walk. Even Tony Zannotti's wife would have needed a calculator to figure out how to get the tying run to the plate, but Terry Francona was taking no chances. He called on Alan Embree to get the final out.

"It felt like Embree spent twenty minutes warming up," Jeremy Perelman said.

It didn't take long after that. Embree threw one ball to Ruben Sierra, then threw a sinker that did exactly what it was supposed to: It dipped below the sweet spot of Sierra's bat, inducing an easy ground ball to second. Pokey Reese fielded it cleanly. He flipped it over to Doug Mientkiewicz. Mientkiewicz squeezed it.

And it was over. At 12:01 A.M., one minute after October 20 had become October 21, the Red Sox were officially declared champions of the American League. Eighty-four years and nine months after dealing Babe Ruth to the Yankees, fifty-five years after that awful lost weekend in 1949, twenty-six years after Bucky Dent, fifty-three weeks after Aaron Boone . . . they had made it. They had arrived. Since 1918, they'd won four pennants, meaning they'd beaten the Yankees to the finish line four times in eighty-six years. They'd never done it staring into the whites of their eyes, though.

Not until now.

Trot Nixon shouted at the bleacher creatures in right field who'd tormented him all series long before sprinting in to join the most joyful baseball pile anyone had seen in a good long time. The clubhouse celebration spared no amount of glee, corks popping and champagne flowing everywhere.

Larry Lucchino, the Red Sox' CEO, one of the men who'd helped add a new spin to this old rivalry, who'd helped to kick the whole thing into overdrive with his famous "Evil Empire" observations, stood just outside the celebratory storm and took a great whiff of fulfillment from what he'd just seen.

"This is really satisfying because we remember the Yankees' accomplishment last year and it's particularly sweet to do it here and celebrate in the same place," Lucchino said. "Someone sent me a hat recently that read, ALL EMPIRES FALL. I refused to wear it. But I might change my mind tonight. I may put it on for a few hours."

The Red Sox fans in attendance at Yankee Stadium, so overwhelmed all night, now engineered something of a palace coup, commandeering the lower bowl of Yankee Stadium just behind the Red Sox' third-base dugout. For a time, they tried in vain to drown out the final few replays of "New York, New York"—the Liza version this time, the Yankees-lose rendition—and when the Yankees finally pulled the plug on that, you could hear the Sox fans lift their voices to the sky.

"*Thank you, Red Sox!*"

"*Thank you, Red Sox!*"

"*Thank you, Red Sox!*"

As they watched with horror from their perch high above home plate, a few of George Steinbrenner's underlings started to fume. These people weren't going home! They looked like they might stay all night, waiting for every one of the Red Sox to come out of the dugout, salute them, spray them with champagne. This was unseemly! This was outrageous! And surely the boss wouldn't approve of this.

So they went to see him in his office, and they lodged their formal complaints, and George Steinbrenner listened very carefully to every last one of them, and then he shook his head and leaned back in his chair.

"Keep the lights on for them as long as they want to stay," Steinbrenner said quietly. "They've earned it."

EPILOGUE

Yogi Berra was right, of course.

From a distance, you could certainly appreciate what the Yankees and the Red Sox meant to major-league baseball and to the sport's fans across the summers of 2003 and 2004, in the same way you could value what they'd meant to each other since that first little conflagration at the Huntington Avenue Grounds in 1903. From the safe remove of a living room, a box seat, or a saloon stool, you could catch glimpses and snippets. You could feel the reflected heat. You could bask in deflected glories.

But you really *do* have to go through it to know what it's like to go through it.

For me, the education process started with those rotating baseball caps in the spring of 2004. It ended with a cab ride through the streets of Boston late on the evening of October 23, right after the Red Sox had beaten the Cardinals 11–9 in game one of the World Series. The cabbie did not speak English very well. But he spoke the language of baseball fluently.

"This World Series, it is nothing, no excitement," he told me. "I wish the Yankees would come back. I wish that series was a best-of-seventeen, not a best-of-seven."

I asked him if he'd followed the American League Championship Series.

"From far away, from my taxi," he said. "But it looked wonderful."

From up close, it looked even better, sounded even louder, felt even more like an endless inferno of passion and hatred and energy and ardor. Over the course of two years, thirty-eight regular-season games and fourteen playoff games, I saw every one live, in person, from a press box seat. I may have wandered the fringes a bit—visiting clubhouses, sitting in dugouts, wandering the grounds at spring training complexes, talking to dozens of Yankees and dozens of Red Sox and dozens of fans who spent so much of these two wonderful summers following every punch, every counterpunch, every juke, every jab.

The night Aaron Boone went deep off Tim Wakefield, I was in the Yankees' clubhouse, drenched with champagne, watching the staid New York Yankees let their hair down for one memorable night. There was nothing corporate, nothing businesslike in that midnight hour. What they'd done, beating the Red Sox? It meant the world to them. It *mattered*, in a way that was hard for any of them to describe.

It became fashionable in the summer of 2004, before the Red Sox went on to beat the Yankees and then win their first World Series since 1918, to find alternative words for *rivalry*, synonyms that would better describe the relationship these teams had with each other. Rivals, after all, are supposed to take turns sipping from victory's jug. This wasn't a rivalry at all, people would argue, but a feud, a dispute, a quarrel, a grudge. Those who would say this weren't in the home team clubhouse in the earliest hours of October 17, 2003. They didn't see grown men, millionaires all, gush tears of joy over beating the other team in this allegedly one-sided relationship.

"We just beat the Red Sox," Derek Jeter told me that night, right after he'd been doused with a full bottle of champagne by Jason Giambi. "And that means we beat the best there is."

The Red Sox always believed they were the Yankees' equals, even as the summer of 2004 seemed on the brink of teetering into the abyss, even after their remarkable late-summer surge failed to carry them past the Yankees in the American League East. There was one moment that proved rather telling, though, and that was the evening of September 26. The night before, the Yankees had beaten Pedro Martinez and all but guaranteed themselves the East Division title. That was the night Martinez declared, "I just tip my cap and call the Yankees my daddy," and added: "I just wish they would fucking disappear and never come back." This should have been the lowest possible moment in the team's season: First place was gone, Pedro's confidence was shot, the MFYs were set to rampage one more time all over Red Sox Nation with their muddy boots and dirty hands.

And yet . . .

Early on this Saturday evening, just before the clubhouse was closed to outsiders, Martinez showed up with a friend: a twenty-eight-inch-tall actor named Nelson de la Rosa. He'd appeared on the big screen in *The Island of Dr. Moreau,* and was something of an icon in the Dominican Republic. Martinez, a Dominican icon himself, brought him to work this night to meet some of the fellas.

And what followed provided the outsiders still in the clubhouse a stunning look inside the Red Sox' world. It's one thing to hear Johnny Damon or Kevin Millar extol their team's slacker image, to hear them describe the clubhouse, as Millar did in the spring, as "the frat house just before the cops knock on the door."

It's something else to be in the middle of it.

But here we were.

Martinez brought de la Rosa into Terry Francona's office, and the look on Francona's face alone—horror mixed with curiosity mixed with wonder mixed with a typically polite Francona greeting of "Welcome to Boston, Nelson!"—would have provided a year's worth of comic relief in most clubhouses, maybe a millennium's worth in the Bronx. But Francona was only the warm-up. Derek Lowe came over and tried to wind de la Rosa up, like a toy soldier. Doug Mientkiewicz yelled, "We gotta get him a uniform!" and Johnny Damon bellowed, "The curse is gone!"

Manny Ramirez and David Ortiz, dressing in their corner of the clubhouse, were both instantly dazzled. "Hey, Millar!" Manny screamed across the room, pointing to his crotch, then pointing at Millar. "This dude's got a bigger one than you do!"

Pitcher Curtis Leskanic sized de la Rosa up, then proclaimed: "I shall call him . . . Mini-Me!"

After a few minutes, it was time for reporters to leave, to head back up to the press box. And every one of them asked the same question: "Did we really just see what we just saw?"

Yep. We'd seen it, all right. We'd seen all of it. Within this rivalry—and yes, no matter how you define the word, it's perfectly proper to call this a rivalry now—you never knew what to expect. Midgets. Mystics. Hexes. Poxes. And more terrific baseball in two years than most baseball fans get to see in two decades. The Yankees and Red Sox are partners in an enduring, endearing, wonderful baseball tale, one that gets more complicated—and more alluring—every year.

Max Frazee surely appreciated that.

Frazee was a forty-nine-year-old construction worker who lived in lower Manhattan and made his way to Yankee Stadium for game seven of the 2004 American League Championship Series with specific rooting interests in his mind—and not the kind you might expect from the great-grandson of Harry H. Frazee. No, as he walked among the fans outside, he smoked American Spirit cigarettes and wore a Yankees cap.

He delighted in talking about how most of his mornings now included at least one playing of Aaron Boone's home run on his DVD player.

"It makes me smile," he explained.

Several years earlier, Frazee and some other family members had been invited back to Fenway Park for a pregame function, and when they were introduced they were showered with boos and catcalls and other assorted ugliness. It was nothing new, really; Frazees have been getting booed in Boston ever since January 5, 1920. But that was enough for Max. The moment he returned to New York City, his home since 1981, the first thing he did was pick up the phone and buy Yankees season tickets.

"One of the most beautiful things in the world is walking into Yankee Stadium," Max said, turning the blade a few more revolutions into the gizzard of Red Sox Nation. "Man, that green grass . . ."

On this night, of course, there would be Red Sox celebrating on the green grass, and while the Yankees fan inside Frazee wanted to weep, there was another part of him that understood how proper all of this was. Finally, after all these years, Max Frazee's great-grandfather could be left alone to rest in peace. Finally, after all these years, the Yankees and the Red Sox could be appreciated as great baseball teams who played great baseball games when they shared a baseball field, and not the products of some mystical coupling. The emperors from the Bronx and the idiots from the Hub, when they got together, knew how to put on a hell of a show.

They always had.

AFTERWORD

The aftermath of the 2004 American League Championship Series was a kaleidoscope of sore throats, red eyes, and empty emotions, no matter which side of the Great Divide you happened to sit on.

In New York City, the denial and subsequent mourning was palpable. The front page of the *Post* screamed: "Damned Yankees!" The *Daily News* countered with this: "See You in 2090." And even the *Times* couldn't help itself: "Monumental Collapse," it cried. Not that it mattered. Yankees fans spent most of the next few weeks ignoring newspapers, news programs, anything that might serve as a reminder of what had just happened to them.

"Hell on earth," is how Frank Russo described it.

In Boston there couldn't have been a greater contrast, mostly because once the Red Sox started winning against the Yankees, they never stopped. The St. Louis Cardinals had come to Fenway Park for game one of the World Series sporting the best record in baseball and an assortment of the most confident and colorless personalities in the sport. After the Yankees, it had been the Cardinals who across the past eighty-six years had tormented the Red Sox the most. Twice, in 1946 and again in 1967, the Sox had faced St. Louis in the World Series, and both times they lost in excruciating fashion, both times in a seventh game. By now, though, most Red Sox fans had reached an amicable armistice with history.

"Here's what I would have liked," Mike Carey said, "I would have liked to take all the Yankees and all the Cardinals and all the players from every team who's shit on us for eighty-six years, make an All-Star team of them, and have these Red Sox take them on. We'd kick their ass, too, as well as we're playing."

It was hard to argue. The Sox steamrolled the Cardinals in four straight games, and when Keith Foulke induced St. Louis' Edgar Renteria to bounce meekly back to the mound at exactly 10:40 P.M., Central Standard Time, on the night of October 27, and when he flipped the ball over to Doug Mientkiewicz, it was over at last. After a wait of eighty-six years, one month, and sixteen days, the Red Sox were champions of the world again. The reality was jarring at first. Soon, though, the Red Sox were everywhere: magazine covers, late-night television shows, cereal boxes. It was impossible to escape the odd, ubiquitous reality of this brave new baseball world.

Red Sox fans surely took to it. On the day before Halloween, over 1 million of them flooded the streets and boulevards of downtown to salute the Red Sox with a parade that would have lasted the rest of the calendar year if it was up to the citizens of Boston. The route began outside Fenway Park, wound through Copley Square, then on to Cambridge across the Charles River. Fans started arriving as early as 3 A.M., without complaint. It had been only two weeks earlier that the Yankees had pancaked their Sox, 19–8, and seemed on the verge of authoring another sinister chapter in this rivalry.

Now, the fans stood and shouted themselves hoarse. They saw Pedro Martinez (in what turned out to be his final public appearance as a Red Sox player) carrying a sign that read "Idiots Rule." David Ortiz, the messiah for whom the Red Sox had searched for eight and a half decades, flashed his twenty-one-karat smile everywhere while everywhere the fans chanted "Whose Your Papi?"

And then there was Manny Ramirez, who would have earned some of the loudest cheers anyway, but who pumped the decibel level to ungodly heights thanks to the sign he'd brought to the parade with him: JETER IS PLAYING GOLF TODAY. THIS IS BETTER.

There wasn't a soul in New England who was about to argue with Manny about that one.

Nothing lasts forever, however, not even something as complete and as compelling as a Red Sox World Series championship that had kept New England sleepless and bleary-eyed for weeks. Business was business, after all, and besides, the only reason the Red Sox had been able to scale the sheer cliff from 0–3 down to the Yankees to the top of the baseball firmament was because they'd been cold, bloodless, and fearless at the July trading deadline. Red Sox fans understood this. But it was still jarring to see the procession of October heroes make their way to the door so quickly.

There was Dave Roberts, the man who stole second base as a pinch runner in game four against the Yankees, who set everything into motion. He was traded to the Padres on December 20 for three players and $2.65 million in cash. There was Doug Mientkiewicz, who'd recorded the final put-outs of both the ALCS and the World Series (and who would cause a serious stir when it was revealed that he'd kept the Series-clinching ball for himself), traded to the Mets for a minor leaguer on January 27, the same day he reached an agreement to lend the prized baseball to the Red Sox for one year. There was Orlando Cabrera, the centerpiece of the Nomar Garciaparra deal, who on December 20 signed a four-year, $32 million contract with the Los Angeles Angels of Anaheim, five days after the Red Sox had decided to fork over four years and $40 million to Renteria—the man who'd made the final out of the World Series—to play shortstop for them. There was popular role player Gabe Kapler, who signed a one-year deal to play in Japan for the Yomiuri Giants, though he would return to Boston in July before rupturing his left Achilles tendon during a game in Toronto in September. There was Derek Lowe, who'd come up so big in the playoffs after such a dreadful regular season, who won all three clinching games in the postseason, who cashed in with a $36 million free-agent deal with the Dodgers.

And, most difficult of all, there was the news on December 16 that Pedro Martinez had decided to sign a four-year, $54 million contract with the New York Mets, officially ending one of Boston's most ardent love affairs between star and fans. Martinez wasn't the same pitcher who'd dominated the American League for the better part of seven years, and he would be a clear No. 2 pitcher on any staff that included Curt Schilling. Plus, at age thirty-three, he had shoulder issues that sufficiently concerned the Red Sox to prevent them from offering a fourth guaranteed year. In fact, Larry Lucchino scooped Pedro and the Mets on their glorious announcement two days early when he said, "Pedro was a great member of the Red Sox team for seven years, and a certain Hall of Famer. He will be missed, and we are disappointed to have lost him to the Mets and the National League."

Change abounded in Boston.

But it resounded in New York, where the Yankees were reeling from what was alternately called the "greatest comeback in baseball history" if folks were feeling charitable, or the "greatest choke in baseball history" if they wanted to tweak the Yankees. Within hours of watching his team lose game seven—and instructing his underlings to allow the partying hordes of Red Sox fans to stay in his stadium as long as they wanted—Steinbrenner issued his valedictory on the season, in the form of a press release delivered through his public relations adviser, Howard Rubenstein: "You can be assured we will get to work and produce a great team next year. Of course I am disappointed because I wanted a championship for our fans and for our city."

The changes wouldn't come at the top: Brian Cashman and Joe Torre would remain as general manager and manager. No key players would be shipped into exile: Derek Jeter, Alex Rodriguez, Hideki Matsui, Gary Sheffield, Jorge Posada, Jason Giambi, Mike Mussina, Mariano Rivera, and an aging but still active Bernie Williams would return to form the core of the Yankees. But there would be moves. There would be additions. There would be deletions. And by the time they were finished, the Yankees would become the first team in the history of professional sports to build a team with a payroll in excess of $200 million.

Kenny Lofton was the first to go, traded to the Phillies on December 3 in exchange for journeyman pitcher Felix Rodriguez. The Yankees addressed their pitching needs soon thereafter, signing both Florida's Carl Pavano and Atlanta's Jaret Wright to free-agent contracts, although they misread the market when they failed to pick up a one-year, $8 million option on Jon Lieber, who emerged as the Yankees' most reliable starting pitcher toward the end of the '04 season; Lieber wound up signing a three-year, $21 million contract with the Phillies, for whom he would win seventeen games in 2005. On December 8, the Yankees decided not to offer arbitration to second baseman Miguel Cairo, opting instead to sign Tony Womack of the Cardinals to a two-year, $4 million deal. And on New Year's Eve, the Yankees took a trip back to their recent, glorious past when they signed Tino Martinez to a one-year deal at $3 million to back up Giambi at first base.

But the biggest game the Yankees were hunting was the same woolly mammoth they'd pursued at the trading deadline in July. Randy Johnson fulfilled every piece of George Steinbrenner's typical wish-list order form: he was a shoo-in Hall of Famer, having amassed 246 victories and over four thousand strikeouts with an ERA just north of 3 in seventeen seasons with the Expos, Mariners, Astros, and Diamondbacks, picking up five Cy Young Awards along the way, emblematic of the best pitcher in the league. He was six-foot-ten, he was imposing, he had one of the game's great nicknames—The Big Unit—and even though he would turn forty-two in September, he still threw his fastballs in the mid- to high-nineties, and featured a slider that snapped nastily as it whizzed past hitters.

In December, the Yankees believed they'd completed a three-way, ten-player deal with the Dodgers and Diamondbacks, in which the primary components would be Johnson going from Arizona to New York, Javier Vazquez going from New York to Los Angeles, and Shawn Green going from Los Angeles to Arizona. New York City was electric, as this came just a week after the Mets had introduced Pedro Martinez. But on December 22, the Dodgers pulled out of the deal, citing Vazquez's alleged unwillingness to take a pretrade physical, although everyone involved in the trade believed it was merely a case of the Dodgers getting cold feet and wanting out of the deal. Of course, Yankees fans had grown accustomed to one overwhelming fact in the Era of Steinbrenner: what George wants, George usually gets. And so it was that just before the New Year, the Yankees and Diamondbacks resuscitated talks on their own and quickly agreed to swap Johnson and Vazquez, with the Yankees tossing in two other players and $9 million in cash. A few weeks later, with a fresh two-year, $32 million extension in hand, Johnson was introduced to the New York media—though not until Johnson had a much-talked-about confrontation with a television cameraman named Vinny Everett during a stroll down Madison Avenue, on his way to a hospital to take his physical.

"Don't get in my face," Johnson snapped at the cameraman, "and don't talk back to me."

Johnson apologized, but the Yankees didn't much care. If he could treat the Red Sox from a pitcher's mound in a few months the way he'd treated poor Vinny Everett on a city street, that would be perfectly all right with them.

They couldn't get out of each other's way, and that would have been the case even if they tried to.

Within minutes of the Red Sox winning the 2004 World Series, it became apparent the Red Sox and the Yankees would waste little time renewing hostilities in 2005. For one thing, the preliminary American League schedule revealed they would face each other on Sunday, April 3, at Yankee Stadium, the very first game of the regular season, televised nationally on ESPN, the Sox and Yankees getting a one-day jump on the rest of major league baseball. But that would only be the appetizer. Exactly eight days after that, the teams would reconvene at Fenway Park for the Red Sox' home opener. This meant that when the Sox received their World Series rings, and when they lifted a championship banner high over Fenway Park for the first time in eighty-six years, the Yankees would be front and center, in the ballpark, forced to watch every bit of pomp, every ounce of circumstance. Not everyone was thrilled with this scheduling quirk.

"When we play there's so much on the field and on the table already," Joe Torre would say with a shake of his head and a crooked half-smile on his face. "Now, you're not only making us the first game of the season, you're making us each other's home openers, too? I think it's great for the fans. But it does make you wonder if enough is ever too much, you know?"

First things first, though. When the Yankees reported to their spring training headquarters in Tampa, they were met with a barrage of Red Sox questions, to the point where Derek Jeter, one early Florida morning, took a reporter aside and asked with a smile, "Y'all do know that we have other teams on our schedule this year, right?" Mostly, they handled the Sox questions with aplomb, giving props to their bitter rivals, offering hopeful talk that maybe the two of them could settle matters once and for all with a rubber series in October. The Yankees rarely cause a lot of smoke or commotion in the preseason. They are too corporate, too careful, too studied for any of that.

The Red Sox?

That was a different matter entirely.

From the moment the Sox reported to their training camp in Fort Myers, they were predictably chirpy, chatty, and charming, filling notebooks with their pithy observations and doling out sound bites. But early in the game, it was apparent they'd reported for work with oversized chips on their shoulders, too. And most of their anger was directed at one person.

Alex Rodriguez.

Not only were the Sox still smoldering from the "slap" play Rodriguez had attempted against Bronson Arroyo in game six four months earlier, and not only were they annoyed by how unapologetic A-Rod was in the play's aftermath, now they had some extra ammunition, too. Just before the start of spring training, Rodriguez had granted one day of full access to Bob Klapisch, who was not only a first-rate baseball columnist for both the Bergen *Record* and ESPN.com, but was still a terrific pitcher in a highly competitive amateur baseball league in New Jersey. Rodriguez had invited Klapisch to train with him for a day, and it yielded a splendid story. But it also included this observation from Rodriguez:

"I know there are six-hundred-and-fifty or seven hundred players who are sleeping this morning. Either that, or they're taking their kids to school. But there's no way they're going to be up running the stairs or doing what I'm doing."

Actually, Curt Schilling had manned the rifle first, uttering his famous "freakin' junior high school play" comment on a national radio program referring to the slap play. Rodriguez had deferred making a retort until January 22, when he finally said: "I just hope he continues to talk about me and my teammates. It's going to give us great motivation to beat him up in the future."

Schilling, never shy, promptly responded: "If that's what he needs (for motivation), cool. I don't care what Alex says. When someone says that, you consider the source." He also talked about how the biggest link in the chain of events culminating with the Sox' championship was the day the Red Sox *didn't* get A-Rod. "The biggest move, when all was said and done, was the non-move. I think if we get A-Rod, we don't get there. I don't question that for a second. He's a Hall of Famer, sure. But after getting to know people who (a) play with him and (b) have played with him, I don't think it would have worked here."

And that was *before* A-Rod cleared his throat and told Klapisch about his arduous work habits. Trot Nixon was first in line to take a few swings at the Yankees' human piñata.

"He said he's doing all this while six hundred players are still in their beds," Nixon began. "I said, 'What's wrong with me taking my kid to school? I'm not a deadbat dad, you clown.' I work out for three hours in the weight room, and I hit for another two or three hours, a father of two. What makes you so much better?"

A few seconds later, Nixon continued: "He said the next time, instead of slapping the ball out of Bronson's hands he's going to run him over. It's like, OK. You're a clown."

And Nixon *still* wasn't done.

"He's done some great things on the field. He's one of the best baseball players in the game and probably will be when it's all said and done. But when people ask me about the Yankees, I tell them about Jeter and Bernie Williams and Posada. I don't tell them about Rodriguez. He can't stand up to Jeter in my book or Bernie or Posada."

When Nixon finally finished, his teammates practically fell over themselves to get in on the fun.

From David Wells, the ex-Yankee who'd signed on with the Red Sox in the off-season: "He's a five-tool player, one of the best out there. But I remember reading about his press conference when he first got there. He said, 'We,' like he's won three or four rings. and that kind of disturbed me. Because I would never put myself in a situation. He shouldn't put himself in that category. You've got to earn it."

From Kevin Millar: "I played against him for twenty games. I know one thing. A lot of us in this locker room, when we watch a guy like

Derek Jeter play over and over again, he's a winner. I don't know if Rodriguez grasps for respect, but you don't need to tell people you're an upper-tier player. You don't need to tell people that you work out seven hours a day. That's an article that rubbed guys wrong. When you're a professional, you do your work."

And even newcomer Matt Mantei, a relief pitching import from Arizona who was two thousand miles away from the frays of 2003 and 2004, raised his hand and asked to be heard: "I don't like the Yankees, I don't think anybody does, except the Yankees. It's true, though. That's the bottom line, everybody in baseball wants to beat the Yankees. Everybody goes into the game against them with a little more adrenaline, a little bit better prepared."

The fires had been duly fanned and the hype duly amped. It took George Steinbrenner, of all people, to walk into the breach and ask for sanity.

"We will play the game on the field," Steinbrenner said.

Soon enough, mercifully, they would.

The season dawned as the two previous ones had: with the Yankees and the Red Sox the smart-money favorites to take half of the American League's playoff slots, putting them in perfect position to set up a third straight meeting in the AL Championship Series, if all broke properly in the playoffs' opening round.

It should have been too cold to play baseball on the Bronx evening of April 3, but the mere presence of the Yankees and the Red Sox walking onto the Yankee Stadium field exactly 165 days after they'd sprinted off was enough to add a simmer and a boil to the proceedings. The presence of David Wells, formerly one of the most popular Yankees of all time, only heightened the already combustible setting. Once, Wells had thrown a perfect game for the Yankees, in 1998, and during his second tour with the team he'd thrown seven masterful innings of four-hit ball against the Red Sox in game five of the '03 ALCS at Fenway Park, after which he'd famously proclaimed: "Whenever they are ready to get rid of this place, let me push the button." Wells' back had broken down a week later in the World Series, and then he broke a handshake agreement with the Yankees and opted to sign for bigger money with the San Diego Padres for 2004. Now he was the Red Sox' Opening Day pitcher thanks to Curt Schilling's nagging ankle problems, which meant he found himself in an odd place: working his favorite ballpark in the hated red-and-blue vestments of Boston. Wells wondered if he would be forgiven this, given his long-standing love affair with Yankees fans.

That mystery lasted all of three seconds, the amount of time it took Yankee Stadium to recognize Wells the Heretic as he hopped out of the visiting dugout alongside third base and made his way to the bullpen. He was booed. He was cursed at. Yankee Stadium even serenaded its erstwhile idol with several choruses of "Boo-mer sucks!" And it lasted across every pitch of Wells' mostly uninspired 4⅓ innings, during which the Yankees gleefully pounced on their ex-teammate on their way to a 9–2 victory behind Randy Johnson.

"I guess you can change uniforms, but you can't change into *that* uniform," Wells said quietly, a few hours later. "Hey, it is what it is. The greeting wasn't great. But there's nothing I could do about that. I couldn't control that. I knew what I was up against. I needed to pitch better than I did tonight. I had a bad night."

Two days later, Mariano Rivera had an even worse afternoon.

It wasn't Yankee Stadium's finest hour. For ten years, Rivera had been one of the most respected—revered, even—members of some forever Yankees teams. Since 1997, he had been the best closer in baseball, and was by general consensus considered the greatest relief pitcher in baseball history. That was true despite what had happened the previous October, when he blew saves on back-to-back nights, games four and five (though he'd been put in an all-but-impossible spot in the latter game, entering with the tying run already on third base; he surrendered a sacrifice fly that evened the game). Rivera wasn't perfect, but he was as close as was humanly possible.

"Money in your fucking pocket," was the way ex-Yankee David Cone once described him.

In the first week of the 2005 season, though, Rivera made a terrible mistake: he spent a couple of days acting painfully human, at the worst possible moment against the worst possible opponent. On April 5, in the season's second game, Rivera threw a 95-mph fastball that would have bored a hole through Posada's glove if it hadn't first been intercepted by Jason Varitek's bat, which launched it into orbit instead. That tied the game with one out in the ninth, though Jeter would rescue Rivera with a walk-off home run leading off the bottom half, off Keith Foulke.

The next day, nursing a 3–2 lead, Rivera's wheels began to spin off. It had already been a surreal day. First, Boston manager Terry Francona was rushed to the hospital for what was at first believed to be a possible heart attack, though it was later found to be a reaction to stress. Later, Jeter was taken to another hospital for a CAT scan after he was hit in the helmet with a pitch. But it was Yankees fans who suffered headaches, and resulting brain cramps, when Rivera endured a twenty-four-minute, thirty-eight-pitch adventure that he brought about himself with uncharacteristic wildness but that was exacerbated by a key error by Alex Rodriguez. The Sox scored five runs to win the game 7–3, and Rivera was booed off the mound by Yankees fans.

"After everything he's done in this ballpark," Yankees coach Mel Stottlemyre fumed, "I was shocked."

Rivera himself was significantly less furious.

"There are always about twenty thousand Red Sox fans here when we play them," he said. "Maybe it was only Sox fans who were booing."

Ironically, five days later, it was only Sox fans who were cheering him, as he was introduced before the Red Sox' home opener. In what was the most hotly anticipated regular season game—and the hottest, hardest-to-get ticket—in the ninety-three-year history of Fenway Park, there was a palpable, if temporary, warming of the Cold War between the combatants. During the goose-bump-raising ceremonies that commemorated the Sox' race to glory, as the players received their rings, as an extra-large banner was unveiled that covered the entire left-field wall, as former heroes like Johnny Pesky and Carl Yastrzemski and Carlton Fisk were cheered, there was a splendid absence of anti-Yankee vitriol.

"This day is supposed to be about what the Red Sox accomplished," Joe Torre said. "It's not supposed to be about what the Yankees didn't accomplish."

So it was that the Yankees remained in the dugout and watched the entire ceremony, a gesture that even Red Sox fans had to admit was both classy and respectful. "I've been on the other side of the field when we've gotten our rings before. I've never watched one. But they deserved a day like this," was how Derek Jeter explained it. "Of course, I was probably a little jealous, too."

The best part of the day came afterward, when the Yankees were introduced to raucous boos (it was back to normal fairly quickly), with one exception: when Mariano Rivera stepped forward and his name was announced, Fenway rose as one and gave him a standing ovation. Red Sox fans have great memories and better senses of humor. This was in recognition of the two blown saves the previous week, the two others the previous October, and the fact that he'd blown ten of his previous nineteen save opportunities against the Red Sox.

Again, Rivera took it all in stride.

"They've waited eighty-six years," he chuckled later. "I had no problem at all with that."

The Yankees were also kind enough to fulfill the role of designated patsies, getting blasted by the Red Sox, 8–1. That actually sent the Yankees spiraling into a shocking tailspin that culminated in a 6–3 loss to the Oakland Athletics on May 6, after which their record stood at 11–19. That left them a staggering nine games behind the surprising Baltimore Orioles, and six and a half games behind the Red Sox. And even though they righted themselves with a ten-game winning streak soon thereafter, the Yankees had started to look old, fragile, and terribly vulnerable. This was most evident in late May, when the Red Sox visited

Yankee Stadium for the second time. After the Yankees won the opener, 6–3, for their sixteenth win in eighteen games, it was the Red Sox who found themselves buried, sitting in fourth place with a 25–22 record, a game and a half behind the second-place Yankees.

But something changed the next day. For one thing, the Red Sox obliterated the Yankees, 17–1. For another, it sent the Yankees into another deep funk, and this one threatened to knock them completely out of the playoff picture. The Red Sox were soon playing full-throttle baseball. Manny Ramirez, after a terrible April, was back to his old self. The pitching staff, despite an extended absence by Schilling, was doing just well enough, thanks to Tim Wakefield's rubber arm and newcomer Matt Clement's hot start, and the fact that Wells soon settled into the unlikely position as ace of the Sox staff.

And then there was David Ortiz.

Big Papi was already a folk hero in Boston, his legend and his legacy secure after his heroics the previous autumn. But in 2005, he would blossom into a full-blown star of the first order, hitting an even .300 with forty-seven homers and 148 RBIs. Not only was he teaming with Ramirez (.292, forty-five, 145) to form the deadliest 3–4 punch in baseball; it was Ortiz' knack for late-game clutch heroics that made him so special. He'd even perfected the art of the walk-off home run, the way he flipped the bat away at impact, then discarded his helmet while rounding third, the better to protect himself from rabid teammates as he jumped on home plate.

"I've never seen anything like him," Johnny Damon marveled. "But then I don't think anyone has ever seen anything like him."

The Red Sox took two of three from the Yankees and by late June were primed to own the American League East. On June 26, they pounded the Phillies, 12–8, for their seventh straight victory. They were 44-30, in first place by two and a half games, with a six-and-a-half-game lead (seven in the loss column) over the reeling Yankees. That day, in the *Boston Globe*, columnist Dan Shaughnessy summarized the feelings of most New Englanders, who were now fully ennobled by the belief that whatever hex the Yankees may have once held over the Sox, it was now not only a thing of the past, it might well be fully reversed.

"It's OK to say it," Shaughnessy wrote. "Don't worry about jinxing them. The 2005 Red Sox are going to win the American League East. By a landslide. Come late September, this is going to look like Secretariat at the Belmont in 1973. After looking up at the Orioles for two frustrating months, the Sox moved into first place Friday night and they are there to stay. Stop worrying about the Yankees, Orioles, and Jays. It's not even going to be close."

Millar echoed Shaughnessy's point as only he could: "We're going to the Series, boys!" Millar crowed. "We're back! The fuckin' Sox are on a roll!"

"This is the place we thought we'd get to," Johnny Damon added. "It was just a matter of time. This team is playing great and I'm proud of what we've accomplished."

What Damon couldn't possibly know was that that weekend in Philadelphia would represent the high-water mark of the season. Oh, the Sox' lead in the A.L. East would reach a season-high four games a week later, but that was over the rapidly fading Orioles, whom nobody, least of all the Red Sox, truly viewed as a serious threat (the O's would soon have a manager fired, would lose Rafael Palmeiro to the biggest steroid scandal in the whole steroid-scarred summer of 2005, and would plummet to a 74–88 record by season's end). No, that seven-game loss-column lead the Sox held over the Yankees would soon erode, and it would happen quickly. By the All-Star break, the Yankees had already pulled themselves up to within two and a half games, and when the teams returned from the three-day break they would reconvene together, naturally, at Fenway Park.

That night of July 14, two magnificent events would converge, and when they did they would yield the signature Red Sox–Yankees moment of 2005. In the top of the ninth inning, in a 6–6 game, at precisely 10:04 P.M., the door to the Red Sox bullpen opened and out stepped Curt Schilling, making his first appearance in nearly two months after recuperating his still-bothersome ankle. Fenway went berserk. Schilling was returning, for now, in a new role: closer. All the innings Keith Foulke put on his shoulder the previous October had caught up to him, he'd been ineffective most of the year and now was being shut down for good thanks to a bum knee. So Schilling volunteered.

Gary Sheffield promptly greeted him with a double off the Wall.

And now here came Alex Rodriguez.

So far, it had been a season relatively devoid of extra-curricular Yankees–Red Sox tension. During the Yankees' first trip to Fenway, on April 14, Sheffield had nearly gotten himself involved in a grisly incident when a Red Sox fan named Chris House had leaned over to try and grab a ball Sheffield was chasing in the outfield. House's elbow had connected with Sheffield's face, and Sheffield's first reaction was to fight back: he shoved House before thowing the ball back to the infield, but that was the extent of his retaliation, a display of restraint that Sheffield later admitted was inspired by the alarming Indiana Pacers–Detroit Pistons melee that had brought ugliness to the NBA five months before. It was a frightening Fenway moment but nothing more; surely in the recent history of this feud, it was barely a blip.

This was more than a blip.

This was Rodriguez facing Schilling, and Schilling facing Rodriguez. Fenway Park was so electric it could have powered the Prudential Tower for a month. Everyone inside the building understood *something* unforgettable was about to happen. They waited for the drama to unfold.

It lasted exactly one pitch.

Schilling threw a slider, but it was a terrible slider, one that hung up fat and flat, all but begging Rodriguez to make it disappear. A-Rod complied. It flew far over the Wall, and a shroud of silence silently fell over Fenway, and for added Yankee pleasure, Mariano Rivera came into the game and retired the Red Sox quietly, 1-2-3, in the bottom of the inning. No standing ovations this time.

True to his personality, Rodriguez betrayed no public pleasure in his moment of triumph. Goaded by reporters, he demurred.

"That stuff," he said, "is over."

The race for the AL East, however, was far from done. By the time the weekend was complete, the Yankees had won three out of four and they were exactly one-half game out of first place. They were dead even in the loss column.

The fuckin' Yanks were the ones on a roll now.

It didn't last, of course. The rest of the summer, the Red Sox and the Yankees danced an uncomfortable dance with each other, and with a rotating cast of special guest stars. Neither could put distance between themselves and each other; nor could they put any distance between themselves and the other contenders for the AL wild card berth, the Oakland Athletics and the Cleveland Indians. On July 18, the Yankees beat the Texas Rangers and the Red Sox lost to the Tampa Bay Devil Rays, and the Yankees were all alone in first place for the first time since April. They stayed there exactly one day. Soon, the Red Sox were again threatening to fulfill Shaughnessy's prophesy. An eight-game winning streak in early August padded their lead over the Yankees to four and a half games; a subsequent six-game tear nudged that to five full games on the morning of August 14.

The Yankees were in big trouble. Five behind the Sox, three behind the A's for the wild card, their pitching was in utter disarray. Pavano had been lost for the season. Wright had been lost for several different chunks of the season. Mike Mussina would soon suffer elbow troubles. Chien-Ming Wang, a rookie from Taiwan and a surprise star of the first half, was shut down for six weeks with a bad rotator cuff. Johnson was an enigma: he would go 5–0 against the Red Sox but 0–2 against the lowly Devil Rays. Tony Womack had been an epic bust, necessitating the call-up of rookie Robinson Cano to play second base.

And yet . . .

"I'm not settling for the wild card," Derek Jeter said one day in August. "There's no reason we can't compete for the division. No reason whatsoever."

It seemed like a captain's dying wish to his troops in mid-August.

Only a funny thing happened.

Starting in mid-August, the Yankees finally began hitting their stride. Pitching fill-ins Aaron Small, Shawn Chacon, and Al Leiter plugged holes when necessary. The bats, always robust, churned out runs at a frantic pace. And Mariano Rivera, after all his early struggles, was enjoying the finest season of his career; he allowed exactly one earned run on the road all year.

By September 11, the Yankees had pulled themselves into the lead in the wild-card race. They were still three games behind the Red Sox after splitting the first two games of a three-game set at Yankee Stadium, but they were in the thick of the playoff hunt. Jeter still talked of winning the division, and it still sounded implausible. But that afternoon, in one of the best pitching duels Yankee Stadium had seen in years (probably since the Pedro Martinez–Roger Clemens 2–0 epic in May 2000), the Yankees won a 1–0 classic, the only run coming in the first inning on a fly ball that Jason Giambi hit off Tim Wakefield, one that traveled 314½ feet to barely clear the 314-foot sign in right field. Randy Johnson was spectacular, shutting the Sox out for seven innings before experiencing calf cramps.

There were twenty games left. The Red Sox led the Yankees by three. Suddenly, a schedule that had been obviously constructed to squeeze as much melodrama as possible between these two teams—two home openers, the first series after the All-Star Game—was now certain to come down to one final three-game series at Fenway Park, the last three games of the season.

And that's exactly what happened.

Sort of.

The Yankees blitzed through the next seventeen games, winning fourteen, forcing the Red Sox to be perfect. And they weren't: there were stumbles against Tampa Bay and Oakland, and three costly losses to Toronto. The Yankees officially passed them into first place on September 21; by the time the teams met up at Fenway on the evening of September 30, the Yankees led by one game, and fans in both cities had officially reached a fever pitch.

This was everything they could have asked for. For one, it was an historical salute to the 1949 season, when the Red Sox had gone to Yankee Stadium on the season's final weekend needing to win one of two games, won neither, and constructed one of the more painful chapters of the eighty-six-year legacy that spanned 1918 and 2004. For another, the fact that the Indians were very much in play for the wild card—tied with the Sox, one behind the Yankees entering the final weekend—conjured 1948, when all three of those teams entered the final weekend with a chance to win the pennant.

And it also hearkened back to 1978, to a time when only one team in the AL East would qualify for postseason play. The Indians had three games against the Chicago White Sox, who had officially wrapped up the AL Central, and home-field advantage, and officially had nothing to play for. There were boundless possible scenarios. If Cleveland took two out of three (as expected), then the Yankees would need to do the same to eliminate the Red Sox. If the Red Sox won two out of three, it would force a one-game playoff between the Yankees and Red Sox on Monday afternoon at Yankee Stadium, with the loser playing the Indians the next day in a one-game playoff to determine the wild card. In many ways, the weekend promised to be filled with more drama than both pervious ALCS combined.

And wound up delivering none of it.

It was stunningly anticlimactic. First, the Indians, in full panic mode, gagged away all three games against the White Sox (who were right at the beginning of an autumn dash that would see them win sixteen of the final seventeen games they played, including a four-game sweep of the Houston Astros in the World Series). That meant that when the Yankees, behind Johnson, drubbed the Red Sox 8–4 on Saturday, they clinched the division title for the eighth straight year (guaranteeing Boston an eighth-straight second-place finish). And it meant, when the Red Sox, behind Schilling, splattered the Yankees 10–1 on Sunday, they earned the wild card. Of course, that still left open the very real possibility that the Sox and Yankees would meet in nine days to start a third straight ALCS Armageddon.

"I think it's inevitable," Alex Rodriguez said that Sunday in Fenway's cramped visitors' clubhouse, as the Yankees prepared to take a six-hour flight to Anaheim, where they would open against the Angels in the best-of-five Division Series. "We know that to get where we want to go, we need to go through the Red Sox. And I think the Red Sox know that for them to get where they want to go, they need to go through us."

It sounded wonderful.

It never happened. It never came close to happening. The White Sox swept the Red Sox right out of the postseason in three games, the Red Sox' final out coming—irony of ironies—via a ground-out by Edgar Renteria. The Yankees lost in five to the Angels thanks to weak efforts from their superstars, Randy Johnson getting knocked out of game three in the third inning, Alex Rodriguez hitting all of .133 for the series.

If anything, the lack of an Act III only underlined how remarkable it was that the Red Sox and Yankees had provided the first two, to say nothing of all the preliminaries they'd delivered going all the way back to 1903. As badly as both teams want the public to believe that the nineteen games they play against each other every year mean the same as the other 143 games on the schedule, it's clear that they take a significant toll: the attention, the hype, the intensity, the all-consuming nature of a rivalry this big in a twenty-four-hour, talk-radio, Internet-message-board culture. Perhaps, in the end, they exerted so much energy and so much effort fighting for the championship of each other that there was little left with which to wage a run for that *other* championship—the World Series.

As both teams cleared out their clubhouses prematurely, there was talk that the Yankees might look different in 2006, and that the Red Sox might look radically different, and that it might mean the Emperors and the Idiots might be ready to take a break from each other and from the rivalry's white-hot spotlight for a while.

Not that anyone really believes that, of course.

Not for a minute.

INDEX

© *Charles Wenzelberg*

ABOUT THE AUTHOR

MIKE VACCARO is a leading sports columnist for the *New York Post*. He has won more than fifty major journalism awards since 1989 and has been cited for distinguished writing by the Associated Press Sports Editors, the New York State Publishers Association, and the Poynter Institute. A graduate of St. Bonaventure University, he lives in New Jersey.

Printed in the United States
by Baker & Taylor Publisher Services